Marina Caparini, Otwin Marenin (Eds.)

Transforming Police in Central and Eastern Europe

Process and Progress

LIT

Bibliographic information published by Die Deutsche Bibliothek
Die Deutsche Bibliothek lists this publication in the Deutsche
Nationalbibliografie; detailed bibliographic data are available in the
Internet at http://dnb.ddb.de.

ISBN 3-8258-7485-0

© LIT VERLAG Münster   2004
Grevener Str./Fresnostr. 2   48159 Münster
Tel. 0251-23 50 91   Fax 0251-23 19 72
e-Mail: lit@lit-verlag.de   http://www.lit-verlag.de

Distributed in North America by:

Transaction Publishers
New Brunswick (U.S.A.) and London (U.K.)

Transaction Publishers   Tel.: (732) 445 - 2280
Rutgers University   Fax: (732) 445 - 3138
35 Berrue Circle   for orders (U. S. only):
Piscataway, NJ 08854   toll free (888) 999 - 6778

CONTENTS

List of Tables and Figures

PART I

INTRODUCTION

Police Transformation in Central and Eastern Europe: the Challenge of Change

Marina Caparini and Otwin Marenin[1]

Introduction

The idea that policing is vital to democratic countries and to countries in the process of democratisation has slowly but firmly taken hold of politicians, scholars, policy-makers and the police themselves. The provision of security – the sense among citizens and communities that the routines of their lives are, to a reasonable degree, protected by the actions of social control apparatuses of the state – is one of the basic demands laid against the state by its society.

The police occupy a crucial political role in any society – by virtue of the realities of their work (their structural position in state-society relations, and by what they do and how they do it), and by the symbolic representations of their work and its impacts upon the political and social discourse (Manning 1997). The police are part of the system of governance (Shearing 1996). They are very important to the processes of state creation, the reproduction of peaceful social relations, the peaceful resolution of conflicts and the creation of social identities and bonds which underpin political life (Loader and Walker 2001).[2] Conversely, ineffective, arbitrary or repressive social control undermines the legitimacy of existing state–society

---

1. Otwin Marenin, one of the co-editors, became involved in this project when he spent the autumn of 2002, as part of his sabbatical leave, at DCAF in Geneva. He would like to thank the people working at DCAF for their unfailing kindness and help in getting settled in and becoming part of the working environment at DCAF. They made the visit worthwhile. He would especially like to thank Theodore Winkler, the Director of DCAF, Phillip Fluri, the Deputy Director, and Heiner Hänggi, for enabling him to spent a pleasant, stimulating and productive four months in Geneva. Last but not least, Marina Caparini was instrumental in getting me settled in and connected to DCAF projects; she proved to be an able and skilled scholar and co-editor and, more importantly, a good friend; and she was always a pleasure to work with.
2. Concluding their review of the literature, Loader and Walker (2001: 20) think it a reasonable argument that, 'through their presence, performance and voice, the police are able to invoke, affirm reinforce or [even] undermine many of the prevailing cultural characteristics of particular political communities, thereby serving as a vehicle thought which such communities may be imagined'. This seems a large catalytic burden to place on the police.

relations, complicates efforts to promote development and severely limits the (re)building of democratic forms of governance and order. In short, the police matter beyond their merely functional work. The actions of the police will both reflect and affect societal changes and the meaning and legitimacy which society vests in state authority.

In changing societies (developing states, states in transition to democracy, failed states) the need for creating effective and legitimate security systems is self-evident. There can be no expectation that people are secure and their persons and property safe if they are surrounded by turmoil, violence, ethnic and religious hatreds, or corrupted state institutions (Caparini, 2002; Duffield, 2001; Hendrickson and Karkoszka, 2002; Neild, 2001; Winkler, 2002; WOLA, 1999–2000). As Winkler (2002: 5) notes, 'without security there can simply be no sustained development, nor any progress towards democracy, stability and peace'. A minimum of social order, political stability, economic well-being and a sense of human dignity are essential prerequisites for societal and individual survival and growth. The police are one of the agencies which can help create and sustain these threshold conditions. In Bayley's (2001: 5) succinct summation, 'security is important to the development of democracy and police are important to the character of that security'.

Democracy, loosely defined by a few emblematic principles of social life, political participation and shared values, has become the stated goal and end-state towards which societies in transition or development are struggling, and much transnational support for reforms is conditioned on acceptance by recipients that democratic societal systems are a worthy and desirable goal. Progress is measured in establishing the institutions and processes which define a democratic polity (McLaughlin, 1992).[3] Salient among indicators is the character of the policing system being brought into existence, for the nature of policing experienced by society is democracy (or non-democracy) in action.

A democratic police and a democratic society exist in symbiosis. Without a supporting democratic context – a culture of tolerance and trust, a supporting legal framework and a system of functioning criminal justice institutions – democratic

---

3. As Schmitz and Sell (1999: 39–40) note, democratisation must mean more than just copying from democratic countries, which can lead to: 'structures and organisations that are "empty", although they are formally democratic. They are frequently created before they are really needed and do not respond to domestic political requirements. Instead they are a copy of ideas from outside or from international cooperation partners.' Conversely, analysts of democratisation must look beyond the rhetoric and institutions to assess whether effective democratic practices are being built in a society. That is a slow process which must have roots in society. Schmitz and Sell (ibid., p. 33) identify the major dynamics of the process. Democratisation 'is the result of a complex interaction of international and domestic factors where initially competitive claims about the better social order are exchanged, and significant pro-democratic actors appear. In the course of time a gradually emerging democratic setting slowly re-frames the interests and behaviour of actors.'

police cannot be created. Yet, at the same time, if the police behave undemocratically, claims that state and society are democratic or moving towards democracy rest on shaky ground (Hills, 2000; Tanner, 2000).

The sections below will (a) enumerate the principles and practices of good policing which have emerged through processes of reform, transnational exchanges and the creation of international regimes; (b) summarise some of the lessons learned on police reform and its implementation, or at least the lessons thought to have been learned so far; and (c) describe the objective of this project and book, which is to examine what has been done and what has not yet been achieved in reforming the policing systems of transitional societies as judged by generally accepted principles and practices of democratic policing.

Democratic policing

Policing systems are given great power, extensive authority and a good deal of discretion in the day-to-day application of their authority and skills. The police can protect and they can also use force, even deadly force, sometimes with impunity. The police can serve the interests of the few or can support the basic preconditions which enable all members of a society to live a reasonably secure personal and community life. Being powerful, the police must be controlled. They must be held accountable for their actions. They cannot be granted the authority to determine the conditions and assessment of their work, yet they must be given enough leeway and autonomy to exercise their discretion and judgment on when and how to employ their expertise and powers to promote a just, secure and stable social order.

In democracies, maintaining this balance between autonomy (or developing trust in the police which underlies the granting of autonomy) and supervision (or the subtle yet essential distrust and monitoring of any organisation or individual given great power) presents the most formidable challenge in police reform. The police must be given enough power and authority to do their work but not enough to risk harm to the well-being of society and individuals. The normal response to this dilemma, in theorising and policy on democratic policing, stresses three notions: legitimacy, professionalism and accountability. The goals of democratic police reform (or creation of a democratic policing system), then, are sustained legitimacy, skilled professionalism and effective accountability. All three conditions must exist before policing can be considered democratic; and all three must work in harmony. Professional behaviour and accountability sustain legitimacy; accountability helps professionalise the police; legitimacy grants the police a necessary degree of professional autonomy.

Legitimacy is an essential trait for any state institution, including the police, which seeks to function efficiently. Legitimacy allows governments to make difficult decisions without needing to expend much time and effort in persuading or forcing groups or individuals to accept policies which are not in their (immediate) interests. A legitimate police force has gained the trust of its communities and of the state. The public has had a chance, based on experienced interactions with the police and accurate descriptions and assessments (which requires transparency) of their occupational cultures and behaviours by outsiders (e.g. scholars, those involved with policy, journalists), to evaluate how well the police do their job. If the job is well done, according to the expectations and norms of society, the police sustain the trust they have earned. If the police fall short of those public expectations and standards in the performance of their duties, they will lose public trust and confidence. Legitimacy judgements incorporate and balance morality and norms with effectiveness and security. A legitimate police force not only protects society; it does so in a just fashion (Reiner, 1996).

The creation of legitimacy tends not to be an even-handed process. It is a profoundly political process as different groups, in the process of granting or withdrawing legitimacy from the police, will have distinct sets and priorities of norms which they value differently and will seek a balance between security and justice that favours their sentiments and interests. There is, as well, unfinished business. Legitimisation is an ongoing process and the level of legitimacy gained by the (new) police and the state will reflect the changing political dynamics of the country.

Professionalism, in its largest sense, argues that the police have accepted the need for balancing effectiveness and justice; that they have acquired the skills on how to reconcile both demands in the varying conditions of their work, and that they apply such skills consistently. In practice, balancing justice and effectiveness requires the capacity to make reasoned judgments. A professional police should not engage in the arbitrary (discriminatory), sporadic, corrupt or abusive exercise of their powers. The (limited) autonomy granted to the police is based on trust by society that the police will have internalised a set of values, a code of ethics and professional conduct which embodies a democratic balance. They can be trusted to exercise self-control.

Yet things can and do go wrong. Some (a few) police will be corrupt, will misuse their powers, will violate their code of conduct and agency and external regulations, and will engage in criminal conduct. In short, there will be violations of prescribed conduct as is true of any other occupation with a large membership and the capacity to exercise discretionary powers. The police can be trusted, but not too much. Accountability to outsiders is crucial. In a democratic society, the police have a duty to explain themselves when challenged or asked about their conduct. They have to accept the reality that others will judge their performance and have a right to do so.

Supervision is essential and its mechanisms can take many forms (Stone and Ward, 2000). Their effectiveness, as are police reforms in general, is heavily conditioned by the societal contexts in which they operate and the history of police–society interactions (Goldsmith and Lewis, 2000). It has become accepted as a principle that multiple internal and external supervision and accountability mechanisms are much to be preferred, both for effective control of police behaviour and for public legitimisation.

Accountability and civilian supervision should not only function to discipline the police after misconduct on their part: they serve the positive functions of preventing small-scale abuses and corruptions from escalating and becoming entrenched in the thinking and habits of the police as normal aspects of their work. The potential vicious cycle of corruption, violence and self-protection can be broken by supervision (Mendes *et al.*, 1999). Supervision not only constrains; it improves policing.

One should add effectiveness as an important criterion of democratic policing, though the term refers not to a specific characteristic of the police, but rather to the impacts of their work on the well-being of their society. Democratic police forces must still prove themselves to their publics. In transitional countries, crime and organised transnational crime will experience a steep increase, threatening the safety and comfort of citizens and the stability of economic and political institutions. Even a professional and accountable police force will not become legitimised if it fails in its major functions of maintaining order, neutrally enforcing laws, and providing security and protecting people in their persons and property without discrimination or bias.

These three goals reflect the by now general consensus on the basic principles for democratic policing. As Bayley (2001: 76) has noted, 'the elements of democratic police reform are no longer problematic'. Some principles can be found in academic discussions of what democratic policing should be like; some are stated as codes of conduct for police officers anywhere (e.g. Council of Europe *Code of Police Ethics*; the UN *Code of Conduct for Law Enforcement Officials*, and the UN *Basic Principles on the Use of Force and Firearms by Law Enforcement Officials*; CIVPOL *Principles and Guidelines*; and the OSCE *Code of Conduct on Politico-Military Aspects of Security*); some are elaborated in policy documents produced by NGOs or government agencies (e.g. the 'Budapest Recommendations' in Kadar 2001); some appear, almost incidentally, in more general discussions of democracy and democratisation.

The basic terms and phrases overlap. Authors, codes, recommendations differ mainly in their phrasing of norms, their ranking of desirable or necessary traits and the implied priorities among principles. Commonly mentioned traits, which point to general and more specific traits, include: non-partisanship (political neutrality); representativeness in the composition of personnel that reflects the society; integrity; fairness; accountability; transparency; sensitivity; moral consensus; civilian control; a public service orientation; obedience or commitment to the rule of law; concern for human rights; responsiveness to civic society; impartiality; minimal, last resort use of force; accessibility; separation from military forces and cultures; or general order (e.g. Amir and Einstein, 2001; Bayley, 2001; Das, 2000; Independent Commission, 1999; Jones, Newburn and Smith, 1996; Marenin, 1998; O'Rawe and Moore, 1997; OSCE, 2001; Sheptycki, 1996; UN, 1994, 1996; US Congress, 1996; USGAO, 1994; Walker, 1993).

These terms are connected to the three basic conditions sketched above. For example, non-partisanship, moral consensus, responsiveness to society or representativeness are basic factors in sustaining legitimacy. A partisan police, which favours, or is perceived as favouring, particular social and political groups, especially if numerically small, or which mainly serves the state, will have little legitimacy in the eyes of the general public. Moral consensus points to the notion that what the police stand for, the laws they enforce and their manner of enforcing them, must be in some accord with dominant societal values. Responsiveness to society reflects the demand that the police listen to and take into account what society wants them to do. A non-representative force, especially in divided societies, will always be suspect, no matter how effective and professional its actions.

Professionalism refers to particular values, skills, occupational orientation and policies of a police service. The principles of fairness, integrity, sensitivity, concern for human rights, impartiality, commitment to law and the use of minimal force are core elements in any conception of professional and democratic policing.

Accountability encompasses the notions of transparency, democratic and civilian supervision and control, and separation from the military (though this last assertion can be contested). Transparency is an essential foundation for accountability. If one cannot tell what the police are doing one cannot hold them accountable. It will become more and more difficult to maintain opaqueness as technological developments and their widespread use will make it more difficult for the police and their supporters to resist any demands for transparency. Access to technology, specifically the Internet, is becoming widespread. Arguments that information cannot be released or made almost universally available are contradicted by existing websites on which extensive information can be posted. And if the official bodies of the state do not post, or release, non-classified information (and the use of classification should be strictly limited) to the public, others will post speculations, rumours and complaints. Unless offset by open documentation and transparency, non-official information will undermine police credibility and public support. It is in the interest of governments and the police to pre-empt speculation by providing reliable and accurate information on a regular basis to the public.

Accountability means that the governments (and their agents) will explain and justify publicly the way they use their power. When problems arise and things go wrong, accountability suggests that corrective action will be taken (Schacter, 2000). Democratic control over the police means that the police are governed by a clear internal chain of command and are ultimately responsible to civilian authorities and subject to supervision by those who are outside the police organisation.

Accountability mechanisms can and do take many forms which vary in effectiveness by contextual support, the activities of the police and the specifics of the issue in dispute. Internal or managerial accountability structures need to be in place within the police organisation. Internal review processes to investigate alleged police misconduct and public complaints exist within any system of professional policing. However, their utility may be constrained by the fact that police officers judge their peers and may be influenced by considerations of collegiality.

External supervision mechanisms are needed precisely to offset that possibility and to reassure the public, and thereby legitimise supervision and democratic control, that accountability is pursued in a serious and visible manner. Supervision through various means can help to identify systemic problems and possible solutions and can recommend or require needed changes in police practices and procedures.

The police should be accountable to each of the main constituent sectors of the state. The executive power exercises direct control from the central, regional or local levels of government, determines the budget, general guidelines and priorities of policing activities and regulations for police actions (although the police should retain operational independence). The legislative power exercises parliamentary control by passing laws that regulate the police and their powers, as well as parliamentary ombudsmen or commissions who may launch investigations into complaints by the public. The judicial power both monitors the police and prosecutes them through civil and criminal proceedings when necessary. Other institutions sanctioned and supported by governments, such as investigative commissions, ombudsmen-type offices, civilian review boards, performance audits and risk management techniques (Chan, 1999; Johnson, 2003), or research bureaus, add to the panoply of possible mechanisms.

Democratic control of the police may also be exercised in informal bottom–up mechanisms that derive from and are supported by the grassroots levels of local communities. Such mechanisms, essentially political activities reflecting local issues, needs and conditions, rely on the existence of social capital – the capacity and willingness of members of civil society to take independent action, to participate in their own governance, and to demand changes from their governments and instruments of government.

The effectiveness of accountability mechanisms depends vitally on the attitude of political and bureaucratic leaders towards accountability: the executive must consent to institutionalise self-restraint and be committed to answering to institutions empowered to oversee its actions. Civil society can also play a critical role in articulating demand for transparent and accountable government.

In short, defining what democratic policing should be like in its occupational cultures, operational policies and relations to state and society is no longer problematic. A basic agreement on general principles exists among progressive police officials, policy-makers and scholars. The real difficulty now is how to implement democratic policing. The main policy and the practical question that needs to be addressed is how to create and sustain organisational arrangements, managerial strategies, personnel policies, training and educational programmes, operational supervision, internal control and accountability mechanisms and interactions with outsiders (public, media, academics, political agencies) which embody democratic policing. In discussing the process needed to move towards democratic police systems and forces, some of the themes may be extracted from the now voluminous literature.

Achieving reform

Principles, not models

There is no one model of democratic policing that can be bought off the shelf. There is no one set of organisational arrangements, managerial strategies, operational policies, accountability mechanisms or structured relations with society and the state which embody democratic norms and expectations. There are some specific policies and practices which reflect democratic principles and which can be inspected and adapted. Lessons can be learned, good practices can be described – but these are always solutions developed in different societal settings and whether they are applicable to the conditions of change experienced in another society has to be assessed, mainly by the people who will have to live with the policing system undergoing reform. Karstedt (2001, 2002), interpreting Braithwaite and Drahos (2000), refers to this process as transnational 'modelling', the adaptation of the experiences and lessons from other places to the functional and symbolic conditions of a society. (For a more general discussion of six lessons about democratisation, which echo police reform generalisations, see Grugel, 1999).

Policing itself is changing continuously in democratic societies and states. New foundation ideologies are rethought (e.g. community policing and risk-based policing). New policing strategies (e.g. relations with informal social control and civic society; social capital augmentation) are being developed. Accountability mechanisms appropriate to changing times and expectations are the order of the day. Basic organisational arrangements (centralisation, decentralisation, devolution) are tested or develop incrementally. If basic conceptions of good or democratic policing are continuously being rethought in democracies, clearly there can be no precisely specified model. But the basic values, principles and goals of democratic policing can be shown by examples and case studies, and these might provide lessons for innovation. This then leads to a second theme.

Adaptation and sustainability

Adaptation has a negative and a positive side to it. A central feature of developing and transitional countries is the existence of police forces which have a history, much of it non-democratic. All the countries included in this book were communist in ideology, though of different variants. And all were either part of the Soviet Union or under its hegemonic control. Before reforms promoting democratic policing can be conceptualised and implemented, existing features which militate against reform must be eliminated. There are no blank slates on which police reform can be inscribed.

In the transitional countries which were subjected to Soviet hegemony, policing served the needs of the state and ruling group, and was heavily politicised and militarised in orientation, structure and often equipment. Before reforms can be undertaken with the hope that they will be sustained and legitimated, existing policing systems have to be depoliticised, demilitarised and decentralised.

Adaptation of democratic principles to local conditions requires decisions both on what to do away with (or what will disrupt or oppose efforts at reform) and what to put in place that is new, whether these be personnel, occupational orientations, legal policies or administrative structures.

Much of adaptation has to be left to the imagination and energy of stake holders in reforms, that is, the people who will have to live with the new police. These include the political leadership, civic society as generally understood, but also the police themselves. International advice on lessons and practices can serve only as a resource, not as the vehicle for reform. The need for adaptation, and corresponding limits on external advice and assistance, is much greater for ideological and strategic rethinking and less so for the incorporation of technical skills into the systems being reformed. If adaptation is not controlled by local stakeholders, reforms will not be sustained.

Contexts and leverage

Adaptation requires a precise specification of the context which has sustained the existing or prior policing system. Reforms of policing affect fundamental political and ethical values. In police reforms there will be some who will win and others who will lose out. New and effective democratic policing redistributes power, resources, rights and privileges. Protection becomes available to those groups who may have been repressed. The police begin to service the majority of the population equitably. Ultimate political control of the police which rested in the state and those who controlled it migrates to civic society. There will always be some resistance to police reforms.

Implementing reforms is not a self-executing process. Someone has to do it and do it consistently, persistently, and with an acute awareness of the social and political consequences of reform which extend beyond the police themselves. Understanding where the resistance will come from and, as far as possible, preventing issues from arising which might symbolise resentments and losses are necessary tasks for reformers. Disarming potential opponents to reform, including the police, is another, as is gathering the resources to sustain reform efforts.

Remember justice

Reforms are often advocated in a climate where crime and fear are prevalent and growing. There will be a tendency, and this is often the major incentive for international assistance, to achieve reforms that will make the police more capable of dealing with crime effectively, especially organised crime. In that process of improving police effectiveness, so it is argued, concern for matters of justice will of necessity be relegated to the background, even if it is only on a temporary basis. Of course it will be said, justice is important, but this is not the time to stress policies which sustain justice but might hamper crime control.

However, reforms develop inertia once they become institutionalised and part of the occupational and managerial policies and culture of the police. Justice relegated to a second-level priority, even though only temporarily, will remain relegated. The necessary democratic balance will be permanently tilted towards effectiveness. In the short run, effectiveness may lead to feelings of legitimacy in the general population. In the long run, effectiveness by itself is not persuasive enough to sustain legitimacy.

The notion that effectiveness and justice are locked in a zero-sum game, that placing priority on one will lead to a loss of the other value, is increasingly challenged by scholars, reformers and the police. As Neild (2001: 34) notes: 'respectful policing is effective policing. A respect for human rights does not hamstring the criminal justice system, but is vital to public order and law enforcement.' (See also Bayley, 2002.) Police policies which lack an element of justice will increasingly isolate the police from their society, forcing them to rely on coercion, intimidation and fear to do their work. The public will not willingly cooperate with a force which it fears and disrespects.

One practical implication for reform is that the police cannot perform their job in isolation or without support from other social control institutions. Reform must be of the criminal justice system as a whole, with the police being just one part of the system. Legal reforms, prosecuting offices which make efficient and fair decisions, courts which function, sanctioning systems of various sorts, and reintegration mechanisms need to support the police in their work. The police often object to the workings of other criminal justice institutions, especially courts, when judges and prosecutors insist that legal limitations on the power of the police be observed by the police in investigations, interrogations, arrests and the use of force. Those are necessary constraints within a system that abides by the rule of law and seeks to promote justice as well as safety.

Not words but acts

In the end, reforms must show up on the street, in the normal work of the police. It is comparatively easy to devise plans for reform, to state new missions, goals and values. The tough part is implementing plans on a sustained basis. Assessments of reforms must step beyond the rhetoric to observe what actually has changed where it counts, in the behaviour of police leaders, mid-level managers and street cops.

Two corollary points follow from this observation. For one, police reform must be based on the police, on understanding the police and their work. The question to be asked is why personnel hired by the state to do a job would be willing to abide by the reforms, accept new ways of looking at their occupational arenas, and learn and apply new skills and attitudes for interacting with the people they serve. Reforms only gain life when carried out. That requires that reforms, and policies implementing reforms, make sense to the police who must implement them within the realities of the work they do. In short, the police, who know more about what the job concerns than outsiders, even though they may currently have the 'wrong' attitudes and values, have to be participants in the planning and design of reforms. They have to be brought in to buy in.

Secondly, the fundamental intermediary goal of reforms is a police culture which incorporates democratic values. Without that culture, there will be nice plans, cogently designed policies, soothing rhetorical flourishes – but little actual implementation on the street. Creating a democratic police culture is a hard task, but an essential one.

Relations to shadows

A common development in transitional countries is the emergence of 'shadows' – that is, informal, non-state-based ordering organisations of varying legitimacy. If the police are inefficient, whether it is because they are corrupt, not trusted, or they serve partisan interests, informal ordering and security mechanisms will be invented to do what the police have failed to do – provide a minimal level of order and sense of security. Shadows may take many forms, but most commonly occur as community-based informal justice, or vigilante type, processes; or as private security organisations hired by economic enterprises, which also drain a significant share of experienced police personnel, being typically much better paid than state police; or as criminal groups which impose order to protect their activities in often brutal and exploitative ways, but also find some acceptance among the public for which they are the only, even if criminal, source of stability. The police, from top to bottom, must find a way of dealing with these shadows in a way which helps legitimate shadows and undermines or replaces illegitimate ones over time.

A long-term process

Reforms take time and patience. For one, nothing will work out quite as planned and expected. There have to be adjustments on the fly. Secondly, as noted, there will be resistance which has to be undermined but in such a manner that the losers will be seen by others as unreasonable and illegitimate in their objections, as protecting their interests rather than looking out for the common good of society and the state. Third, even enthusiastically received reforms will suffer a decline in energies and the active support given to them as time goes on. The routinisation of reforms requires the occasional 'red' campaign to stir up enthusiasm again. Fourth, the pacing of reforms must fit local conditions so as not to 'overwhelm' either the police or the public (Gottlieb *et al.*, 1998: 84). Fifth, as Zhao (1996) has argued convincingly in the case of community-oriented policing in the USA, police organisations seek to shape reforms towards their interests and are much more likely to adopt reforms that do not challenge the existing internal distribution of power and authority within the organisation. And sixth, reforms must become managerial practice. Leadership personnel circulate. A system to teach, or indoctrinate, new leaders as they rise through the ranks has to be developed.

Police reform in Central and Eastern Europe

The collapse of the Soviet Union, the expansion of Europe into a vacated political and economic space, autonomous domestic political dynamics which cleared the way for a structural rearrangement (in varying degrees) of powers and rights of the state and civic society, and new international and domestic threats to security created immense pressures to reform a discredited security system inherited from the old order. That system, including the police, lacked legitimacy. The Soviet Union collapsed as completely and quickly as it did because it was hollowed out from within. It had no passionate supporters outside the favoured elites and their hangers-on. Instead, the state and party achieved compliance and acquiescence by an apathetic society, and groups who objected were forcefully and visibly repressed. The state rested on fear, and political opportunism and a large number of people rejected state rule altogether (through underground economic activity, informal social control, crime and the wholesale manipulation of rules and laws through corruption, evasion and informal networks; for a discussion see Los (1988) and Shelley (1984)). The use of the security services for policing dissent and maintaining surveillance of society contributed much to the slow leaching of legitimacy. Reforming the security sector and the police, that element of the sector most widely encountered by publics, became a priority.

Most of the articles in this book were presented at the workshop 'Police Reform in Central and Eastern Europe', which was organised under the auspices of the Geneva Centre for the Democratic Control of Armed Forces (DCAF) and took place in Prague, the Czech Republic, on 8–9 November 2002. The country chapters examine how such reforms have fared over the last 14 years since the dissolution of state socialist regimes in Central and Eastern Europe and the collapse of the Soviet Union. What has really changed in systems of policing? The basic goal of the papers was to assess where we are right now in police reforms in these countries. What has been done and what remains to be achieved in order to make policing system more democratic and effective.

The focus on democratic reform reflects the mandate of DCAF, which was established to encourage, within a context of good governance, the reform and democratic control of the security sector in transitional and developing countries. DCAF promotes the exchange of information on good practices, lessons learned and effective policies on democratic control of security forces, including the police.

Accountability – and the concomitant requirements for transparency of security forces, the development of the necessary skills among civic society, the media and legislative bodies to assess security performance, and the willingness to challenge, confront and control powerful agencies of the state – lies at the core of DCAF's mission and conception of democratic reform and good governance. As policing systems change, supervision, accountability and control mechanisms need to change as well. For example, the movement towards community policing in the USA and UK has led to demands for new forms of participation, cooperation and control among the police and the communities they serve and protect (Greene, 1993; Greene and Pelfrey, 1997). Existing external control methods will shift in their priority, accessibility and impact as the mission of the police force, and its basic strategies, shift from crime control to crime prevention, from working autonomously as professionals to partnership and co-production, from detachment to involvement in civic society. Similar changes in the salience and effectiveness of accountability methods will have to occur in transitional societies as reforms take hold.

Participants had been selected by the editors based on their familiarity with the policing systems of their countries. Some were known to us personally; some we knew by reputation and publications; some were recommended to us by outside experts. Once they agreed to our invitation to write and present a paper, we asked them to submit the papers to all participants some time before the Workshop. Four authors could not attend due to conflicts in their busy schedules.

In terms of countries, we wanted to cover a large and representative sample of former socialist states, now in the process of transition. For some, it proved fairly easy to find a respected researcher/scholar to write an assessment; for others we had some difficulties and could not find anyone. The inclusion of East Germany (which of course does not exist any more) was based on two considerations. We felt that East Germany, and the changes in the policing system it experienced when absorbed into Germany, would allow a constructive and illuminating comparison of how policing systems change when the context of change is fundamentally different from other states. And, secondly, we knew of a respected scholar willing to contribute to a topic on which very little has been written in English.

We asked contributors to focus on normal or routine policing, that is on work which takes up the vast majority of police energies and time in any society. The police perform many tasks, some quite specialised (e.g., intelligence gathering, specialised teams to deal with public disorders, enforcing administrative regulations). The organisation of specialised work differs significantly from normal 'street' policing, specifically in the reasons and methods for interacting with the public. We were interested in the kind of policing that people are most likely to come into contact with, as victims, as offenders, as people in need of services, information and help.

Prospective authors were invited to follow a set of three general questions. The first was to describe reforms and changes since 1989 in five areas:

(1) *Goals:* What were the goals of reforms as stated by reformers? What policing rhetoric and ideologies, what mission of the police were stressed? Where did the pressures from reform come from? Where did opposition arise?

(2) *Legal status and powers of the police*: What was the mandate, the roles and functions of the police? What legal protections for the police and for public were incorporated into law?

(3) *Organisational structures and policies*: What changes in organisational arrangements have taken place? How have personnel practices changed? Have efforts been made to increase the representativeness of the police?

(4) *Operational policies and work patterns*: Have police resources been directed to implement democratic patterns of work? What roles and functions of the police have been emphasised? What policies to shape and control discretion by officers are in place? What efforts have been made to create an appropriate occupational culture?

(5)   *Supervision and accountability mechanisms:* What external and internal supervision mechanisms have been adopted and implemented? How are complaints against the police handled? What actions of the police have become subject to supervision?

Secondly, authors were asked to assess and evaluate the implementation and success of reforms:

(1)   *Democratisation:* To what degree have reforms moved the policing system towards a professional, service-oriented, accountable and effective police force? What efforts were made to depoliticise and demilitarise the police? Has the notion of service taken hold in the cultures and working practices of the police, or moved the police towards that goal?

(2)   *Legitimisation:* Are there any indications of how legitimate policing structures and practices are in the eyes of the public? What are the relations between the police and civic society? What are the relations with non-state security services?

(3)   *Problems and obstacles:* What obstacles exist to further reforms? What problems remain to be addressed?

(4)   *Integration of reforms in state–society relations:* How do the police fit into the larger political and social changes which have taken place? Have policing systems been a hindrance or a support for societal changes?

Thirdly, what insights for theory and policy do the descriptions and evaluations of police reforms suggest?

The reforms contemplated, advocated and implemented in these countries have drawn heavily on the experience of Western democratic countries and on developing international norms and standards of democratic and accountable policing. Reformers in all countries have become intimately familiar with the expectations of international and regional bodies, external states, international and domestic NGOs, private consultants and scholars, and foreign police officials. Candidate countries to the EU have been told what it would take to upgrade their policing system to acceptable standards; international visitations and assistance by a vast army of consultants, aid donors, NGO representatives and police officials have introduced widely accepted norms and policies on how to democratise policing systems and what the end-product should be in practical – that is policy and operational – terms. Lessons extracted, so far, largely from the experience of Western democracies, on 'what to do and how to do it' (Bayley, 2001) have been passed on through this large diversity of channels of advice and assistance. (Bayley offers a useful and concise summary of 87 basic lessons and corollaries.)

Fourteen years of experience in these 14 countries provide insights into the utility and applicability of such lessons. Have they worked in these countries? Do some and not others? Do lessons have to be modified, and in what ways? What lessons have been learned about the lessons themselves?

So far, the flow of information, advice, best practices and lessons learned has been largely a one-way street from West to East. But as transitional societies undergo change and consciously reform security institutions, and as the experience with reform lengthens, good practices and lessons will be learned from that experience as interpreted by policy-makers, police officials, scholars and analysts. Such lessons may start to flow back and may lead to modifications of existing views on what works in reforming the police, converting a largely one-way street into a circle of mutual learning (Pagon, 1996), a reciprocal flow of information, a feedback loop in which all who study and practise policing participate and share information and advice.

Lessons embody, or are based on, theoretical notions of how to produce change in policing ideologies, organisations and practices, which can be also be quite resistant to reforms. We asked contributors to consider what theoretical insights for police reforms might be gained from the experience of transitional countries.

The Workshop proved extremely valuable. Each author presented her/his paper. Two other participants had been asked to be lead commentators on a paper. After the presentation and initial comments a free, respectful and often quite vigorous conversation ensued during the formal panel sessions, conversations which continued during informal activities. The coming together of 12 experts – who were either practitioners or scholars, or both – in the field of policing created an intellectually rich environment which it would be difficult to duplicate. Similarities and differences in the experiences of their countries, questions of analysis and interpretation, the issue of standards for evaluating changes and performance (what really was new and what had not changed?) – easily recognised as core issues to be discussed in each chapter, quickly led to critiques and challenges, to continuous discussions on perspectives for description and analysis which should be adopted, policy choices to focus on, lessons to be drawn, evaluations to be conducted.

The editors culled general guidelines for rewriting papers from these discussions which were communicated to the participants after the Workshop. Some of the initial guidelines suggested by the editors to participants were modified slightly as a result of this process. The goal of the guidelines was to provide a more cohesive framework for harmonising descriptions and analyses across chapters, thereby assisting readers in making comparative assessments of reforms. Contributors revised their papers accordingly.

We hope this project will help illustrate some of the challenges and dynamics of reforming policing systems in former communist countries, outline the various approaches and courses of action taken in these countries to promote democratic reforms, and assess the difficulties that are being encountered on route. The descriptions and assessments presented in these pages should help policy-makers, practitioners, scholars, donors and police officials at international and national levels gain a better understanding of the requirements and obstacles to democratisation and good governance for an institution which so directly and visibly embodies the power of the state and affects the well being and security of individual citizens. We are grateful for the participants for helping all of us take some long steps down that road.

The chapters which follow provide a snapshot in mid-2003 of the state of policing systems and the implementation of reforms in these countries in transition to more democratic forms of governance. We will summarise general conclusions in the final chapter, and point to unresolved issues of policy and research.

References

Amir, M. and Einstein, S. eds. 2001. *Policing, Security and Democracy. Volume 1: Theory and Practice; Volume 2: Special Aspects of Democratic Policing.* Huntsville, TX.

Bayley, D.H. 2001. *Democratizing the Police Abroad: What to Do and How to Do It.* Washington, D.C.

Bayley, D.H. 2002. 'Law enforcement and the rule of law: is there a tradeoff?'. *Criminology & Public Policy*, vol. 2, no. 1.

Bayley, D.H. and Shearing, C.D. 1996. 'The future of policing'. *Law and Society Review*, vol. 30, no. 3.

Braithwaite, J. and Drahos, P. 2000. *Global Business Regulation.* Cambridge.

Caparini, M. 2002. 'Lessons learned and upcoming research issues in democratic control of armed forces and security sector reform', in Born, H., Caparini, M. and Fluri, P. eds. *Security Sector Reform and Democracy in Transitional Societies.* Baden-Baden.

Chan, J.B.L. 1999. *Governing Police Practice: Limits of the New Accountability.* Melbourne.

Das, D. 2000. 'A world perspective', in Das, D. and O. Marenin, eds. *Challenges of Policing Democracies.* Newark.

Duffield, M. 2001. *Global Governance and the New Wars. The Merging of Development and Security.* London.

Goldsmith, A. and Lewis, C., eds. 2000. *Civilian Oversight of Policing. Governance, Democracy and Human Rights.* Oxford-Portland, Oregon.

Gottlieb, G., Krözsel, K. and Prestel, B. 1998. *The Reform of the Hungarian Police. Processes, Methods, Results.* Holzkirchen, Germany.

Greene, J.R. 1993. 'Civic accountability and the police. lessons learned from police and community relations', in Dunham, R.G. and Alpert, G.P., eds. *Critical Issues in Policing: Contemporary Readings.* Prospect Heights, IL.

Greene, J.R. and Pelfrey Jr., W.V. 1997. 'Shifting the balance of power between police and community: responsibility for crime control', in Dunham, R.G. and Alpert, G.P. eds. *Critical Issues in Policing: Contemporary Readings.* Prospect Heights, IL.

Grugel, J. 1999. 'Conclusion. Towards an understanding of transnational and non-state actors in global democratization', in Grugel, J., ed. *Democracy Without Borders. Transnationalization and Conditionality in New Democracies.* London and New York.

Hendrickson, D. and Karkoszka, A. 2002. 'The challenges of security sector reform', in SIPRI, *SIPRI Yearbook 2002: Armaments, Disarmament and International Security*.

Hills, A. 2000. *Policing Africa. Internal Security and the Limits of Liberalization*. Boulder.

Independent Commission on Policing for Northern Ireland (Patten Commission). 1999. *A New Beginning: Policing for Northern Ireland*. Norwich: The Copyright Unit, St Clements House

Johnson, T.A. 2003. 'Police accountability: a European perspective'. *ACJS Today*, vol. 26 no. 1, 7ff.

Jones, T., Newburn, T. and Smith, T.J. 1996. 'Policing and the idea of democracy'. *British Journal of Criminology*, vol. 36, no. 2.

Kádár, A., ed. 2001. *Police in Transition. Essays on the Police Forces in Transition Countries*. Budapest.

Karstedt, S. 2001. 'Comparing cultures, comparing crime: challenges, prospects and problems for a global criminology'. *Crime, Law and Social Change*, vol. 36.

Karstedt, S. 2002. 'Durkheim, Tarde and beyond. the global travel of crime policies'. *Criminal Justice*, vol. 2, no. 2.

Loader, I. and Walker, N. 2001. 'Policing as a public good. reconstituting the connections between policing and the state'. *Theoretical Criminology*, vol. 5, no. 1.

Los, M. 1988. *Communist Ideology, Law and Crime*. London.

McLaughlin, E. 1992. 'The democratic deficit: European Union and the accountability of the British police'. *British Journal of Criminology*, vol. 32, no. 4.

Manning, P. 1997. *Police Work: The Social Organisation of Policing, 2nd edn*. Prospect Heights, IL.

Marenin, O. 1998. 'The goal of democracy in international police assistance programmes', *Policing: An International Journal of Police Strategies and Management*, vol. 21, no. 1.

Mendes, E.P., Zuckerberd, J., Lecorre, S, Gabriel, A. and Clark, J.A., eds. 1999. *Democratic Policing and Accountability. Global Perspectives*. Aldershot.

Neild, R. 2001. 'Democratic police reforms in war-torn societies', Washington, D.C. (reprint from the *Journal of Conflict, Security and Development*).

O'Rawe, M. and Moore, L. 1997. *Human Rights on Duty. Principles for Better Policing – International Lessons for Northern Ireland*. Belfast.

OSCE. 2002. 'Council of Europe and OSCE Joint Final Report on Police Accountability in Serbia', First Draft, Strasbourg: Co-operation programme to strengthen the rule of law, 10 Sep. 2002. Report written by John Slater and Harm Trip.

Pagon, M., ed. 1996. *Policing in Central and Eastern Europe. Comparing Firsthand Knowledge with Experience from the West*. Ljubljana.

Reiner, R. 1992. *The Politics of the Police*.2nd edn. Toronto.

Schacter, M. 2000. 'When Accountability Fails: A Framework for Diagnosis and Action'. Institute on Governance, Policy Brief no. 9 (May 2000).

Shearing, C. 1996. 'Reinventing policing: policing as governance', in Marenin, O. ed. *Policing Change: Changing Police: International Perspectives*. New York.

Shelley, L. 1984. *Lawyers in Soviet Work Life*. Brunswick, NJ.

Sheptycki, J.W.E. 1996. 'Law enforcement, justice and democracy in the transnational arena: Reflections on the war on drugs'. *International Journal of the Sociology of Law,* vol. 24.

Skolnick, J.H. and Fyfe, J.J. 1993. *Above the Law: Police and the Excessive Use of Force*. New York.

Schmitz, H.P. and Sell, K. 1999. 'International factors in processes of political modernization. towards a theoretical integration', in Grugel, J., ed. *Democracy without Borders. Transnationalization and Conditionality in the New Democracies*. London and New York.

Stone, C.E. and Ward, H. 2000. 'Democratic policing: A framework for action'. *Policing and Society*, vol. 10.

Tanner, M.S. 2000. 'Review Article. Will the State Bring *You* Back in? Policing and Democratization'. *Comparative Politics*, Oct. 2002.

United Nations. 1994. *United Nations Criminal Justice Standards for Peace-Keeping Police*. Handbook prepared by the Crime Prevention and Criminal Justice Branch. Vienna.

United Nations, Mission in Bosnia-Herzegovina, International Police Task Force, Sarajevo.1996. *Commissioner's Guidance for Democratic Policing in the Federation of Bosnia-Herzegovina*. Mimeo.

United Nations. 1997. *Human Rights and Law Enforcement. A Manual on Human Rights Training for the Police. Professional Training Series No. 5*. Geneva: High Commissioner for Human Rights. Centre for Human Rights.

United States Congress. 1996. 'Democracy, rule of law and police training assistance'. Hearing before the Committee on International Relations, House of Representatives, 100th Congress, First Session, Washington, D.C.: GPO.

United States General Accounting Office. 1994. 'Promoting Democracy: Foreign Affairs and Defense Agencies Funds and Activities – 1991 to 1993', Washington, D.C.

Walker, N. 1993. 'The international dimension'. In Reiner, R. and Spencer, S., eds. *Accountable Policing: Effectiveness, Empowerment and Equity*. London.

Winkler, T. H. 2002. 'Managing Change. The Reform and Democratic Control of the Security Sector and International Order'. Geneva: DCAF Occasional Paper no. 1. Available at <www.dcaf.ch>

WOLA (Washington Office on Latin America). 1999–2000. *Themes and Debates on Public Security Reform. A Manual for Civil Society*. Washington, D.C.

Zhao, J. 1996. *Why Police Organizations Change: A Study of Community-Oriented Policing*. Washington, D.C.

PART II

CENTRAL EUROPE

Chapter 2

The Czech Police: Adopting Democratic Principles

David A. Jenks

Introduction

It has often been argued that one critical·method of ensuring social order in emerging democracies is the development of a criminal justice system that can help maintain order without reverting to the totalitarian tactics used by previous regimes. The implementation of this objective proved difficult for the Czech police following the fall of Communism in 1989. During that pivotal year, the police remained one of the few public institutions to continue their support for the communist party, even after others had enthusiastically rejected it and earnestly embraced the democratic reforms. The precipitating event in November of 1989 was a rumour about police brutality at a student rebellion, an altercation that sparked the conflict that eventually toppled the regime.

How successful have the Czech police been in adopting and incorporating a democratic policing style in an organisation that had long favoured an authoritarian one? Because of the complexity of the issue of democratising a police force, this discussion has been broken down into three distinct sections. The first presents a description of general developments in Czech policing since 1989; the second provides evaluations of reforms, challenges remaining and likely future developments provided by key informants for this study, all high level officials in the Czech criminal justice system. The third identifies the key democratic principles that apply to police organisations generally, and assesses these within the context of the Czech police experience. Illustrative examples and general conclusions are also provided. It seems likely that gaining a clear understanding of their progress can make a contribution to the body of police research, as well as to Czech policy-makers who remain extremely concerned with the outcome of their efforts aimed at the implementation of democratic ideals. Thus, the study serves as an important case study of police change in the Czech Republic, a topic of considerable interest throughout Central and Eastern Europe, as well as for outside observers.

The 'metamorphosis' of the Czech police after 1989

Havelka (1997) has described the political, social, and economic transition in Czechoslovakia as being characterised by a 'principle of openness', due to the lack of guiding principles for the changes. Czech leaders were left to their own devices in determining how to move towards a democratic society. At that time, the Czechs faced circumstances similar to those of their post-communist neighbours, all of whom were looking to the West for examples of democratic societies. While all of these transitional states, including Czechoslovakia, could observe a myriad of examples of existing democracies, there were no illustrations of how they might actually become one. The process of democratic development was unspecified, something they would be forced to work out on their own initiative.

While the central government remained in a quandary about how to proceed, the agencies operating under government auspices were even more confused. There existed considerable pressure for the reformation of certain organisations, including the Czech police; alterations were thought to be necessary in order to facilitate the evolution of the new social order. Given the need to improve their poor reputation, police officials felt they could not afford to wait for the government to approve new democratic laws and regulations before initiating a major public relations campaign. It was during these uncertain times that the initial steps were taken towards transforming the police.

Czechoslovakia's new leaders found themselves facing the conundrum of how to reorganise the Ministry of the Interior quickly. This was no easy task, as no other organisation had remained as loyal to the communist past as the police (Lundberg, 1993). Three months after the revolution, the new Minister of the Interior abolished the *Statni Bezpecnost* (or STB – the secret police). Former STB officers were immediately relieved of duty and required to return all equipment, including their firearms, to the ministry. Several commissions were formed to help regulate and evaluate the new police force. These supervision boards comprised community members and former police officers who had been forced from the department in 1968 because of their support for the Prague Spring uprising (Lundberg, 1993).

A major goal of the reformers was to achieve a significant reduction in the power of the Ministry of the Interior. Some aspects of this reformation proved very simple. For example, the military counter-intelligence section was moved to the Ministry of Defence. However, the reform of the ministry was complicated by the fact that suddenly the two republics (Czechs and Slovaks) that comprised the federation had each demanded the right to govern their own people. In response, republican leaders decided to create regional as well as municipal police forces, units that would be more capable of responding to local needs than the national police (Lundberg 1993). These complications prolonged the dispersion of power from the federal ministry.

These early attempts at reform took place under extreme circumstances including a demoralised force and a complete lack of legal guidance. Public confidence in the police was then very low (Burianek, 1998), and the crime rate was rising (Criminological Institute, 1996). While this apparent rise in crime certainly reflected, at least in part, the fabricated and artificially low figures that had been reported under communism, it was a crucial factor in explaining increasingly negative public perceptions of the police. The public seemed to view the changes in the crime rate as real, however, interpreting them as a reflection of police ineffectiveness and incompetence, and further reducing their confidence in that organisation. The task of establishing and then maintaining a safe society without public support posed a formidable challenge.

It was not until late 1990 that the Federal Assembly passed a law granting the Czech and Slovak Republics the right to establish their own police forces (Lundberg, 1993). Additional laws regulating the police were not passed until July 1991. These new laws left the federal Ministry of the Interior in charge of the federal police force, while greatly reducing the responsibilities of that force. The actual distinction between the federal and republican forces was unclear, however, and for several years debates raged over jurisdictional issues. It was not until the break-up of Czechoslovakia in 1993 that the debates were halted with the dissolution of the federal police.

The reform of the police in the Czech Republic was made more difficult by the ever-changing political environment. For example, Tomas Hradilek resigned early in 1990, only two months after he had been appointed Minister of the Interior. His departure was the product of rumours of his previous ties to the communist party. His replacement was Tomas Sokol, a 38-year-old attorney and former defender of dissidents who had been serving as the Prague Municipal Prosecutor (Lundberg, 1993). Notwithstanding the chaotic political environment, the ministry moved towards implementing several sweeping organisational changes. One of the first of these was the separation of the police from all other ministry activities. In order to accomplish this goal, the ministry was broken up into five distinct divisions. The police division retained most of its employees, who constituted nearly one-half of all ministry workers. The four other divisions each comprised approximately equal proportions of the remaining workers. These divisions handled ministry affairs that fell outside the powers of the police such as those related to elections, policy changes and administration.

Within the ministry and the government, the process of 'lustration' led to persons who were carrying out government work being removed and replaced if they had any known close ties to the previous communist regime. The lustration process took place not only within the government, but throughout Czech society (Rosenberg, 1995). As it was designed, lustration was supposed to embrace due process protections, including a careful reading of STB and personnel files, as well as formal hearings and the giving of testimony. Although legislation was passed on the federal level to guide the procedure, the Czech police did not even bother to undertake the task of formal reviews before removing suspected communist collaborators. As a result, many individuals were dismissed from all divisions of the ministry without first being afforded the protection of the required formal hearings.

Other difficulties related to the police reform were associated with equipment problems. By September 1991, the Federal Police possessed only 22 cars equipped with radios, 3 radio-telephones, 22 bullet-proof vests, and no central computer, relying instead on handwritten reports that were passed among stations (British Delegation, 1991). Smaller departments implemented car-sharing programmes when vehicles were available and patrolling on foot when they were not (Sacher, 1991). The few cars that the police had were so antiquated that they could not compare with those used by the emergent criminal gangs that had recently moved into Czechoslovakia. Jan Kozlik, the former director of the Czech Federal Police, commented, 'We have to deal with criminals who are better organised than the police' (Lundberg, 1993: 4). Another obstacle arose in the spring of 1991 when many agencies were forced to vacate premises that had been appropriated from the Catholic Church during the communist period. For example, with the return of the Malostranska police station to the St Nicholas Church, the city of Prague was forced to relocate its criminal police from the monastery from which they had operated since the 1950s.

Another challenge for those directing these reform efforts was the recruitment and retention of competent personnel. Prior to 1989, the state of Czechoslovakia employed 23,000 sworn officers (Criminological Institute, 1996). After the revolution, the republican and local forces were authorised to add an additional 8000 officers over two years, new positions that resulted from lustration and the new responsibilities the republican and local police forces gained from the federal police after 1991. Despite this authorisation to hire new officers, however, recruits were difficult to find. As of March 1992, the republican forces sustained 3000 vacancies. Even today, staffing shortages continue to be a problem for the Czech police.

The Police Act of 1991 defined the role and organisational structure of the police. For the first time in more than forty years, the federal and local police were considered civilian organisations. The hierarchy of command contained a police director appointed by the parliament, and a police chief who was responsible to the minister. The Police Act laid out specific guidelines for the new departments as well. Each department was to contain divisions for criminal investigation, uniformed officers, traffic, protection of public figures, economic crime and administration.

The duties of the police were now clearly identified in an effort to define their new role in the emerging democratic state. These charges included the protection of persons and property, the detection and investigation of criminal activity, the maintenance of public order, the direction of traffic, and the maintenance of essential information (Lundberg, 1993). High-ranking officers were banned from involvement with any political parties (Rosenberg, 1995).

At the time of their passage, these new laws were seen as temporary, designed to give police direction until more permanent legislation could be enacted. This did not occur until after the adoption of a new national constitution, however – an event that was initially scheduled for completion in May 1992, but that was not actually adopted until after the break-up of Czechoslovakia in 1993 (commonly referred to as the Velvet Divorce) into two independent states, the Czech Republic and the Slovak Republic. Special consideration in these new laws was directed at the relationship between the police and judiciary. Another focal area, and one that came as no surprise considering the earlier history of the police, delineated acceptable police procedure for dealing with public protests. For example, it was stipulated that police would have to obtain authorisation from the municipal council before any action could be taken to disperse a public gathering. This provision limited the authority of police administrators, thus reducing the possibility of police abuses.

Perhaps not unexpectedly, there was some opposition to several provisions of the Police Act. For example, concern was expressed in response to the provision that left police officers under the authority of the military courts. This was viewed as being inconsistent with the avowed emphasis on maintaining a police force under civilian rule. Some observers have noted that the perception of the police as an oppressive government force may have actually been bolstered by this provision (Kolar, 2002).

Although it was formally adopted in 1991, the Police Act document – representing the first serious effort to reorganise the police in the Czech Republic – was not actually distributed to police agencies throughout the country until 1993 (Lundberg, 1993). Earlier, its dissemination was left to the discretion of commanding officers, who often did not perceive changes in the law between 1989 and 1993 as being permanent. This problematic situation was exacerbated by the circumstances of policing in an unstable legal environment. It was not until after the break-up of Czechoslovakia and the adoption of the Czech Constitution in 1993 that the legal waters were eventually calmed (Burianek, 1998).

Those who had planned these alterations were well aware that modifying the law would not, by itself, alter the behaviour of police. Consequently, it was acknowledged that training needed to be overhauled for both police officers already in service and for new officers. Prior to 1989, all police training facilities had been located outside of the Czech Republic, with the main school located in what is now the Slovak Republic (other training was conducted in various communist countries), and had largely consisted of military training procedures. Following the Velvet Revolution, the Ministry planned to establish four police schools to be located in Prague, Brno, Jihlava, and Pardubice. A comprehensive curriculum was designed and was to be instituted late in 1993. However, due to the turmoil that resulted from the break-up of Czechoslovakia that year, the changes were not actually implemented until mid-1994.

The new police training strategy was designed to emphasise the service aspects of police work, incorporating topics such as ethics and communication, and was modelled on the training provided in Western countries. A former Deputy Minister of the Interior reported:

> After 1989 we tried to halt immediately the teaching procedures as they existed. We know that what we have embarked on now is a long-term process. What we want is to

depoliticise the whole system, to put more stress on individual qualities, to put more stress on ethics, to put more stress on the ethical qualities of each individual. We want to teach them not only the things which concern the police as such, but also some general topics so that they would know more about the world, so they would be able to communicate with others (cited in Lundberg 1993: 2–3).

Within the new training structure there were three different levels of certification provided: basic, advanced and university-equivalent. Following the Velvet Divorce, university training was provided for all new officers in the new police academy that had been established in Prague. Although officials recognised the need to retrain serving officers, no plan for this was ever developed.

Western policing styles were also reflected in the application and selection procedures for police recruits. Several tests that gauged a candidate's suitability for police work were administered prior to admission to the new schools. Under the previous system, all that had been required was a background check to determine one's loyalty to the communist party. The new process required that applicants take four basic tests. These tests judged the prospective recruit's physical health, psychological health, professional qualities and education. It also incorporated a thorough background investigation that was specifically designed to lead to the disqualification of any former communist collaborators. The emphasis on service needs permeated the entire process. The minimum age requirement for new applicants was 18 years.

Public perceptions of the police

It was widely known that the public perceptions of the police immediately following the Velvet Revolution were extremely poor. Given that they had served as the front-line representatives of the oppressive communist government, this was perhaps inevitable. In order to reverse these negative perceptions, police officials first turned to cosmetic changes. In an attempt to visually distinguish the new police from the old, officials changed the appearance of the standard uniform. In Prague, for example, officers switched from olive drab and red to new blue and grey uniforms. Similar changes were made with police vehicles. The older, often militaristic Soviet models were taken out of service and sleeker, more attractive cars, such as Renaults and Mercedes, were purchased from Western neighbours. The insignia on all equipment was changed from 'public security' to 'police', and although the new cars remained white, they featured green stripes rather than the former blue and yellow.

Most of the proposed changes could not be implemented as quickly as officials had hoped, due to budgetary constraints. For example, the requirement that all officers carry personal identification in the form of a badge with a number, would have cost the ministry over 500 million Koruna, or US $17.6 million (Lundberg, 1993). Although these costs were high, especially considering that the entire economy was in a state of considerable flux, it was determined that these changes were necessary in order to rehabilitate the tarnished image of the police and regain the public's trust. The Czech police implemented the plan methodically as all new officers were issued identification badges upon completion of training, and badges were distributed over time to serving officers.

Other changes were made at the administrative level. The Police Act of 1991 formalised the promotion of a new psychological mentality for the police. Minister Ludvik stated, 'we wanted to put the individual policeman back in touch with the citizens, to take a new approach, more personable, more human than before' (cited in Lundberg, 1993: 10). The act addressed this issue directly, attempting to revive the sense of individual responsibility that police leaders felt had vanished under Communism. It also heralded a return to the police being scrutinised by the public and removed the veil of secrecy they had upheld and under which they had operated during the communist regime.

The tasks of altering the outlook and attitudes of officers, as well as those of the public they serve, were daunting and required explicit initiatives defining appropriate police behaviour. Similar to the requirements mandated by the Miranda decision in the United States, the Czech police had a duty to inform citizens of their rights in any arrest situation. Whenever a police officer challenged an individual, the officer was required to clearly state his/her identity and, when possible, to provide identification, usually in the form of a badge or identification card. Individuals could not be detained by the police for longer than 24 hours unless they were charged with a crime. Standard evidentiary procedures were instituted mandating the documentation of all personal items in the possession of anyone who was detained. Violent prisoners could only be physically restrained for up to two hours and those in detention were to be given the opportunity to eat every six hours.

Other individual liberties, such as a right to privacy, were also addressed. The police were now required to obtain a warrant in order to place a citizen under surveillance. The warrant application had to include the precise address, dates of use, a previous history of surveillance for the specified person, and in the case of phone lines, the number(s) to be monitored. The Minister of the Interior, in an effort to ensure that the command staff would still have a detailed understanding of these invasive activities, could approve the application but the actual surveillance would have to be conducted by the police. The Police Act established use of force guidelines for officers to follow. The specific instruments and holds to be used by police were associated with the resistance levels on the part of suspects. For example, verbal resistance could not be met with batons as that would be considered an unreasonable response and the officer would be disciplined. Guidelines also restricted the use of force against pregnant women, the elderly, the handicapped, the ill and juveniles. Any use of force on the part of the officer was to be immediately documented and reviewed, and the state was to pay reparations to individuals who suffered damages due to police actions that were found to be unwarranted.

One official expressed concern at how difficult it was to change the public image of the police. He stated that: 'Police are still viewed as people who would abuse power. But the STB no longer exists. We are only policemen' (Maryska,

1991: 3). The negative view of the police stemming from personal experiences following the Velvet Revolution also hindered changes in perceptions as people related tales of police ineffectiveness. In Prague, for example, complaints of noise emanating from busy bars and dance halls that were adjacent to flats and houses flooded police stations on a nightly basis, yet on-duty officers claimed they did not have the resources to address the problem. One commentator noted that this led to the cynical belief that even if crimes were reported, the perpetrators would neither be caught nor reprimanded (Maryska, 1991).

Despite these difficulties, there were some early indications that the reforms were having their desired impact. A public opinion poll first conducted in 1990 and then again in 1992 by the Institute for the Investigation of Public Opinion indicated that public confidence in police, although still very low, had increased. Asked whether they trusted the police, 50% of the respondents replied in the affirmative in 1992, compared with only 30% who had done so in 1990, while the numbers for those who did not trust the police dropped from 60% to 34% during that time period (IIPO, 1992). Another study revealed that confidence in the police rose steadily through 1995 and then levelled off at around 70% for 1996 and 1997 (Burianek, 1998). In these polls, satisfaction with the police was higher among respondents in small towns than it was for those living in the cities (Institute for the Investigation of Public Opinion, 1992; also Burianek, 1998). It was clear from these early public opinion polls that attitudes towards the Czech police were changing, and in the desired direction.

Perceptions of reforms

To assess the success of reform, the author interviewed 12 key informants knowledgeable in the workings of the Czech police. Informants were asked, among other questions, what they saw as the major challenges the police still faced and what would be likely developments in Czech policing. Information from informants is supplemented with data when these are available and with the evaluations of other observers.

When asked about the successes and failures experienced in accommodating democratic principles, informant responses focused on the challenges that still face the Czech police as they continue the transition. For example, Mr Petr Zelasko (Commander in the Police Presidium and former head of the Juvenile Division) argued that staffing was of the utmost importance for the police:

> Well, I'm not satisfied with the [staffing] process. I have always said that in this kind of very specialised department the staff have to be true, well educated, well experienced professionals, 45 years old on average. They might not be able to run fast, but bright thinking is necessary. What happened was that these specialists often left to work for a higher salary in the private sector and we could not find anyone of similar proficiency from other units who would be willing to replace them. After all,

we do not have much to offer – no apartments for their families ... That results in a very young staff.

Mr Zelasko expressed concern that the majority of well-trained, experienced professionals who had worked their way up through the police organisation were now leaving for more money and better benefits at private institutions, although no specific examples were provided. Given that the youth and inexperience of the present force were among his concerns, a renewed organisational focus on education and training for the younger officers might help to alleviate these problems. Mr Zelasko expressed concern that without adequate funds to compensate officers for remaining with the organisation, the problem was not likely to be resolved.

Dr Miroslav Platil (Deputy Chief of the Prague Police) identified two challenges that he thought were vital for the police to consider. The first was the need for domestic forces to keep pace with those working in other similar international cities. The second was to increase their efforts at international cooperation as the nation prepares to enter the European Union. He stated:

> I suppose the ... police are not doing bad compared to other national police, although it is not easy to compare due to varying legislative structures. Still, I believe that as soon as we can say that we have control over all of Europe, as soon as all the police forces manage to communicate fast in one language using connected databases – and that is not an idea of a police continent; I'm talking about effective protection of and services for citizens as well as for foreigners – as soon as we define European police standards, which will make it possible to catch a criminal wanted in the Czech Republic anywhere else in Europe, then – despite a variety of legal backgrounds – we will make an efficient, cooperative police force and that would be a true victory. We would finally be able to face the wave of criminality coming from the East. Crime knows no boundaries and we must keep with it.

Dr Platil's second point referred to the domestic situation:

> To handle the increase of crime, make it decline through a good prevention programme. That's fundamental. Then there is a large amount of high-impact economic/financial crime (suspicious money transfers, numerous bank crashes) moving society that needs to be resolved. Last, we need to finish the reform of career promotion rules and make the police work interesting for prospective newcomers and experts. One of the recent steps was a decision to grant the Police Academy the status of university.

While both points related to direct challenges faced by the Czech police, he did not mention many other problems that had surfaced during the last few years.

During his interview, Mr Jiri Kolar, President of the Police Presidium, identified a wide variety of important topics the police should be concerned with. These ranged from police corruption to officer turnover. He stated:

I personally consider generational turnover the most important step ahead. That is something very important for any police force, otherwise they cannot go ahead. Our colleagues in Hungary and Poland were quite reserved regarding this change, since they were concerned about a possible collapse, yet I still think that such a turnover is substantial for future development. The negative aspect of that is higher criminality among young policemen under thirty years of age or serving less then ten years. In the beginning, when the recruitment was so massive, we took in a lot of unreliable people. But the rate of 300 hundred accused policemen each year is not significant enough to stop the generation turnover.

Referring to the number of accused officers, Kolar noted that each year only 300 officers had complaints filed against them either by businesses or private citizens for illegal activity. About half of these accused officers were dismissed with cause, and only 10% of them were later charged with a crime. He also commented on the police/community relationship:

Besides the united service issue, we would like to maintain or even improve the good police-community relationship. Czech people are used to evaluating the police by statistics/quantity, which is not good. We strive to have them trust in the police force – that is the direction which we want to follow.

When he was asked about the future, Mr Komorous (Commander of the National Drug Squad) reduced the various challenges being faced by the police to simple economics. He provided an example of how effective his officers were, even with limited resources:

The economic background and equipment of our unit is terrible. Even though it has improved over the years, we are still strongly dissatisfied. No officer from the West would serve for the salary we have. Every time Fred Geiger [a frequent consultant and former German officer] from Berlin visits us, he says that the ideal combination would be a Czech policeman with American technologies. Since, as far as enthusiasm goes, we are better than American policemen. The American policeman is a spoiled policeman. They're used to sitting in a car that actually goes, switch on the computer which generates 80% of background information for him, for each model situation he has a handbook, but our policeman has to manage with his own intellect.

As the foregoing comments demonstrate, informants agreed generally on the basic challenges the Czech police face. However, it was hoped that discussions of other specific issues could be provoked. For example, it had been anticipated that police corruption would be raised as a concern, and specifically the brutal treatment of Romany suspects, but it was never mentioned. This omission could be attributed to the backgrounds and small number of informants. No Romany officials were included among the key informants, nor could there have been, for the Romany are not represented on the police force and that minority group prefers relatively minimal involvement in police affairs. Dr Maresova, a researcher at the Prague Criminological Institute who had specifically studied police abuses among minority populations, seemed reserved when she commented briefly on the issue of mistreatment of minorities by the police:

> It is true to some extent. Just ... sometimes it is questionable whether it is really a manifestation of racism. Anyone who lives in the Czech Republic long enough finds out that the problem with the Romany exists. No doubt. It is obvious when we look as the police relationship with any other (Vietnamese, Chinese) community. Even though the police attitude to those communities is also generally intolerant, it is still better than the relationship with the Romany, due to numerous negative experiences with Romany offenders. The official trend is to be aware of and hide the external displays of intolerance, but as a matter of fact I don't see any big changes in the approach.

The sentiments of ill will to Romany harboured within the ranks of the Czech police seem to be echoed by the populace. Although there are a growing number of individuals who recognise the Romany situation as unjust, recent opinion polls showed a majority of respondents supporting police treatment of minorities (Institute for the Investigation of Public Opinion, 2001). As Police Presidium President Jiri Kolar mentioned, the Czech police have begun talks on dealing with this issue, but serious change within the organisation will likely not occur until there is a stronger show of support for that change within the community at large.

Prior research on this issue as it relates to the Czech police was much more limited than was true of any of the other areas of inquiry. After conceptualising the Czech transition as a long-term process, the direction it might take in the next decade was considered. While no specific conclusions can be drawn solely from the interview responses, it was a shared opinion of the informants that the Czech police are a progressive, democratic agency striving towards self-improvement. This claim should be subjected to close scrutiny, however, rather than simply being accepted at face value.

The laundry list of ills the respondents identified in follow-up responses are, for the most part, minor and really beg the question of what real issues they face. There is no doubt that the Czech police are facing some difficult organisational problems. For example, crimes committed by the Romany are a major problem, but so is police (and public) prejudice against the group. Together, these may be considered to comprise the 'Romany problem'. The claim by the informants that the Romany themselves were the problem was a shallow denial of the existence of racial prejudice against this group and, when challenged, one informant shied away from the issue to discuss what she termed 'more important' considerations. Regardless of the nature of Romany involvement in criminal activities, there remains tremendous hostility against the entire group within the police ranks, and command personnel are going to have to deal forcefully with this issue. Otherwise, democratic policing cannot be achieved. There were also no mentions of abusive behaviour, denial of rights, or corruption, other than in a very general sense by Kolar when he dismissed 300 annual accusations against officers as 'trivial'.

Principles of democratic policing

Before systematically assessing the successes and failures of the Czech police in their accommodation of democratic principles, the key elements of a democratic policing style must be identified and defined. To date, the most comprehensive explanation of democratic policing has been developed by Bayley (2001) through a grant from the National Institute of Justice. Based on the work of several international projects (Marenin, 1998; United Nations High Commissioner, 1996; United Nations International Police Task Force, 1996), Bayley described four normative prescriptions for what police organisations must do to facilitate the transition towards democratic policing. They include the following:

(1)   Police must give top operational priority to serving the needs of individual citizens and private groups.
(2)   Police must be accountable to the law and not the government.
(3)   Police must protect human rights, especially those that are required for the sort of unfettered political activity that is the hallmark of democracy.
(4)   Police should be transparent in their activities.

Prior to using these principles to measure the success of the Czech police in adopting democratic values, it is important to define them for this purpose. The first, assigning top operational priority to serving citizens and private groups, is assessed here by noting the extent to which police have been responsive to diverse audiences. Potential measures of police performance in this domain include an assessment of complaints filed against officers, the number of officers charged criminally, the number of civil lawsuits filed against police, and the number and type of disciplinary actions taken by the Ministry of the Interior including fines, suspensions and dismissals. While these figures are now available, they were not recorded earlier under the communist regime and were only sporadically tracked prior to 1998. Another promising measure would include tracking the number of calls for service and subsequent response times. This data could be broken down further to compare these response times with demographic considerations, the nature of the calls and complainant satisfaction with the services rendered in the future, but currently these data are not collected.

The second principle, that police must be accountable to the law rather than to the government, may be defined by the extent to which they apply the law, rather then arbitrarily making decisions, and the extent to which their judgments are upheld by the courts. Other possible measures for the second principle could include the role and degree of involvement of police officials in the drafting and enacting of legislation, as well as donations made to political parties on their behalf. This would require access to political documents that are not currently available to the public, however.

The protection of human rights described in the third principle may be measured in terms of the extent to which the Czech police protect activities that are essential to the practice of democracy. These activities include 'freedom of speech, association, and movement; freedom from arbitrary arrest, detention and exile; and impartiality in the administration of law' (Bayley, 2001:14). There are many opportunities to assess the behaviour of the police in this regard, and especially in circumstances when public protests occur. These situations have proven problematic in the past, as evidenced by the International Monetary Fund (IMF) debacle.[1] Direct observations of these events and their later analysis can be completed with the assistance of newspaper accounts, discussions with reporters, officials, bystanders and others. Assessing the number of individuals detained and the reasons given for their arrest, along with the disposition of the cases can provide additional information pertaining to progress in this dimension. The fact that the Czech Police currently keep no records of wrongful arrest is telling in this regard (Kolar, 2002).

The fourth principle calls for transparency of police activities. The degree to which this is being achieved can be measured by how open the police are about their activities and how they handle requests for access to sensitive information. This could be operationalised in terms of the number of complaints filed against police officers and the ease with which those complaints can be filed. Another indicator would simply be the public availability of basic statistics on the police forces, e.g. force numbers, gender breakdowns, budgets etc. In addition, reporters could be contacted, and especially those working for leading newspapers, television stations and magazines, in order to determine their views regarding police openness.

Although specific data are not currently available with which to conduct a comprehensive analysis of each of these principles, a preliminary assessment can be made. Each of the principles is addressed below, with an emphasis on the police in Prague, since there is more information available on the Prague Police force than on other municipal and rural forces.

Principle 1: Police must give top operational priority to serving the needs of individual citizens and private groups

It seems clear that the Czech police have made some progress towards accommodating the first principle. A dramatic organisational change has occurred in terms of the department's responsiveness to individual citizens. While it is of vital importance to respond quickly to emergency calls for service, the key informants interviewed by the author repeatedly stressed that the vast majority of crimes reported to police since 1989 have been non-violent property offences, a

---

1. Recently the Prague Police were on the world stage as protesters rallied against the IMF and World Bank meetings in September 2000. In that melee, police confronted protesters with mounted patrols and water cannons, tactics seldom utilised in similar protests in the West, and tactics that may be viewed as excessive.

development that one would expect as material wealth increases and as citizens gain confidence in the police. The Czech police have proven responsive to several citizen-initiated concerns as well. For example, special units were recently assigned in Prague to both the Old Town Square and Wenceslas Square in order to help prevent crime and to facilitate the reporting of minor thefts that frequently occur in the areas popular with tourists. A major change occurred in 1997 when Chief Bornik of the Prague Police introduced complaint desks at each of the city's police stations. Complaints from citizens, including those against officers, are now routinely recorded and investigated. Finally, there has been no indication that the police favour any one political party or interest.

While the Czech police appear to have become more responsive to individual complainants since 1997, these changes were not immediate. Initial media reports following the events of 1989 illustrated that police were having difficulty responding to all calls for service (Auster, 1992b, 1992c; Kilmova, 1992; Levy, 1991). Auster (1992c) wrote:

> The openness with which professional scam artists, prostitutes and thieves operate on Wenceslas Square has long served as testimony of the lax, sometimes invisible, law enforcement that followed the breakdown of the Communist regime's police structure.

Taking a broader perspective, Levy (1991) stated:

> We are living in the left bank of the 1990s. For some of us, Prague is a second chance city: for others a new frontier where anything goes, everything goes, and often enough, nothing works.

These and other negative assessments of police inaction in 1990 and 1991 could be seen as reflections of their reluctance to appear repressive, although it soon became clear that officers would have to maintain order, regardless of public perceptions (Auster, 1992c, 1992d). The existence of these crime problems illustrated that the adoption of this principle was a process that was by no means complete. Auster (1992a) described one of the earliest reactions to what had been described as a 'crime wave' in 1992:

> 'There will be a new face for police', Ruml [former Minister of the Interior] said. 'The most important thing is to organise the police well, so that they can function efficiently.' The most dramatic example of Ruml's influence so far was last month's comprehensive police sweeps around Wenceslas Square and Prague's other heavily trafficked areas. In the end, police stopped 520 people and arrested 313, including 13 wanted suspects. They were charged with everything from pickpocketing to carrying concealed weapons.

Although numerous changes have been initiated to aid the police in serving the public, a number of problems have persisted. During one interview, Petr Zelasko spoke repeatedly of the necessity for the Czech police to direct more resources to their responses to calls for service. This commitment would demonstrate the police support of the principle that responses to citizens should be their top priority.

By fostering a more response-oriented organisation, the Czech police could demonstrate their support for democratic principles. Although they have made strides towards achieving a more democratic model, two major areas will have to be addressed in the future. First, the organisation must be made accountable to the entire population, without consideration of race, religion or nationality. Secondly, the police must strive to improve how they serve marginalised populations.

The Romany are still treated by many police officers as second-class citizens, and are routinely targeted as suspects. On the other hand, the Czech police have rigorously adopted service-oriented policing for other groups in the population, and have made plans to continue to expand these practices. For example, they have increased foot and bike patrols in the town centres, and have hired public information officers as well. According to Jiri Kolar, 'we will serve the needs of the public and protect the outcome of democratic changes'. As noted above, democratic policing in this part of the world has not produced equal treatment for all citizens. This has been demonstrated time and again in Prague as minorities, and particularly the Romany, have been targeted for 'special attention' by police. Auster (1992e) wrote:

> On Oct. 9, a group of off-duty police officers fought with several Romanies at the discotheque, Unimarket, in District 5 of Prague. Two officers suffered stab wounds and one Romany was shot four times, but survived.

The writer revisited this point in another article where he stated (Auster, 1992f):

> Romanies are convicted for proportionally more crimes than other segments of the population. Statistics for 1991 attribute nearly 20 percent of crime to Romanies, although they are less than 3 percent of the population.

As noted, rather than using these statistics as justifications of the officers' actions, the author cited them as evidence of prejudice directed against the Romany.

In one particularly telling example, the Ministry of the Interior discovered a significantly higher rate of animosity expressed towards Romanies by officers of the Czech Police and trainee officers than was found among Czech high school students. The ministry quickly responded to this finding, urging the police academy to introduce special courses on ethnic minorities with the intent of increasing the cadets' understanding of, and compassion for, minority groups. The report was commissioned in response to a rising number of clashes between white and non-white citizens, and predicted increases in the Czech Republic's ethnic minority populations. Since 1995, ethnic relations courses have been required of all police recruits. However, as of November 2001, no comprehensive evaluation had yet been conducted of these efforts to determine if they were having the intended effect. Jiri

Kolar acknowledged that although the evaluation had been planned for some time, funding was not currently available to undertake the project.

Principle 2: Police must be accountable to the law and not the government

The second democratic prescription appears to have been implemented in the Czech Republic. The informants pointed out that the Czech police organisation cites the Police Act of 1991 as the legal basis for its actions. No mention was made of specific governmental officials or political parties in reference to the rule of law or its application. Despite such claims, caution must be exercised in assuming that all political influence has been eliminated simply because it was not mentioned. Although the Czech Police were working on organisational aspects of the new Police Act, there was no evidence that they had had any particular influence in designing or enacting the laws they must uphold. In addition, the courts must validate all police arrest decisions. Of course, this supervision does not ensure that the Czech police are rigorously adhering to the second prescription, although it does provide some support for the contention. Further evidence of the acceptance of law as the driving force for the police organisation was provided in the interviews when future legal changes were discussed. The pending Police Act of 2002/2003 was described in the interviews with Jiri Kolar and Petr Zelasko as a positive step in reforming both the rule of law and police behaviour.

In one reported incident, the police were confronted with a political dilemma. Chipman (1997) explained:

> Police charged Miroslav Sladek, the chairman of the far-right Republican Party, earlier this year with inciting racial hatred for statements he made at a protest during the signing of the Czech–German declaration in January. 'We can only be sorry that we killed too few Germans during the war', Sladek said outside the Liechtenstein Palace, where Prime Minister Vaclav Klaus and German Chancellor Helmut Kohl were signing the document. [Police] said the file will be passed over to the state attorney by mid-June, after Sladek's lawyer has had a chance look at it. Police also intend to press charges against Josef Krejsa, one of Sladek's Republican deputies, for publishing racist articles in the party newspaper, *Republika*.

Although these events may seem minor, they had explosive potential, as the police were charging someone who had previously been one of their staunch supporters. Before 1989, the organisation would never have adhered to the rule of law and charged a politician, regardless of his/her crime. In this case, charging a member of the Republican Party was not really a risky political move, however, as the group controlled very few seats in parliament and was often simply dismissed as an irrelevant fringe movement.

Principle 3: Police must protect human rights, especially those that are required for the sort of unfettered political activity that is the hallmark of democracy

Bayley's third principle raises a serious concern that pertains directly to the Prague Police, especially in relationship to their activities in controlling public protests during the IMF/World Bank Meetings in 2000. The following excerpt from a report of this incident details some of these actions:

> A number of those detained were not involved in any unauthorized protest activity and a smaller number were simply incidentally present at the scene of the police action to apprehend protesters. The decision to detain them appears to have been arbitrary (Amnesty International, 2001).

The detention of individuals without cause raised serious concerns. The reports of their experiences while being illegally detained were even worse. Amnesty International (2001) reported that the Prague Police routinely denied these detainees access to medical attention or legal representation, and that they refused to provide interpretation for those who could not speak Czech. The detainees were crowded into small cells and held for hours without food or water. While these activities had been common under the past authoritarian regime, they clearly are not compatible with established standards in democratic states. The Amnesty International report depicts an authoritarian police force that, behind closed doors, committed violence and conducted an abusive vendetta. Abuse is, of course, unacceptable in a democracy, and Amnesty International's suggestion that the Prague Police may have indulged in it is certainly troubling. If democracy is to be afforded more than just lip service, Czech government officials can no longer adopt a position that provides unqualified support of police officers regardless of the nature of their actions.

In addition to the events at the IMF/World Bank meetings, Amnesty International (2001) also included the following case that occurred in early 2000 as another example of the failure of the Czech police to deal with all citizens as equals:

> In February in a bar in Nachod, around 15 skinheads shouted racist insults and attacked five Roma and one other man who was punched in the head, breaking one of his teeth. Gabriela Farkasova, Romany Advisor to the District Government Office and a witness to the attack, managed to leave the bar and call the police. Although the Romany victims identified some of the attackers, the police allegedly failed to detain or even properly register their identities at that time. Subsequently, all of the victims were questioned about the incident and helped to identify one of the attackers from the documentation concerning local skinheads. However, the majority of the skinheads were not local and the police did not show the victims photos of any skinheads from outside the locality. Apparently the police treated the incident as a bar brawl rather than a racist attack.

One commentator from the Prague Police, who asked not to be identified, believed that the resolution of most criticism levelled against the organisation hinges on the answer to one question: when will the Czech Republic decide to dispense with its authoritarian past and create judicial structures that remove the responsibility for investigation of wrongdoing from the hands of the accused? Lundberg (1993) raised the same point when discussing police reforms in Central and Eastern Europe just after 1989. The fact that in the Czech Republic the Ministry of the Interior is basically in charge of investigating police abuses allows no opportunity for external evaluation. Without an external review mechanism that can hold police accountable for their actions, little progress can be made towards assuring that human rights will not be violated.

Perhaps even more troubling than the inability or unwillingness of the police to deal with the Romany issue is the utter disdain that government officials have shown towards this important minority group. Mortkowitz (1997) explained:

> Following a Bohemia Foundation address to invited dignitaries, a journalist asked about potential Czech membership in the EU being affected by the problem of Romanies seeking political asylum abroad. The question was greeted with laughter by many of the Czech officials present. This caused one participant to take the Czechs to task on the issue. This is a perfectly fair and legitimate question, he said reproachfully. He added, The Roma [Gypsy] problem is an important one and it needs to be solved. Though saying it should not become a major obstacle to Czech integration in European structures, he emphasised that the Romany issue could become a strategic problem if neglected. The laughter of the Czech officials also shocked a prominent foreign member of the Czech business community, who walked out in a gesture of protest. I was personally offended, said the protester, who wished to remain anonymous. The response calls into question how seriously the Czech government takes the Gypsy question. He continued, the Czech government has announced that they are serious about wanting to solve the problem. But when the issue is raised in a forum, they scoff at it. This raises serious questions about how reliable they are with their statements on the Gypsy problem or any other problem.

Despite the fact that there has long been tension between the dominant Czech population and its Romany citizens, there is some evidence that the Czech police have been taking steps to improve their relationship with the group. In January 2002, for example, Jiri Kolar appointed a task force to study how the organisation could best respond to the specific problems posed by police interactions with Romany. When pressed on the issue of evaluating the effectiveness of academy training directed at reducing prejudice among police recruits, Kolar expressed a desire to evaluate the programme and noted that provisions were in place to allocate funds to address Romany issues in the 2002/2003 Police Act. The fact that this has not been done, however, provides additional evidence that remedying Romany problems may not be high on the list of police priorities.

Principle 4: Police should be transparent in their activities
The preceding discussions of informant interview responses and the other data collected for this project support the notion that police transparency is becoming increasingly evident. While there is room for significant improvement on this dimension within the police organisation, the level of information that is now available regarding their activities has increased dramatically since 1989. While access to information pertaining to the investigation of officers remains limited,

however, police abuses are being actively reported in the local media, and some steps have been taken by the Ministry to identify and reprimand officers who violate organisational rules and democratic principles. The veracity of some of these claims remains extremely suspect, however. For example, the Ministry admitted wrongdoing on the part of police at the IMF/World Bank meetings, but then refused to identify the offending officers by name. Wilson (2001) reported:

> The Interior Ministry has confirmed three cases of police brutality during last September's anti-globalisation demonstrations. But to the frustration of human rights groups and observers, the guilty officers will not be identified or prosecuted. 'Unfortunately, specific persons against whom charges can be brought were not found', Interior Ministry Inspector Mikulas Tomin said. Tomin's team confirmed that police used excessive force against demonstrators on Sept. 26.

Tomin's argument that specific officers could not be identified or punished was countered later on in the same article:

> 'The police force is a hierarchical institution' said Marek Vesely, spokesman for the Civic Legal Observers (Občanské Právní Hlídky or OPH), which monitored police behavior during the September world finance summit. 'Someone must always be held responsible for a criminal act – either the guilty policeman or a superior on duty during the violation.

At this juncture, the Czech police remain content to admit that abuse has occurred, but have not taken the next logical steps that would lead to public identification of the perpetrators and the issuance of reprimands. This serves the interests of the police organisation as a whole by building loyalty within the ranks, as each such incident provides evidence for officers that the organisation will go to great lengths to protect them, regardless of their actions. Furthermore, so long as those investigating these public servants are themselves in the employ of the police organisation, there can be little public confidence in the legitimacy of the process. An untitled opinion piece in the *Prague Post* recently spoke of this issue:

> To say the [Amnesty International] report was expected is an understatement. Legal observers and human rights officials were vehemently critical of police conduct in the days following the Prague riots. At the time, this newspaper criticised organisers – who had promised to ensure peaceful protest – for allowing their fringe members to clash with police in scenes that are now sadly typical of anti-globalisation efforts. Firebombs were thrown, so were cobblestones. These actions remain distasteful and reprehensible. They in no way abet a cause. They encourage the media to portray critics of globalisation as under the tyranny of renegades intent only on picking hooligan-style brawls with any established order. So our criticism stands. But there is a new matter on the table. Amnesty depicts a sinister police force that, behind closed doors, indulged in gratuitous violence and vendetta bordering on torture. Torture is a tough and risky word. That Amnesty would use it, albeit gingerly, suggests that Prague had better take these charges seriously – something that it has so far refused to

do. Instead, government officials have been aloof or arrogant, adopting a 'stand by our boys' position that will not help this country move forward. The centrepiece of most criticism levelled at police begs a basic question: When will this country decide to dispense with its authoritarian past and create judicial structures that remove investigation from the hands of the accused? Here, foolishly, police look into police misconduct; the Interior Ministry is its own watchdog. Vested authority exists to protect the state. Police exist to root out those who would disturb the peace. But when the keepers of the peace abuse their mandate and use closed chambers as a shield behind which to violate basic rights, those who invest them with power must move swiftly to determine what went wrong, and discipline the culprits. While most European nations entrust commissions to study allegations of police misconduct – and in so doing admit the possibility of misconduct – the Czech Republic dissembles.

These sentiments cogently describe a fundamental issue that should be addressed by the Czech police if they sincerely wish to be seen as transparent in their activities, which could be done by a citizen review process or through some other supervision process and institution. Despite the organisation's stonewalling, these events have been discussed in the local media, and even the Ministry has admitted wrongdoing on the part of some police officers. Such critical assessments foster transparency. Detailed, critical information regarding police activities is now available for public discourse and this may prove to be the precursor of real change. In this regard, Vaclav Havel (1989) stated, 'I really do inhabit a system in which words are capable of shaking the entire structure of government, where words can prove mightier than ten military divisions.'

Conclusion

The Czech police operate in a fluid political, social and economic environment. They are called upon to uphold the rule of law, while simultaneously the law is changing. Their ultimate success or failure to implement democratic principles will be intimately tied to the nation's efforts to do the same. The Czech police will continue to confront new challenges as their environment fluctuates. Whether this results in the adoption of more democratic practices or a return to authoritarian methods remains to be seen. Certainly as actors in a much larger system, and one over which they have little obvious control, they will be only partially able to shape their own destiny.

Lessons can also be learned from the numerous countries currently experiencing problems during their respective transitions. In Serbia, for example, the direct involvement of the police organisation in the wars since 1989 has demonstrated an almost complete lack of democratic policing in that country. The involvement of the police in political disputes has only lessened the viability of the police organisation as one that can uphold principles of democratic policing in the future. The Czech police must be wary of attempts to politicise them. The current director of the Department of Crime Prevention in the Ministry of the Interior, Jitka

Gjuricova (2002) pointed out that public opinion regarding the IMF protests in Prague in 2000 was manipulated prior to the event.

While similar research is currently being conducted in a variety of other countries throughout the world, there exists a problem in comparing these studies. There are numerous organisational arrangements, managerial strategies, accountability mechanisms, and standard operating procedures, all of which vary dramatically from one country to the next. There are, however, several key terms that have emerged in recent research around the globe that may prove to be comparable. They include: non-partisanship, representativeness of personnel, integrity, fairness, accountability and transparency. Future research should focus on measuring these and similar concepts in an effort to construct a tool that police organisations could use universally, one which accounts for differences yet can be generalised to apply to other police organisations.

References

Amnesty International. 2001. *Annual Report on the Czech Republic, 2001*. London.

Auster, A. 1992a. 'Ruml vows a new face for Police'. *Prague Post,* 8 Nov. 1992.

Auster, A. 1992b. 'Police probe abuse charges'. *Prague Post,* 20 Oct. 1992.

Auster, A. 1992c. 'Crackdown signals a change in police tactics'. *Prague Post,* 4 Aug. 1992.

Auster, A. 1992d. 'Tougher police image brings lasting change to city centre'. *Prague Post,* 6 Oct. 1992.

Auster, A. 1992e. 'Romanies appeal to Czechs to be sensitive to racism'. *Prague Post,* 20 Oct. 1992.

Auster, A. 1992f. 'Romany coverage isn't their responsibility'. *Prague Post,* 9 Dec. 1992.

Bayley, D. 2001. *Democratizing the Police Abroad: What to Do and How to Do It.* Washington.

British Delegation to the Czech Republic. 1991. 2nd Report. Sep. 1991. London.

Burianek, J. 1998. 'Democratization, crime, punishment and public attitudes in the Czech Republic', in *Crime, Law, and Social Change.* University Park, PA.

Chipman, J. 1997. 'Police complete investigation on Sladek'. *Prague Post,* 11 June 1997.

Criminological Institute. 1996. Statistics of the Ministry of the Interior. Prague.

Gjuricova, J. 2002. Personal interview conducted on 26 Feb.

Havel, V. 1989. Statement to the German Booksellers Association on 15 Oct. 1989. Prague.

Havelka, M. 1997. 'Democracy in the shadow of globalisation'. *Sociologicky Casopis,* vol. 33, no. 3.

Institute for the Investigation of Public Opinion. 2001. *National Report on Crime in the Czech Republic.* Prague

Kilmova, O. 1992. 'Stolen antiques found'. *Prague Post,* 1 Sep. 1992.

Kolar, J. 2002. Personal interview conducted on 28 Feb.

Levy, A. 1991. 'Us'. *Prague Post*, 1 Oct. 1991.

Lundberg, K. 1993. *The Czech Republic: Police Reform in a New Democracy.* Harvard

Marenin, O. 1998. 'The goal of democracy in international police assistance programs'. *Policing*, vol. 21 no. 1. Bradford

Maryska, F. 1991. Editorial. *Prague Post*, 26 Nov. – 2 Dec. 991.

Mortkowitz, S. 1997. 'Cook: Romany issue – not funny'. *Prague Post,* 3 Dec. 1997.

Rosenberg, T. 1995. *The Haunted Land: Facing Europe's Ghosts After Communism.* New York.

Sacher, R. 1991. Report on Eastern Europe. *Radio Free Europe*, 28 June.

United Nations High Commissioner for Human Rights. 1996. *International Human Rights Standards for Law Enforcement: A Pocket Book on Human Rights for the Police.* New York.

United Nations International Police Task Force. 1996. *Commissioners Guidance.* Sarajevo.

Wilson, F. 2001. 'Police brutality actions are confirmed'. *Prague Post,* 14 Feb. 2001.

Chapter 3

The Lady Vanishes:
the Silent Disappearance of the GDR
Police after 1989

Fabien Jobard

Introduction

What was at stake in the German process of reforming its socialist police after 1989? Of course, some of the problems of the German transformation are common to other former socialist countries, i.e. the integration of former agents, reform of former organisations and bureaucracies, the formulation and implementation of new legislation etc. Yet, many factors separate Germany from its eastern neighbours. In terms of constitutional law, the transformation occurred simply with the integration of the administrative regions (known as the *Neue Bundesländer* or NBL) into the constitutional and administrative order of the German Federal Republic (Article 23 of the *West German Constitution*). There was no constitutional reform, merely a Unification Treaty (*Einigunsvertrag*) between the two German states, which was signed in 1990 (Glaeβner and Wallace, 1992; Maier, 1997. For the full text of the Unification Treaty, see Hancock and Welsh, 1994: 353–63).

The method of transformation of the administrative structures that existed in East Germany largely resembled a 'flash of lightning'. On the day of unification, 3 October 1990, one sole political regime was established, that of Federal Republic of Germany, with 16 autonomous administrative regions, referred to as the *Länder* (or States), and thus 16 police forces and two federal-level police forces: the *Bundeskriminalamt* (or BKA – similar to the FBI), and the border and transport police, i.e. the *Bundesgrenzschutz polizei* (BGS) (for details on the German police see Busch *et al.*, 1998; and Rupprecht, 1995).

What lessons can this 'German approach' provide in terms of transforming law enforcement or policing institutions? In answering this question, one ought to consider whether the uniqueness of the German political transition, based on the integral expansion of state structures from the FRG towards former GDR territories, can impart any lessons in police transformation for other states. Given the normative nature of this book (Caparini and Marenin, 2004), which attempts to gain a better understanding of what a democratic police force actually is and ought to be, we shall, in particular, endeavour to understand how the authoritarian regime that existed in East Germany could have led to the introduction and success of reforms, or, to put it terms of 'transitology', to the transition and subsequent democratic consolidation of the police (Stark and Bruszt, 1998; Dobry, 2000; see also Hancock and Welsh, 1994; and Offe 1996 on the transition process in Germany).

Before being able to understand this issue, it is appropriate to include a few words about the GDR police prior to 1989 (for information on the GDR itself, see the Introduction in Fulbrooke, 1995; and for an extensive analysis of the GDR police, see Lindenberger, 1998 and Lindenberger, 2003). The police (*Volkspolizei* or DVP), which consisted of approximately 60,000 full-time officers, was one of the pillars of national defence and was placed under the authority of the Secretary-General of the Communist Party. The DVP, which was organised on a military basis, found itself having to submit to supervision bodies and those conducting political investigations, most notably to the *Staatssichereit* or 'Stasi' (see Fulbrooke, 1995). The Stasi, or 'political police', viewed the DVP *Volkspolizei*, or regular police, as being poorly equipped, especially for dealing with criminal matters. The *Volkspolizei* were primarily responsible for public security and surveillance of local social activities. We will turn first to examine the 'absorption' process, and then address the effects of this very particular feature on the transformation and democratisation of the police.

The process of absorption (1989–90)

The FRG police: the only possible standard for police forces
From a constitutional and political point of view, and in particular after the legislative elections of 18 February 1990 in the GDR, which saw the victory of Chancellor Kohl's party, the West German Government sought unification between the two States to be achieved as quickly as possible, which avoided any institutional changes in West Germany (Glaeβner, 1994; Maier, 1997). Whether the matter is considered from a monetary or administrative point of view, the only acceptable standards had to be those of the FRG (German Federal Republic), which were simply exported. The transformation was to be based on the 'transplant' method. The most crucial feature of the transformation was that of the West German constitutional procedure known as 'administrative mutual assistance' (*Amshilfe*), in which one *Länder* lends its help to another *Länder*; thus each state in West Germay had to provide assistance and share its experience with another state in the Eastern part (e.g., Bavaria and Bade-Wurttemburg assisting Saxony, Northern Westphalia assisting Brandenburg, Schleswig-Holstein assisting Mecklenburg).

Standards and values of the FRG police
In West Germany, the responsibility for policing lies with each state. Hence, one finds as many police forces as states, as well as the two federal forces, i.e. the BKA

and BGS. These police forces, which are placed under the increasingly lenient control of the paired state authorities, are subject to the same rules on penal procedures, but have their own capacities in terms of police administration and public security (*Polizeirecht*). The increasing centralisation of the FRG since the time of Chancellor Willy Brandt (1969–74), the fight against internal terrorism (since 1972), and the increased professionalisation of police forces, encouraged a growing alignment of practices and structures from the 1970s. This was particularly encouraged through the device of the 'Conferences of the Interior Ministers of the Lands' (IMK), held under the authority of the Federal Minister, which brought about *de facto* a form of growing centralisation of the West German police forces, a process which continues even today. Moreover, since the early 1990s, these police forces have been involved in programmes promoting community policing and creating urban partnerships with municipal and local associations (Aden, 2002).

Federal politics and the issue of police reforms in East Germany

Guidelines on police reforms established in the Unification Agreement of August 1990

The 'electoral alignment' of February 1990 in the East accelerated an inexorable process of administrative realignment, based on negotiations between East and West Germany, with a view to monetary union, and then later, constitutional unification. The springtime brought a series of informal exchanges between police officers from the West (whether they were in active service and posted elsewhere or retired officers) and police from the East. These exchanges were institutionalised by the IMK's Resolution of 5 May 1990: an East–West German working group was established with the aim of organising and facilitating cooperation between the policing services of the two states. Partly as a result of the rise in petty crime in the GDR, the resolutions of 28–29 May and 29 June made it necessary for the DVP to align itself with the police structures of the West, and to do this under the guardianship of the Federal School for Police Officers in Münster. These two resolutions set out the expected organisational principles of the police in the West (law conforming to the rule of law and federalisation of the police, professionalisation of recruitment criteria, aligning the standards of training and the rules of public service with those of the FRG, technical and equipment upgrading).

The Resolution of 8 August set out the basic principles for cooperation in terms of training: the obligation for the East German police to adopt the training principles of the West German police, the introduction of professional and democratic criteria for in-service training, the possibility of training East German police officers in West German schools, and sending educators and teaching material from the FRG to the East, as well as the creation of a permanent coordination cell. These programmes offer a radical solution to the major constraint of transitional policies, which is spelling out precisely how the transition is to occur and exactly how the transition is to be consolidated, or in other words, specifying both the short- and long-term aspects of the transition. As they were rushed by the political timetable that was imposed by Chancellor Kohl, the political decision-makers who decided on policing issues risked everything in favour of immediate gains (Glaeβner, 1994).

The question of the lasting effects and possible long-term risks of the transition was not asked in 1990; urgency was the driving force of the reform (for information on the timing of political decisions during the transition, see Offe, 1996; Dobry, 2000; Jobard, 2003). The political imperative of the West German government was not the only factor to mention. In terms of policing and security, two factors caused those responsible to intervene quickly in East Germany: the need to control the rapidly increasing rate of criminality, unexpected both in terms of the number of crimes and the variety of forms they were taking; and, in view of imminent unification, the need to control the East German police forces, which were neither familiar nor well understood.

However, the speed of the political-administrative process could not on its own stifle the moral dimension of bringing the two sides' police forces closer together. The issue of the treatment and the possible integration of personnel from the DVP, who were undoubtedly key means of support for the condemned GDR regime, had to be dealt with, but it was not possible to do so at the same pace as the structural alignment.

The political and ideological dimensions of police reforms

Article 20-EV of the Unification Treaty set out the general entry principles for civil service employees of the GDR into the civil service of the united Germany (*Verbeamtungskriterien*, or appointment criteria for civil servants). Those people who occupied management positions at different levels (national, regional and communal) of the SED, leaders of workers' unions, those in charge of instruction on Marxism and Leninism, and Stasi collaborators would all be excluded.

At first sight, these general provisions were incompatible with the general rules of the DVP: the East German police were formally an integral part of the Stasi, under the authority of Erich Mielke. Applying the EV in its strictest sense would have led to the immediate dismissal of 120,000 officers and a considerable lack of police forces. Thus the option that was followed was to dismiss the most senior-ranking officers in the police command, and to consider the individual situation of other officers, whether active in operational policing or in training, on a case-by-case basis. In order to do this, and right from the time of the absorption of the *Volkspolizei* into the police forces of West Germany, these officers would have to complete individual questionnaires (*Fragebögen*), which would be evaluated by specially designated examining committees. Thus, right from the start, the integration of GDR police forces into those of the West was only a temporary measure.

The absorption process

From March until 3 October 1990, senior police leaders left the *Volkspolizei* en masse, and the organisation adapted progressively to West German police standards.

From the month of October, all of the repressive political police of the GDR found themselves in a hardening situation of structural panic in the face of public demonstrations which were taking place in the county's three largest cities – Dresden, Leipzig and Berlin (Kuran, 1991; Opp, 1994; Maier, 1997). The most spectacular example of the loss of control by the political police was the sudden decision to release virtually all of the political prisoners who were kept in GDR prisons in November 1989 (Dünkel, 1992; Jobard, 2002).

As far as policing was concerned, the situation was not much better. The transition regime, from November 1989 to February 1990, attempted to reform the police by dissolving combat and paramilitary groups tasked with maintaining order (riot police as well as 'workers' armed forces' and other militias), and by creating a police force that was clearly distinct from the army (by dismantling the DVP's military structure and introducing training and functions that strictly related to policing). In February 1990, a circular indicated that in order to reduce the occurrence of *Disziplinlosigkeit* (lack of discipline) and *Nichtdurchsetzung* (non-execution of orders), all policemen opposed to the democratic changes were required to leave the police force. A law that was being discussed, which would remove the capacity to threaten use of lethal force and would introduce the personal identification of officers through individual identity badges, hastened the movement of the DVP towards democratic ways by encouraging massive numbers of officers to leave the police, as well as producing a general feeling of apathy among those officers who remained in service.

In East Berlin, only 9600 officers out of 11,200 presented themselves to the new police service. In Brandenburg, 3000 of the 13,500 police officers left of their own accord. In Thuringen, only 8000 of the 13,000 officers put forward their application. In the end, only 2800 high-ranking police officers (ranging in rank from major to general) out of all of the East Germany *Länder* presented themselves for recruitment (Haselow, 2000). Moreover, this apathy was encouraged by the huge amount of work that resulted from the introduction of freedom of movement and the explosion in the rates of petty crime and general crime, i.e. a 30% rise in the number of complaints registered in 1990 in comparison with 1989; a 220% increase in recorded burglaries; a 75% increase in arson; and a 50% increase in theft and robberies. To these figures, new forms of crime must be added, such as drug trafficking, political extremism (in particular neo-Nazism), for which the *Volkspolizei* were totally unprepared and lacking in relevant training. The traffic situation was particularly chaotic, with a growth of more than 85% in the number of persons killed in motor vehicle accidents. This situation also resulted from the lack of interest of the East German population in their police. In terms of the confidence that the population had in the professional abilities of their police, only 12% of the people questioned in polls said that they were convinced that 'the police were ensuring good control of the criminality' (Schattenberg, 1991).

The result of these trends was that the police services that had been planning to rejoin the FRG became very demoralised. An opinion poll of public security officers, taken between 28 August and 25 October 1990, showed deeply divided support for the social changes among police officers from the former DVP: 50% of the officers claimed to support the 'social changes', whereas 30% claimed to be still undecided. Most significantly, many officers admitted to living with a mixture of profound worry about their social position (96% said they were uncertain about the future of their situation) and had a fear of political collapse (80% stated the belief that social tensions would lead to more serious political conflicts). Finally, half of the police officers polled stated that they were unable to cope with the new working conditions of being a police officer, according to an opinion poll carried out by a group of sociologists, from 28 August to 25 September 1990, on police officers from the DVP who were in active service (Wanderer and Thieme 1990). It was under these conditions of deep professional and political uncertainty that, on 3 October 1990, the *Volkspolizei* was absorbed into the police services of the reunified Germany.

Police unification on 3 October 1990

On 3 October 1990, Germany became a single juridical entity, covering the region from the Rhine to the Oder River: on 15 October, the penal code of procedure of the FRG was extended to the Eastern states (previously, the penal code that was in force was voted by the GDR's law of 1 October, which was largely inspired by the West, retained the force of law), and each state in the East adopted a temporary police law (*Polizeirecht*), based on that of their partner state in West Germany, from 3 October. All the officers who had asked to become officers of their state were granted this, but only according to three specific conditions. They were no longer governed by the statute for civil servants (*Beamte*), but were under an employee (*Angestellte*) statute: their permanent integration was subject to the decision taken by the commissions in charge of selecting personal (*Personalauswahlkommission*, or PAK).

Moreover, in order to control the costs of salaries in a country where the currency had been unified from 1 July 1990, they found themselves receiving just 60% of the salary of their colleagues from the West. Finally, all of the officers were stripped of their previous rank and carried on their service at a lower level of command: the regular officers worked at the lowest level of the hierarchy and their superiors became regular officers and so on (*Herabstufung*). The high-ranking officers and directors who put themselves forward at the point of the integration, were removed from active service and placed on a 'waiting list' (*Warteschleife*), pending review of their records. All of the management duties in the Eastern *Länder* were taken over by police officers from Western Germany.

The new police forces in the Eastern States

From the beginning, the 'absorption' of the *Volkspolizei* into the structures of the Federal Republic of Germany presented two major problems: that of the compatibility of the police officers with the new criteria for policing; and that of the ability of policing organisations to manage their environment (crime and public order) and to manage themselves. Therefore, the problem could be put in the following way: how could they ensure that the decisions taken for reasons of political urgency (a pace imposed by Helmut Kohl) and in the face of urgent societal needs (for public order to be maintained on a daily basis) could avoid undermining the establishment and long-term viability of an efficient and democratic police force? Would it be possible to ensure that the decision, which was forced by the needs of the moment, did not lead to a point of 'no-return' or 'lock-in' (Moe, 1990; Pierson, 2000; Dobry, 2000), and thereby paralyse the future?

The qualification and disqualification process applied to former Volkspolizei agents

The biggest immediate challenge was the management of personnel that the new regime inherited from the former regime. There were three levels to this challenge. First, the officers of the DVP simply found themselves vastly over-manned compared with the police forces for West Germany; moreover, with an abnormally high number of supervisors, the forces were top-heavy. It is estimated that 80,000 dismissals would be necessary in order to ensure a density of police coverage that would be fairly equal in all of the regions of the East and the West of Germany; and this concerned those officers who were still present in October 1990. Then, as has already been mentioned, the officers were, with only a few exceptions, all members of the Communist Party. Therefore careful procedures had to be adopted in order to appreciate the differences in officers' political loyalties. Finally, the officers' professional skills were a long way behind the qualifications of West German officers, and unprepared for the new requirements demanded by the increase in crime. These were the three problems that had to be resolved.

In terms of over-staffing and the command pyramid, the situation was partially settled by the number of police officers leaving the service. Many police forces were dissolved (in particular those that were responsible for controlling exit from the GDR's territory and all of the auxiliary members of the Stasi). Therefore, those who remained had to undergo individual tests that were suggested by the special personnel evaluation commissions.

Professional tests for former agents

The doctrine concerning taking back officers could not be put better than in this memo from Erich Pätzold, the Minister of the Interior of West Berlin in March 1990 (Jobard, 2003):

> The *Volkspolizei* has been a centralised authority, which, for forty years had been based on a Marxist-Leninist view of the state. Tasks and competency are impregnated by socialist design of the police and do not strictly conform to our democratic point of view. [...] But there is strong evidence that the rank and file officers had primarily received a craftsmanship education, together with an '*Erfahrungswissen*' which one should not underestimate. This *Erfahrungsschatz* constitutes the fundamental training on which we have to work: that is why we have requested the implementation of occupational training, based 'learning by doing' [in English in the original text]. [...] Practical skills occupy a crucial position in our work, and in that field, we will have to promote the position of craftsmanship at the core of democratic policing, through the common achievement of police tasks.

This meant that police forces in the West could not do without those from the East, who possessed far better knowledge of the terrain than their Western colleagues. Despite being better trained and trained for a longer period of time, Western police officers were largely ignorant of the local contexts of policing. This measure led the State of Mecklenburg-Pomerania to identify the following objectives for the integration of police officers: to keep only 80% of each class of officers, 20% of supervising officers, and 1% of the directors. These objectives were virtually identical to those for the other states, and were widely achieved. The first measure which aimed to reduce the number of people receiving salaries and was, as has already been stated, the creation of a salary differential between police officers in the East and those in the West, as well as shifting all of the officers from the East down a level in the hierarchy.

The second measure, which had dramatic consequences, was that all officers aged over fifty or having had a career of more than 25 years, and who so desired, were given 'early early retirement', i.e. even earlier than the usual 'early retirement'. Naturally, those officers grabbed the opportunity, which enabled them to escape from the worry of waiting for their results from the Personnel Evaluation Commissions, and to have a permanent status. This was indeed a dramatic decision, which brought about a massive curtailment in the number of the most experienced officers who, moreover, were the most popular among the populations they policed. In Mecklenburg, no officers over the age of 50 presented themselves for inclusion in the new police.

The third measure was testing professional abilities, by examining the professional records and the responses given by officers on their questionnaires (*Frageböge*). Having trained in a useless or obsolete service, lacking training, or possessing insufficient or inadequate training, were the most common reasons for 'ordinary dismissal' (*Ordentliche Kündigung*).

The political test for former agents

As already mentioned, the professional abilities of officers were not the only ones examined. The political biographies of officers were also considered in the acceptance criteria for candidates, and could constitute a motive for 'exceptional dismissal' (*Ausserordentliche Kündigung*). Five major reasons were given for this type of dismissal:

(1) Holding major political responsibilities or belonging to the Stasi: these reasons primarily concerned the highest ranking police officers, who were most affected by this rare form of dismissal.

(2) Performance of tasks in close collaboration with the Stasi or the Party, whether as a one-off case or in long-lasting collaboration.

(3) Committing acts that are contrary to the fundamental rule of law, and in particular, those that undermine human dignity, or any active participation in the brutal repression of demonstrations which took place in Berlin during Gorbachev's visit on 8 to 10 October 1989.

(4) Holding a political vision (*Politische Gesinnung*) that is contrary to the principle of rule of law, or that reflects views prohibited by the FRG.

(5) Intentional false declarations, lies or omissions. It appears that in the eyes of the various commissions, it is vital that the candidate who is accepted recognises his past mistakes rather than intentionally hiding them.

To these requirements set out by the police services one can, of course, add the political examinations carried out by the designated authority within the scope of the law on the handling of the GDR's past, which is referred to as the Gauck Commission (*Gauck-Behörd*). Under the directives of Minister Joachim Gauck, this federal authority was presented with the task of examining the overall individual and collective responsibilities of former inhabitants of the GDR, following a systematic examination of the Stasi and the SED's archives. This meant that a candidate who was accepted into the ranks of the unified police by the Commission of his particular state always ran the risk of being ousted by the Gauck Commission which, through its examination of the individual's Stasi file or the files of a third person, revealed their participation in one or another action that violated fundamental rights.

Organisation of human resources within East German police forces: continuity and breaches

It is extremely difficult to determine exactly whether policemen were expelled for commonplace or 'exceptional' reasons. The examination procedures were drawn out over four or five years (this process involved individually studying tens of thousands of files), which further complicated their evaluation. Even more so, given that decisions taken by the Gauck Commission were still susceptible to falling several years, or even a decade after those of the Commission in charge of evaluating personnel. The final assessment was rendered very difficult indeed.

In summary, it can be said that, depending on the state, and no matter what their level in the hierarchy, about 30% of the officers did not resume their functions; however, most often they made use of 'early early retirement' possibilities. In Berlin, no high ranking officers were employed at the same level of responsibility apart from one, but he was fired a few years later as the result of an investigation by the Gauck Commission. In total, 1056 officers were dismissed. In Brandenburg, the PAK was made up of policemen and state employees, who were chosen by each state's parliament and supervised by a police officer who came from the 'partner' state, Westphalia. Approximately 4000 of the 10,500 active police officers were dismissed for commonplace (or non-extraordinary) reasons or forced to take early retirement. Only 150 police officers were dismissed for political reasons. In Mecklenburg, where the PAK was made up of just two people, 20–30% of the personnel were dismissed under the direct order of the Prime Minister. In Thuringen, 5500 police officers (out of 8000) were authorised to continue, which led to approximately 1750 officers soliciting positions. In Saxony, the figures were around 500 candidates excluded out of the 11,500 applicants. In Saxony-Anhalt, 2300 candidates were excluded out of the 10,000 officers applying (Haselow, 2000).

This devastating loss of police officers led to low morale and personnel shortages in the police services. As was the case for all of the public service, this void enabled those who worked in collaboration with the police of the West to gain access to the most enviable or desirable managerial posts in the police of the East. In the State of Brandenburg, for example, all of the heads of police departments were police officers from the partner State of Westphalia and all of the police constables (*Polizeipräsidente*) were state employees sent from the State of Westphalia, with just one exception. Furthermore, all of them were members of the SPD.

To this human void at the top of the hierarchy of police services were added personnel with inferior qualifications, who, during the first two years, often underwent additional training (in Saxony, this was the case for about 10% of the personnel during 1992). When added to material difficulties, these measures rendered the policing organisations rather fragile.

West German police standards and the East German context: recruitment and training programmes

Police officers who had been admitted to the new policing organisations of the East on a temporary basis (*Angestellt*) were obliged to commit to follow two types of instruction. The first sort of training took place in the field, where, to use a well-known expression, the officers were 'learning by doing'. The second type was the supplementary training which was accomplished in police schools and academies.

The notion of 'learning by doing' was taken the furthest in Berlin, where the government decided to integrate all applying East Berlin police officers into the West Berlin police force. The government decided simply to mix together the 8200 applying police officers from East Berlin with the existing 22,000 West Berlin police officers on both sides of the city. On 1 October 1990, some 2000 West Berlin police officers had to go on the beat and to police stations in the Eastern part of the town; and around 700 of their East Berlin colleagues had to report for work in the Western part of the town (Glaeser, 2000; Jobard, 2003). In this manner, the problem of training was, for the most part, resolved by combining modern professional methods with older traditional methods -- namely establishing contacts so as to be more aware of the realities of life on the streets (these measures can be compared to the knowledge that we have on the institutionalisation and professionalisation of policing in large American cities. For examples, see Haller, 1976; and Miller, 1990).

The additional training was offered by the *Länders'* state police schools and was therefore run by staff who were involved in policing activities in the West, aided by the Police Officers School in Münster (Westphalia). All of the officers were to follow a four-week-long seminar, devoted to teaching about democratic, pluralist and constitutional societies. In West Germany, these four weeks of training were given in the schools of the partner state. The aim of all of this teaching was as much to inform officers about the foundations of the rule of law, as to familiarise the former *Volkspolitzei* with policing and police officers from the West through face-to-face exchanges.

The amount of supplementary and special training on offer varied greatly from one state to another. In Brandenburg, police officers who had reached the ranks of 'supervisors' had to attend about three hundred hours of teaching and this rose to approximately six hundred hours for those at the management level, spread out over a three-year period. One should not forget that the initial training (in a police school or police academy) for a police officer in the West lasts for two-and-a-half years.

However, very rapidly the number of Western personnel who were needed for this teaching overtook the capacities of the police from the West to provide them, to the extent that at times this put their own personnel training at risk. This was all the more the case since, according to current evaluations for Brandenburg, for example, the levels of education of police officers from the East were only about one-third of those of their Western colleagues. Hence, supplementary training was spread out over several years and was often supported by an element of 'on-the-job' training.

A successful graft?

What conclusions can we draw regarding the speed of police reform and its effects in Germany? Within a few months, the two parts of Germany formally had only one type of police. This type of police was legitimate, professional and responsible, the three criteria put forward by Marina Caparini and Otwin Marenin in the introduction to this volume. However, to these three we must also add the criterion of decentralisation. Decentralisation has been the constitutional guarantor of democracy in Germany, since its experiences with Bismarck, Hitler and the GDR.

The efficiency of East German policing

The implementation of West German police doctrines and procedures into the new *Länder*, despite being quite sudden and stark, was extremely efficient. Two points should be considered: the efficiency of the structural alignment of police organisations, and the efficiency of the fight against crime and maintenance of public order.

As far as the bureaucratic structures are concerned, the partnerships between Western and Eastern *Länder* led to the disappearance of a specifically GDR character of the police services of the new Eastern *Länder*. The autonomy of the police in (Western) Germany also gradually led to the relative independence of the institutions compared to the police of the new states. Naturally, the formal laws (*Polizeirecht*) that govern the practices of regular police in Saxony are very similar to the texts that were introduced in Bavaria, its Western partner state. The political proximity of the two *Länder* (largely due to the conservative parties) but also the legacy of institutional imitation, further contributes to their resemblance in legislation and guidelines. It is the same case, for example, for the two states that are the bastions of the social democrats, and thus partners, Westphalia and Brandenburg.

In other words, the police services in the East acquired an autonomy that, while being characteristic of any decentralised service, was still strongly indexed to the practices and habits of the partner states in the West. Thus one finds the same programmes of community policing or municipal partnership in the Brandenburg and in Westphalia, the same programmes of citizen militias being granted police competencies in the municipalities of Bavaria and municipalities of Saxony (Hohmeyer, 1999; *Neue Kriminalpolitik*, 2000; Jobard, 2003).

The issue of the efficiency of the fight against crime should be discussed with great care, given the considerable difficulties in making comparisons in this field: in the end, it does not make much sense to try to find out whether Japanese police are more effective in fighting crime than British police, as the crimes committed differ from one society to another, as do the expectations of different societies (Bayley, 1985, 2001).

In 1997, for example, the crime rate was proportionally higher in the new states: 9400 compared with 7700 for 100,000 inhabitants. In 2001 these rates were respectively 8500 and 7500, which marks a reduction in criminality over the whole of Germany (this has been the case for every year since 1992, apart from 1995 and 2001). This fall in criminality is most marked in the East, thus bringing the criminality rate for each side of the former East–West German border closer together (BKA, 1998, 2001).

Indeed, the rates of certain types of criminal activities remained higher in East Germany than in the West, and this situation sometimes could not be explained – in 2001, for example, thefts with aggravating circumstances represented 22.8% of all of the criminal activities found in the West and 26.7% of those in the East. Other rates could be easily explained by geographical reasons (for example, criminal activity linked to legislation on immigration is stronger in the East than in the West), or by historical reasons (extreme right-related crime is greater in the East than in the West).

Do the police play a specific role in these differences? There can be little doubt that the answer is no; and one should highlight the extent to which the level of autonomy of police organisations, as authorised by the legal federal framework, enables police to adapt their responses to the various forms of delinquency. For example, many hundreds of police forces from the East created brigades and specific services for the fight against the criminality of the extreme right. An example of this is the State of Brandenburg and its MEGA programme, which was specifically designed for the prevention and repression of organised forms of neo-Nazism, including the gathering and the dissemination of their ideas and practices (Koopmans, 1997; Oehlemeyer, 1994).

The day-to-day work of the regular police is much more difficult to evaluate. It is well known that the most substantial activity of the police is maintaining the peace, to a much greater extent than fighting crime (Bittner, 1974, 1990; Shearing, 1984). The essence of the problem is that this enormous part of police work is the least easily assessed and quantified. The methods of intervention that are used by the police in people's everyday lives go to the heart of what people are prepared to put up with from an intervening state authority and therefore also touches the heart of the relations between civil society and the State. From this point of view, the issue of police efficiency could fall under that of legitimacy.

The legitimacy of police forces of East Germany
What, in essence, accounts for the legitimacy of the new police forces which are derived from former ones in the new Eastern *Länder* of the Federal Republic of Germany?

A large part of the answer to this question can be found in what happened with the policy promoting the extension of the authoritative models of the West to the territory of the former GDR. Let us recall the effect of the departure of former officers and directors from the police, as well as the departure of those who were the most compromised with regard to the former regime. One must not forget the ousting for 'extraordinary' (i.e. political) reasons of those who, despite everything, remained after 3 October 1990. One should also not forget the massive departure of the oldest age groups to retirement or to early retirement, which emptied the police forces of the East of all those who, whether willingly or not, had been socialised into the organisations of the party. Finally, one should underline the strength of institutional imitation, which, as mentioned earlier, means that one can no longer distinguish between police of the East and those of the West in organisational terms. These elements strongly influence public perceptions of the police in the Eastern territories of Germany, where it is only with great difficulty that the police could be accused of embodying the dictatorial police of the previous era.

However, two elements should be underlined as strong points of reference, although they do not completely explain how the legitimacy of the new police is understood, nor how political consolidation has been achieved.

On the one hand, we should highlight the effects of the crises or trends towards failure, which brought into question one or another police service from the East. The most revealing example within this context is a fire which criminals maliciously set (hence committing arson) to a camp where asylum seekers were housed in the town of Rostock (in Mecklenburg-Vorpommern) in 1992. An entire fringe of the local population (who had been drinking heavily), responded to the code-word of the heads of local neo-Nazi groups, and assembled around the home. They then set fire to it, while chanting racist and Nazi slogans, under the totally impassive eyes of the local police who, to make matters worse, were considerably late in arriving at the location, thus reinforcing the idea of strong collective racism characterising the former members of the DVP.

The judicial inquiry into these events struggled to demonstrate any racist behaviour among the rank and file, however, it pointed at two institutional shortcomings. On the one hand, these police officers, who were totally inexperienced in dealing with non-conventional demonstrations (which, for the most part, had not occurred in the GDR since the uprising of June 1953), were guilty of non-intervention. Furthermore, on that particular weekend evening, the heads of the Rostock police were far from the scene and were therefore unable to react at all. The heads of the Rostock police, like the heads of all police forces from the East at this time, happened to be police employees of the partner state (Schleswig-Holstein) and were enjoying Friday evening in the company of their families, several hundred kilometres from the event. These failings show the effects created by the administrative organisation of German unification.

What is important to highlight at this point is that the failures of policing in the East arise from a combination of the legacies of past years (in terms of police professionalisation) and the perverse consequences of the reorganisation of the services (in terms of training of personnel). However, it must be emphasised that to this day there has been no convincing research leading to the conclusion of a more frequent or stronger inclination towards criminality (i.e. brutality, racism etc.) committed by the East German police in comparison to their colleagues from the West (one may note the failure to mention this question in reports by Amnesty International and also in the summaries of press reviews; see Korell and Liebel, 2000).

Moreover, opinion polls have demonstrated the blatant differences in the levels of 'confidence in the police'. On a scale between '–5' (no confidence whatsoever) and '+5' (complete confidence), the West Germans awarded their police force with an average mark of 1.9 for the period between 1991 and 1995; the East Germans credited their police with an average grade of 0.4 for the same period (Haselow, 2000: 145). The difference in the figures is significant. First, the numbers show the widespread wariness that East Germans display towards public institutions, whether they are viewed as too 'Eastern' (in which case they may be suspected of continuity with the GDR), or too 'Western' (leading to suspicions or concerns about imperialism of the FRG). Much more subtle instruments would be required to measure the exact perceptions of the role of the police in this transitional period.

However, another structural point needs to be stressed. It concerns the adjustments between society's demands for security and the government's policy on the matter. What are society's real expectations in terms of democratic policing? An 'authentically democratic' police force can only be identified if one takes the trouble to place it in its correct historical context. Thus, it is known that Western police forces have encouraged various models of community policing with the intention of bringing the police and the population closer together, so that police work can better respond to demands of the local population (Greene and Mastrofski, 1988; Brodeur, 1998). Yet it was precisely this model of community policing that characterised the GDR's police forces, to an even greater extent than in any other Western system.

Indeed, the GDR possessed police officers who were assigned to a specific district, or to one or two apartment blocks, in which they resided and worked. By being in close proximity to the inhabitants they also became close to the population, who would call on them at any hour of the day or night – for example, when their children were ill and urgently needed to be taken to hospital. Due to their 'natural' closeness to the population, these policemen, known as *Abschnittbevollmächtig* (or ABV – literally 'district delegates/representatives'), were also responsible for keeping watch over the population. Thus, by being immersed in the community, the ABV collected any information that could be required and handed it to their superiors in the hierarchy, and travelling up the chain of command until it arrived in the hands of the Stasi. Now and then, the ABV were assigned the task of destabilising individuals who were judged to be political deviants (by spreading rumours, harassment, filling their letterboxes with rubbish etc.). Yet, in reality, their *de facto* field of activity, provided by their immersion in the community and its problems, was of not-insignificant benefit for local populations, who knew how to distinguish between them and Stasi agents, the latter being only assigned to political work (for information on the ABV, see Lindenberger, 1999, 2003; for other analogies, see the text on Japanese community police in Bayley, 1985).

However, within the context of the profound social changes that occurred after the fall of the Berlin War, the East German police began showing a specific and growing need for training and for following through with the East German population at the same time as the West German police, whose model was applied to the East, were, in all honesty, looking to export 'their' isolated sections and community policing to the East. What then emerged? ABVs (KoB in 'Western' administrative terms) – but ABVs who were much less efficient, who only rarely lived on the site, who were only available during working hours and who were only available to deal with policing issues within their mandates etc. (Hausmann and Hornbostel, 1997; Hornbostel, 2000). This touches on the bottom line of the notion of the democratic consolidation of policing: should we not pursue true community policing and 'democratic consolidation' through policing programmes that attack 'modern' bureaucracies (modern community police cannot be reached at all times...), as well as by a policing philosophy that impinges on the independence and privacy of individuals? Naturally, the modern forms (both bureaucratic and professional) of 'State Organisations', to use Max Weber's categories, protect private lives and individuals' liberties, while holding the officers at the greatest distance possible from the citizen. However, at the same time, the familiarity, paternalism, and sometimes stifling proximity of officers of the Democratic Republic of Germany offered citizens the possibility of declining individual responsibility within the regime.

Conclusion: Political and historical paradoxes in the consolidation of 'democratic' police systems

In terms of the sociology of democratic transitions, German unification presents a specific difficulty in combining the 'democratisation' process and the 'integration' process, i.e. 'a process whereby a group of people, organised initially in two or more independent nation-states, come to constitute a political whole which can in a sense be described as a community' (Pentland, 1973: 21; Hancock and Welsh, 1994). The main lesson that the transformation of the police brings to the sociology of the German transition is the dual strength derived from absorbing authoritarianism and federalism.

In the case of authoritarianism, paths of opposition or of resistance were smothered from the start under the incredible pace of the transition. In a certain way, the suddenness of the political change, following the fall of the Berlin Wall, nipped in the bud any attempted opposition by officers who were faithful to the regime. The rapid pace of administrative reform then prevented even the smallest mobilisation within the police service, because by their very nature, the changes forced the oldest members to leave and thus cut off the ideological and material resources necessary to support any vague impulse to mobilise.

The speed in changing administrative procedures can also be seen as being representative of one of the key features of the police, which the highly respected police scholar Egon Bittner highlights as being in control, everywhere, of the present moment: police officers must intervene in 'something that ought not be happening and about which someone had better do something now' (Bittner 1974/1990: 249). This is also a dictatorship of the moment, which by engaging its policemen in the most urgent tasks, imposed its own rhythm on the administrative reform, and, in the end, on the 'democratisation' of the institution. In other words, in order to summarise political authoritarianism, one can underline the fact that an undoubtedly democratic transition (as decided by the first free elections in February 1990) was implemented in certain sectors of society, such as the police, in the form of a group of regulations and policies aiming to eliminate uncertainty and mobilisation, even though uncertainty and mobilisation are two pillars of the democratic order (Przeworski, 1986; Guilhot and Schmitter, 2000; Schedler, 2001).

Federalism also plays a pertinent role. In the end, no unification of police forces occurred (except in Berlin), but rather a forced adaptation of the police forces of the five new *Länder* to the models in use by the police forces of the West. Once the years of training were over, these police forces enjoyed the same degree of autonomy that was conceded to police forces in the federal systems, and then followed their own developmental path. It is this flexibility and relative autonomy during the so-called 'consolidation' phase, which, to a large extent, has enabled the violence of the 'transition' to be absorbed.

Thus, it is within this context of plurality of paths open to the East German police that the debate on the stages of the transition must be brought back to the alternatives to 'modernisation/path dependence' (Offe, 1996; Stark and Bruszt, 1998; Dobry, 2000). On the one hand, no other administration is more anchored in social problems or issues than the police, nor is there any administration more profoundly dependent on society's demands which are set out in the very definition of its practices and aims. This being the case, one may recall one of the oldest adages of police sociology, which points out that a community will get the police that it deserves (Banton, 1964). Moreover, any delay or survival of the past in police practices (as long as they can be empirically changed) must not lead one to forget the specificities of the social fabric and the social demands in the various regions of East Germany.

On the other hand, one of the paths to the 'modernisation' of policing from the 1980s onwards was a return to so-called 'village police', foot patrols and community policing, local police and police familiar with the dominant groups in the district. From this point of view, and as far as policing is concerned, the adaptation of police forces from the East to 'Western modernity' seems only able to borrow the ambiguous approaches of policing in the past, which in the GDR were so well embodied in the paternalistic and authoritative model of the ABV. Modernisation, in terms of policing in East Germany, has familiar faces...

References

Aden, H. 1998. *Combatting Crime, Mobilizing New Actors and Tendencies towards a Repressive Roll-back. German Security and Crime Prevention and Policies in the 90s.* Opladen.

Bayley, D. 1985. *Patterns of Policing. A Comparative International Analysis.* Rutgers UP. New Brunswick.

Bayley, D. 2001. *Democratising the Police Abroad. What to Do and How to Do It.* Washington.

Bittner, E. 'Florence Nightingale in pursuit of Willie Sutton', in *Aspects of Police Work.* Boston: Northeastern University Press, originally published 1974, reprinted 1990.

Brodeur, J.P., ed. 1998. *How to Recognize Good Policing?* Thousand Oaks : Sage.

Bundeskriminalamt. 1998. *Polizeikriminalstatistik.* Wiesbaden.

Bundeskriminalamt. 2001. *Polizeikriminalstatistik* Wiesbaden.

Busch, Heiner et al. 1988. eds., *Die Polizei in der Bundesrepublik.* New-York.

Caparini, M., and Marenin, O. 2004. 'Police Transformation in Central and Eastern Europe: the Challenge of Change', in this volume.

Dobry, M., ed. 2000. *Democratic and Capitalist Transitions in Eastern Europe. Lessons from the Social Sciences.* Dordrecht.

Dünkel, F. 1992. 'Probleme des Strafvollzugs nach der Wiedervereinigung', in Kury H. *Gesellschaftliche Umwälzung. Kriminalitätserfahrungen, Straffälligkeit und soziale Kontrolle.* Freiburg.

Fogelson, R. 1977. *Big City Police.* Cambridge, Massachusetts.

Fulbrooke, M. 1995. *Anatomy of a Dictatorship: Inside the GDR 1949-89.* Oxford.

Glaeser, A. 2000. *Divided in Unity. Identity, Germany, and the Berlin Police.* Chicago.

Glaeßner, G. J. and Wallace, I. eds. 1992. *The German Revolution of 1989.* New York.

Glaeßner, G. J. 1994. 'Parties and problems of governance during unification', in Hancock, D., Welsh, H., eds. *German Unification. Process and Outcomes.* Boulder, Colorado.

Greene, J. and Mastrofski, S. 1988. *Community Policing. Rhetoric or Reality?.* New York.

Guilhot, N. and Schmitter, P. 2000. 'From transition to consolidation. A retrospective discussion of democratization studies', in Dobry, M., ed. *Democratic and Capitalist Transitions in Eastern Europe. Lessons from the Social Sciences.* Dordrecht.

Haller, M. 1976. 'Historical roots of police behaviour. Chicago. 1890-1925', in *Law and Society Review* vol. 4, Santa Barbara.

Hancock, D., Welsh, H. 1994. 'Models of unification: integration theory and democratisation', in Hancock, D., Welsh, H., eds. *German Unification. Process and Outcomes.* Boulder, Colorado.

Hancock, D., Welsh, H., eds. 1994. *German Unification. Process and Outcomes.* Boulder, Colorado.

Haselow, R. 2000. *Der Wandel der Volkspolizei zu einer rechtsstaatlich-demokratischen Polizei.* Lübeck.

Hausmann, C. and Hornbostel, S. 1997. 'Von der Volkspolizei lernen oder : Wie neu ist die kommunale Kriminalprävention?', in Kury, H., ed. *'Konzepte kommunaler Kriminalprävention'.* Freiburg in Breisgau.

Hohmeyer, C. 1999. Kommunale Kriminalpolitik in Deutschland. Akteure, Themen und Projekte kriminalpräventiver Gremien'. *Bürgerrechte und Polizei* vol. 3. <www.cilip.de>

Hornbostel, S. 2000. 'Der "Abschnittsbevollmächtigte". Ein fast vergessener Versuch der Kriminalprävention'. *Kriminologisches Journal*, vol. 32, no. 3.

Jobard, F. 2001. 'Weiß neben Schwarz leuchtet besser. Die Zusammenführung der Berlinerpolizei (1989-90)'. *Horch und Guck* vol.10, no. 4. Berlin.

Jobard, F. 2002. 'Singularités allemandes. Les surprises de l'unification du système carcéral'. *Critique Internationale 16*, June 2002. Paris.

Jobard, F. 2003. 'Usages et ruses des temps. L'unification des polices berlinoises après 1989'. *Revue Française de Science Politique* vol. 53, no. Paris.

Korell, J. and Liebel, K. H. 2000. *Urban, Polizeiskandal, Skandalpolizei. Demokratiemangel bei der Polizei?* Münster.

Kuran, T. 'New out of newer. The element of surprise in the East European revolution of 1989', in Bermeo, N., ed. *Liberalisation and Democratisation. Change in the Soviet Union and Eastern Europe.* Baltimore.

Koopmans, R. 1997. 'Dynamics of repression and mobilization. The German extreme right in the 1990s'. *Mobilisation*, vol. 2, no 1. San Diego.

Lindenberger, T. 2003. *Volkspolizei. Herrschaftspraxis und öffentliche Ordnung im SED-Staat 1952-1968.* Cologne.

Lindenberger, T. 1999. 'Creating state socialist governance. the case of the German Volkspolizei', in Jarausch, K., ed. *Dictatorship as Experience. Toward a Social History of the GDR.* New York.

Lindenberger, T 1998. 'Die deutsche Volkspolizei (1945-90)', in Diedrich, T., Ehlert, H., Wenzke, R. eds., *Im Dienste der Partei. Handbuch der bewaffneten Organe der DDR.* Berlin.

Maier, C. 1997. *Dissolution. The Crisis of Communism and the End of East Germany.* Princeton.

Miller, W. 1990. 'Cops and bobbies. 1830–1930', in Klockars, C. and Mastrofski, S. *Thinking About the Police. Contemporary Readings.* 2nd edn. New-York.

Moe, T. 1990. 'The politics of structural choice: Toward a theory of public democracy'. *Organisation Theory. From Chester Barnam to the Present and Beyond.* Oxford.

Neue Kriminalpolitik. 2000. *Polizei und städtische Sicherheitspolitik im Wandel'.* vol. 1.

Offe, C. 1996. *Varieties in Transitions.* Cambridge.

Ohlemacher, T. 1994. 'Public Opinion and Violence Against Foreigners in the Reunified Germany', *Zeitschrift für Soziologie,* vol. 23, no. 3.

Opp, K.D. 1994. 'Repression and revolutionary action. East Germany in 1989'. *Rationality and Society,* vol. 6, no. 1. Thousand Oaks.

Pentland, C. 1973. *International Theory and European Integration.* New York.

Pierson, P. 2000. 'Path dependence, increasing returns, and the study of politics', in *American Political Science Review,* vol. 94 no. 2. Washington.

Przeworski, A. 1992. 'The games of transition', in Mainwaring, S., O'Donnel, G., Valenzuela, S., eds. *Issues of Democratic Consolidation.* Notre Dame.

Reiβig, R. and Glaeβner, G. J. 1991. *Das Ende eines Experiments. Umbruch in der DDR und deutsche Einheit.* Berlin.

Rupprecht, R. 1995. *Polizei Lexicon.* 2nd edn. Heidelberg.

Schattenberg, B. 1991. 'Entwicklung der Kriminalität in den neuen Bundesländern', in Polizei-Führungakademie, *Transformation. Zur Entwicklung in den neuen Bundesländern.* p. 65 (quoted in Haselow, 2000, p. 41).

Schedler, A. 'Taking uncertainty seriously : the blurred boundaries of democratic transition and consolidation'. *Democratisation,* vol. 8, no. 4.

Schmitter, P. and Santiso, J. 1998. 'Three temporal dimensions to the consolidation of democracy',in *International Political Science Review*, vol. 19, no. 1.

Shearing, C. 1984. *Dial-a-Cop. A Study of Police Mobilisation.* Toronto.

Wanderer, L., et al. 'Die Ergebnisse einer soziologischen Untersuchung im Dienstzweig Schutzpolizei der neuen Bundesländer', *Die Polizei*, vol. 83, no. 1.

Chapter 4

Hungarian Police Reform

Éva Keresztes Dimovné[1]

A brief country profile

The small Central European state of Hungary (with a population of 10,149,000 people and a territory of about 93,030 square kilometres) illustrates the profound changes that regime change can bring to the social reality of a country. After the second half of the 1960s, the state Socialist regime in Hungary was characterised as 'softer' than that of other countries in the Soviet zone of influence, most of all because of its moderate economic freedom. In the second half of the 1980s reforms had been initiated, and continued through the round-table talks between the ruling communist elite and the emerging democratic opposition. By 1989 the political agenda was clearly indicating new trends: Imre Nagy, who had been Prime Minister in 1956, was reburied with other victims and revolutionaries of the 1956 revolution; Hungary's western borders were opened before the huge crowds of East Germans who intended to go further to 'the West' through Austria; and on 23 October 1989 the Hungarian Republic was proclaimed. In 1990 the Soviet army left the country and the first free parliamentary election took place, resulting in the victory of the Hungarian Democratic Forum (MDF) and the formulation of a centre-right coalition government in partnership with the Independent Smallholders' Party (FKgP) and the Christian Democratic People's Party (KDNP) (U.S. Department of State 1999).

The legislative and constitutional changes brought about a parliamentary democracy with a multi-party system, a market economy, a rule of law state where the constitutional structure is based on Western models and fundamental rights are respected. New institutions have been established within the constitutional framework of the country, such as the President of the Republic as the head of state, who is elected by the parliament for a term of five years; the parliamentary commissioners (ombudsmen) – guarantors of constitutional rights; and the Constitutional Court, which reviews the constitutionality of laws.

In terms of its international relations, Hungary has joined numerous international organisations and ratified the Statute of the Council of Europe. Also, since 1999 the country has been a member of the NATO alliance, and is expected to join the European Union in 2004.

---

1. The author would like to thank the Service of Personnel Affairs of the National Police Headquarters for their kind cooperation and assistance.

Introduction

The 1989 Velvet Revolution ensured, via the round-table talks, a peaceful democratisation in Hungary. Understandably, the transition period witnessed profound changes in the social, political, economic, legal and cultural framework of the newly emerging democracy. These changes, revolutionary in their scope and intensity, stretched the capacity of the governance system to its limits, especially the legislature's ability to react to emerging societal patterns. Thus, legislation became 'reactive' instead of 'regulatory' and 'anticipatory'.

The acute negative repercussions from the surprising speed and breadth of revolutionary changes had been especially pronounced in the field of criminal justice, a system which proved to be completely inadequate to meet the new democratic requirements and different crime conditions. An indication of the abnormal quantitative and structural changes in crime is the upsurge in the number of registered crimes, which grew by more than 20% in 1989 and by more than 50% in 1990, in contrast to the 3–4% annual average growth in the previous years (Déri-Budai, 1990: 333). A more detailed view of the structure and dynamics of crime is presented in Table 4.1, which indisputably shows a general increase, with some annual fluctuations, in the forms and frequency of reported crime. The crime rate became much higher during transition than the Hungarian public had been accustomed to during the state Socialist period.

As a consequence of this unfavourable trend and the accompanying public outcry about the crime situation, a number of experimental reform initiatives have been launched to 'update' the criminal justice system as a whole, and most of all for the reform of its core institution – the police.

Increasing police professionalism and efficiency became the basic goal for political reformers, a task that had to be achieved in parallel to and not at the expense of democratic values, which remained a socio-political and ideological priority. The practical 'marriage' of these two complimentary tasks, as I will demonstrate, has proven to be elusive during the course of political transition. This chapter presents what has been achieved so far under the notion of 'police reform' and analyses the major reasons for the failure of modernisation to take root, mainly the incremental nature of attempted reform measures and the lack of public and political consensus on how to strike the appropriate balance between the goals of effective and democratic policing.

Table 4.1   Registered crimes according to the main headings of the Penal Code (1991-2001)

Crimes	Against state and humanity	Against person	Traffic	Against marriage, family, youth and sexual morality	Against public admin., admin. of justice, purity of public life	Against public order	Economic	Against property	Against military obligation	Total
2001	0	20,927	19,561	4,642	15,558	74,535	12,412	317,900	159	465,694
2000	0	16,591	19,566	5,059	10,408	76,312	10,986	311,611	140	450,673
1999	0	18,882	20,503	4,668	12,120	71,063	20,318	358,036	126	505,716
1998	1	18,684	22,423	4,589	8,587	75,592	13,454	457,188	103	600,621
1997	1	16,445	21,203	4,619	6,493	65,956	6,543	393,003	150	514,403
1996	0	14,720	20,689	5,153	6,053	48,598	5,409	365,235	193	466,050
1995	4	16,096	24,633	4,460	5,446	55,061	5,064	391,062	210	502,036
1994	19	16,150	26,556	5,095	6,785	43,379	4,085	287,095	287	389,451
1993	9	14,782	29,362	66,492	5,206	31,230	6,146	307,396	312	400,935
1992	7	14,823	33,130	6,497	5,618	27,480	8,913	350,582	165	447,215
1991	2	13,974	29,942	7,712	5,029	18,474	8,347	356,671	219	440,370

Source: Police, Ministry of Interior Affairs, Hungary

Snapshot of police during the pre-transition period and at the start of transition

> In communist countries, the primary task of the police forces, in common with other bodies and institutions, was to sustain the political system and safeguard its functioning. The police operated as a subsidiary force of the state security agency ... Regular police work, such as detention or prevention of crime, was secondary to the task of maintaining the security of the state (Kőszeg 2001a: 1).

In Hungary, the nature of policing during the communist regime fit this picture. However it was not only the politicised role of police that required fundamental changes at the beginning of the transition period. The police also struggled with severe difficulties as noted in various academic studies. Géza Finszter (1990: 3) described the Hungarian police in 1990 as facing a functional and moral-political crisis, including a lack of legitimacy. Attila Bencsik (1991: 7–9) characterised the Hungarian police as an 'anachronistic, bureaucratic' and 'over-centralised' organisation whose main function was to secure political power; the borderline between public security policing, political policing and secret services became blurred. Thus the police appeared to the public as a symbol of oppression. The police were organised to manage their work under conditions of a political dictatorship; crime rates were kept artificially low and the police were ill-prepared to deal with the consequences of societal upheavals or changes in the regime. Police officers were underpaid, had low social status and their contra-selection presented major problems. There was a huge gap between police and the society, including local communities. Their technology and equipment were not up to modern standards (e.g. they had no sophisticated databases or computer systems) and were insufficient in quantity.

In addition the police lacked basic legal status since they were established and regulated by governmental and ministerial decrees and not by a statute passed by the legislature, even though police operations have the potential to severely restrict the fundamental rights of citizens. Before the enactment of the Police Act of 1994, the main 'laws' regulating the police were the 17 statutory rules from 1974 on State and Public Safety, the 39/1974 (XI.1) Decree of the Council of Ministers on Police with its amendments, and the 22 statutory rules of 1963 on the use of firearms by police. Also, some of the norms governing the police and their operations were of a confidential nature, difficult to access by the public, and hence raised serious questions regarding the predictability of legal norms. Only in 1990 were the citizens able to openly access the 1/1990 (I.10) Decree by the Minister of Interior on the Service Regulation of the Police (Szikinger 1996: 2).

The 1993 Project on Ethnic Relations assessing the Pest County Police District and the Hungarian National Police found – among other things – that modern management techniques were only sporadically applied; that the police were highly centralised in structure which limited 'the ability of district commanders to make necessary changes and to be responsive to the changing needs of their district,

district personnel, and local civilians'; that the education system needed to be revised; that the police profession had a low prestige among the public; and that the police suffered from 'a lack of public trust and credibility' (Project on Ethnic Relations, 2000: 4–6).

The goals of police transition

The modernisation of police was on the political agenda from the beginning of the transition, and Hungary has received international help on numerous occasions, which made it financially possible, for example, to entrust Team Consult (a Swiss consulting firm) with an evaluation of the Hungarian Police (Gottlieb *et al.*, 1998). Politicians, academics, police experts and police representatives were involved from the very beginning in formulating what was needed for police transition. The goals of police reform, though, have changed throughout the transition period.

Ferenc Kőszeg, President of the Hungarian Helsinki Committee, has argued that at the beginning of regime change principles such as depoliticisation of the police forces, professionalism over 'political expediency', organisational independence, decentralisation and reducing broad police powers together with promoting respect for human rights were the main goals of police reform demanded by the new democratic political forces (Kőszeg, 2001a: 1–2). Yet the goals of reform were already amended after the first democratically elected government came into office. The principle of decentralisation had been abandoned early and a militarised and centralised police system was later advocated by politicians, and even by police itself, as the most efficient means to combat the increasing rate of crime and to meet citizens' demands for public safety.

Further developments can be traced in legislative instruments regarding the aims of police reform during the transition period. The major instrument of police reform is the 1994 Police Act (Act XXXIV of 1994 on the Police). The General Explanations to the Bill emphasise that among the goals of reform are a police which is 'politically neutral' (non-partisan), whose work is 'prescribed by law in terms of its functions and means', and whose 'activities are legally controlled'. This requirement is derived from the Constitution, international treaty obligations and the European integration process, and is in accordance with the norms of a democratic state governed by the rule of law. The other aim stressed by the General Explanations is that the police should become an 'efficient means in the fight against crime' which is necessary to preserve the country's 'international reputation', and which is required by the 'the demands of the citizenry for public safety and the non-disturbance of public life'. The final aim of the Act is to create the 'stable legal foundations and the legally prescribed "latitude" [discretion] for the efficient and successful operation of the police which will contribute to the maintenance of internal order and public safety'. Thus the Police Act stresses depoliticisation of the police, harmonisation with EU standards and requirements for the rule of law, police efficiency in fighting crimes, and creating a legal basis for police operations and accountability.

One cannot describe the goals of police reform in Hungary in homogenous terms, since, as mentioned before, emphasis was placed on different principles depending on the actual political agenda; thus significant shifts occurred regarding certain key principles. Also, as will be perceived presently, academics and police experts have completely different notions about what should be the necessary aims of police reforms than do party politicians, police leaders or the public.

Description of reforms in the major targeted areas

The duties of the police

Article 40, A, paragraph (2) in Chapter VIII of the Hungarian Constitution – which has been amended fundamentally several times since the transition started but is still based on Act XX of 1949 – declares the major duty of police as 'maintaining public safety and domestic order' – a duty also reiterated in Article 1, paragraph (1) of the Police Act. Article 3, paragraph (1) of the Police Act defines the police as 'the armed force of the state protecting public order and carrying out tasks related to crime prevention, crime detection, public administration, and general law enforcement/ policing'. Article 1, paragraph (2) and Article 2, paragraphs (1), (2) and (4) of the Police Act gives a more specified list of police tasks. These include:

> Crime prevention and detection; misdemeanour authority (prevention and detection of administrative offences); policing of foreigners and refugees; authority regarding instruments and substances dangerous to public safety; traffic authority; policing tasks related to maintaining the order of public places; protection of life and the bodily integrity of 'protected persons'; guarding designated establishments; licensing and supervision of private security guards and of private detective activities; assisting municipal guards; law enforcement tasks; protection from actions directly endangering or violating life, bodily integrity or property of people; counselling and assisting those in need (all these while respecting human dignity and protecting human rights); action against international crime based on international treaties and reciprocal co-operation with foreign and international public order defending organs; and other tasks.

Decree 3/1995 (III.1) of the Minister of Interior (Code of Conduct) further specifies the manner in which to carry out the duties of the police.

Organisation, structure and character of the police

During the communist regime the police had been under the direction of the Communist Party and supported party interests and politics. The borderline between secret services and public safety policing was kept unclear. The first step of police reform, hence, was to separate police from politics, and the police from the secret services. The so-called Dunagate scandal[2] at the very beginning of 1990 gave impetus to drastic changes concerning the structure and powers of the Ministry of Interior. The scandal also affected the police even though it was the security services that were involved and not the police (Wiener, 1996). Apart from personnel changes in the leadership, several legislative amendments were introduced. By force of law at the beginning of 1990 (Article 7, paragraph (2) of Act X of 1990), the national security services were separated from the Ministry of the Interior and placed under the direction of the President of the Council of Ministers (the executive), making it clear that the internal security of the state is not a duty of agencies in the Ministry of the Interior but constitutes functions of national security agencies, and that national security activities are not a function for the police.

Another amendment in 1990 (Article 22 of Act XXII of 1990) separated the National Police Headquarters from the Ministry of Interior by allocating the power to give commands and concrete instructions only to the National Police Commissioner. The Minister of Interior could direct and control police only by regulatory means (Wiener, 1996). The enactment of the 1994 Police Act extended the restricted powers of the Minister of Interior since it gave authority to the Minister to give concrete orders to the police via the National Police Commissioner (Article 5, paragraph (3)), making it possible by the letter of the law that a political figure, the Minister, could influence police operation in specific situations.

Before the enactment of the 1994 Police Act, the notion of decentralisation – preserving the centralised state police for certain duties but, in addition, allocating functions with regard to local public safety policing to municipalities – seemed rather attractive. Yet the Police Act did not bring about fundamental changes in the organisational structure of the police for three main reasons: local governments did not want additional responsibilities without financial support for the new tasks; the top management of the police argued for a centralised system, 'being mostly interested in retaining power and social status'; and politicians and the public thought that efficient policing in the new criminal environment required 'an army-like organisation' (Szikinger, 1996: 5). In consequence, the Police Act of 1994 retained the Hungarian police as a centralised, unified, military type of force.

The National Police Headquarters is at the top of the hierarchy to which the 19 county police headquarters plus the capital headquarters (Budapest, which has the same level status as a county) are directly subordinate. Local police stations represent the lowest level in the hierarchy. By September 2002 there were 153 local headquarters (*rendőrkapitányság*) and 265 local police stations (*rendőrőrs*).[3]

---

2. The Dunagate scandal revealed that the Interior Ministry had continued to gather intelligence on opposition politicians even after the change in regime. See: http://www.coldwar.hu/html/en/chronologies/_4_90.html

3. For more information, see the website of the Hungarian National Police: http://web.bm.hu/rendor/rendor.nsf/93188b8ee4f56e56c1256966001ec8ac/aed87309d8b1 91a4c12568e30041effc?OpenDocument

The Police Act regulates only the 'stable and permanent' central, county level and local organisations of the police, but does not apply to police agencies with special duties which are not part of basic organisational system (Article (3) of the Police Bill). According to 3/1995 (III.1) Decree of the Minister of Interior, the organisation of the police is divided into branches by general services (criminal, public order protection, traffic police, administration, protection of persons and property), specialised services (anti-terrorism, airport security, demolition experts, increased forces of police troops (*rendőri csapaterő*), after-hours duty service, national courier-service) and support services (economic, information technology, personnel, and official services, this latter category including legal, medical services, secretariat and day-to-day administration).

Section (1h) of Article 35 of the Constitution declares that 'the Government shall supervise the operation of the police'. Article 4, Section (1) of the Police Act states that the government directs the police through the Minister of Interior. The National Commissioner of the Police is appointed and dismissed by the Prime Minister based on the proposal of the Minister of Interior, and the candidate is interviewed by the respective parliamentary committee. The National Commissioner of the Police directs the National Headquarters of the Police and controls and directs the operation and professional activities of the police headquarters, which are under his/her own responsibility guided by the relevant legal regulation. According to Article 4, paragraph (3) of the Police Act, the Minister of Interior represents the police at parliamentary sessions and in the government. This provision gave and continues to give rise to concerns about the possibility of organisational lobbying by police. As noted by István Szikinger (1998: 37), a constitutional lawyer and expert on police issues: 'neither the border guards nor other important organisations have achieved that level of an institutional lobby [...]. However the will of the police is expressed and implemented' (translation by the author; see also Kőszeg, 2000: 86).

The principle of depoliticisation

Laws enacted during 1989 and 1990, and the 1/1990 decree of 10 January 1990 by the Minister of Interior (on service regulations for the police) already regulated and restricted certain political activities for persons serving in the armed forces or armed bodies, including the police. For example, they were prohibited from collecting nomination coupons for parliamentary elections at police stations or from members of armed forces when they were discharging their duties; the ban on political party activities on police premises, including the prohibition on discussing party politics during staff meetings; the ban on displaying party badges and symbols on police premises; the restriction on forming and maintaining a political party by police officers; or the requirement that police officers can act as experts or advisers on questions of police service upon request from political parties only with the authorisation by the Minister of Interior.

Following the 24 December 1993 Law (No. 107 of 1993, on certain amendments to the Constitution), Article 40B, paragraph (4) of the Constitution now declares that, 'professional members of the armed forces, the police and other civil national security services may not be members of political parties and may not engage in political activities'. In addition the same principle of restraint on political-party influence is confirmed in several articles of the Police Act and in Act XLIII of 1996 on the Service Relations of Career Members of the Armed Forces (henceforth Act on Service Relations).

The introduction of the constitutional provision referred to above has been challenged by domestic organisations and before the international forum of the European Court of Human Rights, which in the *Rekvényi v. Hungary* decision (Application no. 25390/94, Judgement of 20 May 1999) found no violation either of the right to freedom of expression, nor the right of freedom of association, nor taken them in conjunction with Article 14 (the article concerning non-discrimination) of the European Convention on Human Rights. The Court noted that Hungary experienced a totalitarian regime in the past, a regime, 'which relied to a great extent on the direct commitment of the police to the ruling party', and the Government also contended that, 'given Hungary's peaceful and gradual transformation towards pluralism without a general purge in the public administration, it was necessary to depoliticise, inter alia, the police and to restrict the political activities of its members so that the public should no longer regard the police as a supporter of the totalitarian regime but rather as a guardian of democratic institutions' (*Rekvényi v. Hungary*, 1999: Paragraphs 41 and 44).

Thus the European Court of Human Rights found that the above provision amending the Hungarian Constitution was introduced 'in order to protect the police force from the direct influence of party politics' and 'can be seen as answering a "pressing social need" in a democratic society'. The Court also noted that:

> An examination of the relevant laws shows that police officers have in fact remained entitled to undertake some activities enabling them to articulate their political opinions and preferences. Notably, while sometimes subject to restrictions imposed in the interest of the service, police officers have had the right to expound election programmes, promote and nominate candidates, organise election campaign meetings, vote in and stand for elections to Parliament, local authorities and the office of mayor, participate in referenda, join trade unions, associations and other organisations, participate in peaceful assemblies, make statements to the press, participate in radio or television programmes or publish works on politics (*Rekvényi v. Hungary*, 1999: Paragraphs 48 and 49).

Although in principle depoliticisation of police has been achieved, the police are sometimes criticised by civil society groups as serving political interests. For example, in February 2003, when the police after the first request had denied permission for a mass peace demonstration, civil sector representatives evaluated the denial of the demonstrators' request as a 'political decision' by which the 'police leadership wanted to meet political expectations' (NSZ, February 2003).

Decentralisation versus centralisation

The principle of decentralisation became a victim of politics. The idea of police decentralisation, allocating tasks to maintain local public safety to the municipalities together with the necessary resources and powers, was abandoned in the course of police modernisation. Although before the first free parliamentary election in 1990 there was a broad political consensus on police decentralisation and the National Police Headquarters supported the idea of the 'police under municipalities' to meet local needs, by the end of the debate the Police Act further strengthened the 'centralised' structure (Szikinger, 1998a: 41, 50; Kőszeg, 1992: 167–71). The detailed explanation of Article 3, paragraph (1) of the Police Bill stresses that the tasks enumerated there, namely crime prevention, criminal investigation, public administration and policing, constitute exclusive state functions. The Bill affirms the concept of a unified state police. In other words, the centralised and not the decentralised model of police organisation gained approval.

This regulatory framework on police structure leads – as stressed by the experts (e.g. Szikinger, 1998a: 52) – to ambiguities in the legislation in force, since Act LXV of 1990 on Local Self-Governments assigns to local governments the task of maintaining local public safety. However, the Police Act, in the explanatory memorandum to the Bill, states that policing tasks are solely central state functions.

Though the idea of a 'police under municipalities' has never gained approval in the process of the 'modernisation' of the Hungarian police, it became necessary because of the discrepancy between state and municipal powers concerning public safety, to regulate in greater detail the relationship between police and local self-governments on this issue. Chapter III of the Police Act allows granting, for certain issues, very weak powers to local self-governments, such as, for example, the right to 'express their opinion' on certain issues (such as to the establishment and termination of the operation of a local police station, or concerning the appointment of the leaders of respective police units); a duty of the police 'to inform municipalities' prior to enacting measures affecting the general conditions of local inhabitants; or the right of the municipalities to 'make observations' on certain police measures. The police and municipalities can conclude 'cooperation agreements', especially on financing matters and material resources provided by the municipalities to the police (Kósa-Kálmán 2000: 68–72). Yet it is apparent from the provisions of the Act that in cases of disagreement between the police and a local self-government, the police are in the dominant position. This is reflected in the appointment procedure, since a police authority can appoint its own candidate even against the opinion of the municipality, but must give its reasons (Article 3 of the Police Act). Working with municipalities, police commissioners can establish crime prevention and public safety committees, but in case of disagreement between the committee and the mayor or the head of the relevant police organ, the concerned parties can request the position of the head of the superior police authority (Article 10, Paragraph (3) of the Police Act).

Since 2002, parliament has shown evidence of political will to advance some changes towards the decentralisation of the police. The Alliance of Liberal

Democrats (SZDSZ), in its political party programme during the course of the electoral campaign, advocated and elaborated the idea of community policing as its 'liberal proposal', stating that the governmental duty of public safety should be shared with local self-governments; that policing should be returned to civil administration; that local public safety should become a duty of local self-governments; and, to carry out this new function, they should receive support from the central budget (SZDSZ 2002). In 2002, the SZDSZ having become one of the parties in the new ruling coalition, together with the Hungarian Socialist Party, the long awaited decentralisation of policing may take place, since the liberal agenda, even if very softly formulated, is reflected in the current governmental programme (Cselekedni, 2002).

Demilitarisation versus militarisation

> Hungarian police officers are structured into the same rank order as used by the army. The uniforms are very similar but the colour is different ... The chain of command, duties and rights of the officers, discipline and all other conditions of performing duties have been put into a principally uniform framework by the 1996 Service Relations of Officers of Armed Organs Act. Police officers are soldiers in terms of criminal law. This means they are subject to special provisions of the criminal code in addition to the ordinary ones. Disobedience, for example, is a military offence even if the order has been proved unlawful. The only justification of refusal to comply with orders is avoidance of committing a criminal offence (Szikinger, 2002: 3).

The above quote highlights the fundamental criticism concerning the militarised character of the Hungarian police. The currently existing conditions for following orders and the strong internal discipline, when contrasted with Council of Europe standards, are the first major indicators of the 'militarised' character of the police. Although Resolution 690 (1979) of the Parliamentary Assembly of the Council of Europe on the Declaration on the Police requires (in Point A.4.) that 'a police officer shall carry out orders properly issued by his/[her] hierarchical superior, but he/[she] shall refrain from carrying out any order he/[she] knows, or ought to know, is unlawful', the 1994 Police Act permits disobedience only in the case the officer would commit a criminal offence by carrying out the order. In case the order would constitute an 'unlawful' measure – save for the case of committing a criminal offence – the police officer cannot disobey the order but can only draw the attention of a superior to the nature of the order (Article 12, Paragraph (1) – (2) of the Police Act). Thus, the requirement of strong obedience to an order coming from a superior and internal discipline as these are regulated in the Police Act is not in compliance with Council of Europe standards (Szikinger 1998: 111, 112, 133, and Kőszeg, 2000: 87). It should be noted, as well, that although the Police Act requires the execution even of an unlawful order, earlier regulations, specifically the 1/1990 (I. 10) Decree of the Minister of Interior, allowed disobedience also in cases when the order constituted an 'unlawful' act.

Personnel-related issues: service strength

The number of Hungarian police personnel is increasing. In 1989 there were about 20,000 regular personnel for a population of around ten million inhabitants (Kőszeg, 2000: 86). By the year 2002 the number of career police personnel had reached the figure of 29,610, that is one career police officer for every 343 citizens. Although in 2002 the approved number of police staff was 39,893, by 1 September of that year the number of active personnel was somewhat lower, only 38,349, indicating a shortage. A total of 8707 public servants and 32 civil servants were employed as civilians in the police force.[4] By 2002, around 50–55% of the career members were in uniform. The number of female employees was around 15.5% among the career officers, according to the Personnel Affairs Service of the National Police Headquarters. No data can be collected under current law regarding the ethnic composition of the police. A Roma minority recruiting programme was introduced nationwide to attract young Romani individuals to the police organisation; however, for several reasons, the programme achieved little success. Article 7 of the Police Act, which defines police personnel as career members of the armed forces and persons with civil administration status, intends to further the aim of the demilitarisation of the police forces.

Since the start of the transition period, the police have argued that the efficient struggle against crime and the effective maintenance of public safety require budgetary increases for police and more police officers on the streets. Yet experts on the police have stressed that policing powers have increased, since it is not only the police but also border guards and customs officers who, for example, can undertake crime control functions. István Szikinger (1998: 122) even went so far as to claim that 'taken all round, it can be said that today the potential for public monopoly of coercion is far stronger than in the last period of the dictatorship' (translation by the author).

It is a fact that police leaders continuously struggle with the shortage in the number of police officers. In response to this problem, alternative strategies have been developed to help the situation. For example, in Budapest, which experienced a shortage of about 600 uniformed patrol personnel by February 2003, it became necessary to introduce so-called 'circulating units', a programme of police patrols in eight minibuses circulating around the city ten hours a day in order to increase the presence of police in public places and provide a visible police 'service' on the streets (NSZ, 6 February 2003).

Formerly, the personnel system of the Hungarian police had been heavily criticised for operating as a top-heavy structure, in which 'one-third of personnel are higher-ranking officers compared to the average 10 to 12 percent seen elsewhere' (Finszter, 2001: 148). By February 2003 the Minister of Interior announced a freeze

---

4. Source:
    http://web.bm.hu/rendor/rendor.nsf/93188b8ee4f56e56c1256966001ec8ac/aed87309d8b1
    91a4c12568e30041effc?OpenDocument

on the creation of new positions in the higher ranks of the police apparatus. In the future any new high-ranking positions can only be created with the permission of the National Police Commissioner. It is expected that the financial redistribution across the rank structure as a consequence of this measure will increase the number of lower ranking personnel (*Magyar Hirlap*, 12 February 2003).

Personnel matters and human resource management

> The average age of police personnel is 32 years. Middle-aged officers with great experience are almost entirely absent from the corps; professionals from whom policing could be learned are simply not present. [...] The profession is unattractive and has no ability to hold on to staff (Finszter 2001: 139).

The above quote from Géza Finszter, an expert on the police, best summarises the major problems for police personnel management: policing is still an unattractive profession with continuously high turnover rates. Recently , the rate of turnover of personnel was around 5–7% annually, 'which is not excessively high, but is rather expensive, even for training costs only' (Szabó, 2001: 33). The 'drain' effect was strongest between 1994 and 1996 when around 1600 trained professionals holding a degree from an institution of higher education left the police corps (Kuncze, 2000: 98–9). Searching for the reasons for the drain, one can list low salaries (for some years before it had been a real struggle to receive what the police officer had earned by his/her work when serving overtime during his/her days off); the attractiveness of the newly developing market economy; the emergence of private security and private police agencies; the demanding working conditions; and the lack of a comprehensive human resource management policy.

The 1997 *ex officio* investigation on the human rights situation in the police system, conducted at local police headquarters by the Parliamentary Commissioner revealed – among other findings – that there was a complete 'lack of human resources management policy in the police organisation'; in addition, for 'police officers serving on the "frontlines" neither the direct work conditions nor the social facilities assisting their work (locker rooms, shower rooms, recreation rooms, etc.) represented a quality contributing to the efficient performance of police duties'. Vehicles and bullet-proof vests 'were found to be in an inferior state and actually unsuitable for combat against an increasing crime situation'. Furthermore, 'little attention was being paid to maintaining the appropriate level of training, health, and mental fitness of the officers'. Regarding the state of police buildings, 'it was determined that facilities, including 16 headquarters buildings, were unsuitable for service purposes and could not be renovated economically' (Gönczöl, 1997). The situation of police officers has changed very slowly since that investigation, because in its 2001 report the Parliamentary Commissioner mentioned that, due to difficulties in financing, the human resource strategy for police which had already been prepared was not yet approved (Gönczöl, 2001).

Education and training

The educational system of the Ministry of Interior has undergone significant changes in the past decade. Only applicants who hold the necessary prior education and the required professional qualification are employed in the police. The educational system has two levels: vocational police schools and the Hungarian Police Officer College (Rendőrtiszti Főiskola, henceforth: Police Academy). The police vocational school system was established between 1992 and 1995 and provides a general police education after secondary school graduation (Szakács, 1998: 79). Police vocational schools are established in the main regions. Applicants have to pass a set of required entrance examinations: professional intelligence, psychological and physical tests, a medical check-up, and, in addition to being a graduate from a secondary school, must be at least 18 years old. While at police vocational schools, students receive a stipend and become members of the police only after passing the professional exam at the end of the second year. Higher education for the police is provided by the Police Academy, in the form of a three-year full-time educational programme while in residence or a four-year correspondence course. The entrance exam of the Police Academy consists of medical, psychological, physical conditioning tests and exams on different subjects. The budget of the police higher education system is part of the budget of the Ministry of Interior.

A recent phenomenon is the 'pre-police school' education option for secondary school students interested in becoming police officers. By 1998, already 39 secondary schools had decided to organise special courses for students interested in the police profession. The classes focus on aspects of psychology, sociology, communication, law, administration and history that are relevant to policing. The system is expected to result in a qualitatively different type of police force and personnel (*Budapest Sun*, 19 November 1998).

The last few years have indicated a trend towards centralisation in terms of education as well. As László Szabó (2001: 31, 34–5) has emphasised, this trend in the educational system is intended to coordinate the educational systems of the different branches of law enforcement (police and border guards) because a centralised educational system can better achieve 'the harmonisation of educational aims and demands' in the course of preparations for EU accession. Before the reorganisation, law enforcement schools were either part of the structure and direction of the police or part of the border guards. The law enforcement vocational school system became unified in 1999. Integrating border guard schools into the educational system of the Ministry of Interior affairs is a novelty in Hungary. After the reorganisation, all seven law enforcement schools became subordinate to the Educational Department of the Ministry of Interior (*BM Oktatási Főosztály*).

Police reformers and instructors have proposed a wide variety of further educational facilities and opportunities. Some examples can be found in a recent article by Joszef Boda. Since the early 1990s, Hungarian law enforcement professionals have taken part in different courses abroad, for example, in the United States, Germany, France and the Netherlands. These relationships have become even more regular in recent times. 'By 1994, all county police headquarters had established professional relations with the police in Dutch regions, mainly covering the exchange of professional experiences, training, and language courses' (Boda, 2001: 68). There is strong and regular cooperation between Hungarian and US police agencies, notably with the FBI, but also with British and Turkish police agencies regarding educational and training matters. In addition, Hungarian participation in PHARE must be noted, a programme which seeks to assist accession to the EU by focusing on reforms to law-enforcement and public administration agencies. The number of Hungarian police participants in EU professional and language training courses has shown a steady increase up to 2000: in 1998, 24 Hungarian police professionals took part in such courses; 223 in 1999, increasing exponentially to 1057 in 2000. In 2001, 360 professionals of the police forces participated in EU professional training courses. The trend is similar in language courses: in 1998 only 20 professionals took part, rising to 55 in 1999, 1026 in 2000 and 150 in 2001 (EU-Integration Office, Ministry of Interior, as cited in Boda, 2001: 76).

A major change was brought about by the establishment of the Educational Department of the Ministry of Interior, which since its establishment in 1999 coordinates and directs all education, training and scientific work-related activities for law enforcement agencies, including the police. In addition, the Educational Department of the Ministry of Interior fulfils international educational and training duties, such as the training of prospective peace-keeping police and military police officers (Boda, 2001: 67).

Police vocational schools also take part in international education and exchange programmes. The initiative of the Miskolc school must be mentioned here; since 1998 it has established very fruitful cooperation with Dutch police schools. Police Academy students have the opportunity to take part in training or exchange programmes abroad. In 1991, 65 participated in such programmes, and between 1992 and 2001 the number of the students participating exceeded 200 (Boda, 2001: 60) The founding of the Central European Police Academy (Közép-európai Rendőrakadémia – KERA; or Mittel Europäische Polizei Akademie – MEPA) in 1993 was a continuation and extension of the already existing cooperation between Hungary and Austria, by now involving the police of eight central European countries. The International Law Enforcement Academy (ILEA, or Nemzetközi Rendészeti Akadémia – NRA), based on an agreement between Hungary and the United States was opened in Budapest in 1995. By August 2001, Hungary had taken part 11 times in its training sessions; 222 law enforcement professionals, including 195 police officers, have been trained; and 1814 law enforcement officers have participated in its special courses (Boda 2001: 64–5).

Accountability and control of the police

The present control and accountability mechanisms meet, at least on paper, the standards declared in Recommendation 10 (2001) of the European Code of Ethics by the Committee of Ministers to the Member States. However, at the practical level, police accountability is subject to heavy criticism, especially by representatives of civil society.

Executive control of police is exercised through the Minister of Interior. The Executive discharges its directing function via law-making powers and by issuing decrees and decisions. The budget of the police is part of the budget of the Ministry of Interior. Legislative control is carried out by the parliament. Throughout the transition period either permanent or ad hoc parliamentary committees conducted activities related to police. For example, there was the permanent committee on 'Local Government, Public Administration, Internal Security and Police' during the 1990–94 parliamentary period; the 'Parliamentary Inquiry Committee on the Investigation of the Possible Corruption Cases Regarding the Oil-Scandal Related Cases and Their Link to Organised Crime' (set up for a one year term in the 1998–2002 parliamentary period) and the Law Enforcement Committee has existed since 2002. The Constitutional Court as 'negative lawmaker' is also a key factor. The judiciary controls the police via civil and criminal proceedings.

Internal review mechanisms, on paper, are well developed; however, concerns are justified at the level of practice. Disciplinary powers are vested in the police superior (Article 119 and Articles 125–7 of the Act on Service Relations). Breaches of any service related obligation by members of the regular forces will qualify as a breach of discipline and disciplinary procedures will be carried out. Misdemeanours committed by career police officers during their service and while discharging their duties must be determined in a disciplinary procedure (Article 119 of the Act on Service Relations).

The investigation of any non-military felonies committed by regular members of the police is exclusively within the jurisdiction of the special investigating units of the prosecutor's office.[5] Since, according to the Penal Code, career police officers are considered military personnel, investigations regarding military felonies fall within the powers of military prosecutors (Section 2 of the Appendix to Act V of 1972 on the Prosecution of the Hungarian Republic). The investigation of military offences is vested either in the military prosecutor or, under certain conditions, in the police higher commissioner (II/1995 (II.10) Decree of the Minister of Interior).

---

5. Article 6, Section (1d) of the 5/ 2001 (Ük.6). Instructions of the Attorney General on the Investigating Offices of the Prosecution and the Investigation by the Prosecution.

The police 'conflict-map' for the year 2000 indicates that 509 criminal proceedings were launched against police officers (including military felonies as well), 63 criminal proceedings were launched due to 'atrocities' by the police. Forty of these were assaults committed during an official proceeding, 16 concerned maltreatment of detainees during interrogation, and seven cases concerned unlawful deprivation of liberty. Among military felonies, a high number of such acts as breach of official duty and disobedience of orders were represented (Szeszták, 2001: 31–2). In the same year, 2572 disciplinary proceedings were launched (including both disciplinary and misdemeanour acts). As a consequence of disciplinary procedures, the service of 119 police officers had been terminated, out of which 35 had been terminated via criminal sanction, 25 via disciplinary sanction, and 39 cases by mutual agreement (Szeszták, 2001: 32).

Complaints about police measures and the use of force can be submitted within eight days from when the grievance occurred to the head of the respective police organ, who then has 15 days to issue her/his reasoned decision. There is a possibility of appeal to superior police organs (Article 93 Section (1) – (3) of the Police Act). Decisions on complaints issued after appeal to higher police authority, which qualify as administrative decisions, are subject to judicial review (1/1999 Közigazgatási Jogegységi határozat – Administrative law-harmonising decision by the Supreme Court). The biggest concern with regard to the internal complaint mechanism is that the investigation of complaints remains inside the police organisational structure and that, because of the lack of an independent unit examining the complaint, the sense of professional solidarity among police can hinder the efficiency of serving justice. In practice, only a very low number of complaints against police officers reach the stage where officers are found responsible. 'One-third of the cases reported against police officials are judged to be unfounded and are rejected by the authorities whose duty is to investigate them. A further 80 percent of investigations are unsuccessful' (Kőszeg, 2001a: 4). Another source also indicates the low efficiency of the internal control system:

> Police abuses continued, including use of excessive force, beatings of suspects, and harassment. Police also continued to harass and physically abuse Roma and foreign nationals. In 1999, 2,397 reports of police abuse were filed compared with 2,296 in 1998. Of these complaints, only 377 resulted in court cases, compared with 312 in 1998. In 845 cases, no investigation occurred ... Historically, 10 to 15 percent of such cases result in conviction (US Department of State, Country Reports 2000).

There exists a legally prescribed individual civil liability for regular members of the police forces for damages caused by delinquent breach of obligations while in service. The police authority as an institution also has complete civil liability for damages caused by members of the regular forces in connection with their service, regardless of culpability under conditions specified by law (Act XLIII of 1996). Yet these means are hardly ever employed due to the traditional attitude of affected persons not to come into conflict with the police authority, and due to their reservations towards the administration of the justice system when its own actors are involved.

One of the key external civilian supervision mechanisms is vested in the parliamentary commissioners. These ombudsmen, since the enactment of the Act LIX of 1993, are entitled to investigate grievances related to violations of constitutional rights reported by citizens or arising from their own initiatives. All four commissioners – the Parliamentary Commissioner and her/his Deputy for Civil Rights, the Commissioner for National and Ethnic Minorities Rights, and the Commissioner for Data Protection and Freedom of Information – can enquire about and continue to investigate citizens' complaints related to police activities and operations. The strongest methods currently available to defend constitutional rights are the recommendations issued by the ombudsmen, their access to the media and ability to draw the attention of the wider public to unlawful activities or measures violating the constitutional rights of people, and the annual report presented to the parliament. Complaints concerning the actions and inactions of police submitted to the Hungarian Parliamentary Commissioner and Deputy Commissioner for Civil Rights show an increasing trend. During six months of 1995, 169 complaints against the police were registered; there were 534 in 1996, and 666 in 1997 (Gönczöl, 1997).

The overall number of complaints regarding unjustified police measures lodged at the Offices of the Ombudsman for National and Ethnic Minorities and for Civil Rights had increased in 2000. Of the complaints introduced, only around 30% resulted in court cases while in 70% of cases no investigation occurred. Many cases did not reach the court system and are still pending. (Commission of the European Communities, 2001: 19–20).

The emerging, but not yet strong, civil sector organisations play the role of police watchdog. Examples are the Hungarian Helsinki Committee having been launched in 1996, jointly with the Constitutional and Legislative Policy Institute (COLPI) by means of their Police Cell Monitoring Programme, which has developed ongoing monitoring of police detention conditions (Kőszeg, 2001b: 197–200).

Critical issues remaining in police reform

Respect for human rights
Since the mid-1990s significant changes have occurred in the attitude of the police towards the Roma population and in initiatives of cooperation between police and Roma representative bodies. Regular communication between Roma self-governing bodies and the police had been established on different levels (Csányi, 1999: 114–17). In Nógrád county a new Roma minority protection programme has been implemented since 1996, focusing on discourse and cooperation with minorities (Orbán, 2000: 6–7). Two fundamental police initiatives were established to change

the attitude of the police towards Romani people and to enhance the knowledge by police officers of Roma issues. The first initiative, pursued in all counties, sought to invite young Roma citizens to police vocational schools; however, the programme had little success. In spite of public advertisements for the programme, except in one or two counties, it has remained unattractive for Roma individuals (Orbán, 2000: 11–12). Another police initiative to increase trust and change attitudes towards members of the Roma community inside the police forces has been a 'Romology' course which is taught in police training schools and also in the Police Academy (Canada, Immigration and Refugee Board, 2001: Part 6.2. Police Initiatives).

Despite all achievements and positive intentions to change the situation in the human rights field, as international reports have documented, ill-treatment and misconduct by police officers continue to be a problematic issue, often targeting Romani individuals (see, for example, Human Rights Watch World Report, 2002; Amnesty International. Annual Report, 2000 and 2002; 2001 Annual Report on Hungary issued by the International Helsinki Federation; 1999 Country Reports on Human Rights Practices, Hungary, issued by the US Department of State; 2001 Country Reports on Human Rights Practices, Hungary, issued by the US Department of State). As the 2002 Regular Report on Hungary's Progress towards Accession to the Commission of the European Communities summarises:

> According to the Opinion of the Ombudsman for Minorities the situation concerning degrading treatment by the police has been improving marginally over the past year, but there continue to be reports of ill-treatment and forced interrogation, and, in one case, a police raid on a Roma settlement. Although the data protection law prohibits the identification of individuals by ethnicity, Roma are particularly at risk of such treatment. During 2000, the Public Prosecution Office reported 850 cases of ill-treatment during official proceedings and 283 cases of forced interrogation. As in earlier years, only a very limited number of cases (11 percent) were followed up (Commission of the European Communities, 2002: 27).

Corruption

Corruption is assumed to be highly prevalent, yet confirming corruption is difficult; estimates of police corruption are much higher than the number of detected acts (Pap, 2001). Corruption continues to be a problem and the public is aware of corruption as a problem with regard to the police. The Hungarian Gallup Institute conducted a survey in Hungary in 2000 regarding the opinion of the general public as the clients of public sector institutions and consumers of their services. The survey indicated that the population perceived the traffic police and the Customs and Excise Authority as the most corrupt state institutions dealing with individual members of the public. 'A fifth of the population believes that Ministry officials, officers in other branches of the police ... have to be bribed to ensure that affairs are handled "properly"' (Gallup Monitor, 2000). A survey by the Association of Police Research conducted in 2000, via interviews and discussions with police personnel, found that traffic police and 'investigators collecting bribes from small businesses' were the most typical form of police corruption, and that the climate of white collar crime, tax fraud and evasion, and drug related affairs 'also offer significant opportunities for corruption' (Open Society Institute, 2002: 278, n. 97).

Positive measures against police corruption have been undertaken, such as the abolition of on-the-spot fines imposed by police officers in traffic violations; police officers have to wear badges to be identifiable to citizens; policemen accepting bribes may be reported and immunity is offered to the party reporting; and police programmes include some training on possible responses to proposed corruption. However, these measures can only combat corruption occurring on the surface, and cannot effectively penetrate deeper into the system. The low salaries of police officers sustain the inclination to take small bribes as an additional source of income (Open Society Institute, 2002: 278).

Images and attitudes of police officers

Changing attitudes and behaviour of police officers is a slow process. There have been several attempts to improve the public image of the police by having police officers give lectures in educational facilities, and through various programmes aimed at establishing cooperation between citizens and the police force (e.g. programmes for crime prevention, victim protection, 'telephone witness', or the tourist assistance summer programmes). However, much still remains to be done.

Several surveys have been conducted to assess the understanding, images, beliefs and attitudes of police officers; questions have also focused on their attitude and opinions on human rights standards and legal guarantees during criminal procedures. Survey results are rather surprising. It was found that 'policemen are satisfied with their professionalism', 'they do not believe that police measures employed were too severe', and they 'do not miss the participation of civilians in the control of their operation'. They consider the guarantees of human rights and fundamental freedoms, such as the rule of law and judicial control to be 'obstacles' for their activities (Búzás, 1999: 26; translation by the author). A four-year-long survey conducted by the Police Research Institute, which also included similar questions, yielded similar findings:

> police officers feel that the rule of law state, the legal guarantees of criminal procedures, and the press complicate their work, although public opinion expects a tougher approach from police. Statutes and laws are just hindering the efficiency of their work (Búzás, 1999: 26).

The picture becomes more complicated in the light of citizens' perceptions of the attitudes of police officers. According to a 2003 Gallup poll, 44% of Hungarian citizens have a positive view of the police, whereas only 16% of the citizens have a negative opinion. Those expressing positive views mainly emphasise police courtesy, helpfulness and their friendly approach, whereas the negative features include the fact that the police sometimes do not act when they should, and that they are not efficient enough (Dzindzisz, 2003).

Overall assessment of the police reform and the future

Even though the modernisation of certain key sectors of the police system has achieved progress, such as in education or the depoliticisation of police, more fundamental reforms are lagging behind in the areas of decentralisation, demilitarisation and deeper structural changes. The citizenry has exerted strong pressure on the police to maintain public safety in an efficient manner and to adopt a service-oriented outlook, and this even while the crisis of the police is still ongoing in terms of low salaries, under-motivated personnel, lack of self-esteem among members of the force, and the low moral prestige of the profession.

In the last 13 years there has been no systematic strategy for police reform which was not based exclusively on political interest over criminal policy, or which sought to combine police professional experience with scholarly and expert opinion from relevant social and civil organisations. Géza Finszter (2001: 139–40), an expert on the police, describes the Hungarian situation as a conflict between two competing schools, the 'reformers' and the 'evolutionists', over how to modernise the police. Reformers are mainly academics and theoretical experts who advocate the agenda of 'depoliticisation, decentralisation and demilitarisation', of reconstructing the police as part of public administration. Evolutionists are mainly government officials, politicians and police leaders who target efficient 'functioning, self-confidence and discipline', in other words, relying on the preservation of the special authoritative status of the police. Bridging the gap between the two schools would probably have accelerated police reform by implementing the deeper structural changes that are desperately needed, yet, as demonstrated, it ultimately did not happen. The process of police reform, which has now been going on for nearly fifteen years, still brings dissatisfaction from all sides (police, citizens, scholars and politicians) and expectations for a new day and a new chance, a waiting for a new Godot – 'Tomorrow it will come.'

The government appointed in 2002 proposed that 'another tomorrow' be placed on the reform agenda again. As a first step, a Consulting Collegium for Law Enforcement and Crime Prevention has been established inside the Ministry of Interior with the duty of scheduling reform measures and providing an opinion on them. Among the first planned measures are: structural reforms as part of and within the context of the regionalisation of public administration; sustaining changes in the institutional culture of the police, that is, promoting a change in attitude and communication; a result-oriented assessment of work of individual officers; plus promises for a new model of police financing by making budgetary allocations to police organs dependent on their tasks and duties, thus linking executed tasks with the necessary finances and transferring these to the level where the duties are discharged (Salgó, 2003).

If something is to be said as a conclusion to this overview of police reform in Hungary, it is that even if positive interpretations of police reform might be justified, given the changes from the legacy inherited from the pre-transitional period and the nature of problems encountered after the start of the reforms, there is still room for criticism due to the incoherence and inconsistency of the reform measures which have been conducted so far. Reforms to date have once again left much work for the notorious 'tomorrow'.

References

Amnesty International. 2000. *Annual Report 2000*. 'Hungary'. Available at:
　　http://www.web.amnesty.org/web/ar2000web.nsf/58f967f150817f77802568f
　　500617d07/0992d76a29c28bef802568f20055292e?OpenDocument
Amnesty International. 2000. *Annual Report 2002*. 'Hungary'.
　　http://web.amnesty.org/web/ar2002.nsf/eur/hungary!Open
Balázs, E.. 'Police start their training young'. *Budapest Sun*, 19 Nov. 1998 – vol. VI, issue 46. Online.
　　http://www.budapestsun.com/full_story.asp?ArticleId={287C37E77EDC11D
　　28334000502125134}&From=News
Bencsik, A. 1991. 'A rendőrség fejlesztésének lehetőségei' (The possibilities to modernise the police). *Rendészeti Szemle* (Policing Review), vol. XXIX. no. 4 Apr. 1991.
Benke, M. 2001. 'Policing in transition countries compared with standards in the European Union: Hungary – where dreams are not fulfilled', in Kádár, A., ed. *Police in Transition. Essays on the Police Forces in Transition Countries*. Budapest.
Boda, J. 2001. 'Nemzetközi oktatás és képzés a magyar rendvédelmi szerveknél' (International education and training at the Hungarian law enforcement organs). *Belügyi Szemle* (Review of Interior Affairs) vol. 10/2001.
Boross, P. 2000. 'Rend vagy jogállamiság?' (Order or rule of law?). Comments on the essay of Kőszeg Ferenc. *Belügyi Szemle* (Review of Interior Affairs) vol. 1/2000.
Búzás, P. 1999. 'A rendőrség és az emberi jogok szakirodalmi áttekintése' (Review of police and human rights related literature). *Belügyi Szemle* (Review of Interior Affairs) vol. 3/1999.
Canada. Immigration and Refugee Board, Research Directorate. 2000. 'Hungary: Views of Several Sources on the Situation of Roma. Part 6. The Roma and the Police'. Ottawa. H
　　http://www.irb.gc.ca/en/Researchpub/research/publications/hun09_e.htm#hu
　　n9e-Sect6
Caparini, M. 2002. 'Police reform: issues and experiences'. Paper presented to the Fifth International Security Forum, Zurich, 14–16 Oct. 2002.
　　http://www.isn.ethz.ch/5isf/5/Papers/Caparini_paper_IV-3.pdf

Commission of the European Communities. 2001. Regular Report on Hungary's Progress Towards Accession. Brussels, 13.11.2001. SEC (2001) 1748. http://europa.eu.int/comm/enlargement/report2001/#report2001

Commission of the European Communities. 2002. Regular Report on Hungary's Progress Towards Accession. Brussels, 9.10.2002. SEC (2002) 1404. http://europa.eu.int/comm/enlargement/report2002/#report2002

Council of Europe Parliamentary Assembly Resolution 690 (1979), 'On the Declaration on the Police'.

Csányi, K. 1999. 'A kisebbségi ügyek rendőrségi kezelése Magyarországon' (Ethnic affairs as handled by the police in Hungary). *Belügyi Szemle* (Review of Interior Affairs), vol. 7-8/1999.

'Cselekedni, most és mindenkiért! A nemzeti közép, a demokratikus koalíció kormányának programja.' MAGYARORSZÁG 2002- 2006. 2002. (To act, now and for everyone! The governmental programme of the national centre, of the democratic coalition. HUNGARY 2002-2006). Chapter VIII.B. Point 1-2. http://www.szdsz.hu/2_6.php

Déri, P. and Budai, A. 1991. *Korszerű bűnüldözés* (Modern crime detection). Budapest.

Dzindzisz, S. 'Fővárosi jelenség a korrupció'(Corruption is a phenomenon of the capital). *Magyar Hirlap,* 25 Jan. 2003. Online.
http://www.magyarhirlap.hu/Archivum_cikk.php?cikk=61906&archiv=1&next=0

Finszter, G. 1990. 'A magyar rendőrség válsága'. (The crisis of the Hungarian Police). *Belügyi Szemle* (Review of Interior Affairs). vol. XXVIII, no. 6 (June 1990).

Finszter, G. 2000. 'Rendőrségek a XXI. Században'. (Police in the 21st century). *Belügyi Szemle* (Review of Interior Affairs), vol. 1/2000.

Finszter, G. 2001. 'The political changeover and the police', in: Kádár, A., ed. *Police in Transition. Essays on the Police Forces in Transition Countries.* Budapest.

Gaál, Z. 2003. Rendőrségi létszámstop: parancsnokból van már elég. (Freezing the increase of the number of police personnel: enough higher officers). *Magyar Hirlap,* 12 Feb. 2003. Online.
http://www.magyarhirlap.hu/Archivum_cikk.php?cikk=62648&archiv=1&next=0

Gallup Monitor. Nationwide study of relations between public institutions and their clients. A Magyar Gallup Intezet Web Lapja [The Gallup Organisation Hungary]. http://monitor.gallup.hu/en/gsurveys/010119_pubinst.html

Gönczöl, K. 1997. 'The situation of the professional members of the authorities in terms of human rights', in 1260 Investigations. The Experiences of the Hungarian Parliamentary Commissioner and the Deputy Commissioner for Civil Rights in 1997, part 3.8. http://www.obh.hu/allam/eng/cover.htm

Gönczöl, K. 2001. 'Human rights of conscripted soldiers and of professional members of authorities', in 1217 Recommendations in 2000. Report by

Katalin Gönczöl, Parliamentary Commissioner for Civil Rights. Summary, part 10.
    http://www.obh.hu/allam/eng/cover.htm
Gottlieb, G., Krözsel, K. and Prestel, B. 1998. *Die Reform der Ungarischen Polizei. Vorgehen, Methoden, Resultate. The Reform of the Hungarian Police. Processes, Methods, Results. A Magyar Rendőrség reformja. Eljárás, módszerek, eredmények.* Holzkirchen.
Hungarian Civil Liberties Union. 2000. *HCLU on the Police.* Budapest.
Human Rights Watch. 2002. *World Report 2002. 'Hungary'.*
    http://hrw.org/wr2k2/europe11.html
Hungarian Police website: http://www.b-m.hu/police/
Hungarian Central Statistical Office. 2001. *Statistical Yearbook of Hungary 2000.* Budapest.
International Helsinki Federation. 2001. *Human Rights in the OSCE Region: the Balkans, the Caucasus, Europe, Central Asia and North America Report 2001: 'Hungary'.*
    http://www.ihf-hr.org/reports/ar01/Country%20issues/Countries/Hungary.pdf
Kósa, L. and Kálmán Z. 2000. 'A rendőrség és az önkormányzatok kapcsolata a rendszerváltás után'. (The relation between police and local self-governments after the regime change). *Belügyi Szemle* (Review of Interior Affairs), vol. 10/2000.
Kőszeg, F. 1992. 'A rendőrség megújulása?' (Reform of the police?), in: *A váltás rendszere. Tanulmányok a kormány politikájáról.* (The system of change. Essays on governmental politics). Budapest.
Kőszeg, F. 2000. 'Rendőrség és politika' (Police and politics). *Belügyi Szemle* (Review of Interior Affairs), vol. 1/2000.
Kőszeg, F. 2001a. 'Introduction', in: Kádár, A., ed. *Police in Transition. Essays on the Police Forces in Transition Countries.* Budapest.
Kőszeg, F. 2001b. 'Monitoring Police Detention: Experiences with Civilian Supervision of Law Enforcement Agencies', in: Kádár, A., ed. *Police in Transition. Essays on the Police Forces in Transition Countries.* Budapest.
Kuncze, G. 2000. 'Jogállamiság vagy rend?' (Rule of law or order?). *Belügyi Szemle* (Review of Interior Affairs), vol. 1/2000.
Népszabadság (NSZ). 6 Feb. 2003. 'Nyolc rendőrcirkáló a fővárosban. Hatszáz egyenruhás járőr hiányzik Budapest utcáiról, részben őket igyekeznek pótolni az új egységekkel' (Eight police 'circulator' in the capital. Six hundred police patrols are still needed in the streets of Budapest, the new units are partly their substitute). Online
    http://www.nepszabadsag.hu/Default.asp?DocCollID=94169&DocID=87599 #87599
Népszabadság (NSZ). 9 Feb. 2003. 'Rendőrséget bírálja a korábbi adatvédelmi biztos.Tiltakozik az Európai Szociális Fórum' (Police criticised by the former data protection commissioner. The European Social Forum protests). Online.

http://www.nepszabadsag.hu/Default.asp?DocCollID=94454&DocID=87826
#87826

Népszabadság (NSZ). 13 Feb. 2003. 'Salgó a demonstrációkról' (Salgó about the demonstrations). Online.
http://www.nepszabadsag.hu/Default.asp?DocCollID=95316&DocID=88406
#88406

Open Society Institute. 2002. *Monitoring the EU Accession Process: Corruption and Anti-Corruption Policy in Hungary (2002)*. Part 8.1: 'Police'.
http://www.eumap.org/reports/2002/content/50/348/2002_c_hungary.pdf

Orbán, S. 2000. 'A cigány kisebbségi önkormányzatok és a rendőrség együttműködése 2000-ben' (The cooperation between the Gypsy minority self-governments and the police in 2000).
http://web.bm.hu/rendor/bun_m.../bc43184c1127fdb4c1256b540075775a?

Pap, A.L. 'Street Police Corruption. A Post-Communist State of the Art'. Paper presented to the Third Socrates Kokkalis Graduate Student Workshop, Kokkalis Programme on Southeastern and East-Central Europe, John F. Kennedy School of Government, Harvard University, 9–10 Feb. 2001.
http://www.ksg.harvard.edu/kokkalis/GSW3/Andras_Laszo.pdf

Prestel, B. 1991. 'Interjú Dr. Bernard M. Prestellel A magyar rendőrségről' (About the Hungarian Police. Interview with Dr. Bernard M. Prestel). *Rendészeti Szemle* (Policing Review). vol. XXIX, no. 9 (Sep. 1991), 25–30.

Project on Ethnic Relations. 2000. *Towards Community Policing: The Police and Ethnic Minorities in Hungary*. Budapest.

Rekvényi v. Hungary (Application no. 25390/94). European Court of Human Rights. Judgement of 20 May 1999.
http://hudoc.echr.coe.int/hudoc/ViewRoot.asp?Tname=Hejud&Id=REF0000
1055&Language=en&Item=0&NoticeMode=1&RelatedMode=3

Rzeplinski, A. 2001. 'The police in the constitutional framework: the limits of policing', in: Kádár, A., ed. *Police in Transition. Essays on the Police Forces in Transition Countries*. Budapest.

Salgó, L. 2003. 'A Magyar Köztársaság Rendőrsége reformjának alapvetései' (Fundamental statements on the reform of the Police of the Hungarian Republic). Speech delivered on 20 Feb. 2003 by the National Police Commissioner on the occasion of the jubilee of the periodical Belügyi Szemle (Review of Interior Affairs). H
ttp://web.bm.hu/belugy/hir2002.nsf/262067e6e5c6411dc1256b380073fc29/f0
a4315951caab04c1256cd300382fbd?OpenDocument

Szabó, L. 2001. 'A belügyi oktatási rendszer korszerűsítése' (The modernisation of the education system of the Ministry of Interior Affairs). *Belügyi Szemle* (Review of Interior Affairs), vol. 10/2001.

Szabó, M. 'From a Police State to Demonstration Democracy: Policing Mass Demonstrations in Hungary before, during and after the Regime Change'.
http://caesar.elte.hu/ajk/html/tudo/kiadvanyok/academia/szabom-police.pdf

Szakács, G. 1991. 'Reformra szorul-e magyar rendőrtisztképzés?' (Is there any need to reform the higher police education?), in Timoránszky, P., ed. *Rendészeti tanulmányok. A rendőrképzés reformja a kelet-európai változások tükrében* (Essays on Policing. Reforms on police education in the light of the Eastern European changes). Conference Proceedings, Balatonföldvár, 12–13 Nov. 1991.

Szakács, G. 1998. 'A rendőrképzés korszerűsítésének szükségességéről' (About the necessity to modernise police training). *Belügyi Szemle* (Review of Interior Affairs), vol. 1/1998.

SZDSZ. 2002. Esélyt Mindenkinek! A korszakváltás programja. (Chance to Everyone! The programme of the regime change. Alliance of Liberal Democrats).
http://korszakvaltas.szdsz.hu/index2.htm

Szeszták, F. 2001. 'Elemzés a rendőrség 2000. évi konfliktustérképéhez' (Analysis of the police 'conflict-map' for the year 2000). *Belügyi Szemle* (Review of Interior Affairs), vol. 9/2001.

Szikinger, I. 1991. 'Interjú a rendőrségi törvényről Dr. Szikinger Istvánnal' (Interview about the Police Act with Dr. István Szikinger). *Rendészeti Szemle* (Policing Review), vol. XXIX, no. 1 (Jan. 1991).

Szikinger, I. 1996. 'Continuity and Change in Hungarian Policing in the Mirror of Public Security Detention', in *Policing in Central and Eastern Europe: Comparing Firsthand Knowledge with Experience from the West.*
http://www.ncjrs.org/policing/con253.htm

Szikinger, I. 1998a. 'A magyar rendőrség jövője' (The future of the Hungarian police). *Belügyi Szemle* (Review of Interior Affairs), vol. 1/1998

Szikinger, I. 1998b. *Rendőrség a demokratikus jogállamban.* (Police in a democratic state governed by rule of law). Budapest.

Szikinger, I. 2002. 'Armed Control of Civilian Forces in Hungary'. Geneva Centre for Democratic Control of Armed Forces (DCAF). Working Paper series – no. 14. Geneva. http://www.dcaf.ch/publications/Working_Papers/14.pdf

United States Department of State, Bureau of Democracy, Human Rights and Labor. 2000. 1999 Country Reports on Human Rights Practices. Hungary. Released 25 Feb. 2000.
http://www.state.gov/www/global/human_rights/1999_hrp_report/hungary.html

United States Department of State, Bureau of Democracy, Human Rights and Labor. 2001. Country Reports on Human Rights Practices – 2000. Hungary. Released 23 Feb. 2001. http://www.state.gov/g/drl/rls/hrrpt/2000/eur/774.htm

United States Department of State, Bureau of Democracy, Human Rights and Labor (2002). Country Reports on Human Rights Practices – 2001. Hungary. Released 4 Mar. 2002.
http://www.state.gov/g/drl/rls/hrrpt/2001/eur/8264.htm

United States Department of State, Bureau of European Affairs.1999. Background Notes: Hungary.
http://www.state.gov/www/background_notes/hungary_9908_bgn.html

Weber, R. 2001. 'Police Organization and Accountability: A Comparative Study', in: Kádár, A., ed. *Police in Transition. Essays on the Police Forces in Transition Countries*. Budapest.

Wiener György 1996. 'Hatalmi viszonyok és kormányzati struktúra (1988–1994)' (Power relations and governmental structure 1988-1994). Published Online in *Eszmélet* (periodical 'Consciousness'), vol. 36.
http://eszmelet.tripod.com/36/wiener36.html

Chapter 5

Challenges and Changes to the Police System in Poland

Emil W. Plywaczewski and Piotr Walancik

Introduction

Poland (*Polska*) lies at the physical centre of the European continent. The total area of Poland is 120,727 square miles (312,683 square kilometres); its population in 2002 was 38.6 million. Its capital is Warsaw. Its current frontiers, stretching for 2198 miles (3538 kilometres) were drawn in 1945 and presently border six countries. In the west, Poland borders Germany along the Oder (Odra) and Lusatian Neiss (Nysa Łuzycka) rivers. In the south, the borders mainly follow the watershed of the Sudeten (Sudety), Beskid and Carpathian mountain ranges which separate Poland from the Czech and Slovak Republics. In the northeast and east Poland borders Russia, Lithuania, Belarus and Ukraine. The Baltic coast forms the northern frontier.

Since the Second World War, Polish society has been transformed by two great movements: the growth of a dominant, urban, industrialised working class and the continuing drift of peasants from the rural areas into towns and cities. The aging agricultural population, which remains working the land, is under strain. Emigration has been a permanent feature of Polish life for most of the last two hundred years, and roughly one Pole in three lives abroad.

In 1990 Poland experienced rapid political change. The changes that happened so far have not, however, altered Poland's need to grapple with the uncertainties of further political and economic transitions. Also, in 1990 the Polish government decided to move the Polish economy towards a free market system.

In 1990 the parliament passed a new Police Act which sought to create a police organisation which would be adequately prepared to fight crime within the new democratic political framework. The national police force currently numbers over 103,000 (in 2002), is mostly male (females constitute 10% of the uniformed police) and is controlled and commanded by the Ministry of Interior Affairs and Administration. The Polish police operates three main types of services – criminal; preventive; and organisational, logistic and technical support. The police also comprises the Court Police, police schools, the Higher Police School, prevention units and anti-terrorist sub-units, and research and development units. Besides the police, the Ministry of the Interior Affairs and Administration also controls the Border Guards and the Fire Brigade.

The concept of democratic policing

The democratic political transformation initiated in Poland in 1989 had an influence on police structure and functioning. Transformation occurred in all spheres of public life and altered inter-relations among the state's institutions.

The 1992 Provisional Constitution, and regulations of the 1952 Constitution which continue in force, catalogue the basic principles of the Polish Republic's political system and establish Poland as a democratic state governed by law. The principle of rule of law, introduced to the 1952 Constitution by the amendment of 21 December 1989, affects the functioning of the police and other state security agencies. The new Polish Constitution was enacted on 2 April 1997.

The new principles of policing, along with effective administrative control over the police, meet the needs of a democratic society. These changes had become necessary by the thrust and direction of political reforms, including those within the police, and by the need to cooperate with other states (especially European ones) in the maintenance of internal security and the successful prevention of trans-border crime, in particular that of an organised nature.

Needless to say, democracy has both advantages and disadvantages. Among the latter are the inefficiency of institutions, corruption and other forms of social pathology. All the same, to paraphrase Winston Churchill's words, though democracy is the worst of all possible systems of government, no-one has ever come up with a better one.

Charles de Montesquieu's model of government with its basic tripartite divisions of powers and functions strongly influenced the drafters of the Polish Constitution and helped alter the understanding of executive power which, at present, is wielded by the President and Government of the Polish Republic. Montesquieu's model also contributed to changes in that part of government administration (which includes the police force) called the special administration.

Organisational challenges

In a democratic state, the role of the police is to provide protection against internal and external threats to the state and to secure the peaceful functioning of society. On the other hand, the fundamental responsibility of the state with regard to the police is to maximise its capacities for the prevention and control of crime and other undesirable phenomena, and to minimise the risk of the police being used in conflict with principles of democracy. When considering the position of the police in democratic society, three issues need to be examined: the legal status and role of the police, control over the police, and the political disengagement of the police.

Legal status and role of the police

In a democratic society, the authority and basis for police actions should be among the most important legal acts passed by the legislature. In democratic Poland, police work was for the first time regulated by the Police Act, adopted on 6 April 1990 (*Journal of Law*, 1995). Under this act, the police were separated from other organs of internal affairs and administration. According to chapter 1 of the Act, the police are a uniformed and armed force serving society and designed to protect the safety of the people and to maintain public safety and civil order (Galster *et al.*, 1996). The police carry out the following responsibilities:

(1)   Protect the life of the people and their property against illegal attempts.

(2)   Ensure public safety and civil order in public places, public transportation, road traffic, and on water.

(3)   Initiate and arrange measures aimed at preventing crimes and misdemeanours in cooperation with state and local bodies and public organisations.

(4)   Detect crimes and misdemeanours and pursue offenders.

(5)   Supervise municipality and city guards and private security.

(6)   Control compliance with order and administrative regulations to be observed in public places.

(7)   Cooperate with police services of other countries and their international organisations.

The police were made responsible to the Minister of Interior Affairs and Administration, who is their supreme authority within the state. As a member of government, the Minister is responsible for enforcing all statutory tasks in the field of public safety and order. Of some importance for the functioning of the Polish police is the fact that the force falls under the authority of one of the so-called presidential departments. The appointment of the Minister of Interior Administration lies with the President, while the nomination is by the Prime Minister. The Chief Commissioner is the head of the force and acts as an agent of the national state administration, responsible for protection of the people and maintenance of public safety and civil order. He reports to the Minister of Interior Affairs and Administration and is appointed and dismissed by the Prime Minister on request of the Minister of Interior Affairs and Administration. The Chief Commissioner is constitutionally responsible to the Tribunal of State, which is a special judicial organ that deals with cases concerning infractions of the Constitution committed by the President of the Republic, members of the government, the General Inspector of Fiscal Control, the Attorney General, heads of central administrative departments, and members of the National Broadcasting and Television Committee.

Regarding police reforms in Poland over the last twelve years, two comprehensive police reforms took place in 1995 and in 1999. The first of these reforms, in 1995, strengthened the legal image of the police as the force which serves the community rather than a militarised force. As a result of this:

(1)   Boundaries have been set between the following types of police forces: criminal service, prevention service, with a notice that the police also consists of police schools, prevention squads and anti-terrorism squads;

(2)   The local police have been abolished;

(3)   The service to provide administrative, logistics and technical support to the police activities has been established;

(4)   The Court Police has been established within the police – and authorisation has been given to the Chief Commander of Police to establish in justified cases, upon agreement of the relevant minister in charge of internal affairs, other types of police forces;

(5)   The possibility of using firearms by police officers has been extended by providing a more precise list of cases which justify the use of firearms;

(6)   The scope of intelligence and operational activities has also been extended.

From the standpoint of combating particularly dangerous crimes, the most important were those regulations that fully recognise the importance of certain operational police activities in detecting crimes and their perpetrators. The controlled purchase (Police Act, Section 19a) and controlled delivery (Section 19b), as well as control of correspondence, and the use of operational techniques which make it possible to acquire information secretly and record evidence, introduced by the amendments, are examples of these operational activities.

The above-mentioned techniques of police operational work are used most of all in cases of particularly dangerous crimes. Controlled purchase can consist in secretly buying or receiving things either derived from crime (subject to confiscation), or which, according to the law, cannot be produced, possessed, conveyed or traded, as well as in accepting or giving material profit. On the other hand, controlled delivery can be used in order to supply documentary evidence for such grave crimes as traffic in explosives, weapons or drugs. Moreover, these activities can be carried out to identify people involved in crimes or to seize the object of crime, and, according to the code of criminal procedure, the techniques aimed at gathering information that eventually may be used as evidence in criminal proceedings (Waltos, 1996: 359).

In addition, Section 19 of the Police Act expands the circumstances under which the police can use technical means to obtain information secretly and record clues and data of evidential value. In connection with these changes, the police and, in some particularly justified instances, persons other than police officers, have been authorised to carry and use documents which prevent their identification when carrying out these activities (Daszkiewicz, 1996).

The final change in law requiring some discussion is Section 20[2] of the Police Act. It empowers the police to take, collect and use for detection and identification fingerprints, pictures and other data concerning people suspected of intentional crimes or prosecuted on indictment who are trying to hide their identity or are unidentified. This section expands the procedural, forensic and operational powers of prosecuting agencies and provides the authority for setting up and maintaining necessary identification data files, e.g. photo and fingerprint records, and for using them in criminal proceedings (Kudrelek and Lisiecki, 1996: 18–21).

The new legal regulations resulted from new threats faced by Polish society. There arose much controversy as regards their interpretation, procedures and ethics. Nevertheless, they are of extreme importance given the new criminal reality. On 25 June 1997, the legislature enacted the Law on the Crown Witness (known in the United States as 'granting immunity to a witness'), which seeks to break down the solidarity of criminal groups by providing special protection for witnesses who inform on criminal groups of which they were members (*Journal of Law*, 1997). All of these changes equipped the police with more efficient tools and means in their fight against the crime wave.

The second police reform was even more significant. It took place on 1 January 1999 and introduced changes, as part of general administrative reforms in Poland, to some acts which specified the competencies of state administration authorities (Central Police Headquarters, 2000: 12). As a result of this reform, several changes took place within the police. In connection with the decentralisation of the functions of the State within the administrative regions (*województwa*) and counties, the police – while still remaining separate from the general State administration and retaining their character as a centralised force under the command of the Chief Commander of Police – has become a part of the *województwa* and county 'joint administration' by joining the government (State) administration at the *województwa* level, and the self-government administration at the county level. As a result of this, the police – within its statutory limits – reports to the regional administrator (*wojewoda*) at the *województwo* level, while reporting to the head of county *(starosta)* at the county level. The authority of government administration and self-government administration at the *województwa* and county level, respectively, results in the power held over the police by both the regional administrator and county head in terms of police activities as well as personnel and financial issues.

Another effect of the general administrative reform of the police was that powers regarding police activities exercised by *wojewoda* and county heads relate mainly to preventive actions of the police. The *wojewoda*, being the representative of the State government within the *województwo* territory, has the task of ensuring public safety and order within his jurisdiction. To implement this objective, the *wojewoda* has his/her own support services and also the police. The *wojewoda* defines the threats and specifies, among other things, the directions for the actions of the police, while the *województwo* Chief of Police performs the activities necessary in order to ensure public safety and order within the *województwo* territory. A similar situation occurs at the county level – where the *starosta* specifies the needs regarding public safety and order, while the County (Municipal) Chief of Police performs the activities to satisfy these requirements.

Moreover, with regard to financial issues, the authorities of the joint administration have the possibility to participate in the costs of police operations, especially by financing jobs in prevention units (district constable precincts), county (municipal) police headquarters and police stations, on the basis of agreements signed between the county or municipality and the relevant *wojewoda* and an approval by the Chief Commander of Police.

Other results of the administrative reform include the introduction of a catalogue of job positions in the police, along with a related motivational pay system. There have also been changes to the police school system. It has been assumed that the fundamental way to bring about professional improvement of police officers will be through significantly deepening their professional specialisation.

The police reforms implemented so far were aimed at providing the police in Poland with the status of a decentralised force, close to local communities, especially within the sphere of crime prevention. They were also aimed at establishing an autonomous force, independent from the joint administration within the sphere of crime detection. And thirdly, the reforms aimed to create a centralised force within the sphere of the fight against organised crime.

The new structure was supposed to reflect the administrative division of local government, but was primarily introduced in order to bring police officers closer to the public. More police officers were to be deployed to the districts and the police stations, and more officers were to be allocated to work on the streets. The new and primary goal of the force, according to former Commander In Chief, General Jan Michna, was 'to become a tool in the hands of the public' (Haberfeld *et al.*, 2002: 150). It seems that this move was the right one if one considers certain poll results. According to a public opinion survey conducted in October 2002, for example, 72% of the population trust the police, 68% regard its work as good or very good, and 56% feel safe in their place of residence after dark (*Wizerunek Policji w oczach opinii publicznej* 2002).

New organisation of the Polish police

The present structure of the police in Poland meets all formal requirements necessary for a democratic state and the rule of law. Given the roles and powers exercised by police officers, their activities must be evaluated by standards of effectiveness in protecting the people's life, health and property as well as by the observance of human rights and freedoms.

Figure 5.1   The Organisational Chart of Polish Police

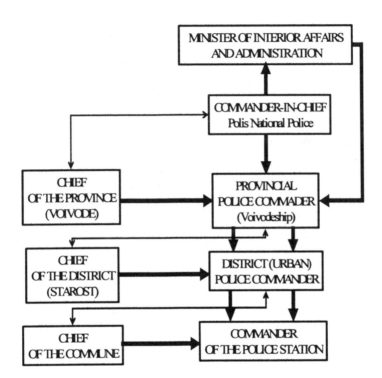

Control over the police

Control over the police is one of the fundamental features of public life in democratic states. External control is perceived as one of the main factors which guarantees conformity to constitutional principles by law enforcement agencies. The forms and scope of control over the state's administrative agencies (including the police force) are defined by constitutional laws and acts and statutes at a lower level. In Poland, the police are controlled by parliament, the Chief Board of Supervision, courts, prosecutors, the Ombudsman, as well as by society in general through public control institutions regulated by law (such as local administrative agencies). It should be mentioned that in Poland the police are also controlled by an internal control agency, the Internal Affairs Bureau (*Biuro Spraw Wewnętrznych*), which was created in May 1998 for the purpose of detecting crimes committed by police officers and police employees and to uncover social pathologies in the police community. The Bureau collects and analyses data on crime among the ranks of police officers and police employees.

Moreover, influence on the police is exerted by district courts and local administrative agencies and authorities, for it is they who approve candidates for the posts of police commandants of regional *(wojewódzwo)* and district headquarters and police stations. Every year, police commandants must present reports about their work, and they must inform their *wojewoda,* their regional and local authority councils, about the state of public order and safety of the area. In the case of threat to public order or other major disorders, reports and information must be submitted immediately to the supervision bodies mentioned. The police must accede to every request for information at other times. This requirement establishes democratic control over the police and promotes a dialogue between them and civil authorities.

Political disengagement of the police
The principle of political disengagement of the police is explicitly expressed in the Police Act. In accordance with this principle, police officers cannot belong to any political party; on joining the police they automatically cease to be members of a party. They must execute only orders issued by constitutional state agencies and they cannot submit to party discipline. In addition, some restrictions have been imposed on police officers as regards their involvement in non-police associations. They must inform their superiors about their membership in national associations. To become members of foreign or international associations and organisations, they must obtain the permission of the Minister of Interior Affairs and Administration or another authorised person. However, political disengagement is not total. Police officers enjoy the right to vote and to belong to trade unions.

The question can be raised whether or not existing legal regulations provide adequate protection against police officers' involvement in political activity. The answer is yes. Further restrictions would violate the constitutional principle of the equality of citizens. The police exist by the authorisation of the community which they serve. In a democratic country their role is to protect society and the state against internal threats and, in some situations, external dangers. On the one hand, the police must reflect the democratic nature of the society they are part of; society should have confidence in the police, support them, and be ready to bear the costs of their maintenance and accept the price and tradeoffs for being safe. This postulate, that the police are part of society but are also partly autonomous, requires maximum openness by the police. Their structures and procedures must be clearly visible in order to ensure that the promotion of public safety and the development of police policies are subject to the legal control and accountability mechanisms of the competent state authorities.

Operational challenges

Common crime

The ongoing transformation of society and the state in Poland has changed the nature and structure of crime. New forms of crime and danger have appeared. However, the comparison of current crime patterns with those of the 1980s may result in misleading conclusions. Criminal policy of that time was strongly influenced by political and ideological factors and criminal statistics were subject to manipulation. A steady increase in the number of reported crimes in the 1980s coincided with a slow decline in the legitimacy and functioning of the political structures of the Polish People's Republic. According to the Police Headquarters (KGP) (*Przestepczosc w Polsce 1989 – 2000*, 2001), the crime rate in the years 1980–89 increased by 53%, from 946 to 1446 per 100,000 inhabitants. The increase was caused, among other factors, by an acute crisis in the operation of prosecution agencies which were then involved in political arguments with the opposition, as well as by a growing demoralisation of administrative authorities.

But it was in the years 1989–90, at the time of the shift from a socialist to democracy-based market economy, that the most rapid growth of crime occurred. Crimes jumped by 61.3%, from 547,589 in 1989 to 883,346 in 1990. In 2002 1,404,229 crimes were committed. The corresponding increase in the crime rate was from 1446 in 1989, to 3634.8 per 100,000 inhabitants in 2002. The clock of crime is ticking faster and faster. While in 1990 one crime was committed every 36 seconds on average, in 2002 one crime was committed every 23 seconds. Criminal offences, which account for the majority of offences, were committed every 41 seconds in 1990 and every 29 seconds in 2002.

Table 5.1   Crime rates 1998–2002 by offence category

	1998	*1999*	*2000*	*2001*	*2002*
Homicide	1072	1048	1269	1325	1188
Rape	2174	2029	2399	2339	2345
Bodily injury	19,496	17,849	18,429	16,968	16,775
Assault and battery	13,034	12,756	14,363	14,369	14,194

a.   crimes against the person

Theft	211,651	243,537	309,846	314,820	314,929
Theft with assault, robbery, Extortion	34,225	44,775	53,533	49,862	47,808
Burglary	355,176	369,235	364,786	325,696	304,625

b.   crimes against property

| Road traffic offences | 34,442 | 20,505 | 19,894 | 138,817 | 163,012 |

c.   traffic offences

| Criminal offences (total) | 931,037 | 1,020,654 | 1,133,162 | 1,107,073 | 1,083,854 |
| Economic crime (total) | 78,611 | 60,393 | 84,260 | 103,521 | 109,698 |

d.   totals

| Total | 1,073,042 | | | 1,390,089 | 1,404,229 |

e.   aggregated totals

The clearance rate decreased over this period, continuing a downward trend observed since the beginning of the 1980s. In the years 1980–89, the clearance rate decreased from 77.5% to 55.5%, and in 2002 was 54.9%. The numbers may not be completely reliable (Siemaszko, 1996: 220–7), but they do reflect the efficiency of prosecution agencies, which at present are in a deep crisis due to numerous problems of both organisational and financial natures.

Table 5.2   Detection rates by offence category (selected categories)

	1998	*1999*	*2000*	*2001*	*2002*
Homicide	86.3	85.7	87.0	87.5	89.4
Rape	87.0	83.7	85.9	83.9	85.3
Bodily Injury	90.8	89.2	89.7	88.6	89.1
Assault & Battery	78.7	76.3	77.4	77.6	77.2

a.   crimes against the person

	1998	1999	2000	2001	2002
Theft	25.7	20.7	21.5	21.7	21.2
Theft with assault, robbery, extortion	59.6	52.6	53.7	52.7	50.6
Burglary	27.6	23.5	23.3	22.3	21.5

b.   crimes against property

Road, Traffic Offences	92.3	91.5	92.0	98.9	99.0

c.   **traffic offences**

Criminal Offences (Total)	45.5	40.3	42.3	42.8	42.5
Economic Crime (Total)	86.7	96.7	96.8	96.7	96.6

d.   **totals**

All Offence Categories	**50.5**	**45.0**	**47.8**	**53.8**	**54.9**

e.   **aggregated totals**

Although after 1990 state policy on prosecuting and punishing criminals became relatively stable in comparison with that of the 1980s, the state was faced with new types of crime, especially organised crime, brought about by the new political and economic situation (Plywaczewski, 1997: 109). Following the rapid growth of crime in 1990, the situation stabilised somewhat with a steady upward tendency. In comparison with 1990, in 1995 the number of crimes on record increased to 974,941, which is by 9.4%, and in 2002 to 1,404,229. It should be mentioned that over 163,000 of crimes recorded in 2002 were traffic offences, including driving under the influence of alcohol (which until December 2000 was treated as a misdemeanour). Thus these fluctuations do not exceed criminological norms and should not be interpreted as downward trends.

It is evident, however, that some unfavourable phenomena in the crime structure intensified. There has been a considerable increase in crimes against life, health and property, and their perpetrators have become more violent, aggressive and ruthless to victims. To give an example, in the years 1990–2001 the number of murders nearly doubled – from 730 to 1325 (in 2002 this number decreased to 1188 cases). The above data also include murders committed by juvenile delinquents; their number grew from 17 in 1990 to 21 in 2002.

Migration

Issues related to foreigners constitute one of the biggest problems within the context of unification processes in Europe. Changes within the European Union and efforts by post-communist countries to join the EU have added a new dimension to the migration of people. More possibilities for travelling exist for inhabitants of former Eastern bloc countries, and for many reasons: tourism, family, business and economics. Such travel can result in permanent migration. Moreover, these countries, especially the former USSR republics and Poland, are used as transit routes by refugees and migrants from Asia, Africa and the Near East who are heading towards Western Europe and other developed countries such as the USA or Canada (Plywaczewski, 1995; Rzeplinska, 2000).

Poland plays a major role in these migrations because of its size, geographical location and desire to join the European Union, as well as its political transformations (processes of democratisation) and pace of economic development. So far, Poland has mainly been a transit country but it is presently becoming a destination country as well. This is demonstrated by the growth of new ethnic groups, e.g. Armenians, Vietnamese and Chinese, as a result of the legal and illegal flow of foreigners into Poland (Sklepkowski, 1996: 215–21).

Migrations through and into Poland are a new social phenomenon which can have a great and long-lasting impact, as has been the case in Western Europe. Immigration to Western European countries resulted in the permanent settlement of many ethnic minorities which, in turn, brought about considerable consequences of a political, economic, social and criminal nature (Korybut-Woroniecki, 1993: 86).

Responses to challenges

International influences

In the 1990s Poland has reached an inglorious position among other countries with respect to crime figures. First of all, it has become a transit country for international drug trafficking along the so-called Balkan and Asian routes. Poland is also the main smuggling route to the East for cars stolen in Western Europe. One can observe a recent escalation of criminal activity by international groups in the former Soviet Republics. Drug production and trafficking, money laundering, trade in arms and radioactive materials, and the smuggling of stolen cars, cigarettes and alcohol are all problems which police forces in this part of Europe are faced with more and more often.

Due to its geographical location, Poland plays a crucial role in the development of these criminal phenomena. Moreover, the number of foreigners suspected of committing crimes in Poland has been steadily increasing for a few years now.

Given this situation, individual actions undertaken by the police forces of different countries to fight the criminal world cannot be very effective in the long run. What is needed is transnational police cooperation at different levels and a search for new structural solutions with respect to the functioning of international police organisations. It is also important that legal standards in the area of extradition, money laundering and drug crime become harmonised. However, the matter which is of utmost urgency is that a uniform internal security strategy throughout Europe be worked out. Rainer Schulte (1995: 12), the director of the Police Executive Academy (Polizei Führungsakademie) in Münster-Hiltrup, Germany, has outlined the need for cooperation in three fields of European police relations. He advocates that cooperation be encouraged within the contexts of the European Union and the Schengen agreements, and that bilateral cooperation be cultivated among the countries of Europe.

Existing boundaries do little to restrain the expansion of contemporary crime and that makes crime one of the major threats to the social and economic stability of the continent. Limiting police cooperation only to the Schengen and European Union partners would be a mistake, particularly when the rapid growth of criminal groups in post-communist Europe makes it necessary for these countries to get involved in the process of creating a uniform European internal security strategy. Thus, in 1990, Poland rejoined Interpol. It is worth mentioning that the Polish presence in international police organisations goes back to 1923, when Interpol was established, but in 1952, for political reasons the Polish government broke off all relations with the organisation.

Apart from being involved in international initiatives, in the 1990s Poland has entered into a number of bilateral agreements with respect to transnational policing matters. According to Schulte (1995: 17), a quick intervention by the police, particularly in case of regional incidents, is possible only because of such bilateral agreements. Among the direct results of these agreements were the establishment of liaison police officer posts in signatory countries, whose work provides the foundation for further international police cooperation. At present, liaison officers representing Belgian, French, Dutch, German, Ukrainian, Italian, Russian, French, Swedish, British and American (FBI) police forces are based in Poland. Most advanced is Polish-German cooperation. In 1991, both countries entered into an agreement to fight organised crime, terrorism and illegal migration, and (a provision added later) cross-border crime.

The success of European integration and an internal security strategy will depend largely on the awareness and professional training of police officers. At this time, a number of regional and bilateral initiatives have been started which seek to promote the exchange of experience-based knowledge about methods and forms for fighting crime, enhancing police–public cooperation, or other aspects of public order protection. In 1992, the Central European Police Academy (MEPA) came into being, originally as a partnership between the Austrian and the Hungarian police. MEPA was joined a year later by the Czech Republic, Slovakia, Poland, Germany and Slovenia, and in 1996 by Switzerland. Its aim is to train police officers in the prevention of and fight against organised crime. Academy member countries are extremely interested in cooperation in various areas, including training, because of the threat posed by international criminal groups operating in this part of Europe. The high status of MEPA was confirmed on 22 May 2002 in Budapest, when Ministers of Interior of eight member countries signed the document entitled 'Common Statement' (*Gemeinsamte Erklärung*), that concerns the organisational activity of the Academy (MEPA, 2001). Another interesting initiative aiming to integrate post-communist police forces are conferences bringing together the commandants of police academies.

Individual professionalism

Police ethics are derived from social ethics in their broadest sense. The basic criteria for evaluating police conduct are part of the moral heritage of the whole society. The ethical standards of the police have to be in congruence with general moral norms. However, although police and societal ethics are based on the same basic norms, this does not mean they are identical. Police ethics are also influenced by the characteristics of the job and by the position and role of the police in a democratic state and society. Moral standards of the police are defined taking into account their tasks, methods and means. Thus, the specific nature of police ethics embodies a different hierarchy of socially approved values, which is reflected in such traits as wearing a uniform, an organisational structure based on hierarchy and submission, special equipment, weapons, the power to use reasonable force against citizens, availability for duty at any time, service loyalty, a special attitude to law, teamwork, discipline, the secret nature of many police activities, frequent contacts with the criminal world (which may bring about unfavourable consequences for the police), the necessity to resort to violence and a statutory ban on getting involved in politics.

Police ethics embodies the moral notion that police methods must be subordinated to the superior values, tasks and objectives assigned to the police by the state and society. Moral standards, for example, require that police officers respect standards of human dignity when enforcing the law. The latter often does not always provide clear guidelines as to proper conduct, which means that police officers must exercise their discretion in conformity with moral principles. Police ethics also regulates relations within the force by encouraging solidarity, mutual assistance, consideration for recruits and loyalty towards superiors. In practice, few cases of violating these standards have been observed in Poland recently.

Of much greater importance are norms regulating relations between the police, society and state agencies. These norms define the core traits expected of police officers. The nature of police work requires that police officers exhibit such qualities as bravery, firmness, adherence to principles, determination, politeness, sensitivity to harm, tolerance, good manners, impartiality and honesty. Operational work requires shrewdness, the ability to mislead the enemy and the capacity to act in secret. Because these required traits are many and diverse, it is impossible to state only a single unchanging profile of the good police officer. The changeability of circumstances sometimes calls for completely different approaches when dealing with citizens and offenders: humanity and strictness, tolerance and non-compromising, trust and criticism. The choice of a given approach depends on the situation and depends on the discretion of the officer. However, irrespective of the situation, the police officer should always obey the law and respect human dignity.

Disengagement from politics is a crucial aspect of police ethics, for it ensures the realisation of the most precious procedural and moral principles underlying the work of law enforcement agencies, namely impartiality, broad-mindedness, and an authentic humanitarianism free of political, religious or racial biases.

Police training systems

The proper fulfilment of statutory police tasks rests, largely, on having good personnel – determined by their recruitment, attitudes and, most of all, their training (Micinski, 1994). Improvements in the efficiency of police training and the structure and methods of teaching are continuously sought after, often through lessons drawn from the police experience of other countries, e.g. France, Germany, the United Kingdom and the Netherlands.

Police training is carried out on a number of levels and consists of the following stages:

(1)   Basic Training   Its main objective is to develop basic skills and practical techniques for performing basic police duties. Graduates of this type of training, which is carried out in police training centres and is given to all recruits, occupy the lowest posts. Since 2001, basic training of Polish police officers has been geared towards acquisition of clearly specified skills. Apart from theoretical knowledge, police officers acquire and improve their practical skills related to the tasks performed upon completion of training. During the training process strong emphasis is also put on shaping police officers' traits, such as self-discipline, integrity, commitment, responsibility and courage. Basic training is conducted in two phases. The first phase of basic training applies to officers in all police services i.e. prevention, criminal and support services, and takes 15 weeks. Upon completion of this phase, police officers in support services may be appointed to a specific job position within the service.

Police officers in prevention and criminal services must go though the second phase of basic training – the specialised training, whose duration differs depending on the expected work assignment. On average it takes about four months. The curriculum for this training phase has been selected to match the specialisation assigned to each specific group of trainee officers i.e., prevention, road traffic, investigative operations, forensic techniques, and operational techniques. It ends with an examination, which is to confirm whether the officer has acquired the professional knowledge and skills necessary for him to perform his tasks at the basic position. The exam also provides the basis to take non-commissioned officer's exam.

(2)   Specialised Training (medium level)   Special training qualifies police officers to perform tasks within particular branches. Police schools, the Police

Training Centre in Legionowo among them, which carry out this type of training equip their graduates with medium-level professional qualifications.

Officers in the prevention service are trained within the specialisations of district constable, duty officer, head of patrolling and intervention unit, or platoon commander of a prevention squad; officers in the criminal service are trained within the specialisations of intelligence-and-operational investigation and inquiry, and economic crime.

The Police Training Centre in Legionowo also provides training to police officers in the services providing the Police with administrative, logistics and technical support, within one comprehensive specialisation. The Training Centre provides also courses for the officers in the prevention service within the scope of road safety, youth delinquency, as well as training for police dog guides and training for criminal service officers with regard to forensic techniques and operational techniques.

(3)   Higher Professional Training (higher and postgraduate studies)
Professional training is carried out at the Higher Police Training Academy in Szczytno, which is a higher vocational school granting a first (university level) degree. Although the school's main objective is to train police officers for their future job, the school also provides educational services for departments in the Ministry of Interior Administration, as well as for the national education system.

Apart from updating knowledge, skills and abilities which reflect progress in policing theory and practice, the school provides its students with the necessary formal qualifications essential for fulfilling the role of commissioned officers and police managers. In addition, the school offers postgraduate studies addressed to university graduates specialising in various fields of activity (in this case connected with the police work and the organisation of the force). Postgraduate training automatically leads to promotion (Fiebig and Plywaczewski, 1995: 46–8).

The professional development system deals with demands addressed to the Higher Police Training Academy (*WSPol*) and other police schools by field police units and the Police High Command through its Personnel and Training Bureau. Such demands take into account principles and needs of personnel policy (promotion, creating reserves) and the level of training carried out in particular schools. In addition, professional development training takes place in those police units which have training personnel and specialists posted to them.

One natural consequence of socio-economic transformations in society can be traced by changes in the police curriculum. At present much emphasis is placed on both theoretical knowledge and practical skills. In connection with the new concept of policing (that the police provide a service), the aim of training is to develop attitudes which are desirable from the citizens' point of view, that is, professional relations between the police and the public in general and between the individual police officer and a member of the public.

Conclusion

At the beginning of the 1990s, democracy spread to vast new territories, mainly as a result of the fall of communist governments in Eastern and Central Europe (Brand and Jamróz, 1995). On adopting democracy, people in these countries seek answers to the following questions: what is democracy? What principles should democratic society be based on? What rules should a democratic state obey? Other questions may concern rights enjoyed by an individual in a democratic society, the status and role of political parties, as well as the status and tasks of law enforcement agencies, the police occupying a special position among these.

The time of transformation in Poland witnessed great organisational changes, which had significant consequences in many areas of social life. The police had to adapt to the changes in their organisation, legal regulations and professional awareness; they had to keep up with societal changes and, consequently, had to undergo a transformation themselves. In 1990 the new management of the Ministry of Interior and Administration realised that the Civic Militia, the armed force of the Polish United Workers' Party, would have to be transformed into a modern, apolitical police in a very short time if Poland were to become the democratic country it aspired to be after 1989. It was not an easy task as, on the one hand, the people's confidence in the new police had to be gained, and, on the other hand, the police had to be taught their new role in the new constitutional order, that of public servants under the law and protectors of society.

Despite the objections of various political circles and public opinion at the time, the decision was made to introduce into the newly created police profound organisational changes, including shifts among managerial staff and the dismissal of discredited people who were unable to work within the new framework. This policy resulted in a shortage of manpower at all levels and reduced police efficiency, which was lowered further by a lack of senior officers to occupy managerial posts in the basic organisational units of the police.

At the same time, the widely supported political, economic and social transformations necessary for the development of democratic freedoms and a free-market economy brought about a rapid increase in crime and changes in its structure and forms. The most dangerous development was that of organised crime of both national and international natures, which started to resemble traditional mafias. The dynamic and practically unhindered development of organised crime resulted from, among other factors, misguided political decisions which reflected a blind faith that social processes would lead to the automatic eradication of this form of crime. Yet decisions taken after 1989 concomitantly hindered the effective reorganisation of law enforcement and criminal justice agencies.

The rapid rise in crime was accompanied by an even greater sense of threat. Fear of crime is dangerous in itself as it leads to more and more repressive, and thus less efficient, criminal justice policies. Fear of crime is aroused not only by real threats but also by the mass media and politicians. In particular, it often appears that politicians seeking to gain power are the ones to stress the fact that people in control now are helpless when challenged by increasing crime. Such rhetoric is quite common, not only in this part of Europe, and results from a misunderstanding of the situation and the failure to react to crime in appropriate ways.

It can be assumed that the increase in crime after state borders have been opened is a normal consequence of the lessening of state control over the movement of people. In addition, communism had eroded informal public control. In a communist country everything was controlled by the orders of superior authority. Now, social control institutions are in a more or less serious crisis, while citizens and local communities do not face up to new challenges since they think that crime prevention is a task to be handled exclusively by an anonymous state bureaucracy. Thus, more publicity should be given to one of the basic theses of victimology, namely that citizens should take care of their own life, health and property, and that it is the obligation of the state to create proper conditions for that. However, people generally limit themselves to criticising the state of safety rather than cooperating actively with law enforcement agencies and criminal justice personnel.

The unwillingness of people to engage in such cooperation cannot be blamed only on the 'heritage' of the previous system. The idea of protecting the individual's rights, a position consistently advocated and put into practice since the beginning of the 1990s, sometimes assumed extreme, even pathological, forms. On the one hand, there occurred an excessive increase in the rights and protections of perpetrators in all stages of legal proceedings; on the other hand, the interests of victims and witnesses of crimes were neglected and they were exposed to various forms of aggression and threats from perpetrators and their supporters, as well as to the so-called 'secondary victimisation' at the hands of representatives of law enforcement and criminal justice agencies. Thus, there developed a major imbalance in the rights of victims and witnesses versus those of perpetrators of crimes. This was one of the reasons for the creeping paralysis of criminal justice. The unwillingness to cooperate with the police resulted in a lack of witnesses in preparatory and court proceedings, which made it impossible to examine cases and bring alleged criminals before the court. This situation led to the introduction of the institution of the 'incognito' witness and to work on drafting a crown witness act.

Yet, the initiatives came too late in the face of a growing and extremely dangerous phenomenon of 'auto-jurisdiction': citizens themselves began to administer justice. A new criminological category came into being – crimes due to settling accounts – resulting from, among other reasons, the calculation that a debt could be regained much faster, cheaper and more effectively in this manner than by means of court proceedings. Generally speaking, Polish courts are in a very serious crisis as the number of cases to be tried increased rapidly with the introduction of a democratic system based on a free-market economy while, at the same time, proper initiatives to respond effectively to these new challenges to the finances and personnel of courts were not pursued. Trials take a very long time and there are vast problems with executing sentences. Without further and substantial aid provided to

Polish courts, it would be difficult to regard Poland as a *Rechtsstaat,* or a state based on the rule of law (Siemaszko, 1996).

The Polish police must cope with even greater problems in trying to ensure the safe functioning of the society. The basic tasks of a democratic state with regard to the police are to maximise their capacities to prevent and fight crime and other socially harmful phenomena and to minimise the chances that their powers are used in conflict with democratic principles. At the same time, crime in Poland has been subject to the process of democratisation as well – criminals can be found in all social classes.

In sum, the issue of how to design police training and work in such a manner that the public can feel assured that the police are working for society and not against it remains unresolved. One should also bear in mind that an increase in public safety and order depends on overcoming the following three barriers: legislative barriers, which can hinder the introduction of the legal solutions necessary for effective crime prevention; economic barriers, which can reduce budgetary resources for law enforcement and criminal justice agencies; and barriers in social awareness, particularly when, in the process of shaping public opinion about suggested solutions, there is a tendency to offer only one-sided presentations of limitations, regulations and prohibitions. It is mainly in the field of social awareness that one can observe the escalation of the potential conflict between the rights and freedom of citizens and measures necessary to ensure their safety (Plywaczewski, 2000: 167).

References

Brand, P. and Jamróz, A. 1995. *Democracy Yesterday and Today.* Bialystok.

Central Police Headquarters (*Komenda Główna Policji*). 2001. *Przestępczość w Polsce 1989–2000* (Crime in Poland 1989–2000). Warszawa.

Central Police Headquarters (*Komenda Główna Policji*). 2000. *The Police 1919–1999 – Tradition and Modernity.* Warszawa (Warsaw)

Central Police Headquarters (*Komenda Główna Policji*). 2002. *Wizerunek Policji w oczach opinii publicznej* (Police in the public eyes). Warszawa.

Daszkiewicz, W. 1996. *Proces karny. Czesc ogólna* (Criminal proceedings. General part). Poznan.

Fiebig, J.and Plywaczewski, W. 1995. 'System szkolenia Policji w WSPol. Stan obecny i perspektywy.' (The Police training system at the Higher Police Training Academy – the present and future). *Policyjny Biuletyn Szkoleniowy* (Police Training Bulletin), vol. 1–2.

Galster, J., Szyszkowski, W., Wasik, Z., and Witkowski, Z. 1996. *Prawo konstytucyjne – zarys instytucji w okresie transformacji ustrojowej.* (Constitutional Law – outline of institution in transition). Toruń.

Haberfeld, M., Walancik, P., and Uydess, A.M. 2002. 'Teamwork – not making the dream work. Community policing in Poland'. *Policing: An International Journal of Police Strategies & Management*, vol. 25, no. 1.

Journal of Law. 1995. vol. 30. entry 179 with further amendments.

Journal of Law. 1997. vol. 114, entry 738.

Korybut-Woroniecki, A.1993. 'Migracyjne problemy' (The problems of migration). *Polska w Europie* (Poland in Europe), vol. 10. Warzawa.

Kudrelek, J. and Lisiecki, M. 1996. 'Nowe uprawnienia kryminalistyczno – operacyjne policji' (New forensic and operational powers of the police). *Jurysta* (Jurist), vol. 5.

MEPA. 2001. *Gemeinsame Erklärung zur Zusammenarbeit im Rahmen der Mitteleuropäischen Polizeiakademie (MEPA – Report)*, no. 2, June 2001.

Micinski, R 1994. 'O nowych zasadach przyjecia do służby w policji' (On new principles of police recruitment). *Policyjny Biuletyn Szkoleniowy* (Police Training Bulletin), vol. 1–2.

Plywaczewski, E., ed. 1995. *Foreigners-related Crime: A New Challenge for Theory and Practice*. Szczytno.

Plywaczewski, E. 1997.'Organised Crime in Poland'. *Transnational Organised Crime*, vol. 3.

Plywaczewski, E.W. 2000. 'The Challenges of Policing Democracy in Poland', in Das, D. K and Marenin, O., eds. *Challenges of Policing Democracies. A World Perspective*. Amsterdam.

Rzeplinska, I. 2000. *Foreign Criminals in Poland* (in Polish). Warszawa.

Schulte, R. 1995. 'Europejska współpraca policyjna' (European police cooperation). *Prokuratura i Prawo* (Prosecution and Law), vol. 4, no. 17.

Siemaszko, A. 1996. *Quo Vadis Iustitia? Stan i perspektywy wymiaru sprawiedliwosci w Polsce* [Quo Vadis Iustitia? The present and future of criminal justice in Poland]. Warszawa.

Sklepkowski, L.1996. 'Polska jako kraj tranzytowy i docelowy nielegalnej migracji. Nielegalne przerzuty przez granic przez granice' (Poland as a transit and target country for illegal migration. Organised smuggling across the border), in Plywaczewski W. and Swierczewski J., eds. *Policja polska wobec przestepczosci zorganizowanej* (The Polish police against organised crime). Szczytno.

Waltos, S. 1996. *Proces karny. Zarys systemu* (Criminal proceedings. An outline of the system). Warszawa.

Chapter 6

A Study of Police Reform in Slovenia

Milan Pagon

Introduction

Slovenia is a small Central European country, situated on 20,273 square kilometres between the Alps, the Adriatic Sea and the Pannonian Plains. It has a population of 1,965,986, of which 87.9% are Slovenes. On average, the population density is 97 people per square kilometre, which is much lower than in the majority of other European states. The official language is Slovene. The majority of Slovenes are Roman Catholics, although there are some small communities of other Christian denomination (Protestants), Muslims and Jews. The capital city is Ljubljana.

In spite of its geographically small size, Slovenia is a convergence point for a range of different landscapes: Alpine and Mediterranean, Pannonian and Dinaric, each of which has its own characteristics and unique features. At the heart of Europe, between Austria to the north, Italy to the west, Hungary to the east and Croatia to the south, Slovenia has always been a crossroads of trans-European routes.

Slovenia used to be a part of the former Socialist Federal Republic of Yugoslavia (SFRY) from its creation in 1945. However, after the death of the President Josip Broz Tito in 1980, the economic and political situation started to become very strained and this ultimately led, ten years later, to the end of the SFRY. The first clear demand for Slovene independence was made in 1987 by a group of intellectuals in the 57th edition of the journal *Nova revija*. Demands for democratisation and resistance against the centralised Yugoslavia were sparked off by the arrest of three journalists from the political weekly *Mladina* and a non-commissioned officer of the Yugoslav Army. In 1988 and 1989, the first political opposition parties emerged, which in the 1989 May Declaration demanded a sovereign state for the Slovene nation.

In April 1990, the first democratic elections in Slovenia took place and were won by DEMOS, the united opposition movement. In the same year, more than 88% of the electorate voted for a sovereign and independent Slovenia. The declaration of independence followed on 25 June 1991. The next day, the newly formed state was attacked by the Yugoslav Army. After a ten-day war, a truce was called, and in October 1991 the last soldiers of the Yugoslav Army left Slovenia. In November, a law on denationalisation was adopted and in December, a new constitution. The European Union recognised Slovenia in the middle of January 1992, and the UN accepted it as a member in May 1992. In February 1999, an association agreement with the EU came into effect and Slovenia also applied for full membership.

Slovenia's constitutional order is parliamentary democracy. The head of the state is president of the republic, popularly elected every five years, for a maximum of two five-year terms. The legislative authority is the National Assembly with 90 deputies. The Government consists of the Prime Minister and other ministers. The Government and the ministers are independent within the framework of their jurisdiction, and are responsible to the National Assembly.

Slovenia is among the most successful countries in transition from socialism to a market economy. It boasts a stable growth of GDP and ranks among the countries with the lowest degree of risk. The greatest number of more than 144,000 registered companies in Slovenia is engaged in trade and commerce, followed by industry, services, real estate, construction, transport and communications. More than 90% of companies are classified as small business enterprises.

In 1999, GDP per capita was $10,078, while the standardised rate of unemployment (ILO) was 7.5%. The relatively small internal Slovenian market directed the orientation of the economy towards export. Slovenia's main foreign trading partners are Germany, Italy, Croatia, France and Austria.

Reforms and changes in the country's policing system since 1989

Before 1991 the Slovenian police were a part of the Yugoslav police. Initially a very centralised police force, the Yugoslav police had gradually become more decentralised, transferring a lot of responsibilities to the individual republics within the SFRY. The first Slovenian law regulating policing and security issues, the Interior Act, was adopted by the Republic of Slovenia in 1967 (all previous laws in the area of policing and security were federal laws). The police functions were performed by the Secretariat of the Interior of the Republic of Slovenia. All of the secretariats of the interior of the Yugoslav republics were supervised by the Federal Secretariat of the Interior in the matters of federal security.

The new Interior Act of 1980 stressed the legality and professionalisation of police work, police–public relations, and respect for human rights and dignity. At that time, the State Security Agency (i.e. the political police) was still a part of the Secretariat of the Interior.

The events in 1990 and 1991, described in the introduction, provided an impetus for a further change of the Slovenian police. Slovenia became an independent state. The political system changed from a one-party regime to parliamentary democracy. Slovenia needed a police suitable to the changed circumstances. What needs to be noted, however, is that the police in Slovenia stood by its people during the conflict with Yugoslavia. They fought against the Yugoslav Army during the ten-day war, in which some of the police officers lost their lives. Consequently, public trust in the police was very high and the changes introduced regarding the police were not nearly as radical as they were in some other countries in the region. This, of course, held true for the regular police (the uniformed police and the criminal investigation police), but not for the State Security Agency. The latter were perceived as the political police and their role in the conflict was questioned by many. These were the reasons why subsequent personnel changes in the police occurred most frequently within the State Security Agency and the least within the regular police.

In 1991, the Secretariat of the Interior was given a new name, the Ministry of the Interior. It was now headed by the Minister, no longer by the Secretary. In 1992, the traditional name for the police under the socialist-communist regime, *Milica* (the Militia), was officially replaced by the name *Policija* (the Police). Within the Ministry of the Interior, the State Security Agency was reorganised and renamed the Security-Information Agency. In 1993, it was renamed again, this time as the Slovenian Security Intelligence Agency, and separated from the Ministry of the Interior.

In 1991, the Minister of the Interior established a task force to undertake a project, initially called 'Public Security' and later renamed 'The Police on the Local Level'. The task force was composed of the Minister's advisors, some of them former police officers (both from the uniformed and the criminal investigation divisions), and others coming from other departments within the Ministry (human resources, analytics, public relations). The main purpose of this project was to ensure that Slovenian police would be comparable to modern European police forces. The two main goals were professionalisation and depoliticisation of the police. The task force made recommendations for a number of changes, described below.

It could be said, therefore, that the main reason for the subsequent changes in the Slovenian police was the political change in 1990, followed by the conflict with the former Yugoslavia in 1991. After the new, democratically elected, government took over in 1990, it started to actively seek the best way to govern the new state. In the area of policing, the changes were largely self-initiated, led by the above mentioned task force. The task force's recommendations were gradually implemented in the period from 1992 to 1998, when the new Police Act was adopted.

The most important innovation introduced by the Police Act was the changed status of the police. Previously, the police force was just one of the units of the Ministry of the Interior. The new Act transformed the police into an independent agency operating under the auspices of the Ministry of the Interior. This changed the relationship between the Minister and the police dramatically. While previously the Minister was the highest person in the police chain of command, directly supervising its operations, he was now replaced in this position by the newly formed post of the Director General of the Police, who is appointed by the government of the Republic of Slovenia on the proposal of the Minister of the Interior. The Director General, at least in theory, is a professional and not a political position. The person in this position should not automatically be replaced with the change of the government or the Minister of the Interior.

The relationship between the Ministry and the Police is defined in Article 2 of the Police Act. To carry out the Ministry's tasks deriving from this Article, in particular the tasks relating to the direction and supervision of police work, the Minister has established the Bureau for Direction and Supervision of the Police, headed by a State Secretary. The Bureau participates in the production of basic guidelines for police work, the preparation of guidelines for the Ministry with respect to its relations with the police, preparation of starting-points for security policy and its implementation, analyses of reports and data on police work, and the preparation of legal and technical acts binding on the police. Another important task of the Bureau is control of the implementation of police tasks by stressing the protection of human rights and the fundamental freedoms of individuals in the exercising of police authority (see http://www.mnz.si).

Pursuant to the law, the police perform their tasks at three levels: state, regional and local levels. Organisationally, it is composed of the General Police Directorate, Police Directorates and police stations. The police headquarters are in Ljubljana, the capital of Slovenia.

At the state level, police activity is performed by the General Police Directorate, with the tasks being as follows (see also http://www.policija.si):

(1)   Monitoring, analysing and assessing the security situation, evaluating the situation in the areas of performing police tasks, directing and co-coordinating the work of police administrations, providing expert and technical aid, controlling their work, ensuring improvement of the system organisation and work methods, taking care of the police functioning in a state of emergency or war, taking care of the lawful implementation of regulations in the area of police work and carrying out measures leading to efficient police functioning.

(2)   Taking measures in the areas of eliminating crime, traffic safety, border matters and foreigners, public order in cases where harmonised activity in a wider area is needed and making decisions at the second level on matters concerning crossing the state border.

(3)   Organising, directing and implementing the protection of certain persons, bodies, buildings, districts, jobs and classified information.

(4)   Conducting forensic and laboratory research and giving expert opinions in this area.

(5)   Caring for the implementation of international agreements in the area of police tasks.

(6)   Co-operating with the police forces of other countries and international organisations in the area of police work.

(7)   Collecting, treating, giving and keeping information in the area of police work and managing the information and telecommunication police systems.

(8)   Taking care of informing the authorised bodies and the public on police work, topical security issues and the security situation.

(9)   Taking care of employing policemen and other police workers, allocating and organising them and conducting expert education and training.

(10) Proposing and implementing financial plans and proposing purchase plans, managing the maintenance of buildings, devices and equipment, providing supplies to police units, deciding on resolving housing issues of police employees and performing tasks in the area of office business.

(11) Defining systematisation and standardisation of material-technical means, equipment of the police as well as premises and their equipment.

(12) Planning, distributing and caring for efficient and purposeful use of funds.

(13) Performing other tasks in the area of police work defined by the law or other regulations issued on the basis of the law.

Within the General Police Directorate, there are the Uniformed Police Directorate (with its sectors taking care of public order, traffic, state borders and foreigners, and the organisation and development of uniformed police; it also includes the flight police unit, the centre for foreigners and the police orchestra), the Criminal Investigation Police Directorate (with sectors for general, white collar and organised crimes, special tasks, computer crime and criminal analysis, and the Forensic and Research Centre), the Operation and Communications Centre, the Security and Protection Bureau, the Special Weapons and Tactics Unit, the Common Services, the Informatics and Telecommunications Service, the Personnel Department, and the Police Academy.

On the regional level, there are 11 Police Directorates, located in major cities across Slovenia. Regional Police Directorates supervise the work of police stations on the local level. There are 98 police stations in Slovenia.

Altogether, there were 6,882 police officers and 716 detectives employed by the Slovenian Police in 2001, which gave the ratio of 274 police officers and 36 detectives per 100,000 inhabitants. Their average age was 31 years. The vast majority (70%) had a high-school-level education, while some 20% had education above the high-school level (associate, bachelor's, master's, or doctoral degrees) (source: http://www.policija.si).

Another important change that took place during this period was a change in police training system. The so-called cadet system of training and education was abolished and replaced with shorter training, more comparable to international systems of police training. Under the cadet system, the candidates for police work had to make this important career choice when they were 14 years old. Immediately following their completion of the eight-year elementary school, they were admitted to the four-year police high school. They had to be in residence at that school for four years, during the age when they not only needed a lot of social contacts but were also very impressionable. In other words, they were taken out of their social environment, placed in an artificial, same-sex environment abundant with police subculture and political indoctrination. After their completion of this school and a probationary period, at the age of 18 or 19, they were vested with police powers and trusted with firearms. The public, not surprisingly, was quite reluctant to be policed by relatively immature individuals who, in addition to their young age, were not properly socialised and were already inoculated with police subculture and particular political views. Under the new system, candidates for police work have to complete a regular four-year high school and gain a few years of work experience before they can even apply for police work. If selected, typically around 20–22 years of age, they attend a year-and-a-half long training programme at the Police Academy, after which they become police officers.

The system of further education for police officers and supervisors has also evolved during this period. Before 1995, the only option for a further education was a two-year College of the Interior. Nowadays, there are two institutions offering further education to police officers. The first one, of a year-and-a-half in duration, is organised within the Police Academy, namely the Higher School for the Police. The second one is the Faculty of Criminal Justice, University of Maribor, which offers a three-year and a four-year course in police and security studies. The Faculty (called the College of Police and Security Studies at that time), used to be a part of the Ministry of the Interior and an affiliated member of the University of Ljubljana, before it became a full member of the University of Maribor.

Another change has occurred in the area of complaints against the police. Under the socialist regime, there were hardly any complaints registered against the police. After 1991, the situation started to change. Due to the role that the police played in the ten-day war with the Yugoslav Army, the police had a high reputation in the public perception, so the number of complaints was not too high initially. This effect, however, wore off gradually, and citizens became more critical of their police. So, let us take a brief look at the citizen complaints against the police in Slovenia, as shown in Pagon and Lobnikar (2001). In 2000, the Police received a total of 1552 complaints, 1240 of which were submitted in writing, 258 in person, 29 by phone, 7 through the Office of the Ombudsman, 5 anonymously, 3 over television, and 10 in some other way. Table 6.1 shows a four-year comparison of citizen complaints against the police.

Table 6.1   Citizen complaints against the police in Slovenia (1997–2000)

Year	1997	1998	1999	2000
Complaints	1,363	1,672	1,853	1,552
Index	100	123	136	114
Processed	1,285	1,575	1,760	1,496
Sustained	213	245	214	201
% of sustained	16.6	15.5	12.2	13.4

Source: Pagon and Lobnikar, 2001.

As can be seen from Table 6.1, the number of complaints is relatively stable over the years. Roughly 5% of all the complaints are dismissed immediately, while around 95% get processed. The ratio of sustained complaints is slowly decreasing.

The police statistics for 1999 show that there were 285.7 complaints per 1000 police officers; there was one complaint against every 582nd repressive police measure; and one sustained complaint against every 4783rd repressive police measure. These data appear to be quite favourable, showing that very few of the complaints against the police are actually sustained.

Another interesting observation is that the police introduced a change in the complaint procedure in the year 2000; they started to require that every complaint be submitted in writing. Other forms of submitting a complaint used before (in person, by phone, through the Office of the Ombudsman, anonymously, over television etc.) were no longer admissible. The public reacted unfavourably, which – paired with dissatisfaction among some of those in charge of processing the complaints within the police – lead to a recent change back to the previous status.

While the police have included the public in processing the complaints, a closer examination shows that the public is still not playing an active role in this process. There is one representative of the public present during the decision-making process in each case, but they are mainly passive observers.

Finally, a few words need to be said regarding the issue of international influences on reforms and changes. Even after the change of political system, the mentality of the police has been changing very slowly in this area. They have been still quite suspicious of any foreign ideas and approaches, although not necessarily on a verbal level. This is one reason why numerous foreign initiatives never really had a profound impact on reforms of the police in Slovenia. The impact of international influences was more or less limited to the operational aspects of policing, such as introducing new techniques or methods to police investigations.

Assessment and evaluation of the implementation and success of reforms

As we said before, changes in the policing system were largely self-initiated, led by the task force appointed by the Minister in 1991. However, there is always a discrepancy between what the police perceive as an appropriate form of policing and what the public wants. A closer look at the situation in Slovenia shows that a change process that started in 1990 and culminated in the adoption of the Police Act in 1998 was done according to the police organisation's own perceptions. Now we are entering phase two, in which the public and police researchers are bringing pressures to bear for reforms.

While the task force's efforts were worthwhile and led to important changes in policing in Slovenia, it has to be noted that the approach was almost exclusively based on experience, and lacked a theoretical background and a clearly defined concept of policing, which is probably why the changes were more successful in their form (i.e. changing the organisational structure of the police, names of the units, etc.) than in their substance (i.e., changing the existing philosophy of policing, police subculture, and the work patterns of the police).

As a consequence, many questions remained unexamined and unanswered. For example, how to reconcile tendencies for centralisation and efficiency with tendencies for decentralisation and community policing? Under the 'old' system, the Slovenian police organisation was quite decentralised to the local level. All police stations in the country were considered community-level units. The commanders at those stations were appointed by the local governments, after such appointments were approved by the Secretary of the Interior. Under the current system, all police stations in the country are state-level units which only operate on the local level. The local government has no say in their operation or in the appointment of their commanders. At the same time, however, the police want to practise community policing, by appointing certain police officers as 'community-level police officers' with no repressive duties, just preventive ones. No wonder, then, that community policing by the Slovenian police is perceived just as another technique within the framework of traditional policing, rather than a completely new, organisation-wide, philosophy of policing.

The hardest blow to the Slovenian Police's confidence came recently in the form of the European Commission's Report on Slovenia's progression as a candidate country. Based largely on the judgments made by some other governmental and non-governmental organisations, the Commission accused the Slovenian Police of being brutal and violent in some cases. The report specifically mentioned two problem areas, namely the use of excessive force against persons in police custody and police brutality towards Roma (i.e., gypsies). These accusations coincide with the accusations made by Amnesty International, the UN Committee Against Torture, the European Court for Protection of Human Rights, the Slovenian Ombudsman, and the Open Society Organisation. All critiques have these common themes: excessive use of force, improper treatment, unnecessary display of powers, and threats (Mekina, 2001). The report also mentioned a European Court of Human Rights' judgment in the so called Rehbock case, in which the Court established that Slovenia violated several provisions of the European Convention on Human Rights because its police treated an EU citizen inhumanely.

The police responded by denying allegations and providing statistics that showed just a slight increase in the number of cases where the police actually used force (between 1% and 7% over the last four years). At the same time, several measures were implemented, including an increased level of control of the use of force, more precise analyses of recorded cases, programmes for increasing the level of human rights awareness, and more training in the area of human rights.

Also, much research by police scholars in Slovenia points to the conclusion that the Slovenian police are still, at least to some extent, characterised by a bureaucratic, centralised and paramilitary organisation and philosophy (Pagon, 1998). Police officers within such an organisation are likely to be rewarded for producing desirable statistics and reinforced for exhibiting obedience and conformity, while the paramilitary organisational structure encourages an authoritarian leadership approach. Police work is mainly repressive and reactive in nature, characterised by its orientation to the past, because the majority of the things the police are dealing with had already happened. The police officers, reinforced by their commanders and the media, perceive themselves as 'crime fighters', the 'thin blue line' between the rule of law and general disorder, constantly at war with criminals, 'liberals', and enemies of other sorts. This kind of police organisation and philosophy has been linked to the misuse of police discretion and reinforcement of police subculture (characterised by cynicism, insularity, secrecy, defensiveness etc.) on the one hand and to public dissatisfaction with the police on the other (ibid.).

A recent review of some police-related research in Slovenia (Pagon, 2002) revealed that even after the changes took place in 1991, the Slovenian police are still not immune to problems such as sexual harassment within the police, negative effects of police subculture (such as the 'code of silence' and tolerance of police misconduct, negative attitudes towards marginalised and less privileged segments of the society), stress among police officers (related to supervisor and co-worker undermining their work), stress among police managers (related to their workload, relationships, work hassles, recognition and organisational climate), police deviance, depression and cynicism.

Issues of police ethics and integrity are still not high on a priority list of police management in Slovenia, and quite often are overridden by more immediate operational and efficiency concerns. However, a proper development of police ethics and integrity is one of the most important steps towards the professionalisation of policing, and one of the most powerful antidotes to police deviance and the neglect of human rights by the police. To set a climate conducive to ethical behaviour in police organisation, police managers have to foster character development and moral habits of police officers by educating and training them in police ethics; establishing a high moral climate through appropriate use of goals, means, rewards, and support; facilitating the development of strong and dense social networks extending into the community; preventing cliques and conspiracies within the police; and establishing both cognitive-based and affect-based trust among all organisational members and between the police and the public (Pagon, 2000). Such an approach would also eliminate the negative aspects of police subculture, an issue that has not been effectively addressed by reform efforts in Slovenia.

The issue of depoliticisation of the police, although partially solved on paper, has not been completely resolved in practice. Although, as previously mentioned, the Director General of the Police is supposed to be a professional, not a political, position, experience has shown that politicians and political parties became actively involved in the process of selecting and appointing the 'right' person for this position. Even institutions not typically involved in selecting the police chief (such as the Roman Catholic Church) were rumoured to be involved in the process. Also, the interpretation of Article 2 of the Police Act (determining the relationship between the Minister and the Director General of the Police) was, at times, influenced more by the political power of the incumbents of these positions than it was by professional and/or legal arguments. As long as this relationship is not clear, the issue of police accountability remains unresolved. There were instances where the police refused to be audited by the Bureau for Direction and Supervision of the Police, claiming that the Ministry's interpretation of the Article 2 was incorrect.

On a more positive note, a study of the attitudes towards community policing (Pagon and Lobnikar, 2001a) conducted with a sample of 95 police officers and 75 citizens in Slovenia revealed that both the police and the public favoured community policing over the traditional, paramilitary style of policing. The most important difference between the two groups was that the public emphasised crime prevention while the police emphasised crime investigation.

There were also differences in perceptions of public willingness to cooperate with the police. Those perceptions were significantly higher in the public than they were in the police. More specifically, the public perceived themselves as more cooperative than did the police in the following areas: crime prevention, evaluating police effectiveness, public order maintenance, dealing with youth offenders, defining the police goals, and dealing with juvenile delinquency. The problem is that such public willingness to cooperate with the police remains an unrealised potential to the extent that the police are not aware of it. It is, therefore, the task for police leadership in Slovenia to actively work on changing their own perceptions. Unless these perceptions change, the Slovenian police cannot fully embrace the philosophy of community policing, with public involvement as one of its most important components (Pagon and Lobnikar, 2001a).

We can conclude by saying that the Slovenian police are in a transition from the old to the new approach to policing. Every transition process has its problems, and so does this one. It would be far too optimistic to conclude that the police in Slovenia have fully embraced the philosophy and practice of community policing. Our analysis shows that there is still enough room for improvement. More specifically, necessary measures should target the following interrelated categories (for a more detailed explanation see Pagon, 2002):

(1)   The philosophy of policing (departing from the traditional paramilitary philosophy, embracing the new philosophy of community and problem-oriented policing).

(2)   Police priorities (increasing the number and changing the structure of police contacts with the community, establishing partnership with the community).

(3)   The police subculture (changing the traditional police subculture, including perceptions of and attitudes toward corruption and toward various parts of the community).

(4)   Police recruiting, selection, and promotion (recruiting and promoting more women and individuals other than the typical-police-personality type).

(5)   The training of police officers (emphasising communication skills and police ethics).

(6)   Police management training (emphasising management and people skills).

(7)   Mechanisms for dealing with police deviance (including violence, corruption, sexual harassment etc.).

(8)   The moral climate within the police (establishing a moral climate conducive to ethical behaviour, developing strong and dense social networks within police organisation, and establishing trust among all organisational members and between the police and the public).

Insights suggested by the description and evaluation of police reforms

The first lesson learned from the analysis of police reform in Slovenia is that any reform should not be done based on experience only, that is, in a theoretical vacuum. The reformers should prepare a strong theoretical background and justification for reforms and clearly define the desired concept of policing, along with values, virtues, and standards of policing.

Second, we have to accept the fact that the question of what kind of police a particular country wants to have is a political decision, far too serious to be left to the police themselves to decide (Pagon, 2002). The answer to this question should be decided in a political process in which all constituents and interested parties should partake. The Slovenian case clearly shows that if the police themselves decide upon the content and the extent of change, it is not likely that any substantive and far-reaching change will take place. Therefore, the philosophy and work patterns of policing are not likely to change in this case.

Finally, once the goals of police reforms have been set, the implementation is mostly a managerial problem. Real change in policing cannot happen within a police organisation having a traditional police subculture, plagued by an 'us versus them' mentality – secrecy, isolation, conservatism, police deviance, brutality etc. Such problems, however, cannot be solved by passing new laws and regulations. They have to be solved by working with people on a daily basis, changing their attitudes and perceptions, managing their experience and the consequences of their behaviour, setting an example, establishing an appropriate moral climate, and managing social relationships. For example, based on their research of Slovenian police, Pagon, Duffy, Ganster and Lobnikar (1998) stress the role of good management and personal skills in combating police deviance. Police managers, who are consistent in their support and try to increase their employees' organisational commitment, well-being, and self-efficacy through empowerment and encouragement, are more likely to be successful in their attempts to decrease counterproductive work behaviours in their organisation. According to Ganster, Pagon and Duffy (1996), the police organisations might be able to improve the well-being of their members by teaching police supervisors to adopt more effective leadership behaviours. These behaviours include being more considerate of police officers' personal feelings, including them in joint decision-making, clarifying their roles, and setting specific performance goals.

References

Areh, I. and Umek, P. 2002. 'Zadovoljstvo z delom pri policistkah in policistih' (Job satisfaction among male and female police officers). *Varstvoslovje,* vol. 4, no. 2.

Ganster, D.C., Pagon, M., Duffy, M. 1996. 'Organisational and interpersonal sources of stress in the Slovenian police force', in Pagon, M., ed. *Policing in Central and Eastern Europe: Comparing First-hand Knowledge with Experience from the West.* Ljubljana.

Lobnikar, B. and Kecanovic, B. 2002. 'Pravna in moralna razseznost clovekovih pravic v policijskih postopkih' (Legal and moral aspects of human rights in police-public interactions), in Mesko, G., ed.. *Vizije slovenske kriminologije* (Visions of Slovenian Criminology). Ljubljana.

Mekina, B. 2001. '*Slovenski policist kot Dirty Harry?*' (The Slovenian Policeman as Dirty Harry?). *Newspaper Vecer,* 3 Dec. 2001.

Mekinc, J., Anzic, A., Lukan, A., Kecanovic, B., Zaberl, M., and Lobnikar, B. 2002, 'Clovekove pravice in policisti: analiza primerov varovanja posameznikove integritete, zasebnosti, pravice do obvescenosti in svobode gibanja' (Human rights and the police: Case analyses of protecting individual's integrity, privacy, right to information and the freedom of movement), in Pagon, M., ed. *Dnevi varstvoslovja* (Days of Criminal Justice). Bled.

Pagon, M. 1998. 'Organisational, managerial, and human resource aspects of policing at the turn of the century', in Pagon, M., ed. *Policing in Central and Eastern Europe: Organisational, Managerial, and Human Recourse Aspect.* Ljubljana.

Pagon, M. 2000. 'Police ethics and integrity', in Pagon, M., ed. *Policing in Central and Eastern Europe, Ethics, Integrity, and Human Rights.* Ljubljana.

Pagon, M. 2002. 'Deviance, violence, and victimisation: Are the police a part of the problem or a part of the solution?', in: Pagon, M., ed. *Policing in Central and Eastern Europe: Deviance, Violence, and Victimisation.* Ljubljana.

Pagon, M., Duffy, M.K., Ganster, D.C., & Lobnikar, B. 1998. 'Understanding police deviance: personal and interpersonal determinants.' *Security Journal,* vol. 11.

Pagon, M. and Lobnikar, B. 2001a. 'Disciplining the police: dealing with police misconduct in Slovenia.' Paper, Academy of Criminal Justice Sciences, 38th Annual Meeting, Washington, D.C.

Pagon, M. and Lobnikar, B. 2001b. 'V skupnost usmerjeno policijsko delo: primerjava med mnenji policistov in prebivalcev' (Community policing: A comparison of attitudes between police officers and citizens). *Varstvoslovje* vol. 3 no. 3.

Pečar, J. 2001. 'Policija in (lokalna) skupnost' (The police and the [local] community). *Revija za kriminalistiko in kriminologijo,* vol. 52, no. 2.

Pečar, J. 2002. '"Policing" in preprečevanje kriminalitete' (Policing and crime prevention). *Revija za kriminalistiko in kriminologijo*, vol. 53, no. 3.

Umek, P. and Areh, I. 2002. 'Policija v očeh policistov' (The police in the eyes of police Officers), in Pagon, M., ed. *Dnevi varstvoslovja* (Days of Criminal Justice). Bled.

PART III

SOUTH-EASTERN EUROPE

Chapter 7

Democratic Government and Administrative Reform: the Transformation of Policing in Bulgaria

Vladimir Shopov

Introduction

Political reforms in Bulgaria began in November 1989 when a tide of fundamental transformations swept Central and Eastern Europe. The years 1990–91 were marked by concerted efforts to draft and adopt a new democratic constitution. The country faced the enormous task of shedding its role as a faithful servant to the former Soviet Union. The years 1992–96 will be remembered for the series of half-hearted reforms in economic and political affairs, which nevertheless led to some progress in areas such as privatisation and institutional reform. The years 1997–2001 saw the emergence of a centre-right government which not only sped up the process of economic and social reform but brought the country closer to the EU and NATO. All major social and economic systems (pension, health care, social security and education) underwent radical reform. Bulgaria began negotiations for EU accession and became a prospective NATO member. In 2003 Bulgaria received an invitation to join NATO and was on the home stretch to concluding its EU accession negotiations.

The transformation of policing and police reform are intimately linked to the process of democratic reform which began in 1989. Indeed, the establishment of democratic government and the rule of law represent the most appropriate contexts for understanding police reform processes. Moreover, the continuous requirement to improve the institutional arrangements of policing spring from the need to address in a more effective manner the security concerns of citizens in a functioning democracy. The dual challenges of elaborating a democratic constitution and an adequate political system while ensuring the rule of law constituted crucial dimensions of democratic reform. The immediate dismantling of the repressive apparatus of the communist regime was an important element of the consensus on necessary transformations which developed in the 1989–90 period. This has ensured general political support for policing reforms even while various governments have had their specific policy objectives. The increasing awareness of constitutional rights and the general increase of personal insecurity in a context of extensive social and economic reform have meant more public pressure for further reform in policing and expectations of effective law enforcement. These continue to be crucial pressures for further reform.

The efforts to transform policing in the overall transition context received a radically new dimension in the mid-1990s when Bulgaria applied for EU and NATO membership. The priority of EU accession has introduced an entirely new dynamic to policing and police reform. Harmonisation of legislation, close scrutiny of administrative practices, introduction of new modes of institutional arrangements, continuous examination of co-operation arrangements – these are only a sample of the novel activities EU accession will bring to the field. In addition, police reform has been an integral part of the effort to transform the entire administrative system of Bulgaria. The police services have seen a series of changes in their status.

Policing in Bulgaria is being viewed from various new angles. One has been the impact of effective policing on development in a post-transition setting. Another has been the role of policing in ensuring a conducive business environment capable of generating growth. Increasing attention is being paid to the issue of personal insecurity and its impact on citizens in a democracy. A further angle attempts to examine another crucial issue – the impact of ineffective law enforcement on the legitimacy of a democracy. This issue is of particular relevance in Eastern European states, which have undergone extensive processes of transition, reform and social upheaval.

A protracted process of reform

The reform of policing in Bulgaria has represented a curious balance of institution-breaking and institution-making. Much effort has gone into dismantling the remnants of the repressive apparatus of the pre-1989 regime. The early transition consensus of the 1990s did accord a great deal of attention to the need to transform the elaborate system of repression.

There has been less consensus on the necessary parameters of reform, manifested in a series of 'waves' of reform. This meant that transformation was often a product of divergent policy aims, thereby preventing the development of a coherent framework informing the entire process of reform of policing. As a consequence, one is able to observe a consensual core implemented, to various degrees, by successive governments in the 1990s and early 2000s. Nevertheless, important divergences in policy do appear depending on whether the Bulgarian Socialist Party (BSP) or the Union of Democratic Forces (UDF) controlled the government. To provide an example, the BSP has always shown some reluctance to open law enforcement to new ideas of policing such as community policing and intelligence-led policing. In contrast, the UDF has been, if anything, all too keen to expose law enforcement to these ideas and practices.

Goals of reform

Before tackling the question of the purposes of reform, let me briefly mention the main primary laws and acts which regulate law enforcement in the country. Since 1989, there have been two generic laws on law enforcement – the Ministry of Interior Act of 1991 and the Ministry of Interior Act of 1997 and its amendments (currently in force). The Constitution also identifies a series of principles which must be observed by law enforcement agencies. There has been much public debate on how effective the current law has been and what changes need to be made to address some structural weaknesses. The current government (in power since summer 2001), as was the case with its predecessor, favours the adoption of a new generic law on policing and law enforcement. Yet the timing of such an initiative remains uncertain.

The core of the reform effort has been to establish a modern policing structure, which provides effective protection of the constitutional rights of Bulgarian citizens and is based on the rule of law. This has also meant creating rational structures, i.e. addressing law enforcement issues as they arise in a transitional society. A further feature of the process has been the emergence of statute-based prerogatives and structures. Transparency and democratic accountability to Parliament and the wider public has also led to the establishment of series of institutions. A further goal has been to ensure improved training and the establishment of fully professional police structures which do not rely on conscripts. EU and NATO accession have also meant new tasks linked to the future responsibilities of a member state. Apart from these discourses of change, there has been an infusion of the community service angle to policing. If anything, this is likely to persist as citizens begin to require effective action from public institutions.

As already mentioned policing reform was always considered central to the entire transition project. This has meant sustained political attention in reforming policing structures in the country. It is to the credit of political actors and law enforcement officers that there has not been a systemic effort to resist change. While successive parliamentary majorities and governments have had different strategies and tactics of change, no one has attempted to reverse the process of transformation.

Yet, this is not to state that there have not been pockets of resistance to change in some echelons of the organisation. Many officers educated and trained before 1989 have found it difficult to adjust to the new requirements of an open, transparent and citizen-oriented service. As a consequence, there have been at least two major waves of officers leaving police services – during the periods 1991–93 and 1997–98. The predominant strategy (when there has been opposition) has been one of quiet resistance rather than active, organised opposition. There are some non-governmental associations of either dismissed or retired officers but these have not played an important role in public life and have had very sporadic links with political parties. These organisations have not managed to establish credible programmes that attract wide public support. Indeed, it is hard to find any evidence of support in sociological surveys for such platforms. Retired law enforcement officers have stood as candidates in parliamentary elections, yet none have registered electoral headway.

Powers and legal status of police

The last 13 years have seen a degree of continuity in the definition of the tasks of the police structures. What has been less constant is the actual division of labour and configuration of linkages among police structures. The 1997 Ministry of Interior Act continues to provide the legal base for the functions of the National Police Service (NPS), defining its authority and mandate. Article 60 of the Act specifies these functions in the following order:

(1)   Ensuring and maintaining public order.
(2)   Prevention and detection of criminal acts as well as their investigation.
(3)   Protection of property and other fundamental rights.
(4)   Ensuring and maintaining the security of buildings, state institutions and others and regulation of road traffic and related activities.

The NPS is also in charge of regulatory activities vis-à-vis private security companies and performs the issuance of identity documents. The National Police ensures the legal compliance of legal entities as well the collation and analysis of information relating to public order and combating crime. The above list represents the most important tasks of the NPS as defined in the 1997 Act.

In addition, the law stipulates some key responsibilities of all law enforcement structures. Article 6 posits the following overall tasks of police structures: maintaining security and public order; countering crime; protection of the citizens' rights and freedoms including their way of life, well-being and property; ensuring fire and emergency safety; protection and control of the state borders; and protection of the national economic and financial system.

There has been a firm consensus on the parameters of the mandate of police structures. Yet, deciding how to translate these structures into working institutional arrangements with clear lines of management and responsibilities has proven an enormous challenge. The mandate of the NPS is clearly defined in an organic law and under the Bulgarian legal tradition no generic task can be defined in a piece of secondary legislation. All tasks are statute-based. As it has already been shown, the protection of the constitutional rights of the citizens is at the very core of the *raison d'être* of policing in Bulgaria. Indeed, this is increasingly the measure against which the activities of the police structures are evaluated. In terms of legal protection, all actions may be challenged in court.

I have already indicated the enormous difficulties encountered in defining working institutional arrangements of policing. To illustrate this point, I would mention that at this time the Ministry of Interior encompasses three more national services, which possess the legal tasks of policing. The National Service for Combating Organised Crime (NSCOC), is legally tasked with the investigation of criminal acts of an organised nature. The current EU definition is so encompassing that, in actual practice, this service is in charge of the overwhelming majority of serious criminal cases. The National Border Police Service (NBPS) is also within the Ministry of Interior and has the task of policing the clearly demarcated border areas and their adjacent area within the country. In addition, the National Gendarmerie Service (NGS) is given the task of policing in out-of-town areas, which further complicates the picture.

The dispersal of policing functions across a number of services does require further analysis. I highlight the phenomenon here only to emphasise the difficulty in arriving at an appropriate institutional arrangement. The analysis and conclusions offered in the paper will be solely based on the experience and activity of the National Police Service as this is the policing institution which citizens encounter most regularly in their everyday life.

Organisational structures and policies of the police
The disintegration of the archaic structure of the all-powerful Ministry of Interior of pre-1989 Bulgaria has been crucial to the subsequent restructuring of policing in the country. The old structure had brought under one roof disparate institutions such as the communist political police, the intelligence service, the counter-intelligence service and the police. The period between late 1989 and 1991 saw the gradual appearance of a democratic configuration with the dissolution of the political police and the law-based establishment of separate intelligence and counter-intelligence services.

The 1991 Ministry of Interior Act essentially split the units of the previous single police service into a number of separate structures under the umbrella of the Ministry of Interior. To give an example, the previous unit on combating economic crime within the police provided the backbone of the new, so-called Centralised Service for Combating Organised Crime. The structure of the so-called 'Internal Troops' entrusted with the protection of the state borders was also preserved. A national police structure was also set up and mandated to ensure public order. Beyond this function, it mainly operated as a migration office tasked to ensure registration of foreign nationals, issuance of identity documents, and other related tasks. According to many experts, the structures created under the 1991 Ministry of Interior Act functioned in an excessively centralised manner without producing the expected outcomes.

The next important generic law dealing with the overall structure of the police forces was enacted in 1997 and this law continues to be in force. In essence, the law transformed the previous centralised services into separate national services collectively managed by the Chief Secretary and the Minister of Interior. The law establishes four services with policing functions, with the national police being just one element in a complex configuration of policing institutions. It comes as little surprise that overlapping of functions is at present the overriding problem of this system. Investigations entail complex modes of inter-agency co-operation and the effective collation and analysis of information and evidence continue to pose serious difficulties. The last five years have seen a sustained public debate on the need to rationalise the present structure of policing. Drafts of a new generic law have been in circulation over the past two years, yet no political agreement on an actual draft is in sight. Increasing attention is being given to the above described problems by the Bulgarian public and the EU, which can be expected to lead to changes in the near future.

It is important to highlight that during the many years of transforming policing, no formal process of disqualification of personnel has been applied. There have been some restrictive legal provisions concerning former members of the communist State Security apparatus but these have not been related to members of the law enforcement agencies. What has become evident is a slow but systemic drain away from law enforcement towards the private security industry. The early 1990s saw a significant number of employees of the former State Security leave the newly emerging law enforcement structures and join the numerous private companies involved mainly in commercial activities. This was particularly evident in the period between 1990 and 1992. This first wave of departing officers was then followed by many, mostly younger officers who left to join the budding industry of private security in the mid-1990s. There is a continuing exodus of officers to this industry but it is difficult to keep a tally. There has been some continuity of personnel, mostly in the more specialised units of the Ministry of Interior. There is some anecdotal evidence of illegitimate links between police officers and private security companies, mainly in the form of certain officers' after-hours employment as private security guards. Legislation has been an issue as private security activity is still not regulated by a comprehensive law but mostly by secondary legislation. Little continues to be done about the flow of officers to these companies. Private security has become a profitable business activity and budget constraints have meant only modest increases of income for police officers.

The main filtering factor of party membership was removed as early as late 1989 and the system of law enforcement has not really faced a problem of representativeness. Many women have been joining the system, yet, representation of women at the more senior levels of the police structures still leaves room for improvement. This is partially balanced by an overrepresentation of women in the administrative layers of the law enforcement system and at the central administration level. There has been less progress in the area of representation of ethnic minorities even though the last few years have seen an effort to implement more inclusive recruitment. Community policing is becoming a central part of training of personnel in ethnically diverse cities. Police structures in many cities (including Plovdiv, Sliven and Vidin) presently employ many members of the local Roma minority. Inclusion of members of the Turkish minority also remains an issue as most of these communities are to be found in villages and small towns. In such instances, recruitment would often entail migration, which few families choose to embark upon.

Informal police cultures and police abuse vis-à-vis the Roma minority are being addressed in an increasingly systematic way, mostly though changes in the training curriculum. Training in protection of human rights, community policing and intelligence-led policing has gone some way to addressing these issues. Social pressure has also been a factor. Yet, police abuse remains a cultural issue and will require a lot of sustained effort and change before it can be addressed in a more satisfactory way.

Operational policies and work patterns

The early 1990s saw an important process of reallocation of personnel in compliance with the new mandate of the police. The reallocations after the adoption of the 1997 Ministry of Interior Act have been most significant and continue to inform many decisions on appointments and recruitment. Indeed, most policy-makers and senior officials regard the current configuration of policing structures as one that will persist over time. Redirecting of resources and staff has been guided by the key perception that crime has been becoming more organised and more complex. As a result, the agency dealing with organised crime has received more funding and more qualified officers have joined their ranks. Indeed, the NSCOC continues to attract better qualified recruits and to receive most training and international support. The agency is increasingly becoming the investigative backbone of the police with expertise in white-collar and organised crime. Any future institutional reorganisations are likely to build upon this agency.

The enormous increase in international co-operation work and responsibility has also had an impact on redirecting of staff. The conditions of EU accession and the transformation of policing of the state borders have led to the complete overhaul of the former 'interior troops' and their transformation into a professional border police. Again, this has meant increased funding and redirection of qualified staff to the emerging border police. There is little doubt that these measures have been at the expense of the national police, which deals with public order and crime in its most immediate forms. Officers, especially from the drugs and economic crime units, have been redirected to the other national services. Indeed, this phenomenon might be on the verge of becoming a structural problem. This has been due to a mixture of external and internal pressures. The EU has been quite insistent on Bulgaria's preparedness for being a future external border of the Union. At the same time, Bulgarian parties and citizens are keenly aware that countering crime requires an effective system of border control and management.

There is not sufficient space to explore in detail the changes in policing work patterns but I will highlight a few. The period 1998 to 1999 saw an attempt to introduce the policy of 'zero tolerance' as utilised by the (then) mayor of New York City, Rudolph Giuliani. While the policy was launched with much publicity, it was never backed up by sufficient staffing and training. There were no budgetary provisions or adequate management decisions to implement the policy. Publicity was sought solely in the beginning and there was no campaign to seek the support of the citizens for the successful implementation of the policy. Consequently, the policy was discarded by the year 2000.

Community policing is another new method of policing in Bulgaria. In contrast to the zero tolerance policy, it is on the verge of being incorporated into national training curricula and actual everyday police practice. The national police have been training many officers to police ethnically diverse areas and some successes have already been evident.

The decrease in the number of so-called 'neighbourhood officers' who serve as immediate points of contact for citizens in a given area points to the evident decline of attention on crime control and prevention. More resources are allocated to investigation and institutional strengthening of newly emerging structures such as the border police.

A number of tools are already in place to control and shape the discretion of police officers. Some relate to the primary legislation, which clearly sets out functions and responsibilities. These include, among others, the generic Ministry of Interior Act and the Act on Special Investigative Techniques. Moreover, there is now sufficient secondary legislation, which regulates in detail the modes of behaviour, tasks and responsibilities of officers. There is a Code of Ethics as well as a series of convictions of police officers who have violated the legal provisions of their position.

Supervision and control of police

Bulgaria has already developed a reasonably elaborate system of law enforcement accountability. At the level of the legislature, there exist two parliamentary committees, which deal with issues of law enforcement. One is the Permanent Committee on Foreign Policy and Security while the other is the Permanent Committee on Public Order and Internal Affairs. The former examines and reviews legislation from a wider foreign policy perspective while the latter can exercise control over the activities of the Ministry of Interior. It exercises control over the use of databases of the Ministry and ensures their proper management. The Committee can call the Minister (as well as directors of national services within the Ministry of Interior) to report on matters of interest to the committee and establish staffed ad hoc committees to review various issues. Question time in the plenary session is also often used to ensure accountability.

The administrative reform package of 1999 introduced a new structure of the central administration of the Ministry of Interior. There exists a clear demarcation of responsibility and mandate between the political and professional administrative levels. Civilian and public control is ensured by means of the political cabinet (consisting of the minister, deputy ministers, head of cabinet, parliamentary secretary and head of press office – all political appointees accountable to parliament). The National Police and the other national services are then accountable to a deputy minister.

The Ministry and the National Police have a nascent internal accountability system. They have separate inspectorates whose main task is the internal investigation of various acts of illegal nature (these include corruption, abuse of office, excessive use of force etc.). Depending on whether a criminal or administrative offence has been committed, various avenues of action appear. If an administrative offence has been committed, a police officer may receive a fine and various penalties, including dismissal. If a criminal offence has been committed, the case is referred to the prosecutor's office to carry out an external investigation and the case enters the normal penal procedure. Complaints by citizens are also investigated by the inspectorates. The establishment and adequate functioning of the internal accountability system has been supported by various international donors, most notably the EU.

While the main elements of a proper accountability system are in place and most of the legislative and administrative measures have been taken, systemic implementation remains a challenge. The practice of civilian control is well established and is an accepted norm. Yet, compliance continues to be mainly due to external threat of administrative and legal sanction rather than self–restraint and a vigorous culture of community service. The consolidation of the internal investigation system will require much further effort and change in organisational culture. External investigations continue to face some obstacles due to the relative impermeability and sense of solidarity (sometimes displaced) of police officers. In addition, an intensive public debate has ensued about the precise definitions of civilian and political control. This has been a product of the awareness of the difficulty of establishing and sustaining effective, yet accountable institutions. The overall institutional structure of accountability seems well accepted by citizens and politicians alike, yet a sense of effectiveness remains elusive.

Policing in the service of citizens?

It would be futile to attempt to quantify the extent to which the reform process has already produced a fully operational, professional police service. The range of institutional reforms (significant depoliticisation of recruitment and promotion, introduction of civilian supervision, overhaul of the training process, introduction of an extensive web of legal provisions regulating police work) coupled with an emerging administrative culture of public–oriented work have created important new sign posts. The amendments made to the Ministry of Interior Act in the year 2000 introduced a series of meritocratic elements in the system of appointment and promotion. The professional/civil service layers of the police forces were clearly defined and a new system of appraisal, promotion and dismissal was introduced. For example, the amendments specifically provide clear guidelines and criteria for promotion, which are solely based on evaluation of performance. Special commissions review proposals for dismissal and assess these on purely professional criteria.

In spite of these efforts, the system shows little sign of the police becoming a service-oriented organisation. The ethics of providing a service remains a phenomenon observed at the more senior positions of the police, and which is trickling down at an unsatisfactory rate. Lower ranked officers often remain largely driven by hierarchical obedience than by an internalised consciousness of service.

The somewhat disinterested, grumpy police officer still walks the street of the country.

There have been important changes in training as curricula have been updated. Modern methods of policing, international operational co-operation, legal studies and language training are increasingly becoming central in officers training. Ethical issues, human rights and service delivery have also become important elements of training at the Police Academy. Despite that, success has been varied. Operational work and legal training have received greater attention while service delivery and effective cooperation still leave much to be desired. There is a clear need for major reform of the Police Academy through its opening to civilian institutions of higher education and NGOs. Re-training of officers also remains an exception rather than the rule.

Accountability also remains a problem. While the necessary institutions are in place, they are not utilised very often. The Parliamentary Committee on Internal Affairs continues to be mostly involved in drafting legislative instruments. Very rarely does it look at the actual practices and management of the police structures. There is hardly any systemic supervision on the actual, day-to-day operations of law enforcement institutions. There are no parliamentary annual reports which examine the state of the police and propose recommendations.

Citizens still tend to underreport small incidents, even theft, and rarely bother to register complaints about the police. In fact, crime registration remains a crucial issue. Small incidents of public order disruption, mischievous behaviour, even property theft, are often regarded with insufficient attention and result in police inaction. Car theft is also often regarded as a fact of life by police officers with consequences solely for the insurance companies. As one can imagine, this type of behaviour does not build public trust in the police. It must be pointed out that this general lack of trust often goes hand in hand with very high public approval ratings for senior police officers. For instance, the current chief secretary of the Ministry of Interior has an approval rating of 70%, a rate that is higher than that for any other public figure (Alpha Research Agency Survey, September 2002).

There is ample anecdotal and factual evidence that officer integrity is a major problem in police structures. Stalling of investigations, sloppy gathering of evidence, lack of follow-up on reported incidents represent just a sample of the problems. Much is being done to address these issues including improvements in promoting well-performing officers, and codes of ethics have been adopted since 1999. There is much evidence of improper linkages to criminal organisations, leakage of information and intentional inaction. The legal provisions to deal with these phenomena have been put in place and success will depend on sustained intolerance of corruption, convictions of officers guilty of such behaviour, and general advances in combating corruption in society. Simplification and rationalisation of rules and procedures would also be beneficial. A related issue deserving attention is the ineffective judicial system, which is not helping in dealing with officer integrity.

The lack of consistency in the application of legal obligations of the police remains an overreaching problem. Implementation of these remains patchy at best. As a consequence, public perceptions of the police tend to focus on its relative inability to ensure security and effective protection of individuals. Gathering of evidence is often done in ways which result in prolonged and, ultimately, unsuccessful prosecutions. As already noted, registration and investigation of small crimes is often treated lightly and without sufficient attention. As mentioned at a number of junctures in this paper, effectiveness is also a major problem. This is often the product of incompetent management and insufficient legal training of police officers.

The full title of this chapter makes an explicit linkage between democratic government, administrative reform and policing reform. Indeed, the transformation of policing could not be understood outside this constellation. Most importantly, policing reform and strengthening of law enforcement structures are now an integral element of governmental programmes and efforts. In addition, citizens' expectations of the police are such that, in many ways, the perceptions of the entire process of reform hinge on the success of law enforcement in making citizens feel safe in an increasingly complex and volatile setting. Moreover, there is some emerging evidence that citizens are becoming more conscious of the need to request decent public services in return for payment of taxes. This will continue to develop in the coming years and will represent an important source of pressure for further change. As politicians come to realise this linkage, policing will continue to pay sufficient attention to matters of effective law enforcement. In addition, accession processes to NATO and the EU are increasingly turning into systemic factors of change informing the policy efforts of the political class.

Policy effectiveness and legitimacy

The experience of policing reform in Bulgaria appears to lead to a number of observations. First, as suggested by Bulgarian politics in the period between 1997 and 2001, good policing policy requires the existence of solid political majorities and governments. Secondly, the external factors of societal expectations and international pressure remain crucial driving forces for change and legitimisation at the same time. It is important to emphasise that public support for change is of key importance in driving forward transformation. Furthermore, over the past twelve years the configuration of factors of change has varied. In broad terms, internal factors have tended to be of greater importance in the earlier stages of transition and change while the later stages have seen an increase in the importance of external factors. Thirdly, reform will not be effective and successful without a functioning judicial system supported by an effective investigation service. The Bulgarian process of democratic transformation has been marred by an ineffectual judiciary, which successive governments have sought to reform with little success. Clearly, in the case of Bulgaria, advances in policing will be dependent on progress in this area.

It is crucial to highlight the linkage between effective policing, citizens' security and democratic legitimacy. Bulgaria continues to have a rather peculiar structure of crime, in which small property crime constitutes about 75–80% of all crime. Yet, this means the great exposure of citizens to violations of their property and rights with little effective recourse. This continues to breed feelings of insecurity among citizens and to undermine the legitimacy of the democratic system. This is a key challenge before policy-makers and law enforcement officers, which will require much further effort and attention. It would be fair to say that such a sense of insecurity is one of the few sources of discontent which might breed desires for authoritarian rule in the new and re-established democracies.

As has been indicated, police effectiveness is hampered by a number of structural deficiencies. Let me highlight one here – the continuous and overriding importance of having strong personalities in the law enforcement system. Again, there is ample evidence of that over the last few years. The 1997–99 Minister of Interior and the current Chief Secretary of the Ministry of Interior serve as examples. There still exists a need for a strong personality (emerging from the ranks of the law enforcement system), who will 'oil the system' and make it function. The presence of such a personality seems to provide motivation within a relatively closed and impermeable administrative culture. The background of budgetary constraints and ineffectual judicial and investigative systems also breed a notion of management that centres on strong personalities rather than systemic implementation of set tasks and procedures. The strong public support for such figures at the helm of law enforcement means other tiers of government support and accept the 'hero's crusade' against crime and disinterest.

An important feature of the actual policy process needs to be emphasised in this context. It relates to the very core of the collective process of making decisions in a polity. There appears to be a situation whereby collective decisions are taken at what one might call 'junctures of policy-making'. These might spurred by crises, intense public debates, or accession requirements. The important element here is that decisions are consequence of specific political situations. This is in sharp contrast to the need to arrive at policy decisions in a sustained, structured environment where these are taken as a result of organised, systemic inputs. In such circumstances, policies are made after an informed, open debate, and are founded on feedback, proper impact assessment, etc. It must be recognised that this shortcoming is not unique to the specific area of policing policy. Policy-making in the new and re-established democracies does appear to exhibit specific features and arriving at *ad hoc* decisions, as it were, is one of them.

Conclusions

A wide-ranging analysis such as attempted here may go in a number of directions in terms of potential conclusions about the transformation of policing. I will begin by an observation, which has wider implications for the entire process of system reform and change management in Bulgaria over the past decade or so. It is linked to the need for a 'taming of the legislative imagination'. Policing and other areas of the public sphere have seen over-legislation, and extensive reconfiguring of institutions and structures. While there was an apparent need to embark on extensive reform in policing in 1997, successive governments have all too often led programmes of administrative and personal reshuffles. The period between 1997 and 2001 has witnessed the most extensive overhaul of legislation and practice in the area of policing. A strong case can be made for allowing time for the consolidation of the already reformed services of law enforcement. The past decade has seen, on numerous occasions, the automatic import and transfer of practices and legislative measures. Such was the case, to a large extent, with 'zero tolerance' policing when neither sufficient staffing nor operational and cultural conditions were present in order to ensure success. On the legislative side, public discussion of freezing the assets of suspects proved to be an untimely and premature attempt to import legislative solutions that were appropriate for an entirely different setting. Yet, such experiences should not preclude open dialogue, debate and exchange of best practices. These should, however, be transferred only when appropriate and sufficient efforts have been made to ensure compatibility with local custom and law.

Having stated this, there is also an urgent need to observe and analyse how effectively institutions of policing are functioning. There must be constant evaluation of the extent to which citizens feel that the 'security deficit' is being addressed, and necessary institutional and procedural changes must be made when inadequacies are identified. These should proceed by piecemeal reform rather than elaborate design of social and institutional engineering. Mention has already been made of the extensive overlaps between the NSCOC, NP and BP. These are cases which demonstrate the pitfalls of frequent and repetitive social engineering.

Police reform has undergone a number of phases over the past decade. At the initial stages of transition, the transformation of policing was an element of the entire overhaul and dismantling of the repressive apparatus of the previous regime. As such, it was a core issue during the Round Table talks of late 1989 and early 1990. The continuous public expectation of provision of security for the citizens in their everyday life has also been a crucial driver of change. As this paper has attempted to show, the pressure for provision of security is, if anything, on the increase. As the state has withdrawn from numerous spheres of social and economic life, ensuring security for citizens is quickly becoming a core service which voters expect of the state and politicians alike. This expectation may usefully be considered as a background factor whose importance has fluctuated. As a consequence, political parties have become keenly aware of the need to satisfy voters' expectations in this area.

The second half of the 1990s saw the launch of the actual process of accession by Bulgaria to the EU and NATO. The requirements of preparation of membership have, over the last five years or so, established a momentum of their own. Civil servants and political appointees alike have largely internalised the rhetoric of accession and significant elements of the law enforcement community have adopted the agenda of EU and NATO accession and transformed it into practical action. It is also important to note that this has been the case with the NSCOC and BP to a greater extent than with structures more immediately linked with policing such as the NP.

EU accession and obligations of membership are likely to continue to be key sources of change for the policing community as well. This area was particularly instructive in terms of change management. While many civil servants in policing and law enforcement had sufficient awareness of EU law and practices, change in policing has mainly been the product of persistent and extensive pressure from the political leadership of the Ministry of Interior. The new crop of post-1989 university graduates and political appointees (through the political cabinets) have been instrumental in introducing EU law and practices. These laws and practices relate mainly to border management and control, training of officers, information systems and recruitment. While much has changed, the administrative culture of the policing community remains rooted in group identity and solidarity rather than a fully transparent and open service fully geared to provide services to the tax–paying citizens of a democratic polity.

Admittedly, one of the important consequences of the terrorist attacks of 11 September 2001 has been the realisation of the fragility of law and order in even the most advanced of polities. This acute feeling of exposure has particularly fertile ground in societies which have been through a full-scale process of transition. The increase of street crime and ineffectiveness of the judicial system have led to high levels of anxiety about crime and personal security in Bulgaria. Thus, an entire new security paradigm is presently emerging – a paradigm in which the military aspects of security are sidelined in favour of a heightened awareness that everyday crime and organised crime pose much more immediate and corrosive threats to society and individuals. Policing, in this setting, assumes central importance and begins to occupy an extremely critical place in voters' perceptions and expectations. Creating a setting and structure for policing that is community-based, effective, fully functional and service-oriented thus becomes a critically important task for political leaders and non-political actors alike. Indeed, failing to address a persistent deficit of security might become one of the main threats to the legitimacy of the democratic polity in the coming decade.

References

Constitution of the Republic of Bulgaria. 1991. *State Gazette*, no. 56, 13 July 1991.
Foucault, M. 1988. *Politics, Philosophy and Culture: Selected Interviews*. Ed. Lawrence Kritzman. London.
Held, D. 1995. *Democracy and the Global Order*. Palo Alto.

Konstantinov, E., ed. 2000. *Административната реформа и полицията* (Administrative Reform and the Police). Sofia.

Konstantinov, E., ed. 2000. *Полицията и предизвикателствата на 21-и век* (The Police and the Challenges of the XXIst Century). Sofia.

Konstantinov, E., ed. 2000. *МВР в навечерието на 21-и век – предизвикателства на реформата* (Ministry of Interior on the Eve of the XXIst Century – Challenges of Reform). Sofia

Minchev, O., Ratchev, V. and Lessenski, M., eds. 2002. *Bulgaria for NATO 2002.* Sofia.

Ministry of Interior. 1998. *Strategy for Countering Crime.* Sofia.

'Ministry of Interior Act 1997'. *State Gazette*, no. 122, 19 Dec. 1997.

National Security Doctrine. 1998. *State Gazette*, no. 46, 22 Apr. 1998.

Programme for European Integration of Ministry of Interior 1998–2000. Unpublished document. Sofia. 2000.

Chapter 8

The Reform of the Romanian Police

Pavel Abraham

Introduction

Romania is located in South–Eastern Europe and covers an area of 238,391 square kilometres, distributed almost symmetrically on both sides of the Carpathian Mountains. Population density is 94.1 inhabitants/sq. km, 55% of whom are living in urban areas and the other 45% in rural areas. Romania's population, descendants of Dacians and Romans, totals 22.4 million according to the latest census conducted at the beginning of 2002. Some 89.4% of the population are ethnic Romanians. The majority of Romanians are Christian-Orthodox (88%), living alongside the followers of other religions such as Roman-Catholics (6%), Protestants (5%), and others (1%). While the official state language is Romanian, the languages of national minorities, such as Hungarian, German, Turkish, Russian and other languages, are also used in day-to-day life in certain areas.

Located at the frontier between two continents, neighboured by Bulgaria to the south, the State Union of Serbia and Montenegro to the south–west, Hungary to the west and north-west, Ukraine to the north, and Moldavia and the Black Sea to the east, Romania was and is an important bridge between Europe and Asia. After it gained national independence in 1877 and following its reunification as a national, unitary, sovereign and indivisible state on 1 December 1918, Romania established itself as a democratic nation, both at home and in the international arena, despite the fact that under the well-known historical conditions, between March 1948 and December 1989, authentic democratic values were suppressed following the establishment of the totalitarian communist regime.

Since 1991, when the entire nation voted in favour of the adoption of a new Constitution, Romania has been a parliamentary democracy. The head of state is the President of the Republic, who is elected by direct vote by the population for a mandate of four year and for a maximum of two terms. The legislative authority resides in the parliament's Chamber of Deputies and Senate, both with equal powers. The 345 deputies and 140 senators are elected for a four year mandate, on the basis of a system of proportional representation. The government (the executive) represents the executive authority and consists of the Prime Minister and the other ministers. The Prime Minister, who is appointed by the President, appoints the other ministers. The government is subject to consent by the parliament.

The Romanian economy, currently engaged in a full-fledged privatisation process, is 30.5% based on industry, 12.6% on agriculture, 5.35% on construction, and 51.5% on services. According to Eurostat, the 2002 GDP per capita was approximately 2,160 Euro.

Brief history of the Romanian police

In Romania, the evolution and the role played by the institutions of internal affairs are closely related to history of the Romanian people and state. Documents attest to the existence, since the Middle Ages, of the *Mare Vornic* (nowadays the Minister of Interior), appointed by the *Voievod* (king) and responsible for the operation of guard services, the maintenance of order, and the judgement of disputes. The *Mare Vornic* had under his command the Master Hunter (*vătaf de vânatori*), the predecessor of the Police Chief, who was tasked with keeping an eye on the homeless and marauders, repressing poachers, and exercising control over the travellers hosted at local inns, especially foreigners.

On 25 March 1834, the Police Service of Bucharest, the *Agia,* was presented with the flag and the seal inscribed with the symbol of the Annunciation, an important Christian holiday of the Romanian people, the Annunciation being the spiritual symbol of protection of Romanian police. Later, on 7 February 1864, Alexandru Ioan Cuza, the ruling prince, promulgated the law on the organisation of the armed power in Romania, by which the National Guard was granted extensive civilian, political and military powers, with a view to guard the national order and independence, as well as to watch and protect the entire territory, and to guarantee law enforcement and institutions.

An important role in defining the place of the Ministry of Interior within the Romanian state administration was given by the Law on the Organisation of Central Administrative Service, of 19 April 1892, which provided for the setting up of the Directorate for the General Administration of Personnel and of the Security Police, as well as the Bureau for General Security.

At the beginning of the twentieth century, the police institution was the subject of a major reform process, initiated by Interior Minister Vasile Lascăr, who is considered the founding father of the modern Romanian police. He, for the first time, raised the issue of the political independence of this institution by taking several steps to convince the legislative bodies to shield the police from political fights, arguing that disarming the country and compromising public order and safety only to gain a few more votes was a crime.

Following the adoption of the 1923 Constitution, the reorganisation of law enforcement institutions began with a view to implementing the principle of the separation of the powers. As a result, on 21 July 1929, the Law on the Organisation of the General State Police was adopted, thus establishing the General Directorate of the Police as the main state organ tasked with the guidance, co-ordination and maintenance of internal order and public safety over the entire national territory.

By the adoption, on 2 August 1929, of the Law of the Ministries and especially of the Regulation on the Organisation of the Ministry of Interior, issued on 25 January 1930, the police institution was given enhanced authority, in addition to maintaining public order and general safety, over the management of local administration.

An important moment in the history of internal affairs was the year 1949 (at the beginning of Communist rule), when the Ministry of Internal affairs was reorganised at both central and territorial levels. The central apparatus was organised into directorates, departments and services – the Secretariat, the General Directorate of the People's Security, the Command of the Troops of the Ministry of Internal Affairs, the General Political Directorate, the General Directorate of the Militia, the General Directorate of Penitentiaries, as well as twelve Regional Directorates and the Directorate for the Security of the Capital City.

Regarding the nature of the attributions and powers vested in them during the totalitarian regime, apart from the tasks concerning the maintenance of public order, the defence of civic rights and liberties, ensuring the personal security of the citizens and defence of their material goods, the units of the Ministry of Interior had been charged with certain political tasks which were in conflict with the very essence of their social role.

Following the events of December 1989 (the overthrow of the communist regime) the activity of the Romanian police has been based on new principles. One of the first measures undertaken in this respect consisted of the total depoliticisation of the institution, which has represented the starting point in the process of reshaping both the components of the institution and the legal framework governing them.

The experience acquired over 165 years of existence, together with the profound transformation which has occurred since 1989, offers to the Ministry of Interior and to the Romanian police a well-defined place in society, consecrating the fundamental role of the police in upholding and strengthening the rule of law in Romania.

Background developments after 1989

During the period 1990–2002, the fundamental goal of the Ministry of Interior was to reform, reconstruct, modernise and optimise its structures, as well as to achieve interoperability with similar structures of the member states of the European Union.

The reform process has been an extensive, deep and long-lasting one, requiring not only a rethink of how to prevent and combat crime, which in this period was especially dynamic and complex, but also, and more importantly, a re-evaluation of the role and place of the Romanian police, and of the other structures of the Ministry of Interior, within Romanian society.

One cannot speak about the reform of the Romanian police, and the transformation taking place, without bearing in mind the situation at the start of the transformation, that is, what this institution was like at the beginning of 1990.

First and foremost, as a result of fifty years of the totalitarian regime established after the Second World War, the Romanian police system was under political control of the Communist Party. Politics played an almost primordial role in the functioning of the police mechanism and mostly at the administrative level, since a political bureau existed within each police unit. Although, more often than not, the obligations and directives assigned for the police by the Communist Party coincided with the actions stipulated by the law, in many cases directives exceeded legal limits, because Party policies had to be observed and implemented, irrespective of the methods and means required to implement them. Party membership was a *sine qua non* requirement to enter the system, and careers and promotions to senior positions were closely related to an official's career and record within the Party. Being a member of the Party and belonging to the working class were prerequisites, not necessarily the only ones, but essential nonetheless for being recruited into the police. The requirement of a 'healthy origin' (i.e. coming from an approved class background) obstructed access to the policing system to any person suspected of being even remotely connected to privileged classes of the old social system or being a member of a national minority.

Another essential characteristic of the police system in the early 1990s was that its organisation and functioning were based on a military model. Almost all personnel were military, and military discipline and regulations were considered the foundation for precise, clockwork-like operation, as were the constraints, which guaranteed that the police functioned in the exclusive interest of the ruling Party. The need to hold a military status resulted in a significant shortage of women in the police force, and those accepted were confined to administrative functions. Obviously, the psychological impact of a military organisation dominant over the society was fully exploited by elements of the Party.

At the same time, the police system was excessively centralised, to ensure a single command for all component structures and, also, to ensure those Party policies were implemented down to the lowest levels. Obviously, the freedom to decide was almost absent at lower levels, being exclusively reserved for the leaders in place, and each initiative, if it proved successful, viable and beneficial, was claimed as their own accomplishment.

The regime's total isolation behind the iron curtain of secrecy and the lack of were also manifested in the police system. While some achievements in preventing and countering crime were made public exclusively for propagandistic exploitation, the state and dynamics of the phenomenon of crime were one of the most important secrets of the Romanian State, kept secret based on the doctrine that there are no crimes under socialism. The number of personnel, their working methods and the means of action, and the organisation and its operations were automatically classified as secret. In some cases secrecy was pushed to extremes, resulting in even the smallest details, some of them quite insignificant, being classified as secrets.

Implicitly, the total lack of transparency led to an absence of communication with society. In fact, the way the system had been established obstructed communication. The status and the role of the police force were strictly enforced and the directives and decisions of the Party were excluded from public debate. Moreover, in the totalitarian period, civil society was limited to an amorphous mass of working people whose most representatives institutions were the syndicates and the Party's organisations. At the same time, because of the tacit limitation of the right to associate, Romanian society lacked its own representative and autonomous institutions. In short, real social and democratic control over the police system was absent, although the Party, the only controlling body, was defined as belonging to and representing the working people.

The closure and rigidity of the police system resulted in weak co-operation with the judiciary. In this respect, even if the law stipulated the functional subordination of police structures to the Public Ministry (which is responsible for representing the general interests of society, public order and citizens' rights and freedoms), this was often not the case in real life.

During the totalitarian period, perhaps one of the most important characteristics of the Romanian police system was mythification. From an overall perspective, one can say that the reality of every other characteristic of the police contributed to the creation of the myth. The fact that the police system was the oppressive instrument of the Party, its total lack of transparency and public communication; that it was an organisation based on the military model which induced a state of fear within the population, all led to public perceptions which overestimated the size and powers of certain segments of the police force. In reality, during the 1980s Romania had one of the lowest rates of police officers per inhabitant, compared with other countries, and the general lack of material resources at the level of the entire society also affected the police system. The material and financial situation of police officers was similar to most of the population; privileges were exclusively reserved for the *nomenclature*, the higher echelons of the Party. Moreover, fear existed not only at the level of the entire society but also within the police system.

It is also worth mentioning that the myth created for the police system was the main reason leading to the mass rage against it in December 1989; the policing system had become a real social lighting rod. Social rage, in effect, accused the police of culpability for past ills, an association, which was resented by the police personnel for a long period, almost resulting in the paralysis of the system.

The reform of the police system

Political, economical, social and human values must clearly be protected legally and that actions opposed to these goals should be sanctioned. Yet keeping, developing and protecting these values should be, first and foremost, the result of complex societal efforts and not follow from a repressive, exaggerated and discriminatory penal policy.

By the fundamental decision taken in December 1989 to adhere to a system of values based upon democracy, the respect for citizens' rights and freedoms, the protection of juveniles, social dialogue and tolerance, Romania had to engage in fundamental reforms in all of its institutions, including the police system. The police had to be transformed into an institution serving the public. Functional and flexible structures had to be developed which could efficiently ensure the discharge of specific duties and would enhance the capability of the police to respond to the changing dynamics of crime and conditions of public order in the country. The capacity of law enforcement institutions and of the police to maintain public order, to protect fundamental human rights and freedoms, and to combat the scourge of crime is, as well, an essential prerequisite for Romania to become part of the 'area of freedom, security and justice', which is the new slogan adopted by the European Union, premised on harmonisation and cooperation in justice and home affairs.

The adoption of the new Constitution of Romania entered into force on 8 December 1991. It declared the Romanian State to be democratic and governed by the rule of law, incorporated and expressed a new clear and reforming vision regarding democracy and human rights, a new vision based on social justice, a vision of justice and humanity which seeks to overcome the repressive and inhumane measures that history has proved inefficient and disruptive of the balance between civil society and the state.

The adoption of Law no. 40/1990, On the Organisation and Operation of the Ministry of Interior, was a first step towards reform. The Ministry of Interior became the central body of the executive with the powers to exercise, according to the law, policies regarding public order, defending fundamental rights and liberties, public and private property, preventing and investigating crimes, bringing in this way its contribution to the establishment of a democratic society in Romania and preserving independence, national sovereignty and territorial integrity.

Generally, it may be said that the governing authorities initially desired reforms in order to show the establishment of the rule of law, a commitment that had been agreed to in 1992 when the government expressed its intention to adhere to standards espoused by the Council of Europe. Consistent external pressures for reform and a concomitant opposition to reform by the police marked this period. After 1996, there was a shift with pressure coming from the police and civil society for the accomplishment of reforms, while the governing authorities maintained a cautious approach due to the costs that reform would incur, overwhelming the possibilities for change during that period.

Presently, the Romanian police system consists of a civilian force – the Romanian Police, having 52,000 personnel; a military force – the Romanian Gendarmerie, having around 18,000 personnel; and the community police – Public Guards with 20,000 personnel who are subordinated to local government, all conducting activities related to public order.

The strategy for reform of the police and other security bodies formulated by the Romanian Ministry of Interior focused on their transformation by reconsidering the goals fundamental for a police force within a democratic society based on the rule of law.

The main objectives of the reform strategy were: communication, demystification, depoliticisation, demilitarisation, decentralisation, transparency, partnership with the community and encouraging it to participate in its own security, establishment of a democratic and efficient accountability system, professional ethics and human rights, and achieving interoperability with similar bodies from European states and elsewhere.

Yet after the adoption of the Law on the Organisation and Operation of the Ministry of Interior in 1990, mostly based on the need for change imposed by the necessities of that moment, the reform process stalled, and only in 1994 was the new Law on the Organisation and Operation of the Romanian Police adopted. The 1994 Law (no. 26/1994) aligned the powers, authority and limitations on the police with the provisions of the 1991 Constitution.

The new law represented the first substantial steps towards reform, succeeding, even though sometimes only partially, in solving some essential problems. First, the status of the police was normalised, especially its role within the rule of law, by defining the Romanian police as the specialised state institution which exercises, within the territory of the state and according to law, powers regarding the protection of the person's fundamental rights and liberties and of the public and private wealth, the prevention and detection of crime, and the maintenance of public order.

This rearrangement of priorities regarding the values that the Romanian police system aims to defend and protect, as well as the stipulation that the activity of the Romanian police will be exclusively conducted on the basis of and with a view to enforcing the law, represented the real starting point of the reform process.

Another important step was the inclusion of a constitutional provision within the 1994 Law on the Depoliticisation of the Police System, by forbidding police personnel from holding membership in political parties and bodies; yet the right to vote remains guaranteed by the Constitution. Obviously, this principle required the establishment of mechanisms to ensure the immunity and the resistance of the system against possible pressures from external political factors.

Beside adjusting the powers and authority of the police, by reconsidering the importance and priorities of protected values, some new powers and duties were introduced, such as the prevention and control of organised crime; control over the regime for toxic and narcotic substances; control of public meetings and limitations on policies for that purpose, such as a new regulation on the use of force and/or firearms; the explicit prohibition of any torture or provoking any physical or mental suffering so as to obtain, directly or through a third person, information or confessions; or to punish a person for an act that a person has committed or is suspected to have committed in order to intimidate that person or increase pressure on that person or a third party.

After the adoption of the Law of 1994, the strategy for the reform of the Romanian police became more consistent and actions were taken within the following strategic directions:

(1)   Preparing the conditions necessary for transforming the Romanian police into an institution with a civilian status, thereby emphasising its role as a public service.

(2)   Increasing the response capacity of the police to meet the requirements of the operational situation, by increasing the flexibility of the organisational arrangements, eliminating intermediary links, and decentralising decision-making to local functional-operative levels while, at the same time, centralising strategic decision-making at the national level.

(3)   Changing the organisational culture and promoting the professionalisation of personnel based on unitary and coherent programmes.

(4)   Optimising the distribution and utilisation of the resources that Romanian society may allocate to achieve the national objectives regarding the ensuring of public order.

(5)   Focusing international activities on accomplishing expected police reforms within the preparations for Romania's accession to the European Union and to Euro-Atlantic structures.

These strategic activities were organised and conducted to achieve the following goals:

(1)   Creating the legal framework required executing specific missions in optimal conditions.

(2)   Institutional reconstruction – the decentralisation of decision-making, responsibilities and the allocation of resources required for maximum efficiency and operational response capacity to the local level.

(3)   Modernisation of working methods and their adjustment to the requirements of a democratic society.

(4)   Assessment and ensuring of efficient and effective logistical support.

(5)   Management of human resources and the protection of personnel (salaries, life and health insurance, bonuses, holiday houses, leisure activities etc.).

(6)   Co-operation with public authorities from the defence, national security, public order and justice sectors.

(7)   New efficient instruments for planning, organising and managing the work of the police to adequately respond to the dynamics of the overall operative situation, even under conditions of austerity.

(8)   Increasing interoperability with similar bodies of the European Union in order to maintain regional stability.

The first legislative steps towards achieving these objectives were taken with the abrogation of all administrative regulations that harmed fundamental rights and liberties. At the same time, relevant international legal instruments, such as the European Convention Against Torture, the European Convention for Protection of the Fundamental Human Rights and Liberties, were signed and ratified.

The legislative reform process sought to accomplish two major goals. First, to create a modern legal framework, elastic and perfectly adjusted to support the authority and exercise of the rule of law, as well as the harmonisation of internal legislation with European Union standards and specific documents initiated at the European Councils of Amsterdam and Helsinki. Secondly, a series of high-level legal enactments were elaborated and adopted (laws, government decisions, government ordinances) to control the organisation and operation of the Romanian police and its major component subsystems, create a firearms and ammunition regime, and counter the illicit traffic and abuse of drugs, precursor drugs, corruption, organised crime, money laundering, trafficking in human beings etc. In addition, a series of internal administrative acts, based on existing law, were elaborated to allow an improved implementation of high-level legal acts and of the tasks of the Romanian police.

Activities developed to promote and observe human rights and humanitarian international law included improved collaboration with the Romanian Institute for Human Rights, the Romanian Association of Humanitarian Law, and with other non-governmental organisations having similar objectives; organising courses on a regional basis; elaborating 120 specific written documents for the Ministry of Interior organisation; concluding protocols with organisations and institutions with interests in this area; and investigating notifications received from individuals or non-governmental organisations on alleged violations of human rights by the police.

Legislative reforms and enactments reached their highest point in 2002 with the new Law on the Organisation and Functioning of the Romanian Police (Law no. 218/2002), as well as with the Law on the Status of the Police Officer (Law no. 360/2002).

The reality of changing social, political and economic relations, both at the internal and the international levels, had made even the relatively new domestic regulations on the police institution outdated. This fact required not only the elaboration of a new Police Law, but also the regulation of the police officer profession, the enactment of provisions regulating police structures and their relations to other public administration authorities, the harmonisation of domestic legislation with legislative and administrative provisions of states with a democratic tradition, with a view to implementing the highest standards in the field.

The new Law of 2002 on the Organisation and Functioning of the Romanian Police stipulates a series of principles and provisions derived from the European Code of Police Ethics. For instance, with regard to police objectives, besides their traditional tasks, new tasks were added, such as: preventing and countering terrorism, illegal migration, illegal traffic in radioactive materials, and aspects on providing assistance and service functions to the public. Law no. 218/2002 stipulated that 'the Romanian Police provides a public service and is carried out in the interests of persons and the community and to support other public institutions, exclusively on a legal basis and through the enforcement of laws'. This provision modified the police role, transforming it into a mechanism for service to the community and reducing the reliance of the police on coercion.

The Law on the Status of the Police Officer is the first legal provision regulating the police officer profession and its relations with other professional communities.

A very important provision of the new Law on the Organisation and Functioning of the Romanian Police stipulates 25 March as Romanian Police Day. The choice of this day was based not only on the discovery of the oldest documentation regarding the first public order bodies which had existed on the territory of Vara Românească, but also on the fact that one of the most important religious celebrations of the Romanian people, The Annunciation, falls on this day. The Romanian Police Day was seen as a means to renew the connection of the police institution with the Romanian people.

Another fundamental provision of the law affirms the demilitarisation of the police institution and the professional activities of police officers, by defining them as civil servants who carry arms and who exercise the authority and powers established by law for the Romanian Police.

The demilitarisation of the Romanian police – for the time being a unique initiative in South-Eastern Europe – is an essential precondition for carrying out the goal of transforming the role the police will play within Romanian society, that is, being a public service without neglecting the judicial function of police. It was based on the premise that a police service which responds professionally to requests from civil society is most likely to sustain civic values. Moreover, the legal obligations to safeguard the individual's civil and political rights, which the police have to fulfil in a democratic society, are quite distinct from those imposed on military personnel.

Fundamental changes of the structure and tasks of the Romanian police were conceived as a gradual process, which had to develop from inside the organisation, be coherently organised, have clearly defined stages and objectives, and be based on logical criteria and on a permanent adjustment to the dynamic of the social reality of Romania.

In this respect, legislative actions to rebuild the police institution sought:

(1)   To continue the reorganisation and restructuring process, to seek to eliminate duplication and intermediary links among police structures, to reduce bloated agencies, to achieve concordance between a unit's tasks and its organisational structure, and to increase interoperability levels with similar agencies of European Union states.

(2)   To correlate the new organisational charts with similar structures of advanced democratic states, according to the recommendations of European bodies, an institutional reform assumed by and required of the Romanian Government as one of the conditions for the country's accession to the European Union.

(3)   To increase the operational efficiency for accomplishing the tasks of police structures by a more rational redistribution of personnel.

On the basis of these priorities, the Romanian police was reorganised into three basic components: Judiciary Police, Public Order Police, and Administrative Police.

The major organisational changes also established the following structures: the Institute for Crime Research and Prevention; the Division for Human Rights; specialised Brigades for Countering Organised Crime, the production, distribution and consumption of illicit drugs, cyber criminality, trafficking in human beings, money laundering, corruption, and trafficking in radioactive materials; cross-border crime units; and Rapid Response Units in Bucharest and in the 13 County Police Inspectorates. The Road Police Brigade was established to control roads and traffic and some functions (e.g., registration, the issuing of permits, and maintaining driving records) were transferred to other bodies. The national Europol office was established in the General Inspectorate of the Police, in order for the Romanian Police to participate in European Union activities for countering organised crime.

A National Body of Police Officers will be established as a legal, autonomous, apolitical and non-profit institution to organise police officers by criteria of professionalism and to promote and defend the rights of police officers.

The Law on the Organisation and Functioning of the Romanian Police stipulates the establishment of a new structure – the Territorial Authority for Public Order – which was conceived and designed to ensure the involvement of civil society in shaping responses towards its own security environment. Civil society will be able to contribute to the elaboration of planned activities; assist in the development of objectives and minimal performance indicators; enhance the protection of community interests to ensure a climate of public safety; notify and propose measures for eliminating deficiencies in police activities; organise consultative meetings with members of the local community and with non-governmental organisations regarding priorities for individual safety and public order; and write a detailed annual report on the efficiency of the police unit's activity, which is to be made public.

In other sections, the new law stresses what may be the most important objective, the proper management of human resources. The basic goal was to change the social role played by the *police officer-soldier,* who used to have at his/her disposal all means of coercion and repression and was expected to carry out, unconditionally, the orders issued by his/her superiors, to that of the *police officer-citizen,* whose defining characteristics are sociability and human qualities.

More than 50% of the Romanian police officers who had served during the communist period left after 1989 – most of them retired before the legal age of retirement, receiving compensatory salaries. Others left the police system for other jobs in public or private institutions. Only those who proved that they didn't have anything to do with the abuses of the Communist regime were allowed to remain in the Romanian police.

Another main objective was the democratisation of internal relations in the police. Additionally, changes were made to educational structures, the duration of courses and the content of syllabi, as well as the elaboration and implementation of 'train the trainer' programmes. A new system of recruiting, selection and appointment of personnel was adopted, based on the diversification of selection criteria by specialisation and activity profiles, as well as an emphasis on merit and non-discrimination.

The reconstruction of the Ministry of Interior's educational system was realised by transforming the School for Active Officers into a university level educational institution accredited by the Ministry of Education and Research. More specifically, the Alexandru Ioan Cuza Police Academy offers four-year courses for training police officers, gendarmes, fire fighters and archivists. Graduates receive a BA-equivalent degree in law, building engineering, or in archival science. The Police Academy also offers two-year post-university courses and a six-year PhD degree in policing specialities. At the same time, the schools for lower-rank police officers were reorganised; they now last two years, being equivalent to undergraduate studies. The institutions for the continuous training and professional advancement of police offers were reformed as well.

The new Law on the Organisation and Functioning of the Romanian Police, taking into account the special importance of the protective role of the police towards the society whom they serve, gave special attention to establishing new directions for police work and the training of police personnel, such as crime prevention, countering organised crime, and humanitarian law and human rights. Particular attention was given to the most sensitive problems, including the use of force, intelligence, investigation and undercover activity, and protection of victims, especially women and minors.

Actions were taken to ensure the optimal balance between leadership and line positions between sworn officers and auxiliary personnel, in order to redistribute personnel in a territory according to specific problems, to reduce the average age of the personnel, to increase their quality and compatibility with specific tasks and missions, to hire minority nationals, to increase the proportion of women in the police forces (currently at about 12–15%) and finally, to align the relations between police officers and citizens with European Union standards. As a result, the number of personnel of the Romanian police increased by 68% in comparison to 1989.

Another dimension of the reform in the field of human resources has been to ensure the social protection of police personnel. The Law on the Status of the Police Officer not only maintained existing rights but also harmonised these with the rights of other professional categories (magistrates and public servants). Legislation also included some internationally recognised rights which guarantee police officers greater stability in accomplishing their tasks, gave them a legitimate social position and, at the same time, sought to insulate them from possibilities for corruption.

The European Police Ethics Code implies that the state should not deprive police personnel of any civil and political rights, with the exception of legitimate constraints linked to the necessity of assuring the proper execution of the police tasks in a democratic society governed by the rule of law. Since the accomplishment of the specific duties involves increased special risks for policemen/women and for their families, this professional category should receive adequate social protection in case of injuries arising from their work. Of course, limitations of some rights and liberties have been imposed based on the permanent and compulsory character of the police service as well as by the demands of the police officer profession, even though the police have been separated from military structures.

At present, specific initiatives exist in the police for: the identification of needs for psychological protection, professional stress management, and the treatment of affected personnel; the socio-professional integration of former students of the proper educational institutions and newly hired, replaced or transferred personnel; the setting up of the National Support House in order to issue loans from the funds that members have contributed; obligatory life and service-related accident insurance from the very moment of hire; reshaping the normative system for motivating and rewarding personnel, according to the European standards in the field (European Social Charter); and reshaping the concept of internal order in the police organisation and the system of rights and disciplinary sanctions.

To align the Romanian police with social democratic demands, initiatives to ensure transparency and public control of the activities of the Romanian police structures (including the use of resources) have been instituted. Norms and regulations on confidentiality have been adapted to balance the protection of operative work needs with the reality of the democratic development of Romania, to support the development of partnership relations between civil society and the Romanian police in order to provide a stable environment of civic safety. The requirements of absolute secrecy, which were often pushed to the edge of the absurd under the totalitarian system, have given way to openness and transparency, and public relations structures and spokesperson positions, have been created within all units.

Periodically, information and communications are provided to the mass media, television and radio shows to inform the public and convey an important preventive message. At the same time, 'open door' activities were and still are organised and representatives of the mass media and civil society have unlimited access, with a few exceptions, to police units or sub-units headquarters, including visits to some places of detention or arrest.

The main objective for disseminating information and facts about the Romanian police and the activities of its sub-units was to provide the public with correct operative information regarding the work of the police, while also stressing citizen training in preventing and countering crimes and other antisocial acts. In particular, the idea has been stressed that the police officer works exclusively in the service of the community and citizens, irrespective of the officer's specific field of activity.

As Romanian civil society develops, acknowledges the rights that it has in a democracy, learns to exercise these, and begins to establish representative structures (as non-governmental organisations, associations and foundations), the police will develop relationships with civil society through different activities, in particular through the Partnership Programme. The main goal of the Programme is to establish permanent contacts and to create a climate of mutual trust in order to facilitate specific police activities, even with regard to persons who break the law.

A recent innovation is the implementation of a new vision that developed in Europe in the last few years – community policing. Concretely, this means the involvement of the entire community in preventing and combating criminality. One of the basic principles of the Romanian police is its transformation into a public service, a goal which reflects a philosophy similar to that supporting community policing. By creating the necessary openings for co-operation with other institutions of Romanian society and involving the public in the process of accomplishing the legal functions mandated to the police, society will perceive the police as a service established by and for citizens.

The alignment to international standards in this field was achieved by the establishment of two structures – the Territorial Authority for Public Order and the Consultative Council – which include representatives from the police and other public institutions as well as civil society, who jointly participate in improving police services by adapting the activities of the police, as guided by the law, to the needs and exigencies of the community.

At the same time, relations between the police and local public administrative authorities were established on a new basis by decentralising the police, thereby creating a foundation for integrating the police into the society and enhancing the efficiency and effectiveness of its activities.

Another aspect of community involvement is represented by short-term partnership programmes in the field of human rights that the Ministry of Interior and the Romanian police concluded with the Ombudsman and with domestic non-governmental organisations for the protection of human rights (the Organisation for Human Rights Defence, and the Association for Human Rights Defence – the Helsinki Committee).

A special activity in the field of public relations, which is also part of institutional management, consists of the internal affairs units in the police which investigate allegations of illegal acts, abuses and misconduct by the police, seek to verify petitions regarding police personnel, and conduct criminal investigation of the crimes committed by police officers.

In pursuing the goal of transforming the Romanian Police into a public service, the means necessary for ensuring the democratic control of police activities were created. First of all, traditional internal control systems were re-evaluated. Control has been exercised hierarchically and through specialised structures, such as the General Inspectorate of Police, the disciplinary councils, the National Body of the Police Officers, the committees and boards for human rights, and the intelligence and internal protection units. Aware of the high priority need to create a climate of mutual confidence between the police and the community and to maintain the integrity of police personnel at acceptable standards, the Romanian police are developing and implementing integrity tests.

The importance of ensuring and guaranteeing effective external control was recognised as well. External control is exercised both by civil authorities (the parliament, the executive, Public Ministry, judicial courts) and by citizens (through mass media, non-governmental organisations, etc.). External control is exercised by the legislature (by the approval of budgetary legislation; the activities of the Commissions for Defence, public order and national security, and for the defence of human rights against abuses, which were constituted as joint commissions of the two chambers of the parliament; the establishment of special investigative commissions; the constitutional provision on questioning the Minister of the Interior by members of parliament); by the administration (by specifying the power and authority of policing structures and by the activity of the Prime Minister's Control Body); and by the judiciary (by supervising the activities of the Public Ministry and by exercising legal actions through administrative proceedings) .

The Court of Accounts exercises permanent control over the way the Ministry of the Interior, including the police, use the public founds allocated to them. Control is also exercised by other state institutions, such as the Ombudsman, the Supervising Authority in the field of personal data protection, the public administration authorities, and other international bodies. Finally, citizens making use of their constitutional rights to complain and receive information may exercise some degree of control over the police.

Aware that an authentic democracy cannot be achieved in isolation from other democracies, special attention was given to the development of international co-operation and relationships with other police organisations. The three main components are: co-operation and relationships with the neighbouring countries, with Members States of the European Union and affiliated institutions (EUROPOL, CEPOL, EUROJUST) and with other states. The capacity of the law enforcement institutions, including the Romanian police, to counter the scourge of domestic and transnational criminality requires that Romania be part of the evolving Area of Freedom, Security and Justice in the European Union.

The existence of serious forms of criminality – such as terrorism, corruption, money laundering, organised crime, cyber crime, trafficking with drugs, arms and human beings, illegal migration – require the permanent attention of national authorities from all the states of the world and close co-operation among numerous professional organisations. All these phenomena represent the main targets of the activities of the Ministry of the Interior (including the Romanian Police) in the area of European and Euro-Atlantic co-operation and integration. The achievement of the objectives of transnational police co-operation – countering organised crime, fraud and corruption in all fields of action – is pursued by legislative initiatives, institutional co-operation and personnel training. To achieve fast and effective co-operation liaison officers and internal affairs attaché positions have been established in some Romanian embassies.

Conclusions

The reform has not been easy. After fifty years of a totalitarian regime that isolated Romania from the democratic world, Romanians needed to rediscover democratic values and how to exercise them, with all the uncertainties and difficulties of a new beginning. There were many obstacles, some subjective, deriving from the mentality of citizens and police officers, the absence of a culture of team-work and the lack of a model to follow, and some objective limitations in terms of financial resources.

As an often-misunderstood democracy experiencing a continuous degradation of its way of life during a prolonged transition period, Romania experienced an alarming increase in criminality after the democratic revolution. The expansion of extremist ideologies, the proliferation of parasitic and contesting groups, decreasing chances for social integration, and growing indifference towards politics, all constitute developments with a high potential impact on internal stability, and which may lead to violent acts and serious disturbances of public order. At the same time, insufficient support is given by citizens to public order bodies.

In the Romanian police, the main prevailing dysfunctions are as follows:

(1)   Delays in the adoption of drafts for legislation sent by the Ministry of Interior to the Parliament, caused by complicated procedures in Parliament.

(2)   Political influence on the process of performing specific policing activities.

(3)   The development of inadequate management of police activities at the level of some central and local units, caused by:

   (a) the preservation of too many professional degrees in the police system;

   (b) insufficient decentralisation of resources;

   (c) lack of unions, as associative forms in the professional activity.

(4)   Gaps in the process of changing the mentality of police officers and ensuring a public service character to police activities, caused by:

   (a) insufficient understanding of the principles related to the protection and serving the community;

   (b) insufficient experience of practices conducive to effective community policing;

   (c) deficiencies in co-ordinating the guarding of public goods and values, inparticular the prevention and combating of thefts of oil products from pipelines and stations, from electric installations and from irrigation systems;

   (d) fluctuations in appreciating the role intelligence plays in discovering criminal places and environment and persons conducting criminal activities, especially by organised crime, caused by centralised and unclear intelligence activities;

   (e) reluctance in calling on civilian structures in Romanian society to support police activities;

   (f) budgetary allocations insufficient for the needs of proper functioning and reform.

However, after an attentive analysis of the reform of the Romanian police we can conclude that it has been successful. The accuracy of this assessment is confirmed not only by the accomplishments and the results obtained, but also by surveys conducted with the population, which placed the police in fifth place among the most trusted state institutions, after the Church, the army, parliament and government (executive), with a trust rate of 48%.

Also, the results of reforms can be appreciated by an analysis of crime dynamics. Statistical data analysing serious acts of violence in some European countries indicate that Romania is a country with a relatively low rate of serious and violent crime. The Interpol reports of 1998 revealed that Bulgaria has a homicide rate of 7.5 per 100,000 inhabitants, Hungary – 4.3, Ukraine – 9.04, and Romania only 2, thus approaching the homicide rate of democratic countries such as Austria – 2, Switzerland – 2.6 or Germany – 3.5. In fact, all indicators measuring crime rates in Romania are similar, demonstrating low levels of serious crime, as well as increased general effectiveness of law enforcement bodies in preventing and countering those phenomena.

One can affirm with some certainty, then, that the implemented reforms have successfully come through the transition process, which is now considered to be approaching completion. But reform will continue, particularly with regard to accelerating Romania's efforts to achieve integration with European structures, as well as to finalise implementation of the concept of community policing.

References

Community Police. 2001. The Publishing House National, Bucharest.

Community, the Police and the Transition. 1996. The Publishing House National, Bucharest.

Government Decision no. 137 regarding the Foundation of the Police Academy Alexandru Ioan Cuza.' *Official Gazette of Romania*, no. 120/1992.

Handbook of Criminal Procedure. 1994. The General Part, The Publishing House Paideia, Bucharest.

'Law no. 21 regarding the Organisation and Functioning of the Militia.' *Official Gazette of Romania, no. 132/1969.*

'Law no. 218 regarding the Organisation and Functioning of the Romanian Police.' *Official Gazette of Romania*, no. 305/2002 (2002a).

'Law no. 25 regarding the Appointment to a Useful Job of the Persons Who Are Able to Work.' *Official Gazette of Romania, no. 232/1976.*

'Law no. 26 regarding the Organisation and Functioning of the Romanian Police.' *Official Gazette of Romania*, no. 123/1994.

'Law no. 360 regarding the Statute of the Policeman.' *Official Gazette of Romania*, no. 440/2002 (2002b).

'Law no. 40 regarding the Organisation and Functioning of the Ministry of Interior.' *Official Gazette of Romania*, no. 146/1990.

'Law no. 94 regarding the Organisation and Functioning of the Court of Accounts.' *Official Gazette of Romania*, no. 116/2000.

Ministry of Interior. 2000. *The Documentary Gazette of the Police Academy* no. 1/2000, The Publishing House of the Ministry of Interior.

Ministry of Interior. 2001. *The White Book of the Ministry of Interior 1990–2000*, The Publishing House of the Ministry of Interior.

'The Constitution of the Socialist Republic of Romania.' *Official Gazette of Romania, no. 65/1986.*

'The Penal Code and The Code of Criminal Procedure of Romania.' *Official Gazette of Romania*, 1997.

'The Romanian Constitution.' *Official Gazette of Romania*, no. 233/1991.

'The Romanian Constitution.' *Official Gazette of Romania*, no. 282/1923.

The Transition and Criminality. 1994. The Publishing House Oscar Print, Bucharest.

PART IV

WESTERN BALKANS

Chapter 9

Police Reforms in Bosnia-Herzegovina: External Pressure and Internal Resistance

L. Kendall Palmer

Introduction

While the major event in police reform for most of the states in this volume is the transition from state socialism, the situation is quite different in Bosnia-Herzegovina (henceforth BiH). To be sure, reforms of police must deal with vestigial organisational structures, procedures, attitudes and laws from state socialist times. However, what has been the primal event for police reform in BiH was, of course, the war(s) that took place in the former Yugoslavia between 1992 and 1995. The police played a crucial role in each of the three major ethnic communities in BiH during these conflicts – from the more positively framed protection of their own group and defence of their home cities to the more negative participation in ethnic cleansing. The war divided the three ethnic groups and their political institutions; the Dayton Peace Agreement legitimated this division but also empowered international organisations – especially NATO, the OSCE, and the UN, as well as a newly minted organisation just for BiH called the Office of the High Representative (OHR)[1] – to bring the people and their institutions, including police, back together. It is the dynamics of these processes, overlaid on the transition from state socialism, that has had the greatest impact on the reform of police in BiH.

Historical overview

Prior to the breakup of Yugoslavia, the police were a key instrument of state control. Their primary formal functions were state security, major criminal investigation, traffic regulation, executive protection, intelligence, and border/customs services:

The typical mode of police interaction with the population was the traffic checkpoint attended by some four or five armed policemen. Citizens were required

---

1. The High Representative is the lead official for implementing civilian aspects of the Dayton Agreement.

to produce mandatory documents, and the function served was population control. Police harassment was common ... Police forces lacked patrol cars and radios, so the checkpoint was a tactic well tailored to their meagre means and overall mission of state control. (Dziedzic and Bair, 1998)

Conflict broke out between the three major ethnic groups – Serb, Croat, and Bosniak[2] – in BiH soon after Bosnian President Aleja Izetbegović declared BiH's independence from Yugoslavia on 29 February 1992.[3] Though police forces in BiH, especially in larger urban areas, were multi-ethnic in the 1980s, the outbreak of the war meant that forces quickly became ethnically homogeneous based on which ethnic group controlled a particular territory.[4] As Bair and Dziedzic (1998) note:

> Owing to the character of the Bosnian conflict, all ethnic communities sought to preserve internal security by expanding their police cadres. This was accomplished through an influx of personnel with little or no police training. The ranks were swollen with individuals having predominantly military preparation, and the flow of personnel between police and military units became quite fluid (the standard uniform for the police was the fatigue uniform of their military counterparts and their basic weapon was the AK-47).

On 21 November 1995, the main parties to the wars in the former Yugoslavia signed the General Framework Agreement for Peace in Bosnia and Herzegovina in Dayton, Ohio.[5] This agreement divided BiH into two entities – the primarily Bosnian Serb Republika Srpska (RS) and the primarily Bosnian Croat and Bosniak Federation (Federation). The Federation was further divided into ten cantons – five primarily Bosniak cantons, three primarily Croat cantons and two 'mixed' cantons. Finally, the parties were unable to decide whether to award the strategically important Brčko District to the RS or the Federation. As a result, Brčko was made an independent district and arbitration would later decide to which entity to assign it. The Dayton Agreement gave most power to the entities (especially in the RS) and cantons (in the Federation), with very little authority to the central state government.

---

2. In the 1991 Census, the ethnic breakdown in BiH was approximately 44% Bosniak (Bosnian Muslim), 31% Bosnian Serb, 17% Bosnian Croat, 6% Yugoslav, and 2% Other.
3. For a full description of the events I here gloss over, see Silber and Little (1995) or Glenny (1992).
4. See URL: http://www.ohr.int/ohr-info/maps/ for a map of the front lines at the end of the war, as well as a number of other superb maps of BiH.
5. The Dayton Agreement was initialled on 21 November 1995, by representatives of the three warring parties in the former Yugoslavia – Slobodan Milošević for the Serbs, Franjo Tudjman for the Croats, and Alija Izetbegović for Bosniacs (or Bosnian Muslims) – in Dayton, Ohio. The agreement established peace in, and the borders of (rump) Yugoslavia, Croatia, and Bosnia-Herzegovina, but its focus was Bosnia-Herzegovina. The US government chose the military base in Dayton primarily for its isolation; the idea was to get the former Yugoslav authorities away from their constituencies and keep them closed in at the base until they could reach an agreement. This strategy spawned a new term, 'Dayton-style negotiations.' For full details of the negotiations, see Holbrooke (1998).

This decentralisation applied also to policing powers, with the Dayton Agreement allocating most powers down to the cantons in the Federation or to the more centralised RS. More specifically, each entity and all ten of the cantons have Ministries of Interior while the Brčko District has a Police Department – all this in a country with a population of less than four million. With regard to policing, the BiH-level authorities only have responsibility for international and inter-entity criminal law enforcement, including relations with Interpol. The RS Ministry of Interior is responsible for all crime prevention and enforcement in the entity. In contrast, in the Federation, the Ministry of Interior only takes care of coordinating inter-entity and inter-cantonal cooperation, especially with regard to terrorism and other serious and organised crimes, protecting VIPs and guarding diplomatic premises, while the cantons are responsible for all other aspects of law enforcement (General Framework Agreement, 1995). In practice, mixed cantons often have two police forces – one for each major ethnic group populating the canton.

While the state and entity constitutions incorporated into the Dayton Agreement delegate police duties to the various law enforcement agencies in BiH, the agreement also, in its 11th Annex, gave power to an external body to monitor and oversee police reforms in BiH. While this annex gives responsibility for maintaining a 'safe and secure environment for all persons' to the signatories themselves, it mandates that the UN IPTF (International Police Task Force) be created in order to:

(1)   Monitor and inspect judicial and law enforcement activities, including conducting joint patrols with local police forces.

(2)   Advise and train law enforcement personnel.

(3)   Analyse the public security threat and offer advice to government authorities on how to organise their police forces most effectively.

(4)   Facilitate law enforcement improvement and respond to the requests of the parties, to the extent possible (Annex 11, *General Framework Agreement* 1995).

One year later, UN Security Council Resolution 1088 (December 1996) expanded the mandate of the UN to include 'investigating or assisting with investigations into human rights abuses by law enforcement personnel'. In addition to the UN Mission a number of bilateral organisations, most notably the US Department of Justice based ICITAP (International Criminal Investigative Training Assistance Program) programme, are active in police reforms in BiH.

The overall goals of reform

In many ways, the conditions following the collapse of the former Yugoslavia and the ensuing war remain in BiH. Three nationalist parties – the Bosniak SDA (Stranka Demokratske Akcije or Party of Democratic Action), the Bosnian Croat HDZ (Hrvatska Demokratska Zajednica or Croatian Democratic Union), and the Bosnian Serb SDS (Srpska Demokratska Stranka or Serbian Democratic Party) – have, to a large extent, retained a hold on the tools of economic and social control, though this grip on power has been loosening. As the writers of the European Stability Initiative put it (ESI, 1999: 1):

> Nationalist leaders have a strategic interest in maintaining the conditions on which their power depends: pervasive separation, fear and insecurity among the general populace; a lack of democratic accountability; breakdown in the rule of law; personalised control over the organs of public order; and the absence of institutions capable of controlling illegal economic activity.

Law enforcement clearly is the key, nay essential, institution in the efforts of these wartime leaders to maintain power. As a result, wartime leaders – democratically legitimised and sanctioned by elections in 1996 when they were the only ones organised and powerful enough to win – have resisted attempts to democratise and depoliticise policing in BiH at every turn.

Into this harsh environment stepped the UN Mission in Bosnia and Herzegovina (UNMIBH),[6] the main force behind police reforms in BiH, with the assistance of other international agencies and embassies. The IPTF Department includes about 1800 police officers from all over the world stationed in all the territories of BiH.[7] UNMIBH hopes to create democratic policing in BiH as outlined in the Bonn-Petersberg Agreement on Restructuring the Police Federation of Bosnia and Herzegovina (25 April 1996) and the Framework Agreement on Police Restructuring, Reform and Democratisation in the Republika Srpska (1998, henceforth the RS Framework Agreement). Both of these agreements were brokered by UNMIBH with local police authorities and outlined, in particular, seven key 'Internationally Accepted Principles of Policing in a Democratic State' (UNMIBH, 1996) which are summarised below:

(1)   Police must be oriented and operate in accord with the principles of democracy; that is, they must always operate consistently with the Constitution and the law, not arbitrarily.

---

6. The IPTF is the main department of UNMIBH dealing with police matters, but the mission also includes departments of Civil Affairs, Public Affairs, and Administration. IPTF officers are police officers from all over the world.
7. For example, in June 2002, the mission included officers from more than forty countries. Causing significant problems for the mission has been the fact that, while many officers come from countries with established democratic policing traditions – France (114 officers), the UK (76 officers) – many other officers come from states with less solid traditions in policing – Pakistan (93), Ghana (98). The appointment process varied from country to country, but appointment was often a political prize, since officers receive a sizable per diem from the UN in addition to their regular salaries from their home countries. One officer from Bangladesh told me that he used the per diem from his first three months to purchase 20 acres of land back home. Once IPTF officers arrive in BiH, they apply for various positions within the mission. They are not chosen by their country or the UNMIBH mission for any particular skills they have.

(2) Police, as recipients of high public trust, are professionals whose conduct must be governed by a professional code of conduct which will ensure that police exercise the highest standards of ethical conduct in the discharge of their duties.

(3) Police must have as their highest priority the protection of life. The application of force by officers should be minimal in all circumstances and deadly force should only be used to protect the life of the police or the lives of other people.

(4) Police must serve the public and are accountable to the public they serve. This means the police must act in such a way that the public knows, understands and accepts the police measures which are undertaken to provide for public safety.

(5) Protection of life and property is the primary function of police operations. That is, the primary concern of police operations must be directed to the prevention of crime that threatens life and property, not crime detection.

(6) Police must conduct their activities with respect for human dignity and basic human rights of all persons – adhering to international human rights standards and avoiding torture or other cruel, degrading treatment of citizens and detainees.

(7) Police must discharge their duties in a non-discriminatory manner. Discrimination on the basis of race, gender, religion, language, complexion, political opinion, national origin, birth, property, ethnicity or other status in the delivery of police services is incompatible with policing in a democratic state. This principle applies to the recruitment, promotion and assignment of police officers as well.

Nearly all of the pressure for reform of the police comes from external actors, or what is called the international community in BiH, especially UNMIBH. In short, UNMIBH hopes to create a democratic police force in BiH – police who respect human and minority rights, are not influenced by politics and politicians but instead serve the public and the rule of law. Some additional pressure for reforms, especially for those that relate to the protection of minorities, comes from returnees – refugees or internally displaced persons who have returned to their pre-war homes or would like to. However, in the postwar situation in BiH returnees have little power; their only recourse is to inform the international community and lobby it to take action.

While the local nationalist power structures have provided the most resistance to reform of the police, the other major factor preventing or delaying reforms is finances. The conflicts in BiH left it a destroyed and impoverished society; it is dependent upon the largesse of the international community for most of the multitude of reforms it must undertake, including those of police. While funding for new police initiatives and equipment was readily forthcoming immediately after the signing of the Dayton Agreement donor fatigue has now set in. For example, the State Border Service, hailed by UNMIBH as one of its greatest achievements, is facing a significant funding shortfall despite large donations from bilateral donors and the new emphasis on border control in the post-September 11 world.

UNMIBH has instituted a number of processes designed to promote reforms. One of the most important has been the development of co-location schemes whereby experienced UNMIBH IPTF officers go out on patrol (or stay in the

174 *L. Kendall Palmer*

station) with local officers. The idea is that experienced international officers will be
on the scene to advise local police in the proper techniques of democratic policing,
as well as prevent the most egregious human rights violations. While co-location in
the field and at crime scenes was one of the first major projects of UNMIBH, co-
location of managerial posts came much later. In February 2001, UNMIBH
launched a new co-location project entitled 'Manage the Managers', which co-
located monitors in the legal, personnel, finance and budget departments. While the
co-location programme has been a qualified success, it has had a number of
problems including international co-locators from countries with appalling human
rights records.

UNMIBH has also developed a policy to evaluate the performance of
individual police officers. 'Performance reports' detail minor acts of poor
performance by officers, while 'non-compliance reports' record major lapses of duty
or violations of the law. When an officer receives a non-compliance report, police
officials must commence internal disciplinary proceedings against the officer (with
UNMIBH IPTF monitoring the proceedings). Officers who receive more than one
non-compliance report may be de-authorised from exercising police powers
(UNMIBH SRSG Report, June 2001).

Another, much different process promoted by UNMIBH has been the
creation of the monthly Ministerial Consultative Meeting on Police Matters
(MCMPM). After the war in the former Yugoslavia, communication and
cooperation between the various police forces, both between new countries and
between forces within BiH, have been nearly nonexistent. This lack of cooperation
has opened vast spaces for organised crime networks to manoeuvre across cantonal,
entity and state borders. On 1 March 2000, UNMIBH established the MCMPM, 'to
facilitate inter-entity law enforcement agreements and to establish procedures for the
recruitment and voluntary redeployment of minority police officers' (UNMIBH
SRSG Report, March 2000). Also, out of these meetings arose the Joint Entity Task
Force (JTF), which lays out mechanisms to exchange intelligence and coordinate
plans to halt illegal migrants and human trafficking and other organised crime
(UNMIBH SRSG Report, November 2000). These processes also facilitated the
development of a Joint Coordination Team on Combating Terrorism and regional
policing cooperation.

Changes in the legal status and powers of the police

The most important changes in the legal status and authority of the police are
inscribed in the BiH Constitution, which is annexed to the Dayton Agreement. Most
significantly, Article II.2 of the Constitution notes: 'The rights and freedoms set
forth in the European Convention for the Protection of Human Rights and
Fundamental Freedoms and its Protocols shall apply directly in Bosnia and
Herzegovina. These shall have priority over all other law.' The Constitution also
incorporates a number of other international human rights agreements related to law

enforcement and/or protection provided to citizens from law enforcement personnel and others, including:

(1)   The 1948 Convention on the Prevention and Punishment of the Crime of Genocide.

(2)   The 1949 Geneva Conventions I-IV on the Protection of the Victims of War, and the 1977 Geneva Protocols I-II thereto.

(3)   The 1951 Convention relating to the Status of Refugees and the 1966 Protocol thereto.

(4)   The 1965 International Convention on the Elimination of All Forms of Racial Discrimination.

(5)   The 1966 International Covenant on Civil and Political Rights and the 1966 and 1989 Optional Protocols thereto.

(6)   The 1979 Convention on the Elimination of All Forms of Discrimination against Women.

(7)   The 1984 Convention against Torture and Other Cruel, Inhuman or Degrading Treatment or Punishment.

In addition to the broad protection of these international human rights instruments, the Constitution (Article II, Section 3) explicitly set out a number of rights for citizens of BiH, including:

(1)   The right not to be subjected to torture or to inhuman or degrading treatment or punishment.

(2)   The right not to be held in slavery or servitude or to perform forced or compulsory labour.

(3)   The right to a fair hearing in civil and criminal matters, and other rights relating to criminal proceedings.

To ensure that these rights and others were protected and implemented in BiH, Annex 6 of the Dayton Agreement called for the creation of a Commission on Human Rights to consist of the Office of the Ombudsman and the Human Rights Chamber. These two offices shall consider: (a) alleged or apparent violations of human rights as provided in the European Convention for the Protection of Human Rights and Fundamental Freedoms and the Protocols thereto, or (b) alleged or apparent discrimination on any ground such as sex, race, colour, language, religion, political or other opinion, national or social origin, association with a national minority, property, birth or other status arising in the enjoyment of any of the rights and freedoms provided for in the international agreements listed in the Appendix to this Annex, where such violation is alleged or appears to have been committed by the Parties, including by any official or organ of the Parties, Cantons, Municipalities, or any individual acting under the authority of such official or organ (Annex 6, Chapter 2).

And, most importantly in the post-conflict context of BiH, Article II.8 of the *Constitution* of BiH elaborates that:

> All competent authorities in Bosnia and Herzegovina shall cooperate with and provide unrestricted access to: any international human rights monitoring mechanisms

established for Bosnia and Herzegovina; the supervisory bodies established by any of the international agreements listed in Annex I to this Constitution; the International Tribunal for the Former Yugoslavia (and in particular shall comply with orders issued pursuant to Article 29 of the Statute of the Tribunal); and any other organisation authorised by the United Nations Security Council with a mandate concerning human rights or humanitarian law.

The functioning of these human rights institutions will be discussed in more detail below.

Changes in the organisational structures and policies of the police

Most obviously, the organisational structures of police have been altered to fit the new political geography of BiH. For example, from the end of the war until 1997, the Bosniak police of Bosnia-Hercegovina (the Muslim police) was headquartered in the Ministry of Interior in Sarajevo, worked in seven districts (Sarajevo, Zenica, Doboj, Bihac, Tuzla, Mostar and Gorazde) and was organised into motorised patrols, traffic patrols, criminal investigation units and state security services. Completely separate from these Bosniak forces in the Federation were the police of the Croatian Republic of Herceg-Bosna (CRHB) who focused on state security, criminal investigation, traffic regulation, special operations and intelligence and border and customs services. CRHB police worked in the following districts in western and central BiH: Mostar, Livno, Travnik-Vitez, Derventa, Zepce, Kiseljak, Jajce and Orasje (Dziedzic and Bair, 1998). The RS police had similar training and functions to the police of the other ethnic groups, but there was a stronger emphasis on control of borders, special operations and state security. According to Dziedzic and Bair (1998), the municipal level RS police performed intelligence and paramilitary activities and also provided bodyguards for indicted war criminals such as Radovan Karadzić. After the war, the RS police were headquartered in Pale and had major stations in Banja Luka, Bijeljina, Brčko, Foča, Han Pijesak, Prijedor and Trebinje.

The first task of police organisational restructuring after the war was to create police structures that fit the new political geography of BiH. With the signing of the Bonn-Petersberg Agreement on Federation Police Restructuring in April 1996, UNMIBH fairly quickly inaugurated the new police forces in most of the cantons of the Federation. The exceptions were two Bosnian Croat cantons (Livno and Siroki Brijeg) on the western border of BiH with Croatia that still had aspirations of joining Croatia and had many disagreements with UNMIBH over insignia and other symbols as well as minority recruitment. Progress was not so rapid in the RS where the authorities refused to cooperate with UNMIBH and an agreement on police restructuring was not forthcoming until December 1998, more than two and a half years later. The RS police were later reorganised to fit the judicial territories in the RS; the number of public security centres was cut from nine down to five – Banja

Luka, Doboj, Bijeljina, Srpsko Sarajevo and Trebinje. The hope was that this would allow for better cooperation between the police and the judiciary.

The first major challenge of police reform in BiH was reducing the size of police forces down to acceptable levels comparable to the rest of Europe. Police forces were greatly augmented during the war – the origins of the Muslim army of BiH were in its police force and many police of all ethnic groups were used as paramilitary forces (Bair and Dziedzic, 1998). At the end of the war, the combined strength of the three Bosnian police forces was 44,750: 32,750 in the Federation and 12,000 in the RS (SRSG report, 13 December 1995). The Federation and the RS each had a ratio of somewhere between one policeman for every 60–100 citizens, compared with the European standard of one for 380 (Bair and Dziedzic, 1998).

UNMIBH brokered two key agreements on police restructuring: The Framework Agreement on Police Restructuring, Reform and Democratisation in the Republika Srpska (9 Dec 1998 – the RS Framework Agreement) and Agreement on Restructuring the Police Federation of Bosnia and Herzegovina (25 April 1996 – the Bonn-Petersberg Agreement) – in which RS authorities agreed to cut the size of its police force from 12,000 to 8,500 and the Federation authorities agreed to reduce to 11,500 from 32,750. The Federation had reached its target number of officers before the end of 1997 (UNMIBH SRSG Report, December 1997).

Initially, UNMIBH played an important role in vetting the force(s) in the Federation, assisting in the creation of an exam covering the new Bosnian Constitution, the new police Code of Conduct, and the role of police in a democratic society which all officers were required to pass. A psychological test of all officers was also obligatory. However, the Federation authorities only sent the number of applicants necessary to fill the available spots who they felt were qualified. Only 29 out of 1350 taking the exam failed and just ten were targeted for psychiatric evaluation. As Bair and Dziedzic (1998) note, 'thus instead of "vetting", which implies a process whereby those guilty of incompetence, corruption, or abuse (to include war crimes) are expunged, the process served to "downsize" these forces'. Not surprisingly, this process was abandoned after the first few cantons were completed. As a result, UNMIBH lost any control over the selection of which officers were chosen in the Federation and it had even less power in the RS where there was significantly less cooperation with UNMIBH authorities. Most observers believe that those selected to be tested by UNMIBH were more often chosen for their political loyalty than their policing ability and skills.

Operating in parallel with these efforts to downsize the police forces in BiH was a move by UNMIBH to demilitarise these forces. The role of the new police forces is to serve and protect all citizens, not to defend ethnic groups. Demilitarisation of police forces is an essential aspect of democratising policing. Starting in August 1997 UNMIBH, with the cooperation of SFOR,[8] began frequent weapons inspections of police stations to ensure that local police were only

---

8. SFOR (Stabilisation Force) is the NATO-led organisation responsible for implementing military aspects of the Dayton Agreement.

maintaining the weapons necessary to police their areas – one long-barrelled rifle for every ten officers and one side arm for each officer (UNMIBH SRSG Report, December 1997). Numerous weapons, including anti-tank mines, rocket and grenade launchers, and grenades, were confiscated in the first year of this programme. The UNMIBH demilitarisation programme also extended to the 'special police' of each of the three ethnic groups in BiH. These forces were initially subject to monitoring by the SFOR forces, but after training from UNMIBH and entrance into the certification process (described below) many were transferred to new special police or anti-terrorist forces, though many others came under investigation for possible war crimes (UNMIBH SRSG Report September 1998). Integrating the Federation special forces took considerably longer (because the Federation housed both Bosniak and Croat special forces, while the RS only had Serb special forces), but was accomplished in early 2000 (UNMIBH SRSG Report, March 2000).

Many observers believe that during the vetting process in both the RS and most, if not all, of the cantons in the Federation officers were selected much more based on their political loyalty to the ruling authorities than on their policing knowledge and skills. In reaction to this, UNMIBH officials created a more detailed, three-stage certification process for all police in BiH. The first stage of this process was the registration of all personnel with law enforcement powers. In order to pass on to the second stage – provisional authorisation – officers were required to meet the following criteria:

- applicant must be at least 18 years of age;
- applicant must be a citizen of BiH;
- applicant must have passed the UNMIBH police standards test and the UNMIBH psychological test;
- applicant currently exercises police powers;
- applicant is not publicly indicted by the ICTY (International Criminal Tribunal for the former Yugoslavia);
- applicant has no known criminal record (excluding minor offences);
- applicant did not make deceptive statements during registration.

Once an officer has become provisionally authorised s/he is issued an UNMIBH ID card and is authorised to execute police powers. Final certification occurs when UNMIBH makes a final determination whether the officer meets the standards (professional qualifications and background) to serve in a force that practises democratic policing (UNMIBH IPTF-P02/2000).

In the course of this authorisation process, UNMIBH has created a police registry database. This database, along with the requirement to use UNMIBH ID cards to practise police powers and the mandate from the Dayton Agreement and UN Security Council Resolutions, has enabled UNMIBH to exercise additional control over local police forces in BiH. In particular, UNMIBH has been able to create a detailed policy for removal of provisional authorisation to exercise police powers. In addition to the more obvious removals for serious violations of law, UNMIBH may de-authorise officers who make 'material misrepresentations' to UNMIBH, receive two non-compliance reports from UNMIBH which record serious lapses of duty or violations of the law, or whose acts during the war, 'demonstrate that s/he is unable or unwilling to uphold internationally recognised human rights standards' (UNMIBH IPTF-P-2001). One of the major limitations on UNMIBH's power was that de-authorised officers were often re-hired by the Ministry of Interior. Because these positions in the Ministry did not call for the exercise of police power, UNMIBH'S mandate did not extend to these positions. UNMIBH was then limited to lobbying OHR, the lead agency for implementing civilian aspects of the Dayton Agreement, to remove the official.

Training of police officers has also been adjusted to fit the new realities of policing in BiH. UNMIBH, along with bilateral donors such as the US Justice Department-based ICITAP programme, Germany and Austria, have run extensive training programmes for all current officers and new recruits. Before individual officers are finally certified to use police powers in BiH, they must first undergo six mandatory training courses: human dignity (covering the role of police in a democratic society – originally developed by ICITAP), transitional training (focusing on basic 'democratic' policing skills), traffic awareness, basic management training, computer training, and community policing (UNMIBH, 2000). In addition to these mandatory courses for all practising officers, UNMIBH, ICITAP and others have done training for limited numbers of officers in a number of specialised areas from firearms training to trafficking persons to crowd control.[9]

Much of the training detailed above has been incorporated into the six-month courses at the two police academies (in Banja Luka and Sarajevo), as UNMIBH, again with a great deal of assistance from ICITAP, has helped the local police authorities make the transition from gaining recruits through training in secondary school to an academy system. Cadets first have six months of training at the academy and then a further six months in the field before they become fully fledged officers. Academy training, designed by local trainers in close cooperation with UNMIBH, incorporates the six mandatory courses above as well as other specialised and technical training. During 2002 local instructors took full control of the training at the two academies.

These academies play a key role in UNMIBH's strategy to increase minority representation in the various police forces in BiH, an essential component of UNMIBH's overall strategy to reform and democratise police. The Bonn-Petersberg Agreement (25 April 1996), the RS Framework Agreement (9 December 1998), and subsequent IPTF reviews of policing requirements on the ground, set targets for the number of police officers who are classified as belonging to a minority ethnic group ('minorities') to be deployed in each municipality.[10] UNMIBH's attempts to

---

9. See Annex 4 of the UNMIBH MIP-MAP (2000) for a detailed list of UNMIBH training courses.
10. The concept of minority is a little complex in BiH. According to the Dayton Agreement,

increase minority representation have been three-pronged, with (1) refresher courses for refugee or displaced police officers, (2) a voluntary redeployment programme for officers, sending them back to their pre-war municipality where they were minorities, and (3) new recruits trained at one of the two police academies. Those officers who voluntarily redeploy or are retrained through the refresher course are pushed for senior management posts while new recruits, the vast majority of whom are minorities in their area of deployment, by necessity start at the bottom. The bulk of new recruits must be deployed to areas where they are minorities by the tenets of the RS Framework and Bonn-Petersberg Agreements. The primary exception to this rule is female recruits, who may be from the majority ethnic group in any particular municipality.

Most of the reforms detailed above focus on the integrity or capacity of the individual officer. It is only recently that UNMIBH has begun to make systematic assessments of policing as an institution. One of the earlier institutional UNMIBH projects, initiated in early 2000, was the Police Commissioner Project, designed to remove undue political influence on the police. A recent report from the International Crisis Group (ICG 2002: 34) succinctly summarises the situation in the Ministries of Interior in BiH:

> Far from observing the conventional Western niceties regarding the respective spheres of ministers (who make policy) and civil servants (who execute it), Bosnia's interior ministers have taken for granted that they should involve themselves in micro-management, down to individual candidates for preferment, recruitment, and discipline.

The Police Commissioner Project is designed to depoliticise policing by removing Ministers of Interior from the minutiae of day-to-day decision-making regarding policing by appointing an independent, professional police commissioner to be responsible for these decisions. In the ethnically mixed cantons, the Police Commissioner Project serves a second purpose. In these cantons, the Minister of Interior is of one ethnicity (either Croat or Bosniak) and the Deputy Minister is of the other ethnic group. Not surprisingly, especially considering the separate payrolls in these cantons, Bosniak officers report to the Bosniak Minister while Croat officers report to the Croat Minister. The Police Commissioner Project is designed to minimise or, ideally, eliminate these dual chains of command by creating one professional (not political) officer responsible for all the day-to-day policing decisions.

Each police commissioner (for each canton and entity) must meet specific standards: a university degree, a minimum of eight years police experience, a minimum of four years senior management experience, and demonstrated ability to

---

there are three constituent people in BiH – Serb, Croat, and Bosniak – none of which should be considered a minority. However, in the context of police reform as well as most other major institutional reform, minority is much more localised and measured at the municipal level depending on the population there.

manage large-scale operations. Further, the commissioner must not be an active member of a political party or have held an executive or representative position in a political party for the last ten years. In order to ensure that the police commissioner is not just another layer of bureaucracy between politicians and police, s/he will be selected by an Independent Selection Review Board composed of seven members – two representatives from the ministry and five representatives from civil society from legal science, criminology or human rights and not representing a political party (UNMIBH Policy IPTF – P06/2001 A).

Another recent institutional addition to the UNMIBH agenda has been the Systems Analysis Project. This project, launched in December 2001 and under the auspices of the Human Rights Department of the UN mission, aims to promote the efficiency, transparency, and accountability of the police. The project evaluates each police administration in BiH according to the following criteria (Annex 5, UNMIBH MIP-MAP 2002):

(1) Organisation and management structure.

(2) Personnel structure and career advancement.

(3) Functional roles and responsibilities.

(4) Training and human resources development.

(5) Internal and external disciplinary mechanisms.

(6) Operational, auxiliary and technical support procedures.

(7) Procedures for inspection of foreigners and prevention of trafficking and organised crime.

(8) Criminal investigation procedures and crime prevention/criminal justice interface between police and prosecutors.

(9) Relationships with other law enforcement agencies, courts, and other official bodies.

(10) Procedures for deprivation of liberty.

(11) Budgetary control procedures and financial management.

(12) Legislation, regulations, and standard operating procedures.

Besides conducting evaluations of police administrations by these criteria, the project also sets up local change management teams to implement recommendations made during the course of the analysis. Unfortunately, this project was only developed very recently. While the first evaluation of the Brčko police took several months, the remaining systems analyses were crammed into an eight-month period or less, allowing only several weeks per force. Many observers, both internal and external to UNMIBH, believe that the project is designed much more to validate UNMIBH's work in BiH than to reform local BiH police. Not surprisingly, UNMIBH certified all local law enforcement agencies as ready to practise democratic policing at the end of the evaluation.

Changes in the operational policies and work patterns of the police

One of the first major changes in the operational policies of the police after the war involved traffic checkpoints. During the Yugoslav period, the checkpoint was one of the key points of interaction between police and citizens and it served as an essential method of population control (Dziedzic and Bair, 1998). In the context of a deeply divided (by ethnicity) BiH after the conflict, checkpoints served to control freedom of movement; citizens of one ethnic group were harassed when attempting to cross internal borders controlled by another ethnic group, and sometimes were even prevented from crossing into these other areas. One of UNMIBH's early tasks then was to work to increase the freedom of movement necessary in a democratic society, through minimising the impact of these checkpoints. UNMIBH managed this by creating a new policy whereby local police were required to apply to IPTF for approval to hold static checkpoints for more than half an hour at a time – and give evidence that the checkpoints were necessary to prevent or reduce crime, not control movement. UNMIBH was able to implement this policy fairly easily – with the assistance of the NATO-led SFOR troops – despite a lack of cooperation from local police authorities, especially in the RS.

One important new policy fitting with the new ideology and mandate of policing that UNMIBH has been trying to promote is the mandatory deployment of joint – that is, multi-ethnic – patrols in mixed areas. For example, joint patrols between Croats and Bosniaks were occurring in the ethnically mixed cantons VI (central BiH) and VII (Mostar) by the end of 1997 (UNMIBH SRSG Report, December 1997). Joint patrols were fairly quickly instituted in Brčko within a year after the Brčko Final Arbitration Award in March 1999. The Brčko police were the first fully functioning, multi-ethnic police in BiH, as well as the first multi-ethnic institution in Brčko. Unfortunately, the inauguration of joint patrols did little to eliminate the parallel command structures that have plagued policing in the mixed cantons of the Federation.

Although the development of community policing is still slow, despite its encouragement in the police academies and UNMIBH mandatory training courses for officers, there has been a bit of progress with the introduction of bike patrols. The key force behind these has been the US Justice Department ICITAP programme, which purchased a number of bikes and other necessary equipment for the Sarajevo police. After the success of the programme, ICITAP has slowly started to spread it to other police forces in BiH.

Another, and more important, ICITAP project, with the assistance and approval of UNMIBH, has been the development, in all police districts of BiH, of a Book of Rules to guide police behaviour.[11] Because ICITAP, unlike UNMIBH, has

---

11. Though the Systems Analysis Projects make clear some of the problems UNMIBH had with ICITAP 'meddling' in its mandate (UNMIBH IPTF Human Rights Office, 2002a; 2002b; 2002c). UNMIBH was ready to accept assistance from the very competent

no mandate in BiH, it has had to rely on cooperation with local police forces in developing these Books of Rules. As a result, there is some variation (or lack of harmonisation) between the Books in the different entities and cantons; however, police adherence to the Book of Rules may be much better since each police force was actively engaged, with the guidance of ICITAP, in the development of the Book of Rules. ICITAP has certified that each Book of Rules is consistent with the principles of democratic policing.

Changes in supervision and control of the police

Annex Six of the Dayton Agreement called for the creation of a Human Rights Commission to assist the parties to the agreement in meeting their obligations to the various international human rights conventions included in the BiH Constitution. The Commission is composed of two bodies: the Office of the Ombudsperson and the Human Rights Chamber. While, in theory, these bodies exist to handle human rights complaints, including against the police, in practice the long delays and low ability to implement decisions by these bodies lead most of those with complaints, if they decide to publicise their complaints at all, to make their case to one of the many international agencies working in BiH – especially OSCE, SFOR, UNHCR, or OHR.

However, with regard to human rights complaints against the police, this means going to the UNMIBH. The London PIC (Peace Implementation Council) meeting in 1996 called for IPTF to assist local authorities in investigating alleged human rights violations by the police, as well as, where necessary, '[to] carry out investigations of human rights abuses by law enforcement officers' (see ICG, 1999). UN Security Council Resolution 1088 gave UNMIBH-IPTF the powers called for at the London conference. As of April 2002, UNMIBH had 'investigated or assisted with local investigations of over thirteen thousand cases of alleged human rights abuses by law enforcement personnel, of which eleven thousand cases have been resolved' (UNMIBH Achievements, April 2002).

According to an UNMIBH Human Rights official (personal correspondence), Human Rights cases were primarily of three main types (see Figure 9.1), each of which was linked to a different mechanism to identify when mature for closure:

(1)   *Cases of property misuse by police officers:* closed only upon confirmation (by delivery of minutes) that police officers had actually vacated the contested property or upon de-authorisation of the officer unwilling to vacate.

(2)   *Cases of violence against minorities:* closed upon confirmation that the local police had put in place all necessary action to locate and prosecute perpetrators. Achievement of this status had to be left to the judgment of the experienced IPTF Investigators and/or Chief of Regional Human Rights Office.

ICITAP team whenever necessary – ICITAP even trained many of the IPTF officers.

(3)   Cases of police abuse: case closed only after confirmation of an adequate disciplinary action having been administrated by the Internal Control Unit of the police and a parallel action having been taken by UNMIBH in the form of a non-compliance report or a de-authorisation decision. When criminal responsibility was also present, the Human Rights Officer would ensure that the case was brought to the attention of the Prosecutor before closing the case. Full monitoring of the cases during the judicial phase of criminal prosecution was done more on an occasional basis by the Human Rights Office and was considered necessary to close a case only for high profile investigations. In all other cases, the Criminal Justice Advisory Unit, the department of UNMIBH responsible for watching the work of the Judiciary, monitored the rest of the procedure upon closure of the case within the Human Rights Office. These powers of investigation, in combination with the power to write non-compliance reports and to de-authorise officers, give UNMIBH a potent tool to prevent and punish human rights abuses by BiH police.

In addition to these external control mechanisms, ICITAP and UNMIBH have provided much assistance to local police forces in creating Internal Control Units or Professional Standards Units (PSUs). These units provide internal investigation of police officers and forward substantiated cases to police disciplinary committees. Unfortunately, there is little evidence that the idea of Professional Standards Units has taken hold in any of the BiH police forces. Indeed, most PSUs 'co-locate' in stations with the officers they might be investigating. ICG (2002: 38) reports that the PSUs are prone to political influence and quotes an internal US report:

> Although Ministers and Deputy Ministers are appointed by their governments and cannot officially be investigated by their PSU, they sometimes request the PSU to conduct an investigation of the allegations. When the determined facts do not exonerate the official, retaliatory actions might occur.

In other cases, PSUs would not proceed with investigations without pressure from the UNMIBH Human Rights Office.

These problems with PSUs are reflected in UNMIBH's SAP (System Analysis Project) reports (UNMIBH IPTF Human Rights Office, 2002a; 2002b; 2002c), which list a number of problems with their performance, including: (1) station commanders taking action without consulting the PSU, (2) punishments showing evidence of favouritism, (3) numerous cases that lapse because of an abuse of the statute of limitations, (4) the lack of a system for subordinate initiated complaints, and (5) a tendency to change major violations to minor ones.

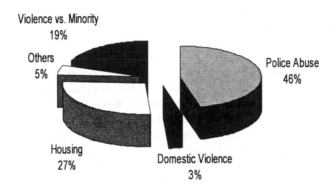

Violence vs. Minority
19%

Others
5%

Police Abuse
46%

Housing
27%

Domestic Violence
3%

🞖 Police Abuse ■ Domestic Violence ☐ Housing ☐ Others ■ Violence vs. Minority

Figure 9.1 Main types of human rights cases according to UNMIBH

Evaluation of the implementation and success of reforms

Movement towards a professional, service-oriented, accountable, effective police force
Measured against standards of policing at the end of 1995 when the Dayton Agreement was signed, police forces have made remarkable progress towards a professional, accountable, transparent, effective, and service-oriented police force.

All law enforcement agencies in BiH have been certified by the UNMIBH Systems Analysis Project. All practising officers have been vetted and authorised via a three-step process. A multi-ethnic State Border Service that has greatly reduced corruption and smuggling across the BiH borders was created by UNMIBH. Freedom of movement across the entire state has been ensured. Bosniak and Croat officers and ministerial officials work together in the deeply-divided Mostar canton, the only integrated ministry in the canton. Bosniak and Croat officers patrol together in this as well as other mixed and divided cantons and municipalities. Two training academies that teach new recruits the principles of policing in a democratic society have been created. The posts of Police Commissioner or Director of Police have been created in all police districts in BiH to minimise political interference in the day-to-day matters of policing.

Despite these significant achievements and others, much work remains to ensure effective democratic policing in BiH. Local power structures have fought tooth and nail against any and all significant reforms to police and have thwarted or minimised the impact of such reforms whenever it was in their power. For example, while forces fairly quickly reduced down to the sizes mandated by UNMIBH, local authorities made sure that those officers chosen to stick around were those loyal to local political officials and not necessarily those most effective at policing. Although local police authorities were willing to sign agreements to increase minority recruitment, the implementation of these agreements has been much more problematic. The RS agreed to increase minority (i.e., non-Serb) representation on its forces to 20% in 1998, but by mid-2002 only 4.9% of officers were minorities. While the representation of minorities within the police in the Federation is much higher (15.5%), it is unclear how these statistics were calculated – i.e. in which municipalities Croats and Bosniaks are counted as minorities and whether SBS officers (fully multi-ethnic) deployed in the Federation count towards this total (UNMIBH SRSG Report, June 2002). In any case, Serb officers remain drastically under-represented in the Federation. Furthermore, although there have been a few successful deployments of senior and middle-level officers through the refresher courses or voluntary redeployment (most notably the Serb police chief in Drvar and the Bosniak Deputy Chief in Srebrenica), the vast majority of minority police were trained through the academies, start at the bottom, and have little influence on the course of policing in their municipalities (UNMIBH Achievements, April 2002). Agreements to limit the number of new majority officers trained at the academy have often been bypassed by the continuation of other training schools (a junior college and secondary school in the RS, for example) or ignored altogether as majority candidates are hired for vacant positions (UNMIBH IPTF Human Rights Office, 2002c). Very little progress has been made in placing minority officers in senior and upper-level positions.

Not surprisingly, this lack of successful integration has meant that, in many places in BiH, the police do not actively protect the rights of minority returnees. For example, during the groundbreaking ceremony for the rebuilding of the Ferhadija

Mosque[12] on 7 May 2001 in Banja Luka (the capital of the RS), police failed to prevent a crowd of local Serbs from rioting, burning seven buses that brought in Bosniaks from across the country for the ceremony, trapping about four hundred attendees of the ceremony, including several high-ranking international officials inside the nearby Islamic Community Centre for seven hours, and even beating one elderly Bosniak to death (ICG Balkans Report, October 2001).[13] While police were not very active in controlling the riot, they were even less successful in the follow-up investigations. The several hundred officers in attendance were not required to write up reports of what they had seen until over a month later, and then only due to intense international pressure. According to an ICG report (ICG Balkans Report, October 2001: 35), 'these reports were written with all the professionalism and zeal of schoolboys made to stay after class to inscribe their apologies on the blackboard.' Further, seven officers initially testified before an investigative judge about a number of participants in the riots but later revoked their testimony claiming they no longer remembered. UNMIBH considered this perjury and later removed these officers.

After recognising the political fallout from the riots and feeling the intense pressure from the international community in BiH, the RS authorities did manage to act, accepting the resignations of the minister of the interior, the security chief, and the head of security in Banja Luka and removing the deputy minister of the interior. Further, a successful groundbreaking ceremony was held on 18 June with extremely high police presence; police arrested a large number of rioters and controlled the crowd with tear gas and water cannons. However, well over a year after the initial riot, investigations have made no progress against the organisers of the protest despite (or because of) many indications of high-level political involvement.[14]

Such lack of protection of minorities and their rights has extended to other areas in the RS, with UNMIBH reporting that it received notification of 316 threats or attacks on minorities in the RS between March 2000 and July 2001. ICG notes that hardly any of these incidents have resulted in criminal prosecutions (ICG Balkans Report October 2001). While UNMIBH suggests that the RS authorities have gotten better at dealing with such minority incidents and public order situations in the last year (UNMIBH SRSG Report June 2002), the moral of this story is, as ICG (October 2001: 37) notes, 'that the RS authorities can only be counted upon to provide security and protect the religious and other human rights of non-Serbs when they know that they must do so in order to escape the wrath of the international community'. While the severity of incidents is significantly lower in the Federation,

---

12. The Ferhadija Mosque was blown up by Serb authorities in 1993 during the war, despite the fact that there was no fighting in Banja Luka. The other 15 mosques in Banja Luka were also destroyed.
13. A similar riot, though with fewer injuries and less damage, but comparable police reaction, took place in Trebinje a few days before the one in Banja Luka. I focus on the Banja Luka riot only as an example.
14. See ICG Report No. 118 (8 Oct. 2001) for a more detailed account.

the problem also remains there especially in Croat dominated municipalities in Herzegovina such as Stolac.

UNMIBH's efforts with the local police registry have yielded some successes. UNMIBH has been able to prevent a large number of officers who have committed major human rights violations from exercising police powers. For example, the most recent SRSG report (8 June 2002) notes that since its last report (in November 2001) it had removed provisional authorisation from 68 officers, 27 for wartime conduct (only seven years after the end of the war). An additional 208 officers are currently under investigation for conduct during the war. However, this points to some problems with the purging process as well. For example, in Bratunac, officers who were engaged as security guards at camps during the war remain on the force; in contrast, no Bosniak officers are deployed in Bratunac despite the fact that it was a Bosniak majority municipality before the war.[15] This discourages minorities from feeling safe returning to the area. Further, many officers who are de-authorised by UNMIBH are reassigned to positions in the Ministry of Interior where they can continue to assert their influence over policing structures. Other former officers have been reassigned to important political positions or key spots in public corporations. It remains unclear how much UNMIBH de-authorisations impact policy, as political parties are likely to appoint another lackey to make decisions.

The Police Commissioner project is an important policy to deal with this problem, as well as other types of political influences on the police. However, it remains unclear how successful it will be. Local political authorities have put up a great deal of resistance to the project. Because of the decentralised political structure of BiH, laws on Internal Affairs had to be passed in all ten cantons, as well as the two entities, establishing the post of police commissioner (or director of police at the entity level). Not surprisingly, there was quite a good deal of variation in the laws across the various political districts. In the end, High Representative Wolfgang Petrisch[16] was forced to impose the law in all of the cantons and the entities, as one of his final acts in office, to ensure harmonisation; as a result, there is concern over how much local authorities will cooperate. In the autumn of 2002, several ministers resigned in Canton X over disagreement about the appointment of the Police Commissioner in that canton. In addition, there is much concern over the level of independence of the Independent Selection and Review Boards.

There are currently very few indications of how the public views the new policing structures in BiH. However, SFOR did conduct a survey on policing in early 2001 (SFOR, 2001). The extensive training of police by UNMIBH and other bilateral donors seems to have paid off – 48.1% of respondents totally agree that the current BiH police are more professional than the pre-war BiH police, as compared

---

15. Interview with a Bosniak member of the Bratunac Municipal Assembly.
16. The High Representative is the head of the OHR (Office of the High Representative) and is the lead international official with regard to implementation of civilian aspects of the Dayton Agreement. The High Rep has the power to remove both elected and unelected officials and impose laws.

to only 24% who disagree, while 44.8% of respondents totally agree that the current police of BiH receive better training to do their jobs than the pre-war police force against 17.7% who totally disagree. Similarly, 52% of respondents totally agree that they would feel comfortable asking the local police for assistance, as compared to only 19% who totally disagree. However, the downside of these numbers can be seen from the answers to another question on the survey, 'I would feel comfortable asking the police from the other entity for assistance.' Only 21.2% totally agree while 42.9% totally disagree. The numbers are quite similar across each ethnic group in BiH. While many citizens of BiH are comfortable with 'their' police, they are much less comfortable with police associated with another ethnic group.

Remaining problems

In addition to the issues outlined above, a number of serious problems for law enforcement in BiH need to be addressed. While ordinary street crime remains remarkably low, organised crime is one of the major problems facing BiH, as Paddy Ashdown, the current High Representative has repeatedly noted. For example, BiH has become an important stop in the trafficking of women from other points in Eastern Europe on to Western Europe. Despite the start of cooperation between entity and cantonal police forces brought on by the MCMPM, the fragmented policing structures and lack of cooperation across them remain a significant barrier to combating organised crime such as trafficking. Another attempt by the international community to deal with this issue was when the High Representative imposed a law on Legal Assistance and Official Co-operation in Criminal Matters between the Federation of Bosnia and Herzegovina, Republika Srpska and the District of Brčko.

However, the problems of organised crime in BiH are not just due to lack of cooperation between local law enforcement agencies; many recent reports, as well as anecdotal evidence, point to the complicity of local authorities and police in trafficking. Indeed, trafficking may provide a major source of financing to political figures in BiH. Evidence suggests the close collusion of BiH state, entity, cantonal and municipal institutions in trafficking. For example, officials from the RS Ministry of Health and Social Welfare have required sanitation inspectors to ensure that all 'girls offering entertainment services' receive HIV tests every month. Raids of brothels are often vetoed by Interior Ministers of cantons, and when they do occur, it often appears that owners have been tipped off ahead of time (ICG Balkans Report, May 2002). The UNMIBH SAP has attempted to deal with the latter problem by creating procedures to minimise the chances of officers not involved in the raids finding out about plans (UNMIBH IPTF Human Rights Office, 2002a; 2002b; 2002c).

At the start of 2003, police reforms in BiH entered a crucial period because UNMIBH pulled out of BiH to be replaced by the European Union (EU) follow-on policing mission. Nearly all of the pressure for reforms has come from UNMIBH, along with other external actors in the international community. Local political officials have done all they can to maintain their control of policing. While

UNMIBH's reforms have begun to have an effect on policing in BiH, there is little evidence that police forces are independent of political manipulation. That is, many question the sustainability of the reforms that have so far been put into place. This is especially true because of the difference in structure between the EU mission and UNMIBH. While UNMIBH had about 1800 international police officers, the EU mission has only about 400. As a result, the EU mission will continue co-location, but only at the managerial levels of policing – primarily co-locating in the ministries, but leaving officers involved in day-to-day policing on their own. Already in January 2003, OSCE and SFOR field staff have reported rumblings that police are returning to their old ways.

Sustainability is also the question with regard to the State Border Service (SBS). Officers were enticed to leave their regular police posts for border control positions by significantly higher salaries. Unfortunately, these salaries may be more than BiH can afford. Despite significant contributions from the international community, funding of the SBS remains a problem. While salaries of SBS officers are rather high for BiH, salaries of the regular police forces are paltry, even by the standards of BiH. Furthermore, in many cases officers are owed back pay. These low salaries can lead to police corruption as police seek alternate sources of income to supplement their regular wages. Salaries are particularly low in the RS, which has only increased the problem of raising the number of minority officers in that entity.

Police reforms and societal and political changes
The dynamics of police reform in BiH largely mirror reforms in other institutions in BiH. In all cases, local powers try to retain control of institutions while the external actors of the international community attempt to reform them. Likewise, local powers continually resist the development of state-level institutions, while the international community pushes them.[17] However, reform of the police may face additional barriers compared to many other institutions in BiH because of their central role in illegal activities that fund the local political authorities.

Insights suggested by police reforms
All major institutional reforms are difficult. In the context of a deeply divided, post-conflict society the difficulties increase logarithmically. The only way to push reforms of police in such a context is through powerful external pressure. Even with such pressure, however, the sustainability of reforms remains a major problem, as external actors never stick around forever. Many observers believe that local officials are playing a waiting game – agreeing to reforms, but obstructing their implementation – until international supervision of policing ends.

Another lesson took UNMIBH quite some time to realise – reforms at institutional level must proceed in lockstep with individual level reforms. Nearly all of UNMIBH's earliest work focused on the individual – eliminating war criminals

---

17. Bosniaks sometimes push for the development of state-level institutions, since they are the largest ethnic group and have no kin state (unlike the Serbs and Croats).

and human rights violators, training individuals in human rights and methods of democratic policing. It was only much later that they took concrete steps to reform police at the institutional level through, for example, depoliticising police with the creation of the post of police commissioner or giving police a full audit through the systems analysis project. The police in BiH would be in much better shape if these projects had been initiated earlier instead of rushed at the end of the UNMIBH mandate.

In a similar vein, reforms of police must proceed in conjunction with overall reforms of the legal system in order to be truly effective. In BiH, there has been little coordination with the judiciary and this has made an impact on the effectiveness of police reforms. When UNMIBH-IPTF has been able to exert pressure on police to reform or act in a way that political authorities disagree with, these political authorities have a second line of defence – the judiciary. While external efforts to reform the police in BiH have been extensive, reforms of the judiciary have been late in starting, ineffective, and lack resources. UNMIBH employees were primarily police officers, not judges or lawyers, and thus were less than ideal for reforming the judicial system. Much evidence suggests that local political authorities continue to have influence over judges, and thus are able to affect the rule of law.

Acknowledgements

Research for this work was supported in part by funding from the National Security Education Program, the American Councils for International Education Research Program in Eastern Europe, the National Science Foundation Democracy and Democratization Program, and the University of North Carolina – Chapel Hill. In addition, I gratefully acknowledge the assistance of Dr Anthony Oberschall, Dr Robert Jenkins, Lynn Whiteheart, and the staff of the International Crisis Group in Sarajevo. All errors remain my own.

References

Alic, A., and Jen, T. 2001. Serve and Protect Your Own'. *Transitions Online.* Available at: http://www.tol.cz
Bair, A., and Dziedzic, M. 1998. 'The International Police Task Force', in Wentz, L., ed. *Lessons from Bosnia: The IFOR Experience.* Washington.
Dziedzic, M., and Bair, A. 1998. 'Bosnia and the International Police Task Force', in Oakley, R., Dziedzic, M., and Goldberg, E., eds. *Policing the New World Disorder: Peace Operations and Public Security.* Washington.

European Stability Initiative. 1999. *Reshaping International Priorities in Bosnia and Herzegovina: Part One – Bosnian Power Structures.* Report of the European Stability Initiative. Berlin.

General Framework Agreement for Peace in Bosnia and Herzegovina. (Also known as the Dayton Peace Agreement). 1995. Available at the website of the Office of the High Representative: http://www.ohr.int

Glenny, M. 1992. *The Fall of Yugoslavia: The Third Balkan War.* New York.

Holbrooke, R. 1998. *To End a War.* New York.

Human Rights Watch. 1998. 'Bosnia-Hercegovina beyond restraint: politics and the policing agenda of the United Nations International Police Task Force', in *Human Rights Watch Report,* vol. 10, no. 5.

International Crisis Group. *ICG Balkans Report* no. 130. 10 May 2002. 'Policing the police in Bosnia: a further reform agenda'. Brussels

International Crisis Group. *ICG Balkans Report* no. 118. 8 Oct. 2001. 'The wages of sin: confronting Bosnia's *Republika Srpska*'. Brussels.

International Crisis Group. 1999. *Is Dayton Failing? Bosnia Four Years after the Peace Agreement.* Brussels.

Perito, R. 'A critique of the OHR Report on a police follow-on mission to UNMIBH and the UN International Police Task Force'. Paper commissioned by UNDP.

SFOR. 8 Mar. 2001. 'Survey on police'. SFOR document.

Silber, L., and Little, A. 1995. *The Death of Yugoslavia.* London.

Somers, S., and Reeves, T. 1996. 'A functional review of the criminal justice system of Bosnia and Herzegovina'. ICITAP Report. Washington.

UNMIBH. 1996a. Agreement on restructuring the Police Federation of Bosnia and Herzegovina. 25 Apr. 1996.

UNMIBH. 1996b. *Internationally accepted principles of policing in a democratic state.*

UNIMIBH. 1998. *Framework Agreement on Police Restructuring, Reform and Democratisation in the Republika Srpska.* 9 Dec. 1998.

UNMIBH. 2000. *MIP Action Plan (MIP-MAP) 2000–2002.* Available at: http://www.unmibh.org

UNIMIBH. 2002. 'UNMIBH Achievements'. Available at: http://www.unmibh.org

UNMIBH IPTF Human Rights Office. 2002a. *Systems Analysis of the Police in Canton VII.* UNMIBH document.

UNMIBH IPTF Human Rights Office. 2002b. *Systems Analysis of the Police in the Federation of Bosnia-Herzegovina.* UNMIBH document.

UNMIBH IPTF Human Rights Office. 2002c. *Systems Analysis of the Police in the Republika Srpska.* UNMIBH document.

UNMBIH SRSG Report Dec. 1995. Available at: http://www.unmibh.org

UNMIBH SRSG Report Dec. 1997. Available at: http://www.unmibh.org

UNMIBH SRSG Report Sep. 1998. Available at: http://www.unmibh.org

UNMIBH SRSG Report Mar. 2000. Available at: http://www.unmibh.org

UNMIBH SRSG Report Nov. 2000. Available at: http://www.unmibh.org

UNMIBH SRSG Report June 2001. Available at: http://www.unmibh.org

UNMIBH SRSG Report June 2002. Available at: http://www.unmibh.org

UNMIBH SRSG Report Dec. 2002. Available at: http://www.unmibh.org

UNMIBH Policy IPTF-P02/2000. 15 May 2000. 'Registration, Provisional Authorisation and Certification'. UNMIBH document.

UNMIBH Policy IPTF-P/2001. 2001. 'Removal of provisional authorization and disqualification of law enforcement agencies personnel'. UNMIBH document.

UNMIBH Policy IPTF – P06/2001 A. 2001. 'Police Commissioner's Project'. UNMIBH document.

Chapter 10

Distinct and Different: the Transformation of the Croatian Police

Sanja Kutnjak Ivković

[T]he militia, according to its Latin root (*miles, militis* – a soldier), is a citizens' or people's army, 'a special armed formation with the purpose of maintaining order in cities and villages' and, in post-World War II Yugoslav practice, 'armed people' as 'the keeper of the [socialist] revolution'. The Greek root of the word police (*politeia* – organised state life) defines a professional institution responsible for public order and the state system and eliminates the ideological overtone present in the earlier name (Kobali and Baloković-Krklec, 1995: 10).

The Republic of Croatia and its police

The Republic of Croatia (*Republika Hrvatska*), once a republic within the former Yugoslavia, gained its independence in the early 1990s. Croatia is both a Central European and a Mediterranean country with a territory of 21,829 square miles or 56,610 square kilometres and a population of 4.7 million. Eight out of ten citizens declared themselves as ethnic Croats and 78% as Roman Catholics (*1997 Croatian Almanac*, 1998).

Croats have been living in South-Eastern Europe for more than thirteen centuries. History has witnessed an independent Croatian Kingdom and a union with Hungary and Austria. The Mediterranean parts of Croatia were periodically ruled by Italy. Following the collapse of the Austro-Hungarian Monarchy in 1918, Croatia became part of the Kingdom of Serbs, Croats, and Slovenians (subsequently renamed the Kingdom of Yugoslavia). After World War II, Croatia became a socialist republic within the communist-dominated Yugoslav federation. Following the break-up of the Yugoslav federation, the Republic of Croatia was recognised as an independent and sovereign country in 1992.

Croatia is currently in transition towards a democratic society and market economy. The road towards democracy has not only been challenging; it has also seriously affected the police (Kutnjak Ivković and Klockars, 2003):

> The journey has been far from smooth: the country has experienced a defensive war against the aggression of the Serb-dominated Yugoslav Army and various

paramilitary troops, the influx of refugees from Bosnia and Herzegovina, a decade-long governance of a strong, right-wing oriented political party, the strengthening of nationalism, a continued legacy of mismanagement of the economy, the transition into market economy, and a high unemployment rate. All these factors shape the environment in which the Croatian police operate and have a strong impact on the state of police integrity.

The Croatian police, one of the youngest police in Europe, are part of the Croatian Ministry of the Interior. The centralised hierarchical structure of the police consists of the Chief of Police (Police Law, 2000) and the headquarters at the top, 20 police administrations in the middle, and approximately 200 police stations at the bottom of the organisational chart. The administrators within the Ministry give orders, coordinate, control, and direct, but rarely perform regular police tasks, according to the Ministry. Police administrations not only 'Monitor the situation in the field, organise and direct police station activities ... [but also] ... take part directly in complex activities' (Kuretić, 1994: 35). The bulk of regular police work is performed at the police stations, which can be classified as either specialised (e.g. airport police stations, border control stations, traffic police stations) or basic. The police presently employ approximately 20,000 sworn police officers, yielding a rate of 4.28 police officers per thousand inhabitants.

The modern Croatian police have had a short but turbulent history. In little over a decade of its existence, the Croatian police had to play a significant role in the defensive war and undergo an ongoing transformation towards democratic policing. On the eve of the war in Croatia in the early 1990s, Croatia was still a republic within the former Yugoslavia. Facing a clash between the need to develop an armed force capable of defending the country in case of an increasingly likely war, in April 1991 the Croatian Parliament passed appropriate statutory changes to facilitate the establishment of the National Guard Corps (NGC) as a police service within the Ministry of the Interior (which was, aside from the Yugoslav Army, the only legitimate armed force on the Croatian territory at the time). The war began soon after the President of the Republic of Croatia proclaimed the results of the public referendum determining that Croatia would become an independent state (on 23 May 1991). Police officers constituted a large portion of the manpower for the NGC, especially in the first few months following their formation. Consequently, for a period of almost two years, the police performed two roles: the defence role and the regular police role (Kutnjak Ivković, 2000).

The war itself and the complex set of related consequences – from the clear separation of the new police from the old Yugoslav militia, the military defence role performed by the police, and the strengthening of the code of silence among the police, to the effects on the country's economy and the level of public confidence in the police – make the road towards democratic policing in Croatia quite distinct and different, despite the fact that some of the encountered problems are shared by virtually every country in the process of transition.

The old Yugoslav militia

To better understand the circumstances that led to this critical phase in the development of the Croatian police and governed its shape and process, one needs to understand the legacy of its predecessor, the old Yugoslav militia. The former Yugoslavia had been a federation for close to five decades (1945–91), during which period the organisation and work of the militia were mostly controlled at the federal level. Several legal statutes in the late 1960s and 1970s, as well as the federal Constitution of 1977, opened the door for shifting the regulation of most functions performed by the militia to the individual republics, while the control of most security-related tasks remained at the federal level.

The Croatian Law Concerning the Interior Affairs Agencies of 1985 regulated the organisation and operation of the militia in Croatia (while still a federative republic within Yugoslavia). According to the statute, the tasks allocated to the militia were far more extensive than keeping the peace, order-maintenance, crime-prevention, and crime-control tasks typical of the police in Western democracies. They included state-security tasks (protection of the Constitutional system), public-security tasks (protection of life and safety of citizens, prevention and investigation of crimes, protection of public order and peace, traffic regulation, as well as border patrol, control of the movement and residence of foreign nationals, regulation of gun ownership and possession), and various other tasks (control of citizens' associations and public meetings, issuance of passports and identification cards, maintaining the citizenship directory and the public registry) (Makra, 1989: 16).

However, as Makra (1989: 17) enumerates, the interior affairs agencies were a part of the system of public protection. Thus, under the justification of the protection of the communist regime, they eavesdropped, followed, and kept files on the potential 'enemies of the state'. Secrecy, mystification, and the lack of public accountability were necessary ingredients for the continuation of such activities, followed by the general arrogance, lack of respect for, and rudeness towards citizens. The militia had the overall reputation of an uneducated, unprofessional force run as a military organisation (Kutnjak Ivković, 2000: 49). While the militia improved the technical skills of its officers over the years, both the rude treatment of citizens by the militia and the lack of public trust in the militia persisted.

Reforms and changes

Overall goals
In the atmosphere of the global trend towards the democratisation of the former communist countries in the late 1980s and early 1990s, as well as pending prospects of joining the European Union, the opportunity to build the new Croatian state and

clearly separate it from the former communist Yugoslavia naturally led to the proclamation of democracy and market economy as the basic guidelines for the transition process. While the defensive war and the processes of democratisation started to occur at the same time, the war drained substantial energies and completely overshadowed the transition processes in 1991–92. The large-scale legal and economic changes necessary for successful transformation into a democratic society and a market economy were temporarily put on the back burner. This hindrance had unexpected benefits: it helped place the Croatian police in the position in which there was a clean break from the old Yugoslav militia.

When the war with the new, Serb-dominated Socialist Republic of Yugoslavia broke out in 1991, most police officers of Serb ethnicity left their posts in Croatia and fought against the newly established National Guard Corps (NGC). According to the 1991 Census, 12% of the general population of Croatia was of Serb origin (Lajić, 1995: 60), while the percentage of ethnic Serbs in the old Croatian militia exceeded 70% (*Halo*, vol. 44, 1995: 5), especially among the administrators and first-line supervisors. Consequently, in the early 1990s, the image of the militia was associated with the Serb-dominated Socialist Republic of Yugoslavia, while, on the other hand, the image of the Croatian police was idealised under the influence of the defence role that they performed.

Public opinion polls reflected these changes: according to the *World Values Survey* (1995), the majority of the Croatian citizens surveyed in 1995 showed a great deal of respect for the Croatian police. The police turned out to be the second most respected social institution (after the Army), commanding more respect than the church, the Parliament, or the legal system.

While independence and the war jointly generated the conditions for the creation of a new police unburdened by the legacy of the old communist militia, the war also slowed the progress in carrying out wider legal and economic changes that would facilitate the transition. Indeed, whereas the new Croatian Constitution – the basic legal document – was enacted as early as 1990, a thorough reform of the criminal justice system and a detailed statutory regulation of constitutional rights (i.e., the legislative reform) occurred as late as 1997. In the early period, from 1990 to 1992, discussions and debates over how to change the police and which values to promote, typical of other countries in transition, were temporarily substituted with the discussions ultimately related to defence, that is, the challenges of rapid hiring and problems in securing adequate equipment and obtaining appropriate training.

Discussions about transition, democratisation, and European integration in general, as well as about the police, their role, and their values in specific, started to surface as soon as the war subsided and the war-related concerns weakened in 1992 (with one-quarter of the territory still remaining occupied until 1995). Politicians and academics used buzzwords such as openness to the public, transparency, accountability, and rule of law, while, at the same time, police administrators focused on professionalism, education, courtesy, and politeness. For example, Željko Horvatić, Professor of Law, stated (1994: 42):

the state has to refrain from the interference into human rights and freedoms, unless it is absolutely necessary. This is written in our Constitution [referring to the rule of law]. On the other hand, especially when discussing the police work, we have to keep in mind yet another concept – the concept of the social state – which on the surface conflicts with the rule of law, while it actually complements it. The social state is the state of all citizens. This means not only that a citizen has to be protected from interference into his rights and freedoms, ... but also that the citizen has to have the state-guaranteed protection of his rights, unless the exercise of these rights is restricted by the law and the performance of the official duties by the state officials, including the police ... [W]e are striving to follow the highest standards [established] by the European Council and the United Nations. All that has to be balanced; that's the rule of law ... That is easier said than done. And that is the role of the police in a democratic society, especially the lawful conduct and the adherence to the rule of law, based on the laws supporting the foundations of the democratic state [and] the division of state and government.

Ivan Jarnjak, a former Minister of the Interior, provided a slightly different take on the same theme – the rule of law (Piškor, 1993: 5):

We are trying to achieve that every Croatian police officer be polite, professional, and follow the rule of the law ... [I]t is very important to the Croatian police that, on the one hand, police officers be courteous and polite toward the citizens, and, on the other hand, that they are respected and accepted by the Croatian people.

In addition, the 'war-is-over' attitude started to dominate the police administrators' views in the mid-1990s, as Drago Matić, head of one of the police districts, had indicated: 'There is no good police officer without a developed love for the homeland and a professional qualification. All of our police officers have proven their love for the homeland in the war, now is the time for professional training' (Rako, 1997: 15).

The issue of democratic policing continued to be a topic of discourse. For example, the Ministry of the Interior itself organised a seminar about 'the functions of the police in a democratic society' in 1994 (see Šintić, 1994). In his opening speech, the then Minister of the Interior, Ivan Jarnjak, discussed the balance between the protection of the rights of individual citizens and the protection of the interest of the society at large. Emphasising that many crucial questions about the police remain open and that there is plenty of room for improvement of the existing system, he added (Jarnjak, 1994: 2):

In a democratic society, these instruments [of crime control] have to provide a balance between the protection of citizens' individual rights and freedoms, and the protection of the interests of the society at large. That balance is the one that reflects the level of democratisation in a particular society ... It is clear that it is not easy to establish this balance, especially in the complex social conditions that have an effect on the police in young democracies, such as ours, by expanding the current tasks and by imposing the new ones ... I argue that the new territorial and organisational structure of the Ministry of the Interior, established on the democratic principles of policing in Western democracies and grounded in our own specific conditions, provides a good basis for the improvement of the new police, especially keeping in mind the formation of the new professional police code of ethics, the expansion of the control system, and a greater degree of mutual trust built between the police and the public.

The democratisation process focuses on five key concepts: depoliticisation, demilitarisation, professionalisation, demystification, and downsizing. Depoliticisation of the police should serve to break the ties between politicians and police administrators which in the past led to the police serving the interests of the communist party and to political interference in everyday police activities, and the recruitment and selection process. Demilitarisation should reflect the idea that the police ought not be a military-type force, but a community-oriented service, characterised less by a military organisational structure and more by businesslike titles for rank and file, as well as by the avoidance of a strict hierarchical system of command. Related to both depoliticisation and demilitarisation is demystification. It should serve to lift the veil of secrecy from police work (justified routinely by the protection of higher national and security interests) and make the police more transparent and accountable.

Depoliticisation and demystification were perceived to go hand-in-hand with the professionalisation of the police: as political interference (justified by the protection of the society's interests) and the level of protection provided by mystification weakened, professionalisation should both develop and enhance police accountability through education and the implementation of various mechanisms of accountability. Finally, as the purposes of the police change and the police no longer need to keep each and every opposition member under surveillance, nor is there any need for the police to assume the defence function, carefully planned and executed downsizing should take place: expenditures should be reduced and the number of employees lowered to meet European standards.

Opposition to the democratisation of the police was rather minimal, if noticeable at all. Moreover, there was no nostalgic sentiment for the 'good old days' and the resistance towards democratisation of the police. The reason was simple: the 'good old days' were associated with Yugoslavia, which by that time had projected a very negative image and thus was utterly undesirable.

Changes in the legal system and powers of the police

The basic legal document – the Constitution – was enacted rather early (in 1990), under the conditions in which war seemed to be imminent and unavoidable. However, the Constitution, as expected, merely laid out the foundation for the legal system and the democratic state. Compared to the set of legal rules typical of the communist era, the new Constitution guarantees quite a different set of rights and freedoms to the citizens. One of these crucial and basic values established by the Articles of the Constitution is the rule of law (Article 3, Constitution, 1990).

In addition to proclaiming fundamental values, the Constitution contains 27 articles specifically addressing 'personal and political freedoms and rights'. A number of these articles are directly relevant for police work; they establish the presumption of innocence (Article 28); require a judicial warrant for an arrest, unless there is reasonable suspicion that the suspect had committed a serious crime and the suspect is immediately handed over to the court in the shortest period of time possible (Article 24); determine that the warrant is required for a search of a residence and that warrantless searches are permitted only when their purpose is to execute an arrest warrant, apprehend the offender, or prevent serious danger to life or substantial damage to property (Article 34); request that the suspect be informed about the charges against him or her (Article 29); prohibit any abuse of the suspects (Article 23); and require their humane treatment (Article 25).

The Constitution laid grounds for the subsequent detailed legal regulation in the form of various statutes and other legislative acts. However, in the meantime the war became a reality and it was pragmatic at the time merely to amend the old laws dating back to the communist regime. In fact, the actual new set of statutes was enacted only in 1997. As Horvatić (1994: 41) emphasises, mere amendments to the old laws were viewed just as the first step:

> We inherited the body of law from the former Yugoslavia. We changed them on the fly. Quickly. But we could not destabilise the legal system by abolishing all the old laws and enacting completely new ones. That was impossible. Thus, we undertook only the interventions which were crucial without hurting democracy. However, the road toward the establishment of the new laws has been a long one and it still continues. Not only in the enactment of the new laws and statutes, but also in the citizens' habits to behave according to the new laws. Because the laws are easy to change, people's habits are sometimes easier, and sometimes much harder to change. And not only [the habits of] the people who are part of the state apparatus, including the police and the judiciary, but also the regular folks on the street who used to live in the system that, I would tend to argue, cherished unlawfulness, as well as solutions beside the law and against the law.

Changes of the existing laws dating back to the socialist regime were made to provide a closer fit with the new social and political conditions, resulting, for example, in the restated version of the Criminal Code in 1996. At that time, the 'mini-reform' was a part of the preparatory stage for the entirely new criminal legislation and reflected some of the future statutory changes (Pavišić and Veić, 1996: x).

At the end of the five-year process undertaken by the Ministry of Justice, a thorough reform of the rules dealing with both criminal procedure and criminal substantive law was carried out in 1997. Focusing on the new political, social, and economic conditions and considering the achievements in the area of comparative law in European and Anglo-Saxon traditions, the legislature promulgated two new statutes crucial for the police: the new Criminal Procedure Code (1997) and the new Police Law (2000).

Compared with the earlier, frequently modified version of the Criminal Procedure Code, the Criminal Procedure Code of 1997 provides a detailed description of the criminal process which features a strong emphasis on the combination of civil-law and common-law traditions. The new Code also contains detailed provisions implementing the citizens' rights established by the Constitution. From the moment a suspect is to be interrogated for the first time (Article 4), the suspect needs to be told about the charges against her/him, receive the Miranda-like warnings[1] about the right to remain silent and to have an attorney present, as well as, if the suspect does not object, have the police notify the family or other persons of her/his choice about the arrest (Article 6; Article 177). Although the police are not entitled to interrogate the suspect when engaging in the pre-investigative procedure (Article 177), if the suspect is arrested or if there is a search warrant to be executed, the police have to inform the suspect about her/his right to remain silent and to have an attorney present. The penalty for violating of these rules, in the form of a modified version of the exclusionary rule (i.e., the prohibition to use the evidence collected in violation of the rules as a basis for the verdicts and/or the court decisions in general), is determined in Article 9. If the court uses evidence collected in clear violation of the rules, such an action constitutes grounds for appeal (Article 367).

The Code also regulates the force used by the police in the pre-investigative process: when the police execute an arrest warrant or engage in an otherwise legal arrest, they are entitled to use only 'The [level of] force necessary for the execution of the arrest and with consequences proportionate to the severity of the crime committed' (Article 96). Article 54 of the Police Law (2000) establishes the police officer's responsibility for using the least level of force necessary. Deadly force or the level of force that could result in serious consequences for the health of the arrestee may be used only on the fleeing felon charged with the crime for which the penalty is at least ten years of imprisonment, or if the suspect's resistance can endanger someone's life or cause serious injury (Article 96).

The Code also prescribes that the police have to bring the arrestee to the investigative judge immediately, at most within 24 hours since the arrest (Article 97). Furthermore, the valid search of a residence as part of the investigative proceedings can be performed only on the basis of a judicial warrant (Article 213), unless the conditions for the constitutional exceptions are met (Article 216). One such exception to this rule is the search to arrest situation: when the arrest warrant is being executed on a suspect, the suspect can be searched without a warrant if there is

---

1. To provide defendants in criminal cases with the protection against self-incrimination guaranteed by the Fifth Amendment and to allow the utilisation of the right to have an attorney guaranteed by the Sixth Amendment to the United States Constitution, the U.S. Supreme Court held in Miranda v. Arizona (384 US 436 (1966)) that 'prior to any questioning, the person must be warned that he has a right to remain silent, that any statement he does make may be used as evidence against him, and that he has a right to the presence of an attorney, either retained or appointed'.

suspicion that the suspect is armed or that she/he will destroy or hide the evidence (Article 216).

Severe limitations of citizens' rights in the form of the use of special investigative techniques, such the wiretapping, eavesdropping, use of undercover agents and agents provocateurs, can be exercised only on the basis of a written order issued by a judge, and then only for a narrow subset of felonies (felonies committed against the state and felonies that violate norms of international law; most serious forms of felonies ranging from murder and aggravated robbery to kidnapping and extortion; and felonies for which the prescribed punishment is at least five years of imprisonment if there is reasonable suspicion that they have been planned or committed by a group of persons or a criminal organisation (Articles 180–1)).

The most recent addition to the new legal system is the Police Law of 2000. This law defines the police and lists their tasks. In particular, the Law defines the police as the 'public service within the Ministry of the Interior entrusted to perform the tasks enumerated in the law' (Article 2) and thus no longer assigns the state-security-related tasks to the police. The tasks, listed in Article 3, now include: protection of life, rights, safety, and health of individuals; protection of property; prevention and detection of felonies and misdemeanours; search for the persons who committed felonies and misdemeanours, as well as their delivery to the appropriate authorities; control and regulation of the road traffic; work on the tasks and issues related to foreign nationals, as determined by the Police Law; control and protection of the state border; and other tasks determined by the Police Law.

The police and their role – a public service oriented towards the protection of life and property – are now defined in a way that corresponds to traditional democracies much more closely. In fact, the first substantive item in the Law (Article 2) defines the police and declares that the police are established to provide protection of the Constitutional and other rights and freedoms of citizens. It further determines that the police are entitled to use discretion and force, and elaborates the ways of exercising these powers (thus determining the boundaries of acceptable police behaviour). At the same time, the Police Law contains articles expanding upon the basic responsibilities determined by the Constitution (Article 20 about personal responsibility; Article 25 about civil damages) by addressing the personal accountability of police officers (disciplinary, criminal) and the civil accountability of the state for violations of citizens' rights committed by the police.

Depoliticisation of the police – the idea that the police should not be accountable to the members of the ruling party but to the public – was one of the aspects of differentiating the old militia and the new police. Some of the earliest changes in the Law on Interior Affairs in 1991 prohibited police officers from becoming members of any political party. The new Police Law of 2000 contains similar norms (Article 95). Furthermore, recent changes in the organisation of the police, including the new position of the Chief of Police, tend to put a buffer between the Minister as a political appointment and the police officers.

Changes in the organisational structures and policies of the police

The Ministry of the Interior 'inherited the communist organisation, mentality and its ways of understanding the police forces' (Morić, 1994: 121). Politicians and high-level administrators wanted to perform a set of dramatic changes to adjust to the new times, but the war intervened. In fact, changes in the organisational structure related to the war, the country's newly gained independence, and the democratic transformation are intertwined and sometimes difficult to pull apart.

To begin with, the country went through extensive changes in the organisation of its territorial units. Once the country was organised into 20 counties, the Ministry of the Interior was one of the first ministries to be reorganised accordingly. Several aspects of these changes can be attributed directly to the new democratic orientation:

> The new reforms also abolished the socialist/communist idea of small districts and strong local governments and their police stations. Because police stations were no longer established on the basis of the organisational principle of serving the district as the smallest territorial unit, police stations could now be established so that, if the organisation of the territory so required, the same police station could perform tasks for several districts ... As a consequence of the emphasis that the Ministry has placed on openness to the public, the organisation of the Ministry is now publicly available ... as are the names of the commanders and their deputies in each of the police administrations (Kutnjak Ivković, 2000: 59).

According to the Police Law (2000), the police are now organised as a three-tier system, with the Ministry of the Interior and the Police Chief on top of the hierarchy, 20 police administrations (corresponding to 20 counties) in the middle, and about 200 police stations at the bottom of the hierarchy. However, rather than promoting a secretive and rigid military-like organisational structure, since the 1990s the Ministry has maintained that the organisation needs to have a certain level of flexibility, making adjustments depending on 'the level of security and on the appropriate ways of adjusting to the arising circumstances' (Morić, 1994: 122). Related to the idea of demilitarisation were the ensuing changes in the system of ranks and assignments.

While democratic societies regard the police as one of the public agencies serving the citizens (as does the new Police Law of 2000 in Croatia), communist regimes regarded the police primarily as one of the mechanisms intended for the protection of the communist regime and its values. The secrecy and mystification of the police, typical of the communist militia, clearly clash with the view of the police as a public service agency. Organisational changes guided by the latter view focus on the greater degree of police accountability. The Police Law requires that the Minister inform the Parliament about the work of the police every year (Article 7) and to discuss the work of the police with the Parliamentary Commission Concerning Domestic Politics and National Security more frequently. The police also have the general duty to inform the public via the media about police activities, as well as to directly inform individual citizens and organisations about specific issues in which they have expressed interest.

The Ministry thus listed openness to the public (as a part of demystification of the police) as one of the primary changes that were carried out as early as mid-1992 and established two new offices, the Public Relations Office and the International Relations Office. The Public Relations Office was established with the dual purpose of providing a summary of the written materials about the police (based on the press-clippings) for police administrators and to conduct public opinion polls:

> The Public Relations Office of the Ministry of the Interior is organised in a way that enables efficient relations with the public through a two-way system of communication: assessing internal and external public opinion and press-clippings. This gives the basis for a more efficient analysis of strategy and tactics in public relations and enables direct communication with the internal and external public through the Ministry's newsletter 'Halo 92' as well as other media and activities, especially aimed at public opinion leaders, that is, reporters from every field of the media (Kuretić, 1994: 44).

In a democratic society, a good working relationship with the public also incorporates the right of citizens to complain about unsatisfactory police work and police misconduct. The Police Law (2000, Article 6) not only guarantees that right to the citizens, but also imposes the duty on the police to react to such complaints. The Police Law expands upon the constitutional rule concerning the personal responsibility of public officials who violate the citizens' constitutional rights in the performance of their duties (Article 20, Constitution 1990). The Police Law regulates the disciplinary proceedings and imposes disciplinary responsibility for such violations. While immediate supervisors are entrusted with the task of operational control over the conduct of their subordinates, the Ministry has established the central Internal Affairs Office within the Minister's Cabinet:

> The Internal Affairs Office was established within the Minister's Cabinet in early 1994 for professional supervision of adherence to legal provisions by police officers as well as identifying and preventing illegal behaviour and non-adherence to the police Code of Ethics. Experiences of police forces of developed countries in Western Europe were consulted when the Office was being established. The performance of the officers working in the Internal Affairs Office is defined by rules for criminal and operative tactics in accordance with special Rules of Conduct (Kuretić, 1994: 47).

Furthermore, the Ministry established the Office of Report Analysis and Development. The purpose of the office is to analyse crime reports and provide reports about crime trends. These reports are published annually. According to the Ministry (Kuretić, 1994: 43), '[a] significant part of the work of the Office is the development of reports which serve to inform the general public on the safety situation in major security areas'.

Personnel issues best illustrate the close connection between the effects of the new state, the war, and democratic changes. In particular, when the war broke out, a substantial proportion of police officers of Serb ethnicity, who constituted the majority of the Croatian police force, left their posts, thus resulting in a set of problems quite unusual and distinct from the problems faced by other police forces in countries in transition to democracy. Because of the strong overlap between ethnicity and political views, the issue of disqualification arose primarily on the basis of ethnic origin. However, while there was a substantial degree of discontinuity in personnel between the old militia and the new police, disqualification was primarily a consequence of self-selection processes, rather than a dramatic, state-imposed cleansing process.

While there was an obvious over-representation of one ethnic group before the 1990s (*Halo*, vol. 44, 1995: 5; Lajić, 1995: 60), the 'ethnic composition of the police now corresponds to the ethnic composition of the Croatian state' (Gledec, 1994: 56). The Constitutional Law on Human Rights and Freedoms and the Rights of National and Ethnic Communities or Minorities in the Republic of Croatia (1992) prescribes that the ethnic composition of the police administration on the territory with the special statute has to correspond to the national composition of the population (Article 44). This was a somewhat challenging issue in the 5% of the Croatian territory that was subsequently reintegrated peacefully because ethnic Serbs constituted the majority in a number of cities/municipalities before the war broke out. As displaced persons began returning in the mid- to late- 1990s, the demographics of the area have been changing. At the same time, groups of Croatian and Serb police officers were sent to either the International Law Enforcement Academy in Budapest or the training centre for joint patrols in Erdut. After the peaceful reintegration was completed in January 1998, law enforcement was operated by means of joint patrols.

As for gender, while the data about the percentage of women in the former militia are not available, women now constitute approximately 20% of the police force, which by far exceeds the representation of women in the police in Austria, the Netherlands, Spain, Switzerland, Turkey or the United States, but is lower than the percentage of women in the police in Finland, Norway, or Sweden (Kangaspunta *et al.*, 1999: 168).

The balancing of various ethnic groups had been related to the war: on the one hand, a substantial proportion of the old militia officers left; on the other hand, circumstances at the time required the rapid hiring of a large number of police officers to fight the war. While the recruits were officially hired as police officers, their main role at the time was to defend the country. The recruitment criteria were unofficially relaxed in the early 1990s and the new police officers received a shortened version of police training. The usual police training of high-school graduates was supposed to last for six months, followed by six months of practical training (Jurina, 1994: 75). In the conditions of imminent war, there was no time for regular police training and the Ministry developed a shortened version with an over-represented section addressing terrorism and methods of dealing with it. Over 6,000 people attended the course within the last four months of 1991 (Kutnjak Ivković, 2000: 51). Once the military activities subsided, the Ministry started requiring police officers to obtain additional education in policing, thus striving towards the goal of greater professionalism.

Some of the changes in the personnel and the material taught during the police courses have been described by Kutnjak Ivković (2000: 78):

> About 90 percent of the professors and instructors have been replaced and 'about 50 percent of the classes in this school [Police Academy] are focused on the appropriate approach of police officers toward citizens—manners, speech, writing, learning foreign languages' ... Students take courses such as sociology, philosophy, and forensic psychology ... Ethical issues are taught in various courses, and there is a separate course on ethics. The rest of the curriculum is devoted to professional courses that combine theoretical issues with practical ones. For example, conducting an arrest is taught in two courses – a course about the rules of police work and a physical education course.

One of the strongest institutions of the police socialisation process in the communist regime was the Police High School (which operated as a part of the Police Academy). It was a four-year institution characterised by a semi-military atmosphere and strict daily routine (*Halo*, vol. 46, 1995: 11). The limits imposed on the students' mobility resulted in their isolation from the society at large, frustration, and low self-esteem, all of which made the socialisation process easier for the instructors. In the 1990s, substantial changes were made in the organisation of the institution: the students were housed in dormitory-style buildings; they determined their own schedule, and could leave the dormitory as they pleased. Instead of spending four years at the Police High School, the students would have obtained the first two years of their high-school education at regular high schools, and only enrolled at the Police High School to complete the last two years of their high-school education. Recently, the Police High School was completely abolished. One of the possible reasons may be that, according to European standards, the Ministry had too many employees (a consequence of the rapid hiring in the early 1990s), and did not need to invest in a two-year education for the additional few hundred future employees.

The high turnover in personnel during a short period of time in the early 1990s had a substantial impact on the code of silence and police culture in general. There were very few officers from the old militia and it seems that the police culture had been mostly developed anew. The new legal rules – establishing the rule of law, personal accountability, and stricter supervision – should have served to curtail the code of silence. At the same time, the conditions prevailing in the larger environment could have had an opposite effect on the code of silence: because the police performed a dual role – the regular police role and the defence role – police officers grew closer, the code of silence strengthened and officers probably became more tolerant of the less serious forms of misconduct. When the author interviewed Croatian police officers as a part of a larger study on police integrity, one respondent pointed to another police officer and remarked: 'He is my buddy. During the war, he saved my life ten times over. There is *nothing* he could do that would make me report him' (Kutnjak Ivković, 1996, original emphasis).

Changes in the operational policies and work patterns of the police

The war had a severe impact on police resources through the defence role assigned to the police and the extent of devastation brought on by the war. Despite the rapid growth of the size of the police, the fact remains that, because of the war, the police had a more challenging task of performing their regular police role. Kutnjak Ivković (2000: 66) described the effects:

> Administrators from one police administration particularly affected by the war remarked that 748 police officers left this police administration; some of them are still on the front. Because of the lack of police officers, the police are not able to 'cover' the whole city. That facilitates crime rates ... In fact, the war caused specific forms of criminality to increase—property crimes, crimes of violence, and weapons smuggling. Furthermore, very few people were left to deal with prevention while the majority had to investigate already-reported crimes [...] The situation became even more challenging at the beginning of the war in Bosnia and Herzegovina in early 1992 when a few million people fled Bosnia and Herzegovina and arrived in Croatia. This, in turn, resulted in an increased number of people in need of police services. Furthermore, 'at the beginning of the war all inmates from several large prisons in Bosnia and Herzegovina were released. Many of them arrived in Croatia as refugees and were caught in criminal activities.'

An additional problem was that many of the police officers assigned to regular police work, especially investigative tasks, had very little or virtually no training and/or experience. Similarly, supervisory positions were occasionally filled with inexperienced police officers. Once the military activities subsided, the police officers provided with an opportunity to receive formal police education have already experienced a curriculum which had been changed from earlier versions.

The Ministry had emphasised the benefits of specialised training and had abolished the 'general practitioner' model. The use of the general practitioner educational model had direct implications for the operational use of police officers.

> Because they were 'general practitioners', the same police officers could deal with the duties related to public order and peace today, with the tasks related to border-crossing tomorrow, or with the tasks related to traffic safety, with the investigation of street crimes, or with the tasks related to drugs and smuggling. (Morić, 1994: 121)

The change in educational policy was designed to have an impact not only on the content of education provided to the police officers, but also the on degree of sophistication of the tasks that could be assigned to them once they return to active police work.

A related change having an effect on the operation of the police is the degree of discretion provided to each police officer. Under the old regime, police officers were waiting for the orders from the 'higher levels' and thus had a severely limited level of discretion at their disposal (Morić, 1994: 121). At the same time, the public did not hold them accountable for their conduct and their mistakes were covered up under the veil of secrecy resulting from the mystification of police work; police officers were only responsible for their work to the 'higher levels'. The legal rules now acknowledge that discretion is part of police work (Article 22, Police Law, 2000), establish rules of conduct (Constitution, 1990; Criminal Procedure Code, 1997; Police Law, 2000), and, moreover, hold police officers accountable for their decisions (Article 20, Constitution, 1990).

Use of discretion by the police officers and more detailed boundaries of appropriate police conduct are specified in various laws. The Criminal Procedure Code (1997) determines the police use of discretion when police engage in typical activities related to criminal cases, including arrests and searches. The Police Law of 2000 not only recognises the use of discretion as a part of police work (see Article 22), but also provides certain guidelines on how to exercise this discretion. Various aspects of the exercise of police authority, from the use of force and search of residences to polygraph examinations, to the collection, analyses, and use of personal data, are regulated by the Law. The use of force – the core element of the police definition – is an illustrative example.

The Police Law (2000) determines that the police are allowed to use force (Article 16) and that the level of force used should be proportionate to the reasons for its application. Seventeen articles of the Law address various types of force (from various tactics and baton use to firearms) and specify the conditions under which each of them may be used. Typically, more aggressive tactics should be used only when less aggressive ones have turned out to be ineffective or clearly could not solve the problem.

The rules are very detailed. In the case of use of firearms against people, after establishing that police officers should use the less aggressive methods first or determine that they are inapplicable, the Law lists four conditions under which a police officer could use firearms (protection of own life or lives of other people; prevention of the execution of a crime punishable with five years of imprisonment or longer; prevention of an escape by a person caught committing a crime punishable by at least ten years of imprisonment; prevention of an escape of a person with an outstanding arrest warrant for a crime punishable by at least ten years of imprisonment, or a person who escaped while serving a prison term for a crime punishable by at least ten years of imprisonment) and instructs police officers to issue the first verbal command ('Stop, the police!') and the second verbal command ('Stop or I'll shoot!') before actually using the firearms (see Article 62).

The newly adopted democratic values have a direct impact on certain other aspects of police work. For example, the focus on greater openness to the public and closer relationship with the local communities led to some changes in patrol work. A former Minister of the Interior, Ivan Jarnjak, discussed his vision of patrols with considerable enthusiasm (Lovrić, 1993: 3):

By assigning the same police officers to a particular district, we would like them to grow close to the citizens, which would be to their mutual satisfaction and benefit. For example, that would mean that a police officer would ring the bell of citizens living on his beat and wish them all the best in the New Year and for Christmas, but also on their birthday, and that the citizens will have the same approach toward their police officers. Therefore, we want to allow them to know each other, to develop a relationship of trust, and for citizens to cooperate with the police officer in the prevention of thefts, crimes, so that they can keep the public order and peace together.

As a consequence of the new focus on greater openness to the public, information related to the police budget is now available to the public. The budget is approximately US $500 million to US $700 million annually. The largest item in the budget (more than one half of the total amount) is salaries (*Halo,* vol. 53, 1996: 18). Resource allocation has been affected primarily by the war and the related consequences. Sixty percent of the equipment and 65 police stations were completely destroyed during the war (*Halo*, vol. 7, 1992: 3). Infrastructure repair and new equipment purchases will likely persist as principal budgetary items for a number of years.

The Ministry tried to address the issue of human resources as well. As discussed earlier, the Police Academy offered police courses to provide police officers with specialised education once they leave their war-related duties. To reduce the sheer number of employees (670 police officers per 100,000 citizens), the Ministry and the state tried to make the numbers more similar to the numbers of police officers in Western democracies (200–400 police officers per 100,000 citizens; see Kangaspunta *et al.*, 1999: 167). Under the policy goal of joining the European Union and the pursuit of downsizing as one of the objectives of the transition, the state initiated the restructuring of the police and the army by trying to cut inessential bureaucratic jobs. In parallel, the overall number of employees was to be reduced from over 30,000 in the police (probably including both sworn and support staff) to about 20,000 sworn personnel. In addition to generous incentives for early retirement and an informal freeze on hiring (e.g., the last generation that attended the Police High School was not hired by the Ministry), one such measure included taking away the police officer status from 3,000 police officers and either firing them for misconduct, providing alternative employment in the private security sector, or putting them at the disposal of the state government for potential employment in other ministries.

Changes in the supervision and control of the police

Numerous accountability mechanisms have been put in place as part of the larger system of control. Any citizen or organisation who perceives that their Constitutional rights or any rights protected by law have been violated by the police has the right to submit a complaint against a police officer or a police unit (Article 6, Police Law, 2000). The Law not only guarantees citizens the right to submit complaints, but also declares that trying to obstruct the submission of a complaint is against the law. If the police try to prevent citizens from submitting complaints, they could be charged criminally, based on Article 112 of the Criminal Code ('violations of rights to submit appeals and complaints'). The citizen should be notified about the outcome of the complaint within 30 days (Article 6, Police Law, 2000).

Each police officer is personally responsible for her/his own conduct and can be held accountable through the means of internal discipline (Article 110, Police Law, 2000; see also Article 20, Constitution, 1990). Violations of official rules can be divided into the less serious ones (e.g., discourteous behaviour towards citizens or police officers, inappropriate wearing of a uniform and ranks, unjustified absence from work for a day; Article 111, Police Law, 2000) and the more serious ones (e.g., leaking of information to unauthorised persons, conduct unbecoming, illegitimate use of official equipment; or two or more less serious violations within a year; Article 112, Police Law, 2000).

Most internal investigations are performed by heads of the respective police units, while the Office of Internal Affairs investigates only a small subset of all initiated cases (e.g., more complex cases, cases against police officers in the police headquarters). If there are grounds for the initiation of disciplinary proceedings, the case is forwarded to the respective supervisor or the disciplinary court for disposition. The police officer has the right to appeal the disciplinary decision. At the end of the investigation, if there is reasonable suspicion that the police officer committed a crime, the case is also forwarded to the criminal police for criminal investigation.

Table 10.1 Disciplinary proceedings initiated against police officers (1992–99)

Year	1992	1993	1994	1995	1996	1997	1998	1999
Number of POs charged with serious violations	1,666	1,988	2,040	1,847	1,279	1114	1161	1293
	72.7%	68.8%	41.6%	36.5%	35.6%	-	-	-
Number of POs charged with minor violations	625	902	2,870	3,214	2,394	N/A	N/A	N/A
	27.3%	31.2%	58.4%	63.5%	65.4%			
Total number of POs charged	2,291	2,890	4,914	5,061	3,673	N/A	N/A	N/A
	100%	100%	100%	100%	100%			

Source: Kutnjak Ivković *et al.* (2002: 65).

**Table 10.2 Outcomes of disciplinary proceedings and criminal cases
initiated against police officers (1992–99)**

Year	1992	1993	1994	1995	1996	1997	1998	1999
Public reprimand	251	401	N/A	336	62	33	N/A	N/A
	18.6%	20.0%		23.4%	6.4%	4.1%		
Fine	915	1428	1,768	983	799	703	796	880
	67.9%	71.3%	92.4%	68.5%	82.3%	87.7%	89.6%	81.9%
Dismissal	182	173	145	115	110	66	80	64
	13.5%	8.7%	7.6%	8.1%	11.3%	8.2%	9.0%	6.0%
Total discipline	1,348	2,002	1,913	1,434	971	802	888	1,074
	100%	100%	100%	100%	100%	100%	100%	100%
Criminal Cases	118	209	287	168	186	129	136	101

Source: Kutnjak Ivković *et al.* (2002: 65).

Disciplinary cases have been initiated each year against 2,000–3,500 police officers (Table 10.1) and disciplinary sanctions were imposed on 800–2,000 police officers each year. While more serious violations constituted a larger percentage of the overall number of disciplinary proceedings (over two-thirds of all alleged violations, Table 10.1) in the earlier years, their percentage decreased to less than one-half in the subsequent years. The smaller percentage of more serious charges seems to be due to the increase in the overall number of less serious charges.

The most frequent sanction given in at least two-thirds of the disciplinary cases was a fine (Table 10.2). Criminal cases were initiated against fewer than 300 police officers each year (Table 10.2). The annual fluctuations are probably also related to the war – the relaxed hiring criteria, shortened police training, weaker supervision and rule enforcement in the earlier period, and the increased number of war-related psychological problems probably all affected the actual disciplinary rates.

In terms of external control, the courts can impose the boundaries of appropriate police work. First, if in the course of investigating a crime the police violate the rules of the Criminal Procedure Code (1997), the court's decision in the related criminal case could not be based on the inappropriately collected evidence and, if it were, that fact could be used as a grounds for appeal (Articles 9 and 367). Secondly, through the application of sentences in criminal cases of police misconduct (such as bribery), the courts set and uphold standards of behaviour they are not prepared to tolerate. However, the threshold of severity of misconduct acceptable to the courts is not necessarily identical to the threshold that should or would be acceptable to the police agencies. Similarly, based on Article 127 of the Police Law (2000), the courts in civil cases participate in the larger system of external control by determining damage awards to the plaintiffs.

Police administrators are accountable to the government not only for the success in the performance of the tasks assigned to the police, but also for the proper conduct of their subordinates in the exercise of their duties. The Minister of the Interior is required to submit an annual report to the Parliament and must meet with one of the Parliamentary committees (Parliamentary Commission on Domestic Politics and National Security) more frequently (Article 7, Police Law, 2000). The Minister is also responsible for the resources allocated from the state budget to cover the Ministry's expenses.

Through the threat of a political scandal, the Minister and other administrators are also accountable to the public. Criticism of the actual state of the freedom of press in Croatia notwithstanding (Freedom House, 2000), the media play a crucial role in disseminating information and discovering cases of potential interest to the public. The Constitution establishes freedom of thought and expression, freedom of the press and other media of communication, freedom of speech and public expression, and freedom of establishment of the institutions of public communication (Article 38). For example, a recent cover-page story accusing one police administration of serious drug-related corruption, published in the magazine *Globus* at the end of 2001 (Ivanović, 2001), attracted considerable attention by the police, politicians and the public to the issue. As it turned out, the investigation that followed focused on individual cases and did not result in any extensive reforms of the police.

Problems in the reforms and changes

Democratisation of the police in Croatia is intrinsically related to events in the larger social and political environment of Croatian society, as are its successes and problems. The mere creation of the Croatian police and the actual beginning of its democratisation process both coincided with the war; as it turned out, the impact of the war has been more dominant in the early 1990s. The human and material resources that could have been devoted to the democratisation of the police were often invested in defence. The imminent war required the creation of a strong police force and left no time for a clear and concise plan of how to democratise the police. Although the right buzzwords were used by both politicians and police administrators, the conversion of these guiding principles into concrete and detailed plans and activities was left to police administrators.

Dramatic interventions into the communist-inherited legal system that would have been crucial for police work were postponed for over five years (in the case of the statute regulating police work, closer to a decade) and the police operated based on the frequently amended and changed laws originally protecting a different set of values. This state of anomie created uncertainty about the actual rules, resulted in the conflicting set of rules, and generated awkward situations. An illustrative, yet extreme, example is that of the Temporary Regulations (Kutnjak Ivković, 2002: 63):

> In 1996 the Ministry of the Interior unofficially replaced the old Yugoslav Regulations Concerning the Public Safety Service Procedures from 1983 with the Temporary Regulations. Because the Temporary Regulations of 1996 contained unconstitutional rules and regulations, they could not be published in the official gazette, nor could they serve as a legitimate source of law. At the time when the Temporary Regulations were unofficially put into effect, the old Yugoslav Regulations were not repealed, which in turn lead toward paradoxical situations. In particular, while the Temporary Regulations were used unofficially in everyday operations, court decisions concerning the validity of police officers' conduct were determined on the basis of official regulation – the old Yugoslav Regulations.

For over a decade, smuggling and corruption were tolerated practices in the Croatian society. Sačić (1998: 14) argues that, according to the experts from the European Union, the old criminal procedure legislation was woefully inadequate for the successful investigation into the dark numbers of corruption and organised crime in general. The Transparency International rankings in the Corruption Perceptions Index in the late 1990s (Transparency International Corruption Perceptions Index, 1999) suggested that corruption of public officials is indeed widespread in Croatia. Josip Kregar, then President of the Croatian Chapter of Transparency International, provided a qualitative description of the state of affairs (1999: 11):

> Corruption is widespread; it is a part of the political system and neither economy nor public services can operate without it; it is supported by cultural norms, we have no systematic defence nor institutions assigned to deal with it; there exists neither a serious standard nor a common belief in honesty [integrity] as a basis for politics, law, [and] public service institutions.

In a society that perceives corruption to be widespread, it is difficult to assume that the police are not affected. Indeed, some studies indicated that the police are considered to be among the most corrupt parts of the state system (see Derenčinović, 2000). A leap from the statement that the police frequently violate the rules for material gain to the statement that they violate the rules in general is not far-fetched. Other circumstances point in the same direction; the police culture seems to be tolerant of various forms of police corruption and use of excessive force (Kutnjak Ivković and Klockars, 2000), disciplinary and criminal cases against police officers are infrequent (see Tables 10.1 and 10.2) despite strong indicators of widespread corruption, supervision was relatively weak as a consequence of the war, and the media were controlled and journalists harassed by the government throughout the 1990s (Freedom House, 2000).

Corruption has also been associated with the leadership of the country; the late President Tudjman had to suspend 33 highly ranked members of his ruling party (the Croatian Democratic Union) because they were under investigation for embezzlement. A study by the Kroll Associates indicated that 'the Croatian programme of privatisation is infected by corruption' (Butković, 1997: 15). Despite attempts to censure the media and prosecute journalists who discovered cases of corruption at the top, it was difficult for the public at large not to note the reality. Indeed, 60% of the respondents in a study conducted by the magazine *Globus* in 1997 agreed that the Croatian government led by the Croatian Democratic Union (which subsequently lost the elections in 2000) did not have the resolve to deal with corruption at the highest levels (Butković, 1997: 15).

Furthermore, the level of confidence in the police and the government decreased over the years. While the police remained one of the three most respectable institutions in 1999, the overall level of confidence in governmental institutions has decreased substantially since 1995, as did the level of confidence in the police. The majority of the respondents (over 60%) expressed 'a great deal' or 'quite a lot' of confidence in the police in 1995; less than one-half (46%) did so in 1999 (European Values Survey, 1999). The high degree of legitimacy associated with the police in the mid-1990s was probably affected by the defence role they had performed. On the other hand, the decreased legitimacy of the police and the government in general in the late 1990s has probably been affected by the overall level of corruption and the perception that the government (and the police) were not as willing to deal with the misconduct of public servants as they were expected to.

Even after the enactment of the new Police Law of 2000, which brought crucial changes, especially in the use of discretion, a number of issues remain to be resolved. For example, the Law determines that the force has to be proportionate to the situation and requests that the less serious types of force be exhausted. As is usually the case, the interpretation of the legal standard – the 'proportionate force' – is left to police administrators, criminal and civil courts, as well as the media and the public. If police administrators are not serious about controlling incidents involving use of force, they will not be able to send the message to their police officers about the application of this legal standard in their work and police officers would be able to use excessive force without being punished for it.

Similarly, whether the circumstances of a particular case satisfy the legal standard of a lawful search or arrest is left to be determined by the courts and police administrators. The mechanisms for accountability are put in place; just as they can find a police officer guilty of a crime, the courts can determine civil damages to a citizen whose rights have been violated by the police. Also, police supervisors have legal grounds for punishing police officers who violated citizens' rights in the performance of their duties, including the arrest and search. The crucial point, however, is that it is not sufficient to put these mechanisms into place. An equally important ingredient of success is actually to use them.

Lessons from the Croatian experience

While Croatia might be perceived as yet another Eastern European country on the road towards a democratic society, its challenges and successes to date make its experience quite distinct and different. Despite the strong influence of very specific characteristics which shatter the 'one-size-fits-all' principle, a number of more general lessons can be drawn from the Croatian experience.

First, although the international community can offer attractive incentives and apply strong pressure, for example in the form of requirements for membership in international associations and unions such as the European Union, it is ultimately up to the country and its specific circumstances to decide if, when, and how it wants to comply with the pressure and utilise the incentives. The threat and expectation of the war in Croatia put defence on top of the country's priority list. The democratisation-oriented changes that did not directly correlate with the war-related efforts ended up on the back burner for at least two years. The size of the police force is an illustrative example: the number of sworn officers first increased as a consequence of the war-related activities, only to be dramatically reduced to a number that more closely corresponds to the European standards once the war-related activities subsided.

Second, the police are an integral part of a larger society and, as such, are strongly affected by the conditions in the society. The war in Croatia had an effect not only on the state of police recruitment, training, and supervision, norms of police culture, and the achievement of police accountability, but also on the availability of equipment and the size of the police budget. Similarly, societal tolerance and acceptance of corruption of public officials, including the high-ranking officials of the ruling party, creates an atmosphere in which corruption is an integral part of the political system, economy, and public services. Unless there are intense efforts of curtailing *police* corruption, the police are unlikely to be immune to it in a society in which corruption virtually becomes a way of life.

Third, the democratisation of the police typically incorporates efforts to increase openness to the public and the extent of public accountability. One way of measuring the success of becoming a more public-friendly police is through citizen surveys or public opinion polls. The Croatian example suggests that the degree of public support for the police and the improvements in the democratisation of the police are not perfectly correlated and that a number of intervening variables may have had an impact on the relation. According to public opinion polls, the level of support for the police was higher in the mid-1990s, when the effects of the war – including relaxed hiring criteria, weaker supervision, stronger code of silence, and investigations of primarily serious types of misconduct – were stronger and omnipresent.

Fourth, establishing a relatively advanced set of legal boundaries for police work and behaviour is one of the crucial, yet insufficient conditions for democratisation. The conditions in Croatia provide illustrations for both. The substantial intervention into the existing communist-inherited legal system was postponed for more than five years. One part of the legal framework involves the Croatian version of the SOP (Standard Operating Procedure) rules. While unofficially used in everyday police work, they were declared unconstitutional and officially replaced with the old Yugoslav Regulations. This mixture of, and discrepancy between, the official and unofficial rules created a state of anomie, which probably contributed towards the extent of police misconduct. Furthermore, even when the law is enacted and it actually provides adequate grounds for prosecution in cases of police corruption, an equally crucial step – the actual enforcement of the law – could be missing completely or could be substantially reduced to include only the most outrageous, disturbing or merely unlucky cases.

References

Butković, D. 1997. 'Tajni izvještaj o Hrvatskoj' (The Secret Report about Croatia). *Globus,* 29 Sep. 1997.

Constitution of the Republic of Croatia. 2000. *Narodne novine* 56/00.

Constitutional Law on Human Rights and Freedoms and Rights of National and Ethnic Communities or Minorities in the Republic of Croatia. 1992. *Narodne novine* 34/92.

Criminal Code. 1997. *Narodne novine* 110/97.

Criminal Procedure Code. 1997. *Narodne novine* 110/97.

Croatian Almanac (1997). 1998. Available at: http://hina.hr.almanah97

Derenčinović, D. 2000. 'Kaznenopravni sadržaji u suprotstavljanju korupciji' (The Criminal-Law Context in Curtailing of Corruption). Zagreb, Croatia. Unpublished doctoral dissertation.

European Values Survey. 1999. Zagreb, Croatia.

Freedom House. 2000. *Freedom in the World 1999–2000: Croatia.* 2000. Available at: http://www.freedomhouse.org/survey/2000/reports/country/croatia.html

Gledec, Z. 1994. 'The police system in the Republic of Croatia', in Šintić, J., ed. *The Functions of the Police in a Democratic Society.* Zagreb, Croatia.

Halo 92 (Vols 1–72). Monthly publication of the Croatian Ministry of the Interior.

Horvatić, Ž. 1994. 'The role of the police in a democratic society: respecting the rule of law and human rights', in Šintić, J., ed. *The Functions of the Police in a Democratic Society.* Zagreb, Croatia.

Ivanović, R. 2001. 'Korupcija u policiji?' (Corruption in the Police?). *Globus,* 14 Dec. 2001.

Jarnjak, I. 1994. 'Izvaci s tiskovne konferencije' (Excerpts from the Press Conference). *Halo 92* vol. 30.

Jurina, M. 1994. 'The Review of the System of Police Education of the Republic of Croatia', in Šintić, J., ed. *The Functions of the Police in a Democratic Society*. Zagreb, Croatia.

Kangaspunta, K., Jousten, M., Ollus, N., Nevala, S., eds. 1999. *Profiles of Criminal Justice Systems in Europe and North America 1990-1994*. Helsinki.

Kobali, D., Baloković-Krklec, K. 1995. 'Policajac XXI stoljeca' (A police officer of the 21st Century). *Halo 92* vol. 46.

Kregar, J. 1999. *Nastanak predatorskog kapitalizma i korupcija* (The Development of Predatory Capitalism and Corruption). Zagreb, Croatia.

Kuretić, Z. 1994. *Ministarstvo unutarnjih poslova* (Ministry of the Interior). Zagreb, Croatia.

Kutnjak Ivković, S. 1996. Field notes.

Kutnjak Ivković, S. 2000. 'Challenges of Policing Democracies: The Croatian Experience', in Das, D. and Marenin, O., eds. *Challenges of Policing Democracies: A World Perspective*. Newark, NJ.

Kutnjak Ivković, S. 2002. 'Opinions about the Police in Eastern and Western Europe'. Paper presented at the 39th Annual Meeting of the Academy of Criminal Justice Sciences. Anaheim, California. Mar. 2002.

Kutnjak Ivković, S. and Klockars, C.B. 2000. 'Comparing Police Supervisor and Line Officer Opinions about the Code of Silence: The Case of Croatia', in Pagon, M., ed. *Policing in Central and Eastern Europe: Ethics, Integrity, and Human Rights*. Ljubljana, Slovenia.

Kutnjak Ivković, S. and Klockars, C.B. 2003. 'Police Integrity in Croatia', in Klockars, C. B., Kutnjak Ivković, S., Haberfeld, M.R., eds. *The Contours of Police Integrity*. London.

Kutnjak Ivković, S., Klockars, C.B., Cajner-Mraović, I., Ivanušec, D. 2002. 'Controlling Police Corruption: The Croatian Perspective'. *Police Practice and Research: An International Journal*.

Lajić, I. 1995. 'Demografski razvitak Hrvatske u razdoblju of 1991 do 1994' (The Demographic Development of Croatia in the Period 1991-1994). *Revija za sociologiju*, vol. 26.

Law Concerning the Interior Affairs Agencies. 1985. *Narodne novine* 23/85.

Lovrić, J. 1993. 'Policija znači život' (The Police Means Life). *Halo 92* vol.16.

Makra, A. 1989. *Organi unutrašnjih poslova i Zakon o krivičnom postupku* (The Organs of the Interior Affairs and the Criminal Procedure Code) 2nd edn. Zagreb, Croatia.

Morić, J. 1994. 'The role of the police in a democratic society: the achievements of the Croatian Police', in Šintić, J., ed. *The Functions of the Police in a Democratic Society*. Zagreb, Croatia.

Pavišić, B., Veić, P. 1996. *Komentar Krivicnog zakona Republike Hrvatske* (Commentary to the Criminal Law of the Republic of Croatia). Zagreb, Croatia.

Piškor, M. 1993. 'Izvaci iz interviewa' (Excerpts from the Interview). *Halo 92* vol. 18.

Police Law. 2000. *Narodne novine* 129/00.

Rako, S. 1996. 'U dosluhu s najnovijim tehničkim dostignućima' (In Tune with the Most Advanced Technological Achievements). *Halo 92* vol. 61.

Rako, S. 1997. 'Izmedju jučer, danas i sutra' (Between Yesterday, Today, and Tomorrow). *Halo 92* vol. 67.

Sačić, Ž. 1998. 'Korupcija i njeno suzbijanje u svijetu i Hrvatskoj' (Corruption and Its Curtailing Across the World and in Croatia), *Policija i sigurnost,* vol. 7

Šintić, J. 1994. *The Functions of the Police in a Democratic Society.* Zagreb, Croatia.

Transparency International Corruption Perceptions Index. 1999. Available at: http://www.transparency.org/documents/index.htm#cpi

World Values Survey – Croatia. 1995. Zagreb, Croatia.

Chapter 11

Macedonia's Police Reform

Islam Yusufi[1]

Since its early years of independence, Macedonia, as one of the democratising post-communist countries of South East Europe, has been engaged in reforming its police structures. The aim of this engagement has been fourfold: (1) to create functioning, democratic and professional civilian-based police forces; (2) to develop community policing structures and capabilities; (3) to strengthen the capability of the police to respond to common and organised crime; and (4) to attain Western standards of professionalism and ethics.

This chapter lays out the scope of these efforts to reform policing and analyses the insights that they provide regarding the efficacy of policing reforms in general. The main purpose of this study is to provide an extensive but not exhaustive review of police reform in Macedonia in order to understand more clearly whether adopted reforms have engendered more democratic forms of policing. The chapter consists of three parts. The first section gives a general description of the police reforms implemented in Macedonia and divides the reforms into four different categories: decentralisation, demilitarisation, depoliticisation and democratisation. The second section assesses and analyses the reforms, obstacles encountered, successes achieved and reforms left undone. It also evaluates the challenges that face Macedonia in the area of police reform. The final section elaborates the lessons that might be learned from Macedonia's experiences.

Description of the reforms and changes in Macedonia's policing

Introduction: the overall goals and phases of police transformation
After the Second World War, Macedonia's police, together with the police structures of the other five constituent republics of former Yugoslavia, was modelled after Eastern European systems. This model, which existed for more than four

1. Islam Yusufi is International Policy Fellow at the Center for Policy Studies. He can be contacted at yusufi@policy.hu The views expressed here are those of the author and do not represent the views of the organisations for which he works. The author would like to thank Marina Caparini, Bart D'Hooge, Meredith Knepp, Otwin Marenin, Stevo Pendarovski and Neda Zdraveva who read the manuscript in its entirety and contributed helpful criticism and suggestions. The remaining errors and deficiencies must be clearly author's alone and in the end, of course, it remains author's study and his responsibility.

decades, was rather militaristic in nature since its ultimate goal was the protection and maintenance of the socialist regime. As a result, the efforts by the governments since 1991 to reform the police have taken the shape of decentralisation, demilitarisation, depoliticisation and democratisation.

Once Macedonia attained independence and initiated democratic processes in 1990 and 1991, the new Parliament and Government coming out of the first multi-party elections started the work necessary to establish new democratic institutions, including the police. This first phase of reforms in the policing area encompassed the following fields:

(1)   Transforming the police from being a part of the police system of the Yugoslav Federation into an independent police structure of the new Republic.

(2)   Organising and structuring the police at national and local levels.

(3)   Setting up the necessary legal framework for the police.

(4)   Transforming the police from a *milicia*, a military-based institution, to a *policia*, an institution for the enforcement of law.

The main objectives of these initial reforms were directed towards creating functioning police structures at both the central and local levels as well as developing professional, civilian-based law enforcement institutions.

The second phase, which lasted from 1992 to 2001, included reforms relating to issues of police structure, organisation and professionalism. The goals of this phase were to create and strengthen the ability of the police to respond to new criminal justice issues, to establish cooperative structures with international counterparts, and to reach Western standards of professionalism and ethics.

The third phase of policing reforms began with the armed conflict between the security forces of Macedonia and irregular units of the so-called National Liberation Army of Albanians in Macedonia that broke out in early 2001, and which introduced disorder and the absence of security into certain parts of the country. The conflict continued until 13 August 2001, when the country's main political leaders signed the Ohrid Framework Agreement. With the Agreement, the government of Macedonia undertook major reforms in the police force. The objectives of the police reforms encompassed in this phase are far more profound, complex and institutionalised as compared to the previous phases of police reforms. The goal was to transform the police from a central structure into a decentralised and civil institution at the service of all the communities in which it operates.

Demilitarisation: the transformation of the police from a milicia to the policia

With its declaration of independence in 1991, Macedonia started to transform its police institutions both organisationally and functionally, but within the context of the existing laws of the former Yugoslavia. Since the new law on internal affairs was not adopted until 1995, the police institutions functioned according to the existing law on internal affairs of the former Yugoslavia.

With the initial reforms in the years immediately following the declaration of independence in 1991, the police eliminated some of the unnecessary structures from the former regime; created new sectors, units and branches; transformed the *milicia* into the *policia*; and transformed the Secretariat for Internal Affairs, formerly part of the federal police of the SFRY (Socialist Federal Republic of Yugoslavia), into the Ministry of Interior (MOI) of the independent republic.

The internal structure of police forces in Macedonia traditionally has been based on a military organisational model and has been closed to any outside influence except the dominant influence of the party. Yet, while the name *milicia* was relinquished very quickly after independence, the concept of *milicia* continued to prevail in the police structures, particularly since the system of rank continued to resemble the hierarchical structure of an army.

The education of police officers is one of the areas that have most influenced the demilitarisation of the police. The Centre for the Education of Personnel in the Field of Security in Skopje, the capital of Macedonia, had a major role to play in the recruitment, education and training of the personnel in Ministry of the Interior. The Centre included both a high school as well as a Faculty of Higher Education on Security. The Centre is the continuation of the Centre for the Education of Personnel for Security and Social Self-Defence established in 1977 in the then Socialist Republic of Macedonia (*Official Gazette*, 30: 1977; 29: 1983; 34: 1983; 36: 1988).

According to the Law for the Establishment of the Centre for the Education of Personnel in the Field of Security, adopted on 26 May 1995, the Centre has the duty to prepare personnel with university level or the highest professional education required to meet the needs of the departments within the Ministry of the Interior and of law enforcement agencies, as well as other departments, organisations and communities (Stojanov, 1998: 7).

The aim of the Centre is to provide quality training that meets the needs of Ministry of Interior and society so that officers are equipped to provide effective and impartial police service to all the citizens of Macedonia. Before independence, the contentious issue with regard to the Centre was the rationality and usefulness of having a special faculty for security. In May 1990, the *Sobranie* (Parliament) evaluated the option of transforming the Faculty for Security into the Faculty of Criminology or into an eventual Institute for Criminological Investigation. In March 1993, the Minister of Interior informed the Centre about the government's decision to abolish the Faculty for Security by 2002. This decision of the government was integrated into a draft Law for the Establishment of the Centre for the Education of Personnel in the Field of Security in 1995. However, the Centre will continue to function as a training centre for police.

Educational institutions for the police play a major role in expanding its role and in improving its effectiveness and accountability. Although observers consider that police education in Macedonia is often better and more extensive than that provided elsewhere in the Balkans, there are some important aspects that necessitate changes or improvements. Human rights and police ethics are not taught as primary subjects at the Centre and as a result students remain ignorant of relevant standards and provisions, both national and international. The core themes according to which education should be restructured include: human rights; Macedonia's society and diversity; professional standards and ethics; and problem-solving (Open Society Institute-Macedonia, 2000, 5–6); communication and public relations; and modalities for forging partnerships with communities (author's interview with OSCE (Organisation for Security and Cooperation in Europe) officials).

Another important aspect that has influenced the process of demilitarisation of the police is the large role other various other ministries have played in police reform. Civilian ministries especially have helped to move policing towards a more civilianised approach. Among them:

(1)   The Ministry of Local Government has assisted by clarifying the competencies and authority of those local governments that tend to co-operate most with local police.

(2)   The Ministry of Justice has contributed to police reforms through continuous adjustments to the Penal and Procedural Code in the light of the reforming processes in the police.

(3)   The Ministry of Defence is another important partner of the police. A major issue addressed jointly by the two departments was to reach a common understanding of the needed regulatory framework that would enable the involvement of the military in the fight against illegal trafficking of immigrants and smuggling of illicit arms.

(4)   The Ministry of Transportation has sponsored secondary legislation aimed at facilitating the implementation of the provisions of the Traffic Code, which has urged the modernisation of the road infrastructure as well as a definition of needed co-operative procedures with the traffic police of the Ministry of the Interior.

(5)   The Ministry of Labour and Social Affairs has had a role in the preparation and implementation of employment programmes, in order to fight the social trend of resorting to crime as a means to make a living. The Ministry of Labour has made efforts to better motivate the police to maintain public order and security by addressing issues such as salaries.

The Ohrid Framework Agreement of August 2001, signed by the main political leaders of the country to end the six-month-long armed conflict in the north-western parts of the country, has also been one of the engines for the demilitarisation of the police as it advocated the fundamental restructuring of Macedonia's police. One of the most important issues included in the Framework Agreement was to invite the OSCE, the European Union, and the United States to increase training and assistance programmes for police, including professional, human rights and other training; technical assistance for police reform in areas such as screening, selection and promotion processes; the development of a code of conduct for police; and planning for the hiring and deployment of police officers (*Ramkoven Dogovor*, 2001).

Reforming the police from a centralised to a decentralised institution

In its reforms that followed independence, Macedonia did not implement decentralisation as was introduced after 1967 in former Yugoslavia, nor did it follow the common European trend of decentralising the police and empowering the local governments in police issues. In 1991 all organisational and functional features of the police remained centralised and the municipalities were not given any authority in respect to the police departments. With the Law of Internal Affairs adopted in 1995 this centralisation was formally legalised and the police, both territorially and in terms of functionally specialised units, retained a centralised structure with police functions concentrated within the competencies of the Minister of Interior. At the district level, police branches were established with an organisational structure similar to that of the central police organisation. During this period, the police were under the influence of the fragile multi-ethnic coalitions and a weak judiciary. As a result, human rights violations committed by the police went unaddressed.

Centralising control of policing within the headquarters of the Ministry of the Interior separated the police from the community that it was supposed to serve and increased its politicisation, since the Minister had authority to appoint or dismiss the heads of the local police branches. Local elected municipalities had no power over the functioning of the police within the communities. This centralisation had negative effects on the struggle of the police against crime; the number of solved cases was only a small percentage of the number of crimes reported.

One of the important changes implemented by the Framework Agreement was the decentralisation of policing. A significant issue included in the Agreement was the appointment of local police chiefs; local elected municipalities were given the authority to appoint the heads of local police branches. Local police chiefs would be nominated by Macedonia's interior minister and approved by municipal councils.

This provision of the Framework Agreement has been integrated into the law on internal affairs; however its practical effects remain to be seen. At the time of writing (early 2003), local police chiefs were not yet being appointed in accordance with the new provisions. However, one can be certain that this change will encourage further decentralisation, will increase local self-governments' authority over police chiefs, and will strengthen the ability of the police to adopt community policing.

Despite the optimism that the decentralisation process has engendered, it also remains to be seen how decentralisation and overall policing reforms will affect the ability of the police to fight crime, particularly because Macedonia's crime rate since independence has been on the rise. In addition to the existence of common crime, economic crime and the illicit trafficking of drugs, arms and human beings have also been present. New sophisticated forms of crimes, some involving organised criminal groups, have also been witnessed.

According to statistical data, during the period 1992–2002, there were 238,274 registered criminal acts in the area of the common, economic and organised crime and the illicit trafficking of arms, people and drugs. In Macedonia, organised crime represents a relatively new phenomenon. Macedonia does not have much tradition and experience in regard to fighting organised crime. Yet, due to its specific geostrategic position, transnational criminal actors and organised crime syndicates represent a serious threat to peace and order in Macedonia.

In the reform agenda of the police, great emphasis has been placed on strengthening basic skills such as improving response time, crime-scene preservation, identifying and interviewing witnesses, and obtaining and safeguarding physical evidence; all of these skills have been poorly absorbed and rarely applied. The Interior Ministry in the course of years has directed its attention towards the identification of and combating all kinds of crimes, with special attention to crime prevention. The Interior Ministry has also pushed for legislative reforms, including the creation of a National Programme for Combating Human Trafficking and Illicit Migration. In addition, the MOI has inserted a definition of the criminal act of 'human trafficking' into the Law for Change and Completing the Criminal Code in 1997 to fight against human trafficking.

Regarding the prevention of illegal financial transactions, a significant step has been taken with the adoption of the Law for the Prevention of Money Laundering in September 2001. With this Law, the Directorate for the Prevention of Money Laundering has been established as a part of the Ministry of Finance (author's interview with Ministry of Finance officials). The adoption of the new Criminal Act in 1996 was also a significant step as it included special provisions on definitions of different types of crimes, including those of an economic nature; previously, many economic crimes had gone unpunished.

In the fight against corruption, the Ministry of the Interior has actively participated in the preparations for the adoption of the Law on Anti-Corruption of April 2002. On the basis of a ministry proposal, the Macedonian government decided to establish the Agency for Combating Organised Crime and Corruption. Later, the government launched the National Programme for Combating Organised Crime and Corruption (author's interview with MOI officials).

The Ministry of the Interior in 2001 became a party to the UN Convention Against Transnational Organised Crime and its protocols for prevention of the illicit trafficking and trade in human beings. Apart from this, the Ministry in 2001 also established the Financial Police for the Prevention and Control of Economic and Financial Crime (author's interview with MOI officials). Moreover, the Ministry of the Interior established a Sector for Forensics. The Sector participates in the conducting of the investigation on the spot of the event, during which it finds and secures materials and other relevant facts; makes laboratorial examinations and analyses; conducts identification of persons and materials involved in crimes; and creates photo and video documentation (author's interview with MOI officials).

With the adoption of the Criminal Code in 1996, the system of statistical monitoring of criminal acts was established for the field of organised crime, which previously had been categorised with other fields of criminality. Since then, organised crime has been a distinct field of statistical collection and analysis. According to these statistics, in the period from 1997 to 2002, a total of 970 organised crime acts were registered. The majority of these acts entailed counterfeiting, corruption, and the illicit trafficking of drugs (author's interview with MOI officials).

With regard to human trafficking, in March 2001 the Transit Centre for Foreigners was established within the framework of the Department for Asylum and Immigration of the Ministry of the Interior, with the aim to secure accommodation for foreigners and victims of the human trafficking until procedures for their repatriation to their home countries have been completed. The Centre has contributed to the more effective and fundamental engagement of the authorised agencies of MOI in the war against human trafficking. The continued problems with law enforcement in Macedonia and the region, where criminal groups have established smuggling routes through virtually uncontrolled areas, have turned Macedonia into both a transit and a destination country for human trafficking and trade in illegal substances. The seriously weakened police and security forces have found it difficult to cope with the rapidly rising levels of this type of criminal activity.

These actions taken in the legislative, executive, administrative and operational fields have not produced the expected results in the fight against crime, largely because the Macedonian police has lacked the community policing capabilities and it has had a limited ability to prevent the criminal acts. The police have been unable to conduct adequate investigations in the majority of common crimes, and have also shown an inability to investigate high profile and politically sensitive cases. The crucial sources of this inability have been the lack of the decentralisation of the police and the absence of community policing features that would give Macedonian police the ability to communicate more effectively with local communities in order to discover the perpetrators of the criminal acts.

However, with the Ohrid Framework Agreement, the process of decentralisation and the development of accountable and professional self-government at local and regional level have gained momentum. This constitutes a major step forward in bringing government closer to citizens and thus reducing the still prevalent public distrust of the state. Giving citizens a sense of ownership of their local institutions and empowering them, through local governance, to manage key issues relating to public security and the police is a major condition for the democratic system of governance to take root in Macedonia. In addition to the development of decentralisation, the development of effective governance practices is also required. Broad participatory approaches to policy formulation need to be built, tapping the potential of emerging civil society organisations.

Accountability of the police and its depoliticisation or de-particisation

Another important issue is the question of the depoliticisation of the police. It is well understood that the police in a democratic society are not allowed to act in favour of one or another political interest in the society (Stojanovski, 1997: 89). The police must remain neutral, which is necessary in order to secure its political autonomy and to underline its obligation to act within its legal framework.

Macedonia emerged from a long period of socialist rule in the early 1990s. Since then the country has made progress towards the creation of a democratic system of governance. The progress made to date is even more notable if one takes into account the specific characteristic of the previous regime. Such regimes destroy the capacity not only of civil society but also of the state institutions themselves, which become mere instruments in the hands of the ruling elites.

The challenge for Macedonia's police is to support the creation of a system of governance that promotes, supports and sustains law and order. Governance can be seen as the exercise of economic, political and administrative authority to manage the affairs of the police at all levels. Governance comprises the mechanisms, processes and institutions through which police and citizens articulate their interests, exercise their legal rights, meet their obligations and mediate their differences.

In all three reform cycles, Macedonia has made progress towards the creation of a system of governance for the depoliticisation of the police. Accountability mechanisms are the means that prevent the police from becoming a politicised institution (Labovik, 1999: 40) and they hold the police accountable to the community that they serve as well. One of the key priority areas identified in the overall reform of police is the development of better accountability and internal police control, mechanisms that provide supervision through police investigations of public complaints against the police.

Macedonian law envisages a number of ways that law enforcement officials may be held accountable for their actions.

(1)   There is parliamentary supervision of the work of the police by standing and ad-hoc parliamentary commissions and committees, including the Commission for Internal Affairs and Defence, which scrutinises the activity of police. However, legislative supervision of the police does not function sufficiently. Although the Commission has received reports on a regular basis from the Ministry of the Interior, its work depends very much on the attitude of the Members of Parliament who sit on the Commission and who tend not to act impartially. Members avoid criticising the interior ministry, which may be headed by somebody from the same party.

There have been cases where the Commission has requested the interior minister to testify before the Commission. However, the minister either has not appeared without providing any explanation or has branded the call for him to appear before the Commission a politically motivated action by the opposition.

The Sobranie (Parliament) can also vote to form a special commission to investigate allegations of police misconduct. According to Article 76 of the Macedonian Constitution, such bodies may be established, 'to ascertain the responsibility of holders of public office'. The government is obliged to take action as recommended by the commission if a simple majority in parliament approves the investigative report. Such commissions have been set up to investigate police behaviour on numerous occasions. However, none of these commissions has resulted in any legal or disciplinary action against police officers.

(2)   Citizens may appeal to the office of the Ombudsman. As an external supervision organisation created in 1997 (*Official Gazette* 7:1997), the Ombudsman can be considered an external and independent complaints authority that has the power to require information from police. However, the Ombudsman's office, until

recent changes adopted in the Law on Ombudsman (*Official Gazette* 60:2003), did not have any authority to oversee any internal police investigation being undertaken and to intervene or require a complaint to be re-investigated.

(3)   There is the Legal Department within the Ministry of the Interior that investigates reports of police abuse and recommends to the Minister disciplinary action concerning members of the police.

(4)   Citizens may bring civil or criminal charges against law enforcement officials in court.

(5)   Police officers are accountable through their senior officers to elected representatives of the community who may tell them, on behalf of their communities, what they would wish the police to do and question their mode of operation as well as their effectiveness and efficiency.

(6)   There is public accountability through NGOs and the media that may be particularly persistent in bringing to public attention cases of police abuse, corruption, and wrongful convictions.

(7)   There is professional accountability by a Police Code of Ethics adopted in early 1990s. However, the text of the Code is very vague and it does not include all the aspects of police functions and responsibilities. The Ministry of the Interior, in consultation with the OSCE and the Council of Europe, plans to redraft the text and include provisions with regard to the sanctions that can be imposed on those police officers who are in violation of the Code (author's interview with OSCE officials).

(8)   Lastly, there is also performance accountability, namely an examination conducted by the police Inspectorate of the effectiveness and efficiency of the police. This links the police to financial accountability. Because they operate on public funds, police should be accountable for how they spend it and their expenditures may be independently and publicly examined and audited.

Despite these many options, very few police officers have been held legally responsible for violating the law. The major problem is that victims of police abuse in Macedonia generally are reluctant to report a violation, due to their low trust in the police and the judicial system (Helsinki Committee, 2001). Very often, those police officers who have been found to have engaged in misconduct have been suspended from work for couple of months, but are then reinstated in their previous positions, as the judiciary often does not take any action to hold members of police responsible for their acts. The public prosecution office or the judiciary can also seek to control the police when a member of the police has committed a criminal offence.

Another aspect of accountability is regular public access to police data, such as crime statistics, victimisation surveys, police activity reports at the local and national levels, data from internal disciplinary mechanisms, and so on. Macedonia has undertaken to design a unified crime reporting form for use in all police stations to enable consistent data collection and stations have been developing systems for reporting data to national police headquarters. However, this information is not disclosed to the media and to the wider public. Information is sent only to the relevant governmental institutions. However, to ensure greater transparency, these data should be made available to the Parliament, the press, civil society, academics and private individuals. This would ensure adequate external supervision of policing, strengthen judicial and parliamentary supervision, and create new forms of civilian supervision.

The process of institution and capacity building in Macedonia has not, however, been without serious setbacks. The inability of the emerging state institutions to deal with the problems which emerged during the transition discredited the new institutions, which were created and fuelled the still existing distrust of the state by citizens. This has weakened the ability of the police to play an effective role in providing security to citizens. Furthermore, poor economic development and few opportunities for economic integration with European countries hampered the development of the police reforms. The crisis of 2001 stretched the capacities of the police institutions to the limit and exposed again the fundamental weaknesses in the system of police.

Democratisation, multi-ethnicity and cooperation with foreign governments and international organisations

Following the initial organisational and structural reforms in early 1990s, the first Law on Internal Affairs, adopted in 1995, gave the police a new definition to fit its role in a democratic country. This was the first legislative step in the democratisation of the police.

Article 1 of the Law on Internal Affairs defined the role of the police. According to the Law, the police have the following authority and obligations:

1. Protection of life, personal security and protection of citizens' property.

2. Crime Prevention, detection and seizure of perpetrators and their handing over to competent bodies.

3. Protection of human rights and freedoms of citizens guaranteed by the Constitution.

4. Prevention of foreceful destruction of democratic institutions established by the Constitution of Macedonia.

5. Maintenance of public order and peace.

6. Prevention of exciting national, racial and religious hatred and intolerance.

7. Securing VIP persons and buildings.

8. Regulating and controlling traffic on roads and other matters related to traffic safety on roads.

9. Control of national border crossings, movements and staying within border areas.

10. Residence and movement of foreigners.

11. Resolving border incidents and other violations of national borders.

12. Placing, controlling and maintaining the insignia that mark the border areas on land and on water.

13. Protection from fire and explosives.

14. Controlling the conditions related to manufacturing, sale, supply, possession and carrying arms, parts of arms and ammunition.

15. Manufacturing, sale, storage, shipment and protection from explosive and other dangerous substances and storage and protection from flammable liquids and gases.

16. Control over the registration of residence and dwellings of citizens.

17. Providing assistance to eliminate consequences caused by natural disasters and epidemics that could threaten the life and health of citizens or their property.

18. Research and development within the field of its competence.

19. Other matters stipulated by the law.

Another issue with regard to the democratisation of the police in Macedonia has been the adequate representation of the Albanian, Turkish and other minority groups in the police. One of the deficiencies of the police in Macedonia has been its lack of minority and women police officers within its organisation. Over the years, a growing number of minority and women police officers have been recruited into the police, however, they have not corresponded to the composition of the minority ethnic groups and women in the overall population of the country.

During the implementation of the Framework Agreement, police reforms, to a great extent, have sought to close this gap in the representation of the minority groups in police. The parties to the Framework Agreement committed themselves to the goal that the police services by 2004 would generally reflect the composition and distribution of the population of Macedonia. Under the agreement, one thousand minority police officers are to be employed by July 2003 and deployed in the regions that are populated by a considerable number of members of minority groups. By July 2003 a total of 1262 minority police officers have been trained. The effectiveness of this project has been highlighted by the successful redeployment of the police in former crisis areas, which has already been completed. In principle, the inclusion of the minority members in the police structures was the proper action for increasing the legitimacy of the police and for better police–community relations.

International cooperation is seen by the Ministry of the Interior as another means for democratising the police. In the years following the independence of the country, the international cooperation efforts of the Ministry of the Interior have been significantly extended and intensified. This activity has been an expression of the broader determination of ministry to strengthen overall international cooperation and its firm resolve for the fast and full integration into international and transnational policing structures. These efforts also reflected the need for more involvement by the Ministry of the Interior in international cooperation in efforts for preventing and fight combating crime, particularly organised crime.

International cooperation has been evident at all levels: membership in international police organisations; bilateral agreements and meetings with the interior ministries of other states; agreements and meetings with specialised international organisations and their functional units; contacts and meetings with diplomatic representatives; and participation in the seminars, courses, training and other forms of the education organised in the country and abroad in cooperation with foreign governments, international organisations, and foreign police organisations and agencies.

In 1995, the Ministry of the Interior became the 174th member of the International Organisation for Criminal Police (Interpol). In the period 1992–98, agreements for cooperation were signed with the ministries of interior of Turkey, Albania, Bulgaria, the Russian Federation and Romania and there have been initiatives for cooperation agreements with ministries of other countries.

With regard to the exchange of information in the areas of illicit trafficking in arms, drugs and human beings, common and economic criminality as well as for other forms of crime, the Ministry of the Interior has established intensive contacts with specialised units of foreign police agencies. In this regard, in the period from 1998 to 2002, the Ministry of the Interior has established direct contacts and mutual cooperation with the ministries of the neighbouring countries and other Balkan and European countries, including Bulgaria, Albania, Greece, Slovenia, Croatia, Serbia-Montenegro, Hungary, Austria, Germany, Switzerland, France, Great Britain, Russian Federation, Ukraine, USA, Canada, and others (author's interview with MOI officials).

Besides these activities, the Ministry of the Interior in cooperation with international organisations and NGOs such as the Council of Europe and the Open Society Institute, has published brochures, such as 'The Police and Human Rights', to assist the professional development of the police in the field of human rights that would be of great help in the fulfilment of the democratic functions of the police.

The heavy involvement of the international community following the signing of the Framework Agreement in August 2001 has also enabled the relatively quick transfer of Western experiences in the area of police reform; as a result, international influence on the Macedonian police became substantial. The already established legal and structural framework of the police and the presence of multinational missions such as that of the OSCE, the EU, NATO and the Council of Europe, whose missions in Macedonia have had the mandate to work for the transformation of law enforcement agencies, have constituted a sound basis for further reforms in the police. Today, the international presence continues to exert influence on overcoming possible resistance to reforms, due to the enormous resources invested by them and their extensive monitoring presence. Memberships and activities in various professional international associations and institutions by the Macedonian police have also offered important avenues for the acquisition of skills and exchange of information.

Regardless of the difficult conditions under which the process of democratisation has taken shape, especially in the period between 1991 and 2002, Macedonia is now well on its way to establish a democratic system of governance. A year after the 2001 crisis, state institutions appear to have stabilised, opening the possibility to engage more actively in capacity building and rebuilding trust between police and society. Eventually, this should result in the professionalisation of the police and the development of participatory methods of governance at all levels, which over time will hopefully lead to 'good governance' of the police in Macedonia.

Assessment of the reforms and current challenges

All of the reforms achieved so far have contributed to the gradual transformation of Macedonia's police into an agency that is defending human rights and fundamental freedoms despite the deficiencies that still exist in all fields of the police reforms.

In general, it should be stressed that the police reforms, despite the ways in which they were implemented and the objectives they accomplished, had their own importance in the difficult period Macedonian society and institutions of law enforcement have been facing during the transition period.

In the field of depoliticisation of the police, there was a slowing pace of reform. In this field, what compromised the process of depoliticisation was the continuous identification of depoliticisation with simple personnel removal and changes of structures, even where this was done based on personal desires and interests, or political interference. The low standards of recruitment transformed the police into a politicised force, without its own legitimacy and unable to face the challenges of law enforcement in a pluralist society.

With regard to the demilitarisation, there was lack of a clear strategy. Also, other factors, such as maintaining the police as a military structure, low standards of professional qualification, and preservation of the old (socialist) military style of policing, all exacerbated problems in the attempted reforms aimed at civilianising the police.

Democratisation together with the decentralisation of the police following the Framework Agreement has been a landmark change in the direction of the development of the community policing in Macedonia. It is too early to evaluate the results and the implications of these reforms. However, one thing is certain and it is that these reforms are far more profound than other reforms as they are set to transform the police from a central structure into a civil institution at the service of the community.

These changes, although a good starting point, did not exert any serious impact on controlling crime and other serious violations of public order because of the instability of the country and the fragility of police structures. Other negative factors were the general economic, social and political crises experienced by Macedonian society. As a result, the police of Macedonia continue to face significant problems that plague efforts to develop democratic forms of policing. These problems include:

(1)Inefficiency: According to official statistics, the percentage of solved cases is very high. However, independent figures show that the percentage of the solved cases is in fact low. The belief that the police would not be able to do something has

caused people not to report offences (Shurbanovski, 2001: 26). The Ministry of the Interior is also over-staffed, both in terms of police officers and civilian staff. There is also, as mentioned above, insufficient representation of minority groups and women in the police. The absence of sufficient minority and female officers continues to impair the efficiency of police forces.

(2)Politicisation: The political parties composing the governmental coalitions compete to reinforce their own positions within the police. Also, the coalition parties continue to directly interfere in the designation of the most important functionaries.

(3)Inter-agency cooperation: One of the major problems encountered in countering the obstacles in police reforms in Macedonia is unregulated inter-agency cooperation and slow bureaucratic procedures that pose a significant obstacle in the investigations, and which compromise the quality of the treatment and resolution of the cases (Taseva, 2002: 118).

(4)Lack of democratic policing culture: There is a lack of discipline and a lack of democratic culture among the police. The most serious form of police abuse is excessive violence inflicted on individuals, either during the arrest or while in detention.

(5)Judicial reform: An immediate problem that has been encountered in police reforms is the slow pace or lack of judicial reform, even as police reforms advance rapidly. It is now clearly recognised that police reform requires parallel judicial reform and that it is frequently hampered, even endangered, by the slow pace or lack of political transformation.

(6)Lack of support for reform: There is a low level of bureaucratic, political and public confidence in police reforms. This in part consists of resistance of high-ranking personnel, who fear losing their positions and privileges. They are especially against the reforms that include more minority and women representation in the police and the reforms that are directed towards more openness in the policing activities. Another form of the opposition comes from political, military and economic sectors with vested interests in the old and new security arrangements by acting against more professionalism in the police, as they feel threatened by the professional and functioning police. The public tends to be against reforms as they see the reforms as a continuation of the 'politics' by other means, in which society will not have any benefit.

(7)Corruption: The endemic corruption among the relatively high levels of police institution and the low level of financial incentives to the personnel has jeopardised the intentions and objectives of the reform, has slowed the pace of change and has reduced the motivation for change.

(8)Inexperience in reform: Another issue is the absence of national expertise on the issue of police reforms. Civil society, in the form of independent experts, NGOs, think tanks, universities and other structures, play a negligible role in police reforms in Macedonia as they lack the capacity to contribute specialised expertise to support serious reform. State institutions remain closed to outside advice. The Ministry of the Interior itself lacks the specialised staff that will help in transforming the police.

As discussed above, much yet needs to be achieved. It is imperative that this reform process develop in a holistic and efficient manner, so that the police may develop in the direction of responsiveness, representation and greater professionalism and thereby provide a thoroughly modern, effective and democratic police service. The challenge for the police as well as the public administration of Macedonia as a whole is to create a system of governance that promotes, supports and sustains law and order while respecting the basic rights and freedoms of citizens.

Following the long period of reform, state institutions appear to have stabilised, opening the possibility to engage more actively in capacity building and rebuilding trust between police and society. Eventually, this should result in the professionalisation of police and the development of participatory methods of governance at all levels, which over time will lead to the creation of good governance practices in policing.

Conclusion: insights that police reforms in Macedonia suggest

Important improvements have been made in Macedonia in the promotion of the democratic forms of the policing that suggest various insights and lessons to the other countries engaged in the transformation of the policing structures. In Macedonia and in other Central and Eastern European countries, policing problems are among the most serious problems. The only feasible police reform strategy is reform of the state, and substituting this goal by any special police reform measures is strategically unjustified. The real question Macedonia and other transitional countries of Central and Eastern Europe are confronted with is whether a given government will be guided by the logic of the fight against police problems or by the logic of general democratic and institutional reforms (Krastev, 1997: 7). Police reforms guided by overall and general public administration reforms, would serve to a great extent to further the overall goals of police reforms and institute a sound basis for sustainable democratic and civil reforms in this area.

There is a general impression, due to the failure of the police to find the perpetrators of the criminal acts, that the present police structure is not able effectively to fulfil its obligations (Stojanovski, 1997: 12). It is imperative that the police reforms be guided by the existing problems that a given society faces. If a society is facing increasing rates of organised crime, police reforms should be directed towards the restructuring of the police in a way that that will best enable it to address the problems and needs of that particular phenomenon. The challenge of police reform is to recast the activities, organisation, management and deployment of resources according to the nature of specific crime problems.

The transformation of police means organisational, administrative, functional, cultural and operational change in the development of the democratic forms of the policing. These processes are ongoing and they should be shaped in accordance with the changes and developments in the society.

New forms of criminality are increasingly sophisticated, posing an ever greater challenge to the police. This is underlined when we talk about a transitional society, which has not yet stabilised the institutions of the system, thus there is a threat that the state itself could be a part of the criminal activities. Therefore, the imperative is to increase the strength of the public institutions in order to better come to terms to the demands of the citizens. This can best be achieved through community involvement in the work of police, and through organising local partnerships between citizens and police. Police organisation is most effective and most easily fulfils its functions when it has the sympathies of the public and when it cooperates with the wider public. It is necessary that the organs of the Ministry of Interior become instruments for democratic development of the society. Only in that way, can the police become a model and inspire confidence, because only then will people cooperate with it and seek it for support and assistance.

For many years the police in Macedonia has functioned as a central organisation due to the general central functioning of overall public administration in the country. If there are greater benefits from having centralised policing structures in a particular context, then they should remain centralised. However, if it is decided that decentralisation will best serve Macedonia's public security needs, this cannot be achieved unless there is overall decentralisation of the public administration. The solution to the centralisation problem depends on the solution in the whole organisational set up in the public administration. As already stated, the Framework Agreement introduced some elements of decentralisation. These changes are vital because changing the police culture requires authority and decision-making to be delegated to much lower levels in the organisation and the police have to become more open and responsive in their dealings with the public.

The militarised appearance of the police for many years has negatively affected recruitment and appointment practices. The principles of a meritocracy and professionalism have been combined with militant attitudes and nepotism, as there were nominations in leading positions of the police institution of persons with elementary, secondary or non-completed education. In other cases there were replacements of capable specialists by inappropriate candidates from the professional and moral point of view. Many appointments to managerial positions were made directly from the party offices of coalition partners and the same has applied to dismissals.

The public creates its image of police based not only on the police's general functions, but also on its concrete actions and behaviour in its dealings with citizens. Every individual's image of the police is based on personal experience and his or her contacts with the police. Thus, the dominant focus of the reforms should be on the human and community relations of the police. Only in this way will citizens trust in cooperating with the police to help resolve conflicts in the community. However, it is the obligation of the police and not of the citizens to initiate this cooperation. The police exist because of the people. One of the measures to create confidence is enabling the various citizen groups to visit police stations, offices and laboratories. The police have always a good story to tell. Policing is always of interest to the public and it is in the best interest of the police to convey an accurate picture to the public of what they must contend with both nationally and locally.

The control by appropriate parliamentary bodies, which already exists, should become regular and efficient. At the same time, new independent civil society institutions of external control and supervision should be introduced without delay as it has been proven that Ombudsman is not enough. Setting up of a particular unit within the Interior Ministry for community policing should substantially reinforce the internal control.

The problems associated with a police officer cannot be addressed adequately without focusing on the problems of overall police agency (Swope, 2001). Police misconduct to a great extent is affected by the misbehaviour tolerated or encouraged by the given police agency. For instance, corruption cannot exist without at least implicit acceptance by the police organisation.

Finally, police reforms cannot yield the desired effects without necessary reforms in the economic and social conditions of a given society. For a police reform to be successful, medical care, local economy, unemployment, income, education, presence of minorities, households headed by single women, household size, home ownership and other social and economic factors should be taken into consideration (Silverman, 2001). Other factors such as graffiti, illegal social clubs, drug-dealers, prostitutes, car window washers, noise and begging, do not attract the attention of reformers in the initial period of reforms; however, if not included in the reform agenda, these factors become contributors to the criminality and disorder and also provide conditions which breed further community decline and more serious crime.

References

Helsinki Committee for Human Rights in Macedonia. 2001. 'Godisen Izvestaj za 2001 godina'. Available at Helsinki Committee for Human Rights in Macedonia website: http://www.mhc.org.mk/mkd/izveshtai/2001gi.htm

Krastev, I. 1997. 'Anticorruption Rhetoric and Reform Policies'. Available at http://www.cls-sofia.org/publications/papers/anticorruption_rhetoric_and_reform_policies.pdf

Labovik, M. 1999. *Depolitizacija i(li) Departizacija na Drzhavnata Uprava vo Republika Makedonija.* Skopje.

Official Gazette of the Republic of Macedonia: volumes 30:1977; 29:1983; 34:1983; 36:1988; 27:1995; 7:1997; 60:2003

Open Society Institute-Macedonia, COLPI, ODIHR. Apr. 2000. *Izvestaj od Misijata za Procenka na Potrebite za Reforma na Policijata vo Republika Makedonija*. Skopje.

Ramkoven Dogovor (Framework Agreement). Annex C. Aug. 2001. Available at Macedonian President's website:
   http://www.president.gov.mk/mak/info/dogovor.htm

Shurbanovski, N. 2001. 'Snemozhuvanje na policijata'. *Annual Edition of the School of Security*. Skopje.

Silverman, E. 2001. Innovative Policing. *International Criminal Police Review, 486*. Available at Interpol website:
   http://www.interpol.int/Public/Publications/ICPR/ICPR486_1.asp

Stojanov, I. 1998. 'Dvaeset Godini Fakultet za Bezbednost'. *Annual Edition of the School of Security*. Skopje.

Stojanovski, T. 1997. *Policijata vo Demokratsko Opstestvo*. Skopje.

Swope, R. 2001. 'Ethics, Integrity and the Police Culture'. *International Criminal Police Review* vol. 483. Available at Interpol website:
   http://www.interpol.int/Public/Publications/ICPR/ICPR483_1.asp

Taseva, S. 2002. 'Perenje pari i finansiski kriminal'. *Edition: Organised Crime*. Skopje.

Chapter 12

Police Reform in the Republic of Montenegro

Željko Šević and Duško Bakrač

Introduction

Montenegro is one of the six former Yugoslav republics located in the south of the Balkan peninsula, positioned between Albania, Serbia, Bosnia-Herzegovina and Croatia. It has a surface area of 13,821 square kilometres and an estimated population of 630,000 inhabitants. According to the 1991 census, the reported population amounted to 617,000, of whom 61.7% declared themselves as Montenegrins. However, there were also some 139,299 Montenegrins living in Serbia. Montenegro has undergone a very rapid transformation from an agricultural country to an urbanised country. In 1953 around 61.5% of the total population were farmers; by 1991 around 58.2% of population lived in large urban centres.

Being mainly a mountainous country, Montenegro was never formally conquered by the Ottoman Turks and to a large extent developed autonomously. It linked its political destiny very closely with Russia and Serbia, and often followed the lead of both states in international affairs. In 1878 it was recognised as an independent sovereign state, which triggered a strong trend of modernisation. A number of young men were sent to study abroad in the hope that they would return to support the development of the country. Independent development took place between 1878 and 1918 when it was declared in Podgorica (Podgorica Assembly) that the country should join Serbia and create a new state of all south Slav nations – the Kingdom of Serbs, Croat and Slovenes. Between the two world wars, Montenegro was neither a political nor an economic entity.

The territory of today's Montenegro was not very compact and the vast share of it belonged to the Duchy of Zetska. After the Second World War Montenegro was established as one of six federal units in new socialist Yugoslavia. However, it is not clear what was the exact criterion for the establishment of the borders of the constituent republics. During the socialist era Montenegro was one of the republics that supported a strong federation and very few, if any, attempts were made to dismantle the federation. After the fall of socialism Montenegro moved towards political pluralism as a number of political parties were created. However, the Democratic Party of Socialists, successor to the former Union of Communists of Montenegro, has been in power since the establishment of the multi-party political system. In that sense, Montenegro is probably the only transitional country in Europe where the former communists have remained in power, unchallenged.

In Montenegro, as in all other former Yugoslav republics, a special political emphasis has been placed on the police. However, very little has been changed in the police organisation, structure and command lines compared to the policing system that all the Republics inherited from the former Socialist Federal Republic of Yugoslavia. An additional problem is created by the fact that two republics that constituted the 'third' Yugoslavia decided in 2003 to redefine their relationship under the tutelage of the European Union. The Constitutional Charter adopted in February 2003, much favoured by the special European Union envoy for the Balkans, Mr Xavier Solana, created a confederation with very few areas managed in common. The Federal Ministry of Internal Affairs and the small federal-level police force ceased to exist. The Serbian Ministry of Internal Affairs took over the personnel and property on the territory of Serbia, while the Montenegrin Ministry of Internal Affairs took over responsibility for some personnel (who initially were sent to the federal police by Montenegro) and the property of the Federal Ministry on the territory of Montenegro (mainly special purpose hotels and sanatoriums). The Organisation for Security and Co-operation in Europe (OSCE) advanced the rather unique plan of organising a border guard as a specialised federal police force (OSCE, 2001), but it has failed to materialise. In practice, the police of both republics control their own border crossings while the land between the border crossings is secured by the Border Guard troops of the Federal Army. However, this arrangement will cease to exist as the Armed Forces of the State Union of Serbia and Montenegro are no longer in charge of controlling the border areas, according to the newly promulgated Constitutional Charter.

Traditionally in Yugoslavia the police and the military were perceived as the main pillars of the stable and long-standing political regime. The first activities undertaken by the newly recognised independent states Serbia and Montenegro in the mid and late nineteenth century to strengthen government structures and the civil service were largely focused on the organisation (and frequent reorganisation) of the police and the army. This tradition was continued in the first Yugoslavia (1918–41) and in the second Yugoslavia (1945–91). While the army has always been regulated by a number of highly specialised defence laws, the police were usually regulated by a single law on internal affairs and other civil service laws were applied as supplementary, whenever it was perceived to be necessary.

From 1996 and the emergence of the conflict between the Montenegrin political leadership and Slobodan Milošević, then President of Serbia, Montenegro has been drawn closer to Western countries and has largely abandoned its isolationist policy and the policy of constant conflict pursued by Milošević. A number of reforms have been introduced but unfortunately police reform has not received the attention it has long deserved. However, at the time of writing (late 2003), a draft national police law is circulating and it is expected that a major change in the police structures will happen in the next year or two. This is to be accompanied by major civil service reforms and reformed labour laws that will influence some aspects of labour relations in the police force. A significant and far reaching reform of the police will soon take place in Montenegro and should represent a fundamental reform rather than merely the updating of police uniforms, something which was done in the mid-1990s following the break-up with Milošević's Serbia. The change in uniforms and their more 'citizen-friendly' outlook have been the main achievements of police reform until today.

Processes of change and reform

Overall goals of reform
All major political groupings in the Republic of Montenegro agree that there is an urgent need to reform the police in the Republic and to redefine its position so the organisation can meet the requirements of the time and the expectations of the general public that it is expected to serve. Generally the police are perceived as a public service that is supposed to serve public safety, to maintain public order and to ensure personal and property safety. At the moment, it is slightly premature to discuss whether good policing is more proactive than reactive, but a number of non-governmental organisations (NGOs) in Montenegro have acknowledged that efforts have been made to improve the public's regard for the police. Such efforts stress the claim that the police are a friendly service. Currently, the discussion of the issue of use of force in order to discharge police duties is still not welcome, especially as the police used force excessively in the past. Even today the term '*Žuta Greda*' (or the 'Yellow Joist') is a synonym for police brutality. *Žuta Greda* is a curve on the Podgorica-Nikšić road where the Montenegrin police confronted the supporters of the current Montenegrin leadership, which then contested the old communist cabal ruling Montenegro and badly injured many demonstrators. This was one of a few turning points in the development of the police in Montenegro since 1989. Unfortunately, all of these turning points arose from political conflicts between former political allies.

The police have traditionally been perceived as a service that has to secure public order and safety. In performing its duties the police can collect and analyse information; undertake other necessary actions to prevent crime; and apprehend culprits who broke the law. It is important that all their actions be taken in accordance with law, and that information that is obtained illegally be inadmissible in courts of law.

A new police force must be citizen-oriented and focused on providing a good quality service to the general public (Council of Europe, 1999). The emphasis of the new police organisation is to be on the community and serving its needs. In performing their duties the police have to adopt a proactive approach and work together with the community. The new political leadership wishes that all these moves be presented as a logical consequence of the overall democratic changes in the country; the police force is merely following this broader social trend. To what extent the new police will meet the expectations of the community is very difficult, if not impossible, to say. In the previous laws on internal affairs (published in 1985, 1994 etc.) the first duty of the system of internal security was to provide security to the Republic, as the bearer of (national) sovereignty, while service to the public (the provision of security to citizens and ensuring constitutional and human rights) were the secondary goals (see Article 1 of the respective laws).

The pressures for reform come from a wide range of social players. The public views these pressures mainly as resulting from the actions of the international community and international organisations operating in Montenegro. However, an important impetus for reform and change in the police comes from within the organisation itself. A number of middle-aged police officers, who mainly began their careers 15–20 years ago, are requesting the further police professionalisation and more stringent criteria for the entry of new recruits. In accordance with general trends in Central and Eastern Europe (CEE), these pro-democracy oriented police officers are usually organised around different NGOs and seek to influence public opinion through activities of the third sector. Significantly, the interest in police reform issues has been demonstrated not only by NGOs, but also other civic organisations that focus their activities on other aspects of social life (child protection, environmental protection, sport organisations etc.). This clearly demonstrates that civil society in Montenegro is developing rapidly and a sense of wider social responsibility is emerging.

It is mainly due to the activity of NGOs that members of the public are requesting a more responsive, effective and efficient police service, but it is still taboo to criticise the police and to have a proactive attitude towards changes in the 'armed government bodies' (the police and army). Political leaders, including the current and former interior ministers, refer to the changes in policing and the reform of the police when they want to score quick political points.

In commentaries justifying the new draft Law on Police (dropping the old-fashioned term 'internal affairs'), the influence of the international community, especially the Council of Europe and OSCE, is acknowledged. Aside from the formal participation of these two organisations in the legislative drafting process, an important factor driving reform has been the training that Montenegrin police have been receiving from foreign police instructors. For instance, the London Metropolitan Police has provided some training in criminal intelligence and countering organised crime in both republics, along with some other consultancy work (and even work with paramilitary police forces, especially before the fall of the Slobodan Milošević's regime in Serbia in October 2000). To a large extent the call for, and actual commencement of, police reform in Montenegro is a result of the synergy between internal and external forces advocating change. In our view, international pressure has been decisive, as the internal affairs portfolio has always been highly politicised and heavily involved in political conflict. The overall liberalisation of political life has helped to place the issue of police reform on the public policy agenda and to enable further emphasis on professionalism within the police.

At present, all political actors appear to be willing to see changes implemented in the police service. This is certainly an important prerequisite for successful police reform, but it is not the only one. The team that prepared the draft law included a number of experts from NGOs who are very supportive of changes and they have been active in building public support for the reforms. The changes in civil service laws that provide protection for 'whistle-blowers' will certainly have a positive impact on the processes of police reform. In the past, a police officer was forbidden to express his or her opinion publicly without prior approval from the Interior Minister. Even local police chiefs were forbidden to communicate with the press and mass media unless authorised directly by the minister. Transparency in the work of the police would clearly facilitate the process of reform itself.

Some political parties (especially the pro-independence Liberal Union) perceive every reform attempt made by the current government as a political move that requires criticism. Consequently, they see police reform as another game of the government and something on which it will not deliver. An additional problem that affects the credibility of reform efforts is the ongoing problem of the Italian investigation of the current Montenegrin President, Milo Djukanović. The domestic and international press have published reports alleging that Djukanović was involved in a smuggling ring run by the Italian mafia, which delivers untaxed cigarettes to Western Europe. A parliamentary commission was formed to investigate the allegations and their report suggested there might be some truth in the allegations. However, due to the ruling coalition's parliamentary majority, the report has been sidelined and taken off the agenda for some time. These political issues can negatively influence reform attempts but should not prevent reform initiatives.

The real problem is, in fact, a serious lack of resources to implement reform (financial, human, know-how etc.). Although historically internal affairs was portrayed as the main protector of the regime, the financial resources committed to it were not particularly vast, due to a fiscal squeeze and a chronic lack of resources in the war damaged economy. Lack of proper police schools in Montenegro also seriously harms the ability of the country to recruit and train new people who will implement reform. Furthermore, a number of police officers left the force when they disagreed with the current leadership or minister, and the ministry has made a succession of highly political police appointments that were designed to ensure blind obedience to the regime of President Djukanović.

Changes in the legal status and powers of the police

Currently police matters are legally regulated by the Law on Internal Affairs enacted in 1994, replacing the law from 1985 which was amended several times after the fall of the Berlin Wall. As previously indicated, it is planned that the current law will be replaced by the Law on Police, a draft of which has been produced by the Montenegrin government in close co-operation with some NGOs and international organisations, especially the Council of Europe and OSCE.

The Law on Internal Affairs (1994) focused on the broader area of internal affairs that includes public safety, state security and decisions on administrative matters that are, by other laws, entrusted to the portfolio of Internal Affairs. The 1994 Law regulated the basic principles behind the organisation of the Ministry and described processes and procedures that are to be observed within the Ministry of Internal Affairs. However, the main changes are set out in the government By-Law on the Organisation and Activities of the State Administration. This By-Law is enacted under the authority given to the Government by the Law on the Principles of Organisation of State Organs from 1993. Article 3 of the By-Law states that the Ministry of Internal Affairs: ensures the security of the Republic; detects and prevents activities aimed at the forceful change or endangering of the incumbent political regime; provides security protection to Montenegrin citizens temporarily employed abroad; protects human life, the personal and material security of citizens, preventing and detecting criminal offences and locates and apprehends offenders; maintains public order and peace; controls traffic on the roads, railroads and water; provides an immigration service and controls the length of stay and movement of foreign nationals; attempts to solve border incidents; provides close protection for certain public officials; secures designated public buildings and offices; provides an effective fire service; regulates the acquisition, holding and carrying of firearms and their parts; regulates trade in, transport of and the production of flammable substances; undertakes criminal investigative operations and crime reconstruction; holds evidence obtained from citizens' residences and regulates other citizenship affairs; deals with applications for public meetings, personal identity cards, 'unique citizen's registration numbers' (*Jedinstveni matični broj gradjanina* or JMBG), names, travel documents and visas; deals with the registration of vehicles and maintains the registration of driving licence holders; controls the import and distribution of foreign mass-media products; performs administrative control in the area of the ministerial jurisdiction; and performs any other duties that may be entrusted to the Ministry by other laws.

As can be seen, the By-Law is fairly exhaustive, although it also has a general clause that the Ministry will perform all other duties that have been entrusted to it by law. The Law on Internal Affairs (1994) regulated the basics of the organisation of the Ministry and relationships within the Ministry as an administrative body. It fairly precisely regulated the authority of 'empowered official persons' in carrying out their duties as entrusted by law. It stipulated in great detail when physical force, qualified physical force or other instruments of force (a police stick, chemical substances, water cannons etc.) may be used. The law also regulated what conditions must be met when an official person is searching premises or an individual. However, these powers were generally defined in the Federal Criminal Code, which precisely regulated what are the actions that everyone involved in criminal investigations is empowered to undertake. The Ministry of Internal Affairs is also expected to co-operate with other government bodies and to provide assistance if the requests for assistance are based on the law.

As the police service requires that particular labour relations be established, the Law on Internal Affairs regulated labour relationships within the Ministry of Internal Affairs in a fairly detailed manner. Of course, labour law and government employment law are to be used as a supplementary source of law if an issue is not regulated by the Law on Internal Affairs. Finally, the financial and disciplinary responsibility of officials is set out in the Law. The stipulated sanctions range from monetary fines of up to 50% of a monthly salary to dismissal in the case of serious misconduct.

The Draft Law on Police is more detailed and regulates many issues that previously would have been found in other laws. After defining basic issues, the Draft Law regulates in greater detail than previously the authority and rights of the police. Operational and tactical actions that can be undertaken by police are clearly stipulated, including some methods that were previously unknown in Yugoslav police practice (witness protection programmes, bargaining with offenders and the like). Control and audit of police work attracted particular attention as well as sources of finance to enable the police to function. The Draft Law also gives a detailed account of who is authorised to enact by-laws and other regulations based on the Law on Police. Interestingly, the Draft Law on Police in its second part stipulates a Code of Police Ethics, which is novel in Yugoslav legislative practice.

The new Draft Law on Police defines 'police affairs' as those that are oriented towards: protection of security and constitutionally guaranteed rights and duties of citizens; protection of property; prevention and detection of criminal offences and other minor (magistrate court) offences; tracking down criminal offenders and bringing them before the courts; maintenance of public peace and order; providing security of public meetings, and other gatherings of citizens; providing security of designated (public) persons and objects; supervision and control of traffic; supervision and security of the state border and execution of border control; control of movement and residence of foreigners; and other affairs designated by law and the by-laws (regulations) enacted upon the authority established by law.

The role of the police in undertaking investigative actions has changed as the main activities have to be either undertaken directly by an investigative judge or upon his/her request and (close) supervision. All police activities must be undertaken in accordance with the Law on Police and other positive legal acts that accord with international standards and all other regulations that ensure the protection of the dignity of the individual, his/her freedoms and rights as a citizen. Interestingly, the new Draft Law on Police exclusively uses the term 'citizens', whereas earlier laws mainly used the expression, 'the people', which was a hangover from the old communist legal terminology that spoke of 'working peoples and citizens'. With respect to the Draft Law on Police, the duties and authority of the police are: to collect and use information; to search transport vehicles, travellers and shipments; to limit temporarily movement in designated areas; to control and establish the identity of peoples and objects; to enter peoples' dwellings and rooms; to secure and search crime scenes; to summon suspects and others; to escort prisoners and accused; to issue warnings and give orders; to use instruments of force; to commandeer temporarily a citizen's motor vehicle or communication device; to collect, analyse and use personal data; to undertake a close body search of individuals; to search flats and other premises; to acquire objects temporarily; to limit personal freedom ('the right of arrest'); to protect crime victims, witnesses and other individuals; to undertake anti-terrorist searches; to access business and financial documents and correspondence; and to exercise all other authority, as stipulated in related laws.

Specific actions can only be undertaken by an authorised police officer following the letter of the Code of Police Ethics. In choosing between given alternatives, a police officer has to opt for the instrument that incurs the least damage to the people and justice, and ensures the achievement of the goals of a certain action. The Draft Law on Police explicitly defines how each police action should be undertaken, leaving very little discretion for interpretation by the individual officer.

The Code of Ethics, which is currently an integral part of the Draft Law on Police, clearly stipulates how relationships between the police and citizens are to be conducted. In general, a police officer must uphold the rule of law and in doing so, s/he should act 'decisively and carefully' (Article 6, Code of Ethics). A police officer is not to undertake actions that can negatively affect his/her reputation, the reputation of the force, as well as actions that may undermine public trust in the police force. The police officer is sworn to keep official secrets, and is forbidden to be a member of any political party. Also, police officers cannot attend meetings organised by political parties unless they 'are entrusted with a certain task' which requires their presence at that time. The Code also stipulates the principles of police education (and training, although not using the latter term) and the relationship between superior and subordinated police officers.

Montenegro has made its first attempt to codify police ethics through the Code of Police Ethics. However, the Code is inconsistent and many loopholes become apparent when systematically examined. It has been incorporated into the Rules of Police Operations, which have traditionally been inward-looking and have not paid much attention to the relationship with outside stakeholders.

The new law established the Council for Citizens' Control of Police Work which, together with Parliament, the government, judicial and specialised units of the Ministry of Internal Affairs (Internal Control), are to supervise and control the work of the police. Internal controls are to play an important role in preventing breaches of law and improving the overall performance of police work. In instances of police misconduct, citizens can complain to the commander of a regional police force and directly to the Inspectorate-General of Internal Affairs. There always is, as well, the possibility of seeking judicial protection from unlawful acts of the state administration, including the police. A police administrative act can be challenged by a citizen in a regular complaints procedure or an administrative court case can be initiated against the actions of a police officer. The state is responsible for compensating the victims of unlawful police actions. Police officers are especially protected in performing their duties and they can enjoy many additional allowances compared to other civil servants. In their formal status they are in the same position as career civil servants and privileges above the minimum level stipulated for civil servants are envisaged because of the nature of police activities (e.g. danger in the line of duty).

Changes in the organisational structures and policies of the police

The Ministry of Internal Affairs of Montenegro entered the 1990s with an organisation and structures that were enacted under republican law from 1985 (amended in 1989 and 1993). The Law of 1994 did not change much, if anything, except to strengthen the role of the portfolio of Internal Affairs in providing protection for the political regime currently in power. The changes to the police were largely initiated by a number of political conflicts in the Republic, and after every such conflict a number of career police officers were forced or advised to leave the service. The Department of State Security was *de facto* above the Ministry of which it was supposedly only a part. This was achieved because the Assistant Minister (Head of the State Security Department) was, in fact (but not *de jure*) a presidential appointee in direct contact with the President.

Throughout the entire period in focus, the Ministry of Internal Affairs was divided into three main departments each headed by an assistant minister. There were two operational departments (State Security and Public Security) and one administrative department dealing with the collection, storage and analysis of data; procurement; and personnel and other general administrative matters. Later in the mid-1990s this third department was, in effect, artificially split into two parts, one focusing on material and technical support for the operational departments and the other continuing to be in charge of all other matters. The Department of Public Security had Divisions of Police and Criminal Investigation, and later a section in charge of the control of state borders (which initially was with one of the regional police centres, Herceg Novi). The structure of the State Security Department has traditionally been kept secret but it was known that they had different lines of work and their structure and remit would change frequently in order to secure a higher level of secrecy and prevent any penetration by another intelligence service.

The territory of the Republic was divided into seven police regions and seven Centres of Public Security (known as Security Centres). Twenty-seven police stations were formed, together with seven parallel Centres of State Security. Two types of centres (i.e. Security Centres and State Security Centres) were formally independent and had to co-operate in order to discharge their respective duties but there was no strict legal requirement for such co-operation. The Centres of Public Security reported to the Head of Public Security Department while the Centres of State Security were, in the first instance, to report to the Head of the State Security Department. The Centre had the Head who was appointed by the Minister and who was assisted by two Assistant Heads (Police and Criminal Investigations) and the Chief of the Administrative Division. The latter did not have the status of an Assistant but performed the duties of one. Every centre had a number of divisions which covered a smaller territory. Often the divisions would be a simple police station and all serious investigation would be undertaken by officers coming from the centre's headquarters.

The 1994 Law on Police kept the same hierarchical relationships that were promoted in Yugoslavia since the mid-1960s. After the cleansing of the police that was undertaken in Yugoslavia following major political conflict about the so-called Brioni Plenum in 1966,[1] the main aim was ostensibly to demilitarise the police and bring it closer to the people. To a large extent those efforts failed but a flatter, non-hierarchical structure within the Ministry of Interior was formally promoted. For police officers who had only secondary school education, positions were in fact ranks. They were moved up the (pay) scale after a number of years but retained the same title (*milicionar / policajac* – policeman). For holders of associate and university degrees the positions were given different types of inspector titles. The main difference between them would not be so much in terms of seniority as of salary. The highest titles were reserved for the holders of certain very senior posts: Head of the Centre, Advisor to the Minister, Assistant Minister, State Under-Secretary (until the early 1990s), Deputy Minister (a post that existed on paper but not in practice, as nobody was appointed to the post) and Minister. All holders of the higher office were entitled to wear uniforms with the insignia of their respective title/position. Flattening the structure within the police force has been a worldwide trend in 1980s and 1990s, but in Yugoslavia these efforts were politically initiated; to ensure the monolithic structure of the police and streamline the communication between the political appointees and direct enforcers.

---

1. Brioni is an archipelago in the northern Adriatic that now belongs to Croatia. It was the first high-class resort in the Austro-Hungarian Empire, as it had a number of villas developed for Austro-Hungarian royalty and nobility. All subsequent rulers had a villa on the island, and the Yugoslav President Marshal Tito was no different. In summer 1966 Brioni hosted a meeting of Central Committee of the Union of Communist of Yugoslavia which aimed at settling accounts with the Yugoslav security system, which was accused of being abusive and damaging for the further development of socialism and 'self-management'. All civilian and military services were subjected to external political scrutiny which led to the ousting of all senior officials and appointment of new leadership in all respective agencies. This inflicted severe damage to the security system, which experienced serious problems in facing the challenges of its time: Kosovar Albanian rebellion in 1968; Croatian separatism (Croatian Spring) in 1970; Croatian terrorist infiltration in 1972, etc. The civilian security services suffered serious losses, while there are claims that the military services were preparing themselves for 'the witch hunt' and took necessary measures to make the most important agent networks, both in the country and abroad, dormant and to protect the identity of all 'outside voluntary' associates. Despite growing literature on this issue, it is still very difficult to establish what happened. Some scholars claim that it was in fact the last serious fight between those who were in favour of decentralisation and separation of the republics and those who were in favour of the strong federal state. The former won and the latter were serious losers, as it will be demonstrated in the quasi-confederal Yugoslav constitution of 1974 (although often praised as the most democratic socialist constitutional act).

The new Draft Law on Police combines both rank and title/position structure. Something similar was undertaken in Serbia in 1995 when the Public Security Department was given ranks while the State Security Department retained the old, ostensibly less formal, title/position structure. The Draft Law on Police stipulates that there will be four titles for police officers (holding a secondary school certificate), three inspector titles for those with an associated degree and three for those with a university degree. Inspector titles were kept the same as those introduced in 1976 but the criteria for receiving titles were tougher in 1976 than in the Draft Law. For the police officers in the Extraordinary Police Unit (*Posebna jedinica policije*), the ranks have also been stipulated: three ranks for those with secondary school, two for those with an associate degree and four for those with a university degree. Based on the range of ranks, it seems that the Extraordinary Unit will act as a border guard, a coast guard and a special anti-terrorist unit. The highest rank stipulated for the Extraordinary Unit is that of general.

Training of the police service was decentralised and was entrusted to the Republics in the early 1970s. Despite this trend, Montenegro did not create an establishment for the education of police officers but recruited those who went to police schools in other republics and then decided to return to Montenegro. Also some police officers may have decided to complete their formation at a military academy and upon graduation serve in special police units or the State Security Department. Traditionally Montenegro relied for its recruits on those who completed a general or specialised secondary education but with no prior knowledge of police work. They would be asked to undergo a three- or six-month police training course and then, if demonstrating satisfactory standing, were offered a position of a police officer trainee (*policajac-pripravnik*). The Draft Law has the same regulations and asks a new entrant into the police force to complete a general state attestation[2] and specialised police officer examinations at the end of their probation period (one year). Both the old law and the Draft Law stipulate that the police force has reserve personnel who may be called up when the need arises. In the late 1990s there was an open conflict between Slobodan Milošević and the Montenegrin leadership controlled by President Djukanović. The Ministry of Internal Affairs in Montenegro drafted a large number of experienced former volunteers from Bosnia and Croatia into its ranks. Often they did not even meet the minimum requirements for appointment as police officers. The total number of police in Montenegro is regarded as secret and many reports point out that official information on numbers is unavailable (e.g. ESI Report, 2001). However, it is currently estimated that there are 3,800 uniformed police officers, including 410 traffic police and 769 border police.

---

2. In the former Yugoslavia all entrants in any kind of public or quasi-public service (for instance, education) were required to sit the general part of the state attestation examination and the special part which differed from one profession to another (for teachers, doctors etc.) and ministries (each ministry had to set a ministry-specific specialised paper).

It is believed Montenegro has a uniformed force of 4,650 overall with an estimated further 10,000 special police force officers (OSCE, 2001).

Both the old and the Draft Law allow the Minister to decide on numbers of police officers that will be admitted into the police following a short course of study. The only difference between reserve and regular, full-time police officers was that the former were not given police identity cards which in theory should make them an auxiliary police force. In many Centres of Public Security reserve police officers were allowed to perform regular police duties on their own without any supervision by an active police officer. This created a lot of friction between police and the public, which was compounded as the vast majority of the public complaints were filed against reserve police personnel, as it seems that reserve police staff was not properly trained to perform duties on their own. Even in the Draft Law the promotion policy would remain entirely with the Minister of Internal Affairs with a slightly tighter regulation regime that is to be enacted by the government. However, with the strengthening of professionalism within the police force, promotion policies should be more open to public scrutiny and perhaps in time police officers will have a body that recommends promotions. However, within the current title/position system, promotion in itself loses its relevance. It is more important to know what is the authority of a particular police officer rather than his or her formal position in the police hierarchy. Certainly, this has been the culture within the Ministry until now and it is unlikely to change in the short term despite formal innovation that has occurred.

In 1989 after the so-called 'People's Anti-Bureaucratic Revolution', the duo of Bulatović (as the Republican President) and Djukanović (Prime Minister) secured political power within Montenegro with the strong assistance of Serbia's Slobodan Milošević. The supporters of Bulatović and Djukanović had a major clash with the special police force at Žuta Greda on the road to the capital, Podgorica. After the duo achieved power, the 'cleansing' of the Ministry of Interior began. Many pre-1989, highly professional police officers left the force voluntarily, usually asking for regular retirement (after thirty years of pensionable service) or early retirement. However, the lower ranks, that generally supported the changes, remained in the force, and thus secured significant professional continuity. Then, in the mid-1990s Bulatović and Djukanović parted company. After Djukanović's political triumph, another 'cleansing' of the Ministry began, especially after a close friend of Djukanović, Vukašin Maraš, was appointed the Head of the State Security Department. Although Filip Vujanović, then Minister of Internal Affairs and now President[3], secured the very minimum of professional management of the Ministry, some aspects of police work were taken out of his remit and co-ordinated by the Presidential Cabinet. Personnel change within the Portfolio of Internal Affairs has traditionally been smooth as those who opposed a new ruling clique either left the

---

[3] Former President Djukanović has become Prime Minister, while in 2003 Vujanović changed his position as Prime Minister to the position of President of the Republic.

Service or were professionally marginalised so that it was the question of months rather than years before they would decide to leave the force.

Especially after the election victory of a wide coalition named 'It's the Victory of Montenegro!' *(Pobijeda je Crne Gore!)*, action has been taken to increase the number of ethnic non-Montenegrins in the police force. This was due to the fact that Albanian and Muslim minority parties joined the coalition and entered the government. However, very little has been done to improve the force's gender balance which currently contains only 160 women with none in the operational units (OSCE, 2001). No specific affirmative action for minorities has been undertaken until now, although it may be initiated in the future under the pressure of a relatively strong women's lobby. As there is presently no comprehensive method for reporting on equal opportunities policy, it is impossible to get information on the ethnic structure of the police force.

It is very difficult to clearly define the current dominant informal culture within the Montenegrin police force. This difficulty is largely because so many experienced officers left the force after 1989 and large numbers of young, inexperienced officers were quickly recruited to replace them but lacked proper police training. An additional problem was that the recruitment of police officers was often carried out when the political situation required an increase in the size of the police force rather than in response to the needs of the service itself. Consequently, feelings of collegiality and brotherhood, common in other police services, are not so strong within the Montenegrin police. The traditional police structures and culture were crushed but without a new system and values being built. To some extent this might be seen to be an enabling factor that may assist the government in introducing the current reforms as it will be building the desired police culture 'from scratch'.

Changes in the operational policies and work patterns of the police

Due to the tensions between the Montenegrin Police and the Yugoslav Army (in fact, mainly the Navy) from 1996 to 2000, the vast resources earmarked for the Portfolio of Internal Affairs were spent on the acquisition of heavy firearms and other military equipment.[4] There were informal reports that the Montenegrin Police have had in their possession 120mm artillery mortars (beside 'normal' 82mm infantry mortars), and anti-aircraft cannons of 40mm calibre. Some of this equipment was shown in public during the NATO bombing campaign against Yugoslavia. As a consequence, little has been invested in the acquisition of really

---

4. At the time it was generally believed that the Federal armed forces were limiting the sovereignty of Montenegro and that the Montenegrin police should be able to defend the rights of an independent Montenegro. In order to be able to counter to the Federal Army, it was decided by the Montenegrin political leadership to equip police with military equipment and ensure that the police, if needed, would constitute the embryo of a future Montenegrin army. All of these issues came to light only after the conflict between Milošević and Djukanović had emerged.

advanced police equipment although some attempts were made by the Department of State Security to acquire sophisticated surveillance technology to be able to 'compete' with the Military Security Service which has traditionally been far better equipped. The Military Security Services have been highly professional and well-trained, both at home (Intelligence and Security Educational Centre in Pančevo, the famous Milatary Outpost 5000) and abroad (in civilian and military educational establishments in both East and West). While both police and military attracted recruits at a fairly tender age (14–15-year-olds upon graduation from primary school), the police have always been less successful in 'indoctrinating' them than the Military Security Services. As a consequence, the police have always been the junior branch. A historical reason for this situation is that former Yugoslav Federal President, Marshal Tito, treated the army as the bastion of his power. In his concept of socialism, the police played a secondary role.

In the armed conflict that took place on the territories of the former Yugoslavia, police forces of all former Yugoslav republics participated but the degree of their involvement differed. While the secessionist republics resorted to the police to confront the federal army, in Serbia and Montenegro the police played a secondary role. Operations led by the Yugoslav Federal Army were regarded as strictly military with little place for the police. As both Serbia and Montenegro have never declared a state of war or national emergency, the police have never been subordinated to the armed forces, something the Yugoslav Federal Constitution of 1992 permits in such extraordinary situations. Therefore in the case of Montenegro it is very difficult to document the Montenegrin police's participation in war operations in Croatia and Bosnia. Even if some documents exist, it is very unlikely that they will be released due to the continuity in control of such forces. However, in the case of Serbia an abrupt change in government meant that the new Government has entirely neglected state official secrecy principles and made many documents available to the public even though some of these would be unlikely to be publicly released elsewhere in the world. In Montenegro the police archives are still closed and probably 'moderated' (documents implicating the current leadership would be destroyed), as it was often the practice in the socialist Yugoslavia for both police and army security structures.

In the early 1990s during and immediately after the conflict in Bosnia and Herzegovina, the police operated in accord with existing operational rules. The main focus of regular police work was on informants and on the work of a block police officer or *pozornik*. The latter was required to live within the community and to know all its citizens, movements in and out of his/her area, and in general s/he had to have a feel for his/her block. Often block police officers were an invaluable source of information to detectives from the Crime Investigation Division when it was necessary to apprehend or locate some suspects. Mobile patrols of two officers are also regularly used and usually called in to respond to public disorder or to assist to block police officers if assistance is required (OSCE, 2001). Very few resources have been allocated to crime prevention or improving relations with the public. However, some NGOs have been trying to improve the overall public perception of the police force. The presence of police officers has traditionally been perceived by the public as the best method of deterring crime.

Police officers are also requested to assist other government bodies in enforcing their own and court decisions and often this is regarded as a routine police operation. Only in a very few isolated cases were the special police units used to implement court decisions. The maintenance of public order is another example of a routine police operation. As organisers of public gatherings are required by law to report their intentions to the police, a middle-level police officer assigned to the event will liaise with the organiser in order to secure a high level of co-operation and the effectiveness of the police personnel thus deployed. Traditionally, if a public event was profit making, it became the norm that the organisers would meet some of the policing costs incurred. Unfortunately since 1989 the police force has been an instrument of political oppression and consequently the main goal of the police was not to secure public peace and order but to secure the stability of the current political regime. This undermined the credibility of the force itself.

Since the Ministry of Internal Affairs is highly centralised, the discretionary powers of the police as a rule rest with senior police personnel. The first level of police management that is empowered to make discretionary decisions is the Head of Security Centres. In Yugoslav administrative law such discretion must be based on and regulated by law. When discretionary powers are given, the law describes the principles that have to be observed when they are exercised. However, if a member of the public suffers from an unreasonable discretionary action of a police officer, s/he will be in a position to require restitution from the government which is ultimately responsible for the work of the police force.

Changes in supervision and control of the police
Although the current Law on Internal Affairs (1994) does not contain special norms regulating the supervision and external control of police, it does embody articles that define internal disciplinary matters. Nonetheless, the police are still scrutinised by outside bodies. First, there is a political responsibility to Parliament and the Minister has to submit a report to Parliament at least once a year. A parliamentary committee on internal security affairs oversees the activities of the police on behalf of Parliament. The Ministry is responsible to the Government for this portfolio and the administrative affairs entrusted to it. The Government periodically considers the reports on the security situation within the Republic. The Government is entrusted by law to enact all the by-laws that are required for the implementation of the Law on Internal Affairs. The current law did not envisage any formal role for the general public. However, relations with the general public, especially those with local government, are traditionally regarded as very important. Although *stricto lege* they do not exist, there are many informal forms of consultation in place.

Chapter V of the new Draft Law regulates the control and supervision of the police force. It is explicitly stipulated that such control and supervision is exercised via elected public bodies, the judiciary, special units of the Ministry of Internal Affairs and through the Council for the Citizens' Control of Police Work (*Savjet za gradjansku kontrolu rada Policije*). Primary control is exercised by Parliament (the Assembly of the Republic of Montenegro), to which the police is required to submit an annual report on its work. However, the Assembly can require other periodic and special reports to be prepared when the need emerges.

Strong emphasis has been placed on the service for internal control. The Inspectorate-General of Internal Control performs such functions autonomously and they comprise:

(1)   Control of the legality of police work and other services and units within the Ministry of Internal Affairs.

(2)   Financial control.

(3)   Control over the work of territorial police units and the other territorial (detached) services of the Ministry.

(4)   Control over the legality and efficiency of programmes, operations and actions undertaken by the police and other services and units of the Ministry of Internal Affairs.

(5)   Control over the exercise of entrusted powers and authorities.

(6)   Other forms of control which may be important for the efficient and legal work of the Ministry of Internal Affairs (Article 142, Draft Law on Police).

The Law also stipulates that the State Under-Secretary – Head of Police – is required to prepare a plan and schedule of actions needed to remedy any negative findings of the Inspector-General. It is necessary to point out that at the moment there is no State Under-Secretary in the Montenegrin Civil Service. However, in the Draft Law on State Administration such a senior position exists but it is not clear what will be the exact remit of such a post. The Council for Citizens' Control of Police is designated as an independent body of high social esteem that will be comprised of five members appointed by the Government. However, it is a requirement of law that listed public institutions and NGOs also nominate members. The organisations explicitly mentioned are the Montenegrin Bar, the Medical Association, the Law Association and NGOs. The Council is to play a pivotal role in planning different programmes on preventing crime; controlling the activities of the police; and overseeing and monitoring the social role and position of the police, its organisation, readiness, and personnel. The Law also requires that the police work closely with local government and report to them when required. *Stricto lege*, there are good public safeguards against the misuse of the police for political purposes but to what extent this will be achieved in practice remains to be seen. As Montenegro has a fairly poor record in the implementation and efficient enforcement of laws, it is difficult to really envisage that these completely novel modes of conduct will be implemented to the full, soon.

However, there are other ways of challenging police decisions. In the case of a minor offence, a magistrate will examine the legality of the police decision if the case appears before the magistrate court. Also the vast majority of police acts are administrative acts and as such are open to examination by a complaints procedure.

Finally, it is possible to initiate an examination of a police action in the Administrative Court. Any claims for damages suffered as a result of an illegal police action can be put before the regular court. However, the problems of ensuring police accountability are considerable as there is a very low level of transparency in the police force and a high level of corruption in Montenegro. Thus to some extent, issues of legality and the correctness of police work are mere rhetoric in a society where there is a systemic failure of public institutions.

Evaluation of the implementation and success of reforms

Professionalism, service-orientation, accountability, and effectiveness
As mentioned, the main question to be asked is whether the police force in Montenegro really has been subjected to reform? There have been a number of changes since the mid-1990s but they have been of a cosmetic nature (change in uniform design and equipment) and have focused on strengthening the police to protect the current political elite rather than to provide security for society at large. In many respects the post-1990 development of policing has made the police more politicised or dependent on daily politics than in the over forty years of Communist rule. One of the reasons for this is that the current political elite has grown out of the old Communist system and many public officials gained their first political experience in the Socialist Youth and Communist Party organisations. The predominant focus on the protection of the political regime (rationalised to the public as the protection of the sovereignty of the Republic) has simply impaired reform attempts. Successive ministers of internal affairs promised changes when appointed but their enthusiasm faded rapidly when they became involved in daily political intrigues in which the police served as the main source of information. An additional problem has been the general political culture that has long surrounded the police. As the country was small, police service has traditionally been performed by the Royal Guardsmen and the police are still perceived as being in the ruler's service. This is embodied in the historical '*perjanici*', the Montenegrin Prince's guard and close protection service known for their extreme loyalty to the sovereign.[5] Some members of NGOs still refer to the overgrown police force using this historical term. The term is used pejoratively with the meaning that police officers

---

5. The literal translation of the term is 'feather holders', in a sense that they followed the Prince everywhere and were the symbol of his power and prestige. This small military outfit served as the Prince's guard and his bodyguards. However, it seems that many clandestine operations mastered by the Prince were executed by them. They were extremely well-trained, eye-catching and it was one of the biggest privileges for any member of a Montenegrin tribe to serve in this unit, even if there was at the time a feud between the Prince and the family of a soldier. Their loyalty was never influenced by the current politics and divisions.

remain the personal servants of the ruler. The lack of any real political consensus to a large extent impedes reform attempts.

Although legal actions have been taken to depoliticise the police force, in practice things function differently. Publicly expressed political support for the ruling group's ideology has meant that their career prospects have suddenly and significantly improved. The police service has been misused on and off, depending on the needs of the political clique in the ruling party or the Government. Explicit *de jure* promotion of professionalism did not really occur as political patronage was widely practised. Periodic 'cleansing' of all those not in favour of the ruling clique and dominant ideology has also contributed to feelings of insecurity among police officers and conversely, their blind obedience was required and rewarded. Theoretically speaking, the promotion of professionalism should contribute to the enhanced organisational independence of the police and ensure that professional standards are upheld. But in practice, it has not been happening. The legislation introduced in the mid-1990s has failed to bring the police closer to the people. In fact, it has alienated the police force from the public and encouraged it to operate as a narrowly focused organisation serving the purposes of the dominant political clique. Although formally responsible to Parliament and the Government, the police are accountable only to the President who acts to a large extent as their Commander-in-Chief.

The old guard within the Ministry of Internal Affairs, who have now almost disappeared, had some sense of the police as a public service for the general public. The never-abandoned practice of 'beat' and motorised patrols with defined patrolling areas, has certainly contributed to the closer relations between community police officers and citizens. It has been reported that long-serving beat officers have been perceived as a cohesive factor in the community and consequently have occupied a prominent role (with the priest and teacher) in the daily life of the local community. Like all countries with Continental European legal systems, Montenegro has endorsed the legalistic model of policing. In the 1980s the development of authorisation processes, the preventive functions of policing, flexible organisational design, regular consultations with local communities and high job satisfaction levels contributed to the emergence of a community-policing model (Dantzker, 1999; Doerner and Dantzker, 2000). Even in the socialist era, the police were there more to maintain order and public safety than to protect the State. The latter was solely in the hands of the Department of State Security and the Military Security Service(s). There was some overlap, especially when faced with certain criminal acts regarded as serious enough to undermine state security. In those cases the investigation was usually taken over by the State Security Department. Furthermore in Tito's era, the Military Security Service(s) were often entrusted with non-military related investigations. With the death of Marshal Tito in 1980 these practices changed as the republics strengthened their powers and the Military Security and Intelligence Services were perceived as the main threat to this informal 'devolution' (in fact the slow but continuous degradation of the Federal state).

In other words, there was previously some sense of service, which was lost in the last decade of so-called 'changes'. The new Draft Law on Police clearly promotes policing as a public service and puts citizens at the centre. With the older idea of the block police officers still operative, there is a hope that the sense of policing as a useful and necessary public service could be revived. However, a police force that wasted the vast majority of resources entrusted to it on the protection of the current political elite could not really develop an organisational culture of social responsibility and public accountability. Public accountability was, in fact, replaced by arbitrary political loyalty to the dominant political clique. According to the Draft Law on Police, this is to be changed. Policing is defined as a public service run by the Ministry of Internal Affairs. However, this Ministry is in charge of conducting other administrative affairs allocated to its portfolio besides police work.

Proactive policing practices are still to be developed in Montenegro (Bakrač, 2003). Police work is still perceived as reactive, and community policing is far from being realised. However, the Draft Law on Police strengthens the formal ties between local government and territorial police units. These are required to co-operate in preparing and implementing different crime prevention programmes. It is presumed that the police will collaborate with all the other social groups in carrying out its legally defined functions. This assumes that the police force maintains good public relations and a regular flow of information to the public and vice versa. However, the Draft Law limits the authority to disclose information only to the minister and the state under-secretary for the police force, or their nominees. It seems that this authority should be decentralised so that heads of territorial units can communicate directly with the public and seek public assistance in crime prevention and control.

Due to the degree of politicisation of the police, the public have lost confidence in them though they do still have a relatively better rating than political institutions (Slavujević, 1997). However, the Army has been on the top of this list for many decades and this seems unchanged even though the Army was also used in the political struggle between the Montenegrin clique and Slobodan Milošević, as reported elsewhere (Šević and Rabrenović, 1999). However, it seems that things are set to change as the group of NGOs sometimes known as *Akcija* (the Action) is conducting a campaign aimed at improving the public perception of the police.[6] A number of adverts have appeared in the leading national and local newspapers depicting a small young boy talking to a kindly police officer, thus promoting the message that the police officer is a friend. It may take some time, however, to change public perceptions of the police to the stage that it is widely regarded as a service to citizens. It will also be a while before it is a common perception that to co-operate with the police and provide the information needed for the prevention and/or control of crime is in everybody's best interests. Due to the usual policy-implementation time-lag, the efforts of the NGOs will also need time before the

---

6. This refers to a newspaper advertisement to that effect.

benefits of more effective and proactive policing and an increased public sense of security are realised.

The efforts to implement the community-policing model advocated by some senior police officers in Montenegro are beginning to emerge. Bakrač (2003) has suggested that the endorsed model of policing has two components: (1) partnership with the community (the proactive, preventive function) and (2) crime-detection (the traditional, reactive function). The proponents of this model are aware of limitations that face the Montenegrin police force in implementing the model. They are fully aware of the need to improve police education, in the first instance, before the model can be successfully established. It is also believed that the introduction of the community-policing model, will significantly improve information gathering and increase citizen's involvement in making the community secure.

Private security provision has been a new development in Montenegro as it is in all other former socialist countries. The provision of (public) security has long been presented as a core public service and consequently only the state in performing its sovereign powers would be able to provide it. However, private security companies began to be established from the late 1980s. At first there were small detective offices and later complex organisations offering the full range of protection services. Initially the owners of private security firms were former or retired police officers but, from the mid-1990s, more people with non-policing backgrounds entered the industry. There are no formal regulations defining the relationship between the police force and the private providers of security services. But in practice there is usually relatively good co-operation due to personal relations between the owners and their former colleagues who are still in the force. They often seem to informally share information, and it seems that this works both ways, in a reciprocal manner. Certainly this area needs more regulation as at the moment it is literally not regulated at all. A higher level of professionalisation usually requires a higher level of regulation and is certainly the case with Montenegrin private security services. In contrast to many other transitional countries, it seems that private security agencies are less involved with the crime rings and the organised crime although this claim is difficult to document due to the lack of statistical information. However, organised crime *per se* is not perceived as a serious threat by the political elite and therefore it received fairly little attention from the police. In fact, it has been reported that in many instances offenders with close links to the ruling elite are unreachable. For instance, the local police in Herceg Novi broke a cigarette smugglers' ring in 1997 and the case is still ongoing before the District Court, and its closure is not anticipated in the foreseeable future (Bakrač, 2003).

Remaining problems

The Draft Law on Police is presented as initiating a process of major reform of the police force. However, due to weak law enforcement performance, it remains an open question as to how the law will be implemented or even understood by those who are to realise the reform, that is, the police officers themselves. An additional problem is that morale within the police force has been low throughout the 1990s as the service was in real terms under-funded despite the seemingly high investment in policing to protect the current political regime.

It is still necessary to introduce affirmative employment practices in order to recruit more officers from national and other minorities (women, the disabled etc.). It is also necessary to strengthen links with local government and re-establish an effective relationship with local communities. The role of public opinion has been strengthening constantly and, consequently, the police have to become more transparent about their work, results and even problems. The role of the public in crime prevention programmes is of utmost importance. Effective relationships with NGOs are also important as such third-sector organisations become more and more influential in Montenegro and hence they are emerging as an important factor in public policy formulation.

Recruitment and retention strategies and policies have to be re-examined and modernised. Currently there is no single educational establishment for training police officers and this deficiency is to be addressed in the future or a firm contract placed with foreign training schools so that a steady inflow of new recruits can be secured. Developing a philosophy of continuous professional development of currently employed police officers is also an important issue yet to be addressed.

Finally, the relationship with the military structures has to change, together with the demilitarisation of paramilitary (special) police units. However, it is not clear whether this change will be feasible as the new extraordinary police unit will be clearly organised along military principles and will be heavily, and in our opinion unnecessarily, armed.

Societal changes and political reforms
The Republic of Montenegro has enjoyed an undivided support from the EU countries since the moment of its break with the Federal Yugoslav Government and the regime of Slobodan Milošević. Large sums of money were regularly transferred to cover a growing budget deficit and fund social programmes. Very few of these transfers were directed towards reviving production and the economy. Social institutions were formally subjected to reform but in practice the reforms were little more than letters on a piece of paper. Programmes to boost the capacity of public services were more or less effective (ESI, 2001). The most efficient ones were those that focused on the education of future civil servants and training of the younger generation. To a large extent reform to date in Montenegro can be assessed as seriously deficient. There is a danger that the current police reform will blend in with other failed reform attempts. It seems that only local government reform is progressing as planned although even there the implementation of much of this has been postponed for some time.

Concluding comments

The question that has still remained unanswered is whether there is any genuine police reform in Montenegro? Clearly, what has been done until recently can, to some extent, be regarded as reforming the police. The uniform and the basic equipment of police were modernised. The former is less threatening and has a more citizen-friendly look. This was something that Dr Archibald Reiss[7] (Rajs, 1920) proposed as early as the late 1920s but had been long neglected by the Yugoslav police authorities (Bogdanović, 2001). The real changes in police practices, policies and procedures are still failing to materialise. The police are required by law to produce an annual report on their work but what is presented is usually very descriptive, and does not paint a real picture. The effectiveness of the police has been systematically considered, but statistics are not always revealing. Official crime reports are often perceived as something that does not show whether the police force is performing its duties properly; it is more an exercise in statistical information.

The changes in the Montenegrin police force are perceived to be mainly the result of external pressures. All previous calls for change by local pressure groups were either suppressed or simply were not brought to fruition. Currently the OSCE and the Council of Europe have emerged as the main champions of police reform. The Draft Law on Police was largely drafted with not only their supervision but also their direct involvement. The growth of the third sector in Montenegro assisted immensely in improving the civic awareness of Montenegrins. Probably this development has been the predominant influence behind the calls for reform in all spheres of the public services, including policing. Usually the high level of co-operative behaviour demonstrated by NGOs contributes significantly to mutual understanding and ensures many positive results. But the question remains as to

---

7. Dr Rudolf Archibald Reiss, a naturalised Serbian citizen Arčibald Rajs (all foreign names are phonetically written in Serbian, while remaining unchanged in the Croatian), was a prominent Swiss criminologist who visited Serbia during the first years of First World War, to investigate claims that Austro-Hungarian, German and Bulgarian troops committed many serious atrocities against civilians in Serbia in 1914 and 1915. He collected much proof of the excessive use of force and genocide (unknown at the time), and published numerous papers on these issues in the West. After the First World War, he decided to remain in the newly formed Kingdom of Serbs, Croat and Slovenians and settled in Belgrade, where he died. Dr Reiss was also the honorary chairman of the Yugoslav Royal Academic Air Club and played an important role in social life of the country. He took Serbian citizenship and became naturalised by the grace of the King soon after the First World War. However, a few years before his premature death he lost favour with the Court. Dr Reiss was born in Lausanne in 1876 and died in Belgrade in 1929. There is a small monument erected in 1931 in the memory of this important scholar and in gratitude for his services to Yugoslavia.

what can be the influence of civil society in an emerging democracy? Despite considerable efforts on the part of the civil society, not much has yet materialised.

The police reform that is to follow the promulgation of the new Law on Police should have full support from all the relevant political groups and should not face any major obstacles caused by politicians and groups outside the police force. But, as we have already pointed out, there is reasonable doubt as to whether the Law will be implemented in full as Montenegro has a poor record in law enforcement. This includes not implementing laws and having an inefficient judiciary system. Recently the EU Commissioner, Chris Patten, mentioned the many anti-corruption initiatives in the Balkans that failed in the past. He argued that it is high time to cease practices in which the Balkan countries pretend that they are on a reform path, and the West pretends to believe them (Pobjeda, 2002).

Another major problem is the current lack of a well-rooted police culture as innumerable 'cleansings' took place in the last decade or so, resulting in too many inexperienced and under-trained police officers entering the police force. Clearly, it is very difficult, if not impossible, to reform a police organisation that is closely linked with day-to-day politics, or in a country where the President (currently again the Prime Minister) is accused in another country of running a mafia smuggling ring.[8] Certainly the statements of the former Minister of Internal Affairs, who lost his place in the reshuffled Cabinet, that he was prevented from reforming the police force by the then President (Mr Djukanović) do not help in regaining public trust in the police.

The introduction of continuous professional development (CPD) is another challenge facing the police in Montenegro. It seems that despite general belief in the police organisation that officers are properly educated and trained, this is not the case. There is an urgent need to provide hands-on training, with particular emphasis on practical police skills rather than providing classical theoretical police education. But, despite all these noted shortcomings, it seems that the overall societal climate favours reform and it is most unlikely that the status quo will remain.

If anything is to be learned from the Montenegrin police reform experience, it is that it is impossible for the police to reform itself separately from the society. Policing is a societal function and the society at large is responsible for giving the police the main directions as to what is expected and what should be the outcomes of the proposed reforms. The police on its own cannot design and implement reforms, and a non-responsive society cannot expect to have democratically accountable and socially responsible police force. Socially disembedded police must serve the current political leadership, as society does not serve as the clear focus of its attention. An open society must endorse policing as a societal function and assist it in the process of democratic-oriented reforms.

---

8. Mr Djukanović is under investigation in Italy for possible involvement with the Sicilian Mafia and Mason's lodges and running a smuggling ring across the Adriatic.

References

Bakrač, D. 2003. 'Community Policing – novi policijski koncept u Crnoj Gori' (Community Policing – A New Police Concept in Montenegro). Seminar paper submitted to the European Centre for Peace and Development of the University for Peace established by the United Nation's Graduate School of Management

Bogdanović, B. 2002. *Dva veka srpske policije* (Two Centuries of the Serbian Police). Belgrade.

Buynard, R.S. 1978. *Police: Organisation and Command.* Plymouth.

'By-Law on the Organisations and Modes of Operation of the State Administration' (Uredba o organizaciji i načinu rada državne uprave). *Official Gazette of the Republic of Montenegro*, nos. 8/93, 39/93, 19/95, 13/96, 24/96, 26/96..

Council of Europe. 1999. *Police Powers and Accountability in a Democratic Society: Proceedings Reports presented to the 12th Criminological Colloquium (1999).* Strasbourg.

Council of Europe. 2001. *An Assessment of the Human Rights, Ethics and Policing Standards in the Federal Republic of Yugoslavia, Serbia and Montenegro.* Strasbourg.

Dantzker, M.L. 1999. *Police Organization and Management Yesterday, Today and Tomorrow*, Boston.

Doerner, W.G. and Dantzker, M.L., eds. 2000. *Contemporary Police Organization and Management Issues and Trends.* Boston

European Stability Initiative (ESI). 2001. *Rhetoric and Reform: A Case Study of Institution Building in Montenegro, 1998–2001.* Berlin.

'Law on Internal Affairs' (Zakon o unutrašnjim poslovima). *Official Gazette of the Republic of Montenegro*, nos. 24/94 and 29/94.

'Law on Internal Affairs' (Zakon o unutrašnjim poslovima). *Official Gazette of the Socialist Republic of Montenegro*, nos. 13/85, 32/89 and *Official Gazette of the Republic of Montenegro*, no. 20/93.

'Law on the Principles of the Organisation of the State Administration' (Zakon o načelima organizacije državne uprave). *Official Gazette of the Republic of Montenegro*, no. 56/93.

'Law on the State Administration' (Zakon o državnoj upravi). *Official Gazette of the Republic of Montenegro*, nos. 45/91 and 8/93

Ministry of Justice, Government of Montenegro. 2002. 'Nacrt zakona o državnoj Upravi' (Draft Law on the State Administration). *Official Gazette of the Republic of Montenegro*, nos. 45/91 and 8/93.

Ministry of Justice, Government of Montenegro. 2002. 'Nacrt zakona o inspekciji' (Draft Law on Inspections).

Ministry of Internal Affairs, Government of Montenegro. 2002. 'Nacrt zakona o policiji' (Draft Law on Police).

OSCE.[9] 2001. *Study on Policing in the Federal Republic of Yugoslavia*. Belgrade.

OSCE. 2002a. *Background Report: Priority Areas for Police Reform*. Belgrade.

OSCE. 2002b. *Assisting Police Reform in FRY – Ensuring a Co-ordinated Approach*. Belgrade.

Pajić, Z. 2002. *Legal Aspects of Security Sector Reform in the Federal Republic of Yugoslavia*. Geneva.

Perišić, M., ed. 2002. *Ministarstvo policije i svi njeni ministri od 1811 do 2001* (The Ministry of Police and all its Ministers from 1811 to 2001). Belgrade.

Pobjeda (a major, government controlled daily newspaper in Montenegro), 30 Nov. 2002

Rajs, R.A. 1920. *Prilog za reorganizaciju policije* (A Contribution for the Reorganisation of Police). Belgrade.

Rajs, R.A. (date of publication unknown). *Principi moderne policije* (Principles of a Modern Police Force). Belgrade.

Roberg, R.R. and Kuykendall, J. 1997. *Police Management* 2nd edition. Los Angeles.

Šević, Ž. and Rabrenović, A. 1999.'Civil Service of Yugoslavia: Tradition vs. Transition', in Verheijen, T., ed. *Comparative Civil Service Systems: Central and Eastern Europe*. Aldershot.

Šević, Ž. 2000, 'Politico-administrative relationship in a transitional country: the case of Yugoslavia'. *Politics Administration and Change*, vol. 33.

Slavujević, Z. D. 1997. 'Kriza poverenja u institucije sistema' (The Confidence Crisis in the Institutions of the System), in Mihailović, S., ed. *Izmedju osporavanja i podrške: Javno mnjenje o legitimitetu treće Jugoslavije* (Between the Challenge and Support: Public Opinion about the Legitimacy of the Third Yugoslavia). Belgrade.

Strategy of Local Government Reform in Montenegro. 1998. Government of Montenegro. Podgorica.

Talijan, M., Arandjelović, D. and Velimirović, D. 2001. *Organizacija i poslovi uniformisanih pripadnika policije* (Organisation and Activities of the Uniformed Police Officers). Belgrade.

---

9. Organisation for Security and Co-operation in Europe – The Mission to the Federal Republic of Yugoslavia.

Chapter 13

Police Reform in Serbia

Marijana Trivunović[1]

Introduction

Serbia is one of two republics comprising the State Union of Serbia and Montenegro. Serbia nominally includes two autonomous provinces, Vojvodina and Kosovo, although since 1999, after armed conflict and NATO intervention, Kosovo has been administered by the United Nations Mission in Kosovo under the authority of UN Resolution 1244.

While a federal-level police organisation exists, its role is limited to border policing, security of foreign dignitaries, contacts with international organisations, and other minor functions. The responsibility for the majority of policing tasks lies with the individual republics. As the purpose of this inquiry is to understand the challenges in reforming daily police operations, this paper will be limited to the Ministry of Internal Affairs of the Republic of Serbia. In view of the UN administration of Kosovo noted above, recent developments in policing in Kosovo will be excluded from the scope of this report.

Serbia was one of six constituent republics of the Socialist Federal Republic of Yugoslavia, which violently disintegrated throughout the 1990s. The ensuing wars, international sanctions, and more than a decade of Slobodan Milošević's authoritarian rule set the stage for police reform in Serbia quite differently from the majority of the states under consideration in this volume. During the 1990s, the police in Serbia did not undergo a reform process that would render it compatible with operating in a democracy: on the contrary, the police strengthened their repressive function, a transformation which ran counter to the general democratic trends taking place elsewhere in the region.

The police, in particular the secret police, engaged extensively in the hostilities in Croatia, Bosnia, and Kosovo, as attested by evidence presented before the International War Crimes Tribunal in The Hague. During the second half of the 1990s, militarisation of the police intensified in response to the escalating conflict in Kosovo,[2] and due to Milošević's distrust of the conscript army. For example, in

---

1. Marijana Trivunović is an Open Society Institute International Policy Fellow, Belgrade. She can be contacted at: trivunovic@policy.hu

2. Under the socialist system, Kosovo was an autonomous province within Serbia, whose status was illegally revoked by the Milošević regime in 1989. In the decade that followed, the political, social, and human rights of the 90% majority Albanian population were

1995 a system of 18 levels of ranks closely resembling those of the army was introduced. The organisation cultivated a strict hierarchy and military philosophy, with the police academy offering courses in military tactics and the theory of military operations. The uniformed police were trained, as well, in how to handle heavy weaponry such as mortars, mines, bazookas and other rocket launchers, as well as how to operate helicopters (Weber, 2001: 44).

By the late 1990s, with the emergence of an armed insurgency movement (the Kosovo Liberation Army or KLA), the police became engaged in full combat operations in Kosovo. Units were equipped with armoured vehicles and supported by helicopters and heavy weapons, such as artillery, rocket units, and anti-aircraft guns. While the majority of the most serious operations were carried out by special police units, independent Serbian media reported that by early 1998 some 20,000 uniformed and plain-clothes police were constantly stationed in the province, with a total police strength of up to 30,000–40,000 if one takes into account the secret police and reinforcements that were also regularly deployed from other locales (*Naša Borba*, 1998).

Milošević also used the police to crack down on the opposition within Serbia proper: to break up mass demonstrations in 1991, in the winter of 1996/97, and prior to the 2000 elections; to harass and beat opposition activists, especially in the final months of his rule; and, to carry out surveillance operations, kidnappings, and assassinations of political adversaries.

Moreover, the police – like all other state structures – became implicated in organised crime to the extent that organised crime was one of the 'pillars' of the Milošević regime. During a decade of sanctions, smuggling was organised to supply the country with oil and other basic provisions, as well as other consumer goods, particularly cigarettes. Milošević awarded control of these lucrative operations to family members and associates in exchange for loyalty and support. The police were instructed to, at the very least, not interfere with these illicit business ventures.

Reform that would redefine the police function according to norms appropriate to a democracy could not begin to take place until a democratic political order was established after Milošević's ouster in October 2000. Even then, the reformist government did not fully confront and reform the existing security apparatus. The October 2000 'revolution' was rather a negotiated transition; a number of individuals who had taken part in Milošević's political and criminal enterprises were spared from being called to account in exchange for not preventing Milošević's removal through violent action. The government would ultimately pay a high price for this bargain: in March 2003, the former commander and top operatives of Serbia's elite police unit (Unit for Special Operations – USO) assassinated Prime Minister Zoran Djindjić, in retaliation for the government's escalating confrontation with organised crime and alleged war criminals, with which the USO was deeply entangled.

---

systematically violated, and Albanians resigned from most state functions, or were forcibly removed from them, particularly the police, creating a *de facto* apartheid system.

While the assassination generated the impetus for a resolute crackdown, it would be naïve to think that a three-month police action, even under a state of emergency as was the case here, would fully extirpate all elements associated with the previous regime and its crimes from the political and economic power structures. Political and social alliances are complex and shifting in Serbia, and the political will to come to terms with crime falters at the prospect of losing political advantage.

Nevertheless, in the final appraisal (capricious political winds notwithstanding), when comparing the results achieved (and achievable) in Serbia as compared to the rest of Central and Eastern Europe, it is important to remember that the positive reform process, at the time of publication of this volume, is only three years under way.

Overall goals of reforms

The document describing the long-term strategy and aims for police reform, officially endorsed by the Serbian government in March 2002, outlines the mandate and the principal tasks ahead as follows:

1.   The Serbian Ministry of Internal Affairs seeks to contribute to the
       establishment of a society where the individual feels safe and secure on the
       basis of the rule of law and respect for human rights enshrined in the
       constitution.
2.   The Ministry should be organised in such a way, and behave in such a way so
       that citizens recognise it as an institution that offers a high quality of service.
3.   The Ministry should engage itself energetically in the fight against organised
       crime, keeping in mind he need and the obligation for international
       cooperation in this domain.

The document goes on to elaborate other specific goals and values, including the following:

1.   Establishing effective civil supervision and control over the organisation.
2.   Building trust and improving its image before the public.
3.   Becoming a professional, depoliticised and effective institution, responsive to
       the needs and demands of a democratic transformation, and founded on the
       principles of the rule of law, a market economy and tolerance among all
       cultural, religious, and ethnic groups.
4.   Decentralising in domains where centralisation does not contribute to
       operational effectiveness.
5.   Greater diversity of its personnel in order to better reflect the ethnic and
       gender distribution of the population.
6.   Better cooperation with citizens.
7.   Transparency, particularly in relation to civil authorities on the republican and
       local administrative levels (MIA, 2002a).

The document further outlines the main strategic areas of reform that encompass virtually all areas of police work, including the legal framework, structural and operational changes, effective internal and external supervision mechanisms, reform of the training and education system, augmentation of technical capacity, and the improvement of the material position of employees. It stipulates specific three-year, five-year, and long-term strategies in every functional area of police work and detailed action plans with detailed projects.

The defined goals for reform reflect the recommendations of international experts, and as such can be considered in line with democratic principles as well as most progressive aims of modern policing. While commendable (not to say impressive), extensive and comprehensive, the stated goals are also inevitably long-term. The speed and effectiveness with which they will be implemented remains to be seen in a few years' time. Nevertheless, initial steps and priorities can be examined more closely.

Initial priorities

The first major reform initiative emerged in response to a crisis, the low-level armed conflict which erupted in the winter of 2000/2001 in three South Serbian municipalities (Preševo, Bujanovac and Medvedja), where ethnic Albanians comprise a significant percentage of the population, and a majority in two of the three municipalities.[3] Among the confidence-building measures undertaken by the Serbian government and the international community, the Organisation for Security and Cooperation in Europe (OSCE) Mission in Federal Republic of Yugoslavia introduced a multi-ethnic policing initiative, with a focus on training and education and with the aim of balancing the ethnic Albanian presence in the police structures of these municipalities, and thus begin to restore the trust of the local population in state institutions. A delicate peace was established within months; the new multi-ethnic policing was positively evaluated by the public and was continued.

The first phase of the training consisted of brief refresher courses for Serbian police officers and ethnic Albanian reservists and former police officers who had been dismissed or left the force during Milošević's rule. Over the first year, through September 2002, the OSCE programme was extended to new recruits, with a total of 357 students – among them 28 women – from Serb, Albanian, and other ethnic communities having completed a 12-week foundation training course and 15-week field training. A total of 600 officers were projected to have been trained by the end of 2002 (OSCE, 2002b: 7).

The OSCE extended its involvement to other areas of policing, based on a needs analysis completed in October 2001 (*Study on Policing in the Federal Republic of Yugoslavia*, 2001). Other international organisations, most importantly

---

3. After the establishment of the international administration in Kosovo, an armed insurgency movement emerged among Albanian community in south Serbia.

the Council of Europe and the Geneva Centre for the Democratic Control of Armed Forces (DCAF), have likewise conducted assessments and elaborated recommendations during the first year, many of which have been reflected in the official police reform agenda. The early efforts included the September 2001 establishment of an Advisory Body, formed in partnership with a local NGO (League of Experts – LEX) and supported by the Danish Centre for Human Rights, whose role was to counsel the Ministry in charting a course for reform. Other bilateral foreign assistance in various aspects of policing has arrived since.

The OSCE has played the most systematic and sustained role in police reform in Serbia, above all in advising on the strategy and implementation plans for reform, and can be regarded as the Ministry of Internal Affairs' principal partner. The organisation has been invited to assume a coordinating function for all donor activities relating to police reform in Serbia. At the June 2002 donors conference, support for the ambitious long-term goals was solicited on the basis of six initial priority areas determined jointly by the OSCE and the Serbian Ministry of Internal Affairs, as follows (OSCE, 2002a):

1. Police Education and Development.
2. Accountability and Internal Control.
3. Organised Crime.
4. Forensics.
5. Border Policing.
6. Community Policing.

To identify the most important priorities, one may note that of the total US $10.8 million projected for immediate needs, US $5.7 million or 53% was earmarked for the Organised Crime Programme and Forensics, demonstrating the international community's emphasis on building capacity to fight crime (OSCE, 2002a: 2).

Combating organised crime and corruption has been rightly considered the top priority by the Serbian government and the general public, as confirmed by the murder of Prime Minister Djindjić. The assassins – former and current members of the police Unit for Special Operations – were demonstrated to be also the top leadership of one of the most powerful criminal organisations whose income-generating activities included kidnappings of wealthy individuals for hefty ransoms and regional drug trade. Indeed, revelations following the assassination indicated that some of Serbia's most renowned war heroes, or rather war criminals, shifted their engagement to other criminal enterprises once the wars ended. Evidence supports the government's claim that the assassination was motivated in considerable part by the police's advances in combating organised crime, and the government's confrontation with the indictees of the Hague Tribunal. In fact, on the day that Djindjić was murdered he was on the way to sign arrest warrants for the very individuals responsible for his death.

Changes in the legal status and powers of the police

At the time of writing of this chapter, a new law on the police had not yet been passed. A draft Law on Internal Affairs had already been elaborated in summer 2001, but underwent continuing revisions for another two years. In late July 2003, the Minister of Interior announced the anticipated adoption of the new law, along with a comprehensive organisational restructuring, for the autumn of that year.

The process has been delayed, in part, by the formulation of a new federal constitution (the State Union of Serbia and Montenegro came into being only in February 2003), which in turn postponed the drafting of the Serbian constitution (anticipated by the end of 2003). The new republican constitutional arrangement may well incorporate elements of decentralisation, which would have certain impact on police responsibilities to local government authorities. There are also indications of evolution in thinking about the most appropriate provisions for civil control and supervision, and that the ultimate solution would be part of a comprehensive multi-layered framework. The OSCE – a key advisor on this issue – engaged an expert dedicated solely to accountability questions in the autumn of 2002, a move that advanced the process considerably.

The areas of legislative changes that have received immediate attention – areas where laws have already been passed – reflect other political priorities for reform. Amendments to the Criminal Code and Criminal Procedure Code in Serbia were passed in spring 2002, abolishing the death penalty and defining new corruption offences, and in December 2002, establishing the provisions for witness protection and undercover agents. Additional contested amendments were introduced following Djindjić's assassination, such as increasing pre-trial detention of up to 90 days for individuals suspected of involvement in organised crime, but this provision was ultimately struck down by the Constitutional Court in response to challenges by domestic human rights NGOs and the advice of international organisations such as the Council of Europe. New legislation on combating organised crime in July 2002 (Law On Organisation and Jurisdiction of Government Authorities in Suppression of Organised Crime) provided for a special public prosecutor and dedicated teams within the Ministry of Internal Affairs. Additional institutional and legislative harmonisation still needs to take place, but there are positive indications that the legislative framework will in the end stand in full compliance with international standards. In addition to the long-awaited law on police, additional legislation on police education and prevention of hooliganism was expected in autumn 2003.

The most important legal and operational change, however, has been the separation of the security services at the republican level from the supervision of Ministry of Interior. In July 2002, legislation was passed defining the State Security Service (the secret police) as an independent body, the Security Information Agency (*Bezbednosno-informativna agencija*), accountable directly to the republican government and the Parliament – the first move towards asserting civil control over highly compromised and traditionally widely-feared institution (Law On Security Information Agency). While the law requires that the agency director, appointed by the government, report regularly to the republican parliament, human rights activists question the constitutionality of some of the legal provisions,[4] while other observers remain sceptical whether depoliticisation has been achieved.

It may be appropriate to mention that similar redefinitions of security services have occurred at the federal level, placing under control of the federal parliament and the government the four security services operating at the federal level: the military security service, the military information service, the service for investigation and documentation, and the security service of the federal Ministry of Interior (Law On Security Services of the Federal Republic Of Yugoslavia, July 2002).

Changes in the organisational structures and policies of the police

Except for the above-noted separation of security services, the core functions of the Ministry of Interior remain unchanged from the previous period. The Ministry of Interior is responsible for the following tasks:

1. Protection of the constitutional order.
2. Protection of life, person, and property of citizens.
3. Prevention and detection of criminal acts and the apprehension and transfer to appropriate authorities of their perpetrators.
4. Maintenance of public order, security of certain persons and objects.
5. Traffic safety.
6. Control of border crossings and border areas.
7. Procurement and possession of weapons.
8. Manufacture and trade of explosives and other flammable substances.
9. Personnel training.
10. Firefighting.
11. Administrative functions such as issuing of citizenship, identity cards, passports, and drivers licenses; residence registration control, and the registration of foreigners (Law on Ministries, May 2002).

The Minister of Internal Affairs, at the head of structure, with the Chief of Police/Assistant Minister below, direct the Public Security Department (PSD), which is comprised – horizontally – of ten Directorates (Crime Investigation, Uniform Police, Traffic Police, Border Police, Aliens and Administration

---

4. Human rights groups, notably the Humanitarian Law Centre, have challenged the constitutionality of some of the law's provisions as being in possible violation of the privacy of correspondence through imprecise definitions and delimitations of concepts such as 'threats to security of the Republic of Serbia' (Humanitarian Law Centre, 2002).

Procedures, Police Fire Prevention, Analysis, Information Technology, Communications, Common Affairs, and Board and Lodging), two special units (Special Anti-terrorist Unit and Gendarmerie), and an Operations Centre.

The special units require some attention. The Gendarmerie, estimated at over one thousand men, represents the transformation of the former Special Police Units, notorious for quelling disorders beyond control of the regular police. Previously, members of the Special Police Units were integrated into the regular ranks of the police, to be called out and deployed in extraordinary situations, disrupting day-to-day police functions. The reconfigured elite corps has a permanent structure of specially trained personnel, including an anti-terrorist unit.

The Gendarmerie assumed the responsibility for all special operations from the Unit for Special Operations (USO), colloquially referred to as the Red Berets, disbanded in March 2003 following revelations that their former commander and top officers murdered the Prime Minister and led one of the most powerful criminal organisations in the country. The lurid history of the Red Berets illuminates this otherwise shocking development: this was the unit responsible for some of the most appalling combat operations (and, inevitably, war crimes) during the former Yugoslav conflicts; this was also the unit that staged a ten-day protest in November 2001, after the arrest and extradition to the Hague Tribunal of two members accused of committing war crimes in Kosovo. At the time, the standoff ended peacefully through negotiations, although, as events would later demonstrate, not entirely successfully.

The Minister also directly supervises a newly formed Directorate for Organised Crime Suppression (Organised Crime Unit), an Inspector General, the Legal Affairs Section, as well as three training and research institutions – the Institute of Security, the Police College, and the Police Secondary School. The Police Academy is an independent institution under the jurisdiction of the Ministry of Education.

Also separate from the PSD and in line with OSCE recommendations, within the Minister's Cabinet, three new bureaus have been established: the Bureau for Co-operation with International Police and Security Services, the Bureau for Public Relations and Media, and the Bureau for Petitions and Grievances.

All the above-mentioned organisational changes are described as an introduction to a forthcoming complete reorganisation of the Ministry of Internal Affairs upon the promulgation of the necessary legal framework, announced for autumn 2003 (MIA, 2002a).

Personnel

According to the OSCE Report on Policing in Federal Republic of Yugoslavia, in 2001, employees of the Serbian Ministry of Internal Affairs numbered nearly

35,000, with approximately 21,000 uniformed officers[5] and 5000 plain-clothes investigators (detectives) or scientific support officers (OSCE, 2001: 34). Compared to the 7.5 million population of Serbia (excluding Kosovo), according to 2002 census results, the above figures suggest a ratio of 2.8 uniformed police officers per thousand citizens. The October 2002 official Ministry of Interior figures published in *Results of the Ministry Realised in the Period January-November 2002*, however, define that ratio as 2.41 per thousand citizens, a figure smaller than the ratio of police per capita in France, Slovakia, Croatia, Bulgaria, and Great Britain (MIA, 2002f).[6] While the official information is unclear because it does not disclose the raw data on which the calculation was based, there are nevertheless indications of reductions in an effort to bring Serbian police structures in line with international standards. Ministry of Internal Affairs regular reports, however, continue to indicate understaffing (71% of 'systematised', or formally designated, positions), and particularly the lack of highly trained and specialised personnel in the domain of criminal investigations (MIA, 2003c).

Personnel changes began to be implemented immediately upon the change of regime in October 2000. The Milošević era Minister of Internal Affairs and Chief of Security Services, both indicted by the Hague Tribunal for their role in the Kosovo conflict, were the first to be removed from power.[7] The newly appointed and current (as of July 2003) Minister of Internal Affairs, Dušan Mihajlović, is the leader of New Democracy, a small party within the ruling coalition, and a former Milošević coalition partner (1994–98).

By December 2002, 405 replacements had been made at the highest-level leadership positions, including heads of directorates, regional secretariats and commanders of police stations (MIA, 2002f). It has been reported that from January 2001 to June 2002, more than 2500 police officers were dismissed (Milin, 2002). News stories of officers dismissed or arrested for past or present crimes remain a regular feature in the Serbian daily press.

Nevertheless, the process is far from complete. There has been no systematic lustration of the police or any other state institution, and the task of identifying, investigating, and prosecuting individuals who have committed crimes or still engage in illicit activities remains a piecemeal process. Human rights organisations such as the Helsinki Committee for Human Rights in Serbia and the Humanitarian Law Centre are particularly concerned that numerous army and police officials who took part in war crimes committed against the non-Serb population in the

---

5. Of these, prior to the establishment of the Gendarmerie, some 6000 would be called away from regular duties and deployed in the Special Police Unit in extraordinary circumstances.
6. In the regular bi-annual Ministry of Interior report for the period January–June 2003, this ratio is revised to 2.74 (MIA 2003c).
7. The former, Vlajko Stojiljković, has since committed suicide, while the latter, Radomir Marković, has been arrested and is standing trial for the attempted murder of former principal opposition leader Vuk Drašković and for the murder of Drašković's associates.

neighbouring countries and in Kosovo, and in the torture of minority members in
Serbia (particularly in Sandžak and southern Serbia) during the previous regime, are
still at large and active, and that many of them still occupy key police and army
positions (Helsinki Committee, 2002: 28). While the operations following the
Djindjić assassination identified and prosecuted a number of these key individuals,
others still remain.

Most comprehensive and serious changes in the organisational structures and
personnel have taken place in southern Serbia, with the introduction of multi-ethnic
policing. The Helsinki Committee for Human Rights in Serbia reported in October
2002 significant gains toward proportional representation of Albanians among the
police ranks, noted below, compared to the Milošević era when no Albanian officers
were in service.

**Table 13.1   Ethnic distribution among general population and police in
southern Serbia**

Municipality	Population (in %)			Police (in %)		
	Serbs	Albanians	Others	Serbs	Albanians	Others
Bujanovac	34,14	54,69	11,17	58	40	2
Medvedja	66,57	26,17	7,26	85,7	12,1	2
Preševo	8,55	89,10	2,35	50	50	-

Source: Helsinki Committee 2002: 30–1; Republican Bureau for Statistics, 2002.

In terms of the police leadership, the head of police/ chief superintendent in
Preševo was an Albanian, in Medvedja a Montenegrin, and in Bujanovac a Serb.
Superintendents of police stations in all three municipalities are Serbs, but they were
appointed in consultation with representatives of the Albanian national community,
a gesture welcomed by the local Albanians. Despite the progress, minorities remain
underrepresented in other regions where they constitute significant portions of the
population, notably in the regions of Sandžak (Bosniaks) and Vojvodina
(Hungarians).

The Helsinki Committee for Human Rights in Serbia notes that the heads of
three out of four Sandžak police departments are Serbs (one is Bosniak,) and reports
the following ethnic distribution of police, as compared to the general population:

Table 13.2   Ethnic distribution among general population and police in Sandžak

Municipality	Population		Police	
	Serbs	*Bosniaks*	*Serbs*	*Bosniaks*
Nova Varoš	90	10	88,41	8,51
Prijepolje	85	15	53,24	43,42
Sjenica	84,16	15,84	76,1	22,40
Priboj*				
Tutin	4,32	94,23	70	30
Novi Pazar	20,46	76,27	70	30

*Data not available
Source: Helsinki Committee 2002: 30–1; Republican Bureau for Statistics, 2002

The Helsinki Committee also noted a positive step in the reinstatement of 23 Bosniak policemen who had been suspended during the NATO intervention due to their refusal to fight in Kosovo (Helsinki Committee, 2002: 31).

In Vojvodina, where according to 2002 census data, Hungarians represent 14.28%, and Serbs, Montenegrins and Yugoslavs combined comprise less than 70% of the total population, police ranks appear similarly unrepresentative (Republican Bureau for Statistics, 2002: 2). In the 36 municipalities polled by the Helsinki Committee, out of a total of 24 heads of police departments, only one was a Hungarian, while the rest were Serbs and Montenegrins. In the same municipalities, five police superintendents (13.89%) were non-Serbs, 20 were Serbs and Montenegrins, while the ethnicity of the remaining 11 superintendents has not been established (Helsinki Committee, 2002: 33–4)

A more active recruitment of women into police ranks has been introduced. During 2002, the first two groups of more than 700 female officers have completed the foundation course and began field training (MIA, 2002d). Women have also constituted roughly 8% of the new multiethnic police in southern Serbia. In the summer of 2002, for the first time, 30% of the student population at the police academy were females (OSCE, 2002a: 28). By the end of 2002, the Ministry of Interior also reported a total number of 6777 women employed within the organisation, or 19.1% of total staff, noting that the recruitment of women in 2002 was five times higher than in the previous year. Of that total, 752 are women operating as police officers, primarily as highly visible 'beat cops' and traffic officers. The Ministry also cites that 251 women occupy leadership positions within the organisation (MIA, 2002a). These numbers represent a modest improvement, but still stand far lower than the gender composition of some Western European police services.

Changes in the operational policies and work patterns of the police

While low-level armed conflict that erupted in southern Serbia shortly following the arrival of the reformist government presented the key challenge to the Ministry of Internal Affairs in the early months of reform, successful moves on the political front combined with responsible actions of the police contributed to the timely de-escalation of the crisis. Ethnically mixed patrols trained by the OSCE, as noted earlier, represent a critical operational change that has largely contributed to confidence-building in the region and the gradual, if slow-moving, normalisation of political and social relations.

Since then, combating organised crime and corruption, including crime linked to the previous regime, has since been viewed as the police's most important task and their greatest challenge, only further emphasised with the Prime Minister's assassination. The most visible and most publicly-promoted operational changes relate to this area of the organisation's mandate. This is likewise the area where strongest international links have been established, beginning with FR Yugoslavia's re-admittance to Interpol in September 2001, and cooperation with other regional police bodies, including the newly created Association of the Police Chiefs in SEE (SEPCA). International support to enhance the organisation's ability to combat (international) organised crime in form of training and equipment are likewise underway. Special trainings to combat trafficking in human beings, particularly trafficking in women, have been offered by international organisations. Indeed, such activities are growing increasingly numerous.

The Ministry of Interior Affairs formed special organised crime teams to investigate a number of unresolved murder cases, attempted assassinations and kidnappings during the Milošević era, but with modest results prior to Djindjić's assassination. The most notable action until then was the October 2002 arrest of individuals suspected of assassinating a police general earlier in the same year. With a spectacular series of actions following the Prime Minister's murder, most of the pending cases were solved. The successes, however, have further highlighted the remaining unresolved cases – among them killings of journalists – which have an unmistakable political dimension.

Before then, widely publicised but far less enthusiastically received actions have included the spring and summer 2002 initiatives to break up the structures of illegal smuggling both at the international level (e.g. South-East European regional police operation to thwart cigarette smuggling in the region), and also at the domestic level in cooperation with the Customs Directorate and a national NGO – Resistance (*Otpor*)[8] – reflecting a desire to rally support for, and present, a new, open and results-oriented government institution.

Initiatives drawing on some community policing ideas have been introduced. Increased foot patrols in areas considered to be particularly unsafe were introduced

---

8. The NGO in question, National Movement Resistance (*Narodni pokret Otpor*), was one of the key civil society organisations mobilising voters to oust Milošević in 2000.

in 2001. Television advertisements explaining that the police are a neighbourhood friend who is there to serve and protect were aired for a brief duration, but discontinued, observers feel, due to a persisting lack of credibility in the eyes of the population. This general trend shifted dramatically in the months following Djindjić's assassination, during the state of emergency and undertaking of Operation Saber, when public enthusiasm soared in response the police bringing in for questioning more than 11,000, detaining over 2700, and bringing charges against 3946 individuals. While the ultimate success of these investigations remains to be seen, the public approval ratings have declined once again with the return to normality and the daily frustrations with the political and economic situation.

Only long-term sustained efforts to combat organised crime and corruption can effect a lasting increase in public confidence, as will ongoing efforts to engender a service orientation among the officers, which at this stage are only rudimentary. Community policing programmes, launched in December 2002 in five districts throughout Serbia considered representative of the challenges facing the police throughout the country, represent a positive step in this direction.[9] Implementation plans include public opinion surveys, consultation with local communities, and the elaboration of indigenous models of community policing appropriate to the selected socio-economic and cultural contexts.

Some symbols of service orientation have been introduced (nametags and new uniforms that are less militaristic in appearance have been distributed), yet their purpose and intent was not thoroughly inculcated among the individual officers. Anecdotal evidence exists – including personal experience of this researcher – that some officers do not feel comfortable having their names publicly displayed and no longer being protected by a shield of impunity of anonymous authority.

In local police stations, posters of smiling policemen proclaiming their new role to serve and protect have appeared. Yet in everyday encounters, experiences vary widely: it is a matter of pure random chance whether a citizen in everyday life will encounter traditional rudeness or exemplary professionalism. The notable exception to any visible improvement, however, remains police treatment of vulnerable groups, particularly the Roma. Furthermore, human rights watchdogs continue to document torture of suspects and individuals apprehended for having committed crimes,[10] although experts estimate that its incidence has decreased.

Steps such as the introduction of a serious and comprehensive code of conduct in April 2003[11] will assist in changing the behaviour of officers only if coupled with meaningful sanctions of misconduct on one hand, and a system of rewards, on the other. Both approaches need further improvement.

---

9. The five community policing pilots have been launched in Zvezdara, a Belgrade municipality; Kragujevac, a mid-sized city; Vrnjačka Banja, a town in Central Serbia; Novi Bečaj, a small town in Vojvodina; and in the three majority-Albanian municipalities in southern Serbia.
10. Humanitarian Law Centre, http://www.hlc.org.yu
11. 'Instructions on Police Ethics and Methods of Police Work' (MIA, 2003b).

There have been palpable efforts to improve transparency and communication with the public. The Minister and other high officials regularly hold press conferences and issue public communiqués, as well as exhaustive bi-annual progress reports detailing not only crime statistics, but also increasingly information on disciplinary actions against officers, the personnel situation (number of women recruited, for example), international cooperation initiatives, and progress in reform. The Ministry of Internal Affairs' website posts useful information about administrative procedures as well as general information about the structure and responsibilities of the police. The site also posts weekly updates ranging from crime statistics and data on police effectiveness, to auctions and tenders, to employment opportunities and recruitment announcements, to responses to complaints and letters of appreciation from citizens. While the effort does not appear entirely systematic, it nevertheless represents a commendable attempt to improve transparency and communication with the public.

Education and training

The OSCE is in significant part guiding the reforms of the system of education and training. In addition to the multiethnic police training in southern Serbia, the OSCE has offered a Modern Policing Course to a number of serving officers in other regions of Serbia. By October 2002, 1169 officers had been trained, with a total number of 2500, or 25%, of all Serbian patrol officers projected to have been trained by the end of 2002 (OSCE, 2002b: 7).

In parallel, the OSCE has been advising the Ministry of Internal Affairs on the comprehensive reform of the educational system, resulting in plans to consolidate the existing three educational and training centres (police secondary school, college, and academy) into a single police education institution. The planning process has been extensive, including evaluations of the existing systems and structures, an assessment of needs, and a detailed project plan and programme to meet those needs. In addition, a management training programme has been initiated to equip the organisation's leaders and managers with the skills required to carry out the reform process over the long term (OSCE, 2002a: 27–8). Courses on ethics and human rights have been delivered by the OSCE as well as national human rights NGOs. Specialised training on combating various forms of organised crime appear to be ongoing.

Changes in supervision and control of the police

The existing, but soon-to-be modified, law on the police (1991 Law on the Ministry of Internal Affairs) stipulates a measure – an inadequate one – of civil supervision. The police organisation was defined as accountable to the Minister of Internal Affairs, who is in turn accountable to the Parliament. In 1997, two bodies were set up for the supervision of security services, but played no such supervision role during the previous regime (Weber, 2001: 54). New solutions are pending.

The initial new draft law elaborated in June 2001 stipulated a permanent parliamentary commission overseeing the work of the police, though by the following summer opinion had shifted towards creating the institution of Ombudsman. In this context, the Ministry of Internal Affairs recommended establishing a separate Ombudsman responsible solely for questions relating to the police. An implementation plan proposed by the OSCE in winter 2002/03 called for a multi-layered accountability system including parliamentary supervision, external supervision in the form of an independent body empowered to conduct investigations, internal accountability mechanisms, as well as community consultation mechanisms. The full implementation process is anticipated to begin in 2003.

In the meantime, some interim measures have been tested. The Council for State Security of Serbia – a seven-member supervisory body was created in January 2002 to co-ordinate activities and set priorities in the security sector – is a purportedly temporary solution implemented in response to the November 2001 protest of the Red Berets discussed earlier. The Council members include the Federal President, the Serbian Prime Minister, five other republican ministers, and the Prime Minister's security advisor. The body issues reports to the President of Yugoslavia, the Prime Minister of Serbia, the Yugoslav and Serbian interior ministers, senior diplomats, the head of the Serbian Parliament, and the chief of the Coordination Body for South Serbia (Stojković, 2002).[12]

Legal experts and human rights activists oppose this solution as it leaves too much authority within the executive. Parliamentary control of state security – as part of the complex accountability mechanism elaborated in the OSCE accountability implementation plan – is broadly held to be the more appropriate solution.

The OSCE plan calls for parliamentary supervision as one in a system of multi-layered measures, as each separate accountability instrument has its shortcomings. Parliamentary committees, for example, may function poorly because they lack the training, experience, or authority to effectively carry out their function. A scandal that broke out shortly following the passage of the federal law on security services (involving the alleged wiretapping of the federal president) illustrated a number of potential deficiencies, ranging from a lack of independence and impartiality of ad hoc parliamentary committees that would investigate potential abuses, to public access to information in such proceedings (*B92 News*, 2002). Proposals for permanent accountability structures for the Ministry of Interior are awaited with anticipation by many observers.

Internally, an Inspector General's office was established within the Ministry of Interior in mid-2002 to manage internal investigations of complaints and

---

12. The list of recipients will probably ultimately include the President of Serbia, a function that had remained occupied by Milan Milutinović, a figure from the previous regime, until the expiration of his mandate in December 2002.

grievances, but it was only staffed by mid-2003, and internal disciplinary procedures remain problematic. While on the one hand, there are frequent, almost weekly reports of police officers being sanctioned for illicit activities or inappropriate behaviour, and while statistical data supports the claim that there is a crackdown on rogue officers,[13] human rights groups such as the Humanitarian Law Centre continue to document allegations of police brutality and torture, particularly against arrested suspects. While investigations of such allegation are inevitably initiated, human rights activists remain concerned that, in many instances, investigations are not thoroughly pursued and that human rights abuses are insufficiently sanctioned.

Implementation and success of reforms

The vision, aims, values and strategy for police reform in Serbia follow to a great extent the recommendations outlined by the OSCE, the Council of Europe, DCAF and other experts. The reform process is in its early stages, and it is moving forward. There exists a comprehensive and managed strategy for reform, and a commitment to the process by the very top police officials. The Ministry of Internal Affairs reform management teams work in close cooperation with the OSCE, obtaining top expert guidance in their efforts. In a number of interviews conducted with the OSCE police reform team in Belgrade, this researcher has found nothing but the highest appreciation for the commitment and seriousness about change from the Serbian police officials. These factors are not to be underestimated; they are the basic ingredients for success.

Funds have been made available by the international donor community to begin the extensive process of reform, but more fundraising will be required to bring it forward as planned. The June 2002 donors conference secured 4.3 million Euro of support, compared with the 10.8 million Euro estimated need for immediate reform measures, plus an additional 16 million Euro projected need for short-term measures (OSCE, 2002a: 2). Additional funding will be required in the coming years, and successful fundraising will inevitably affect the speed with which the envisioned reforms can be implemented.

Yet there are several serious obstacles to police reform in Serbia at the present. One is the unstable political situation created by an unwieldy 18-member governing coalition representing a broad range of ideological/political positions. Djindjić's assassination has only accelerated the inevitable fragmentation of such a construct, prompting an open and increasingly vicious conflict even among the partners in government. By mid-2003, the bitter rivalry between two principal centres of power – the Serbian Prime Minister Zoran Djindjić's Democratic Party

---

13. The Ministry of Internal Affairs cites, for example, that from 25 January 2001 to 28 February 2002, a total of 1302 disciplinary procedures were initiated, with 265 resulting in criminal indictments, 41 arrests, 277 suspensions, 74 dismissals, and 317 disciplinary actions (MIA, 2002a).

and the former federal President Vojislav Koštunica's Democratic Party of Serbia, and the resulting endless delays and bickering over seemingly every detail of state management – transformed into a multi-polar competition for power, jeopardising progress on the previously agreed course of reforms and feeding public cynicism and distrust.

While the fight against organised crime and war criminals has advanced in the wake of the Prime Minister's assassination, the task has not yet been completed. Questions about the current government's link with criminal groups are lingering, and one of the two key Hague indictees, Ratko Mladić, believed to reside in Serbia, is still at large. Until these issues have been completely resolved, the ability of the police to carry out its duties unobstructed by political pressure remains in question. Suspicion lingers that political bartering continues to dictate the success of police in combating all categories of crime, be it organised crime, or, increasingly, high-level corruption of government officials.

The greatest challenge will remain in generating high-level political commitment to relinquishing its lingering influence over the police, and to create the conditions that will transform the organisation into a truly independent institution that applies the law equally to individuals supportive of the government as to individuals in opposition. This aspect of the reform may be the most difficult to track and measure, for it is only the occasional political scandal that may reveal, for instance, the complicity among law enforcement bodies in (concealing) corruption.

Nevertheless, there are many positive developments in the process of police reform in Serbia, with the most promising aspects relating to the daily functioning of the police and their ability to impact positively on the lives of ordinary citizens. Comprehensive transformation of the police organisation will be a gradual process, advanced in part by the natural attrition of existing ranks and the introduction of new, well-trained officers without ties or debts to dubious interests and structures. The planned reform initiatives, combined with a budding service-oriented police culture should, over time, influence public opinion to the positive, shaking the inertia of discontent. Yet success will be measurable only in a few years' time.

General lessons about police reform

With the reform process only in its early stages, and a lack of measurable indicators for the short term, it is difficult to draw definite conclusions. A few preliminary observations might nevertheless be made.

(1) The needs and priorities of police reform must reflect particular histories and political developments. States emerging from personal dictatorships (rather than one-party dictatorships) will inherit different formal and informal structures of power and influence that inevitably shape the challenges confronting the police. Similarly, states emerging from armed conflict, particularly internal strife, will have an additional set of challenges in reforming a police organisation that has participated in such a conflict.

(2)   In settings with high levels of crime, particularly organised crime, 'democratisation' may become a lower priority. In transitional settings in particular, it is critical to ensure that calls for law and order do not become a justification for neglect of fundamental human rights and freedoms.

(3)   Political will, and readiness for change among the top police leadership, appears to be a highly valued factor among police experts advising on reforms in Serbia. It leads to effective collaboration and generates a great deal of enthusiasm for the process. Nevertheless, political will for reform can exist selectively, or only 'up to a point', with compromised high level individuals enjoying protection from prosecution. While there is a great deal that can be done to reform the complete organisation without eliminating such key individuals, the reform process will not be brought forward past a certain point, and there will remain a danger of 'backsliding' if such individuals are allowed to continue to function with impunity.

(4)   Top-level expert assistance is invaluable in planning and implementing reforms. Even more important, however, is that the expertise be available over a longer term, particularly at the start of the reform process. Hastily formed solutions imposed from the outside can have little hope of producing desired changes.

(5)   Reform must have local ownership, for it is the individuals within the organisation who will carry out the reforms over the long term.

(6)   Police reform must be a comprehensive undertaking, affecting all structures and areas of police operations. New values must be reiterated at all levels, from recruitment, to training, to daily operations, to management approaches, to accountability and supervision mechanism.

(7)   Progress in police reform should be tracked systematically over a period of years through a variety of meaningful benchmarks and indicators, including officer attitudes and public approval ratings.

(8)   Accountability and supervision mechanisms should be viewed as a multi-layered system, for no single mechanism can fully respond to the requirements appropriate for a democracy.

(9)   And finally, reform costs. The donor community must be prepared to assist over several years, particularly in poor countries, to sustain a momentum for reform.

References

Advisory Body of the Ministry of Interior Affairs of Republic of Serbia and League of Experts (*Savetodavno Telo MUP RS i Liga Eksperata*). MIO 2002. *Vizija, Vrednosti, Misija, Ključne Oblasti Rada* (Vision, Values, Mission, Key Areas of Activity). Belgrade. Unpublished document.

B92 News. 14 July 2002. http://www.b92.net

Helsinki Committee for Human Rights in Serbia (Helsinki Committee). 2002. 'Serbia', in International Helsinki Federation for Human Rights, ed. *The Role of Community Policing in Building Confidence in Minority Communities: Albania, Bulgaria, Croatia, Macedonia, Romania and Serbia. Report of the to the OSCE Supplementary Human Dimension Meeting on the Role of Community Policing in Building Confidence in Minority Communities,* Vienna, 28-29 Oct., conference report.

Humanitarian Law Center. 2002. *HLC Challenges Constitutionality Of Security Information Agency Act Provisions.* 2 Dec. 2002. E-mail announcement.

Milin, Z. 2002. 'Serbia's Police Reform Introduces Female Officers'. *Balkan Times,* 4 June 2002. http://www.balkantimes.com/html2/english/020531-ZORKA-001.htm

Naša Borba. 23 Feb. 1998

OSCE Mission in FRY (OSCE). 2001. *Study on Policing in The Federal Republic of Yugoslavia.* http://www.osce.org/yugoslavia/documents/report/files/report-policing-e.pdf

OSCE Mission in FRY (OSCE). 2002a. *Background Report: Police Reform In Serbia Seeks and Receives Substantial International Support.* http://www.osce.org/yugoslavia/documents/reports/files/report-police-support.pdf

OSCE Mission in FRY (OSCE) .2002b. *Assisting Police Reform in FRY –Ensuring a Co-ordinated Approach.* http://www.osce.org/yugoslavia/documents/reports/files/PC-paper-10-2002.pdf

Republic of Serbia. Ministry of Internal Affairs (*Republika Srbija. Ministarstvo Unutrašnjih Poslova* [MIA]). 2002a. *Informacija o reformi ministarstva unutrašnjih poslova sa predlogom zaključaka* (Information About Reform of the Ministry of Internal Affairs with Proposed Conclusions). Belgrade, 25 Mar. 2002. http://www.srbija.sr.gov.yu/video/mup_reforma.zip

Republic of Serbia. Ministry of Internal Affairs. 2002b. *Obraćanje Dušana Mihajlovića, ministra unutrašnjih poslova Republike Srbije glavnim i odgovornim urednicima medijskih kuća* (Address of Dušan Mihajlović, Minister of Internal Affairs of the Republic of Serbia, To Editors-in-Chief of Media Houses), Belgrade, 21 June 2002. http://www.mup.sr.gov.yu/domino/arhiva.nsf/pages/jun2002

Republic of Serbia. Ministry of Internal Affairs. 2002c. '*Multietnička Policija*' (Multiethnic Police). *Saopštenja za javnost* (Public Statements), 27 June 2002. http://www.mup.sr.gov.yu/domino/arhiva.nsf/pages/jun2000

Republic of Serbia. Ministry of Internal Affairs. 2002d. *Promocija 80. klase kursa za policajce-žene – Govor ministra Dušana Mihajlovića* (Promotion of the 80th Class of the Course for Women Police Officers – Speech of Minister Dušan Mihajlović. *Aktuelna saopštenja* (Recent Statements) 20 Sep. 2002.

http:// www.mup.sr.gov.yu/domino/aktuelnosti.nsf/pages/aktuelnasaopstenja

Republic of Serbia. Ministry of Internal Affairs. 2002e. '*Opoziv objave*' (Retraction of Announcement). *Statements* [*Saopštenja*], 3 Oct. 2002. http://www.mup.sr.gov.yu/domino/skzn.nsf/opozivobjave

Republic of Serbia. Ministry of Internal Affairs. 2002f. '*Rezultati ministarstva ostvareni u periodu januar-novembar 2002. godine*' (Results of the Ministry Realised in the Period Jan.-Nov. 2002). *Saopštenja* (Statements), Dec. 2002. http://www.mup.sr.gov.yu/domino/skzn1.nsf/17122002

Republic of Serbia. Ministry of Internal Affairs. 2003a. '*Izvestaj o radu ministarstva unutrašnjih poslova Republike Srbije u 2002. godini*' (Report on the Work of the Ministry of Internal Affairs of Republic of Serbia in Year 2002). *Saopštenja* (Statements), Feb. 2002. http://www.mup.sr.gov.yu

Republic of Serbia. Ministry of Internal Affairs. 2003b. *Uputstvo o policijskoj etici i načinu obavljanja poslova policije* (Instructions on Police Ethics and Methods of Police Work). Belgrade, 15 Apr. 2003. http://www.mup.sr.gov.yu

Republic of Serbia. Ministry of Internal Affairs. 2003c. '*Informacija o stanju bezbednosti na teritoriji republike srbije i ostvarenim rezultatima rada ministarstva unutrašnjih poslova republike srbije u periodu od 01. januara do 30. juna 2003. godine*' (Information on the Security Situation on the Territory of the Republic of Serbia and Achieved Work Results of the Ministry of Internal Affairs of the Republic of Serbia in the Period of 1 Jan. to 30 June 2003). *Saopštenja* (Statements). http://www.mup.sr.gov.yu/domino/skzn.nsf/fc9e82a3073a74fac1256c320039 3d62/$FILE/16.07.2003.doc

Republican Bureau for Statistics (*Republički Zavod za Statistiku*). 2002. '*Konačni rezultati popisa 2002*' (Final Results of the Census 2002). *Saopštenja* (Statements) no. 295, 24 Dec. 2002.

Stojković, D. 2002. 'Policing the Police'. *Transitions Online*. 21 Jan. 2002. http://www.tol.cz

Weber, R. 2001. 'Police Organization and Accountability: A Comparative Study', in Kádár, A., ed. *Police in Transition: Essays on Police Forces in Transition Countries*. Budapest.

Zakon o bezbednosno-informativnoj agenciji (Law On Security Information Agency). 2002. *Službeni Glasnik Republike Srbije* (Official Gazette of the Republic of Serbia), no. 42/02.

Zakon o ministarstvima (Law on Ministries). 2002. *Službeni Glasnik Republike Srbije* (Official Gazette of the Republic of Serbia), no. 27/02.

Zakon o organizaciji i nadležnosti državnih organa u suzbijanju organizovanog kriminala (Law On Organisation and Jurisdiction of Government Authorities in Suppression of Organised Crime – Law on Organised Crime). 2002. *Službeni Glasnik Republike Srbije* (Official Gazette of the Republic of Serbia), no. 42/02.

Zakon o službama bezbednosti Savezne Republike Jugoslavije (Law On Security Services of the Federal Republic Of Yugoslavia). 2002. *Službeni List Savezne*

Republike Jugoslavije (Official Gazette of the Federal Republic of Yugoslavia), no. 37/02.

PART V

EASTERN EUROPE

Chapter 14

Police Reform in Russia

Annette Robertson

Introduction

The Russian Federation is the world's largest country, extending across 11 time zones from Saint Petersburg on the Baltic Sea to the Pacific Ocean port of Vladivostok. It is divided into 89 federal (administrative) jurisdictions ('subjects' in Russian), including 49 *oblasts* (provinces), 21 autonomous republics, 10 autonomous *okrugs* (districts), six *krais* (territories), two federal cities (Moscow and Saint Petersburg) and one autonomous *oblast*. In 2000 an additional layer of administration was created with the establishment of seven federal regions, each with its own presidential envoy.

Since declaring its independence in 1991, Russia has implemented wide-ranging reforms to its economic, political and legal systems, with mixed results (Gustafson, 1998). Police reform, however, has yet to achieve the high profile of parallel restructuring processes underway in the judicial and administrative sectors, although all are clearly part of the government programme to modernise and democratise Russia.

Police reform has in fact been on the agenda since the early 1990s, and in 1996 the 'Concept of Development' was adopted for the Ministry of Internal Affairs, of which the police, or 'militia', are part. Reform became the focus of greater attention with the appointment in 2001 of current Minister of the Interior, Boris Gryzlov, the first civilian appointee to the post. President Vladimir Putin expressly appointed Gryzlov on a reform mandate, with the aim of providing a more effective and efficient service, and promoting greater public trust in, and support for the militia. As this chapter will show, however, in spite of many changes to the legal status, organisational structure and operational policies of the militia, Russia has yet to achieve the reforms considered necessary for the development of democratic policing, in particular responsiveness, accountability, defence of human rights and transparency (Bayley, 2001).

Reform and changes to Russia's policing system since 1989

Since the collapse of the Soviet Union, Russia has been striving to overcome the legacy of communism, including highly centralised, militaristic, politicised and authoritarian law-enforcement agencies (Shelley, 1996; Mawby, 1999). The collapse provoked a law and order crisis, which left the Ministry of Internal Affairs (MVD – *Ministertsvo Vnutrennykh Del*) in a very weak and disorganised shape (Handelman. 1995). During the early 1990s, the whole MVD system began to lose power and authority, weakening it as a unified powerful structure. Its decline has been attributed to many factors, both internal and external, including the destruction of central control, anti-government and other mass protests, depoliticisation and irresponsibility within the MVD (Kazakov, 2001), along with escalating crime rates, especially serious crime such as organised, violent and drug-related crime (Dashkov, 1992; Lotspeich, 1996; Kudriavtsev, 1999), leading to increased levels of insecurity and lower levels of confidence in the militia among the public (Morozov and Segevnin, 1996; Zvekic, 1996; Timoshenko, 1998).

The resulting state of crisis served only to highlight the militia's passive role in law enforcement:

> We are witnesses to their obvious confusion. They only register an increasing number of crimes, but fail to prevent them or, worst still to detect them. Instead of adopting consistent measures, department chiefs frequently embark upon conspiracies, where the main aim is to look better in front of the President and Government, to report on time, to present some positive results as important victories (Militsiya, 1993).

Faced with such a predicament, the need for reform of the MVD system as a whole, and especially the militia, became acute. During the early 1990s some measures were undertaken to reform the militia, aimed supposedly at guaranteeing human rights and freedoms, a more resolute fight against crime, and the maintenance of public order and safety. This led to the adoption of numerous legislative and other normative acts[1] and changes to the organisation and functions of the militia, a process outlined by the orders and instructions issued by the Ministry during this time.[2] It soon became obvious, however, that the reform of such

---

1. Legislation adopted included (a) Federal Laws: 'On the Militia' (18 Apr. 1991); 'On Search and Operational Activity' (12 Aug. 1991); 'On Security' (5 Mar. 1992); 'On Appeals about Court Operations and Decisions Infringing Human Rights and Freedoms' (27 Nov. 1993); and 'On Weapons' (5 May 1993); and (b) Presidential Decrees: 'On the Fight against Corruption in the State Service System' (4 Apr. 1992); 'On Measures for the Protection of Human Rights, Law and Order and Strengthening the Fight Against Crime' (8 Oct. 1992); and 'On Additional Measures for Strengthening Law and Order in the Russian Federation' (8 Oct. 1992).
2. Including: Provisional Instruction no. 415, 'On the Order of Acceptance, Registration, Record-keeping and Sanctions in Militia Departments of Applications, Messages and Other Information about Crimes and Accidents' (11 Nov. 1990); Order no. 70, 'On Measures for the Implementation of the Law of the Russian Federation On the Militia' (20 May 1991); Instruction no. 231, 'On the Organisation of the Activity of Community Militia Officers' (11 July 1992); 'The Charter of Patrol Service of the Militia for Public Safety of the Russian Federation' (18 Jan. 1993); and the Manual 'On the Crime Prevention Activity of Militia Services and Divisions' (6 Aug. 1993).

an important government ministry as Internal Affairs should be more systematic, to include all aspects of its activity.

At the beginning of 1996 academics and practitioners prepared the 'Concept of Development for the Internal Affairs Agencies and Internal Troops of Russia' (MVD, 1996), the main provisions of which were agreed with the Russian President and authorised on 20 March 1996 by Order of the Minister of Internal Affairs.[3] The 'Concept' outlined the development of the MVD in the short (by the end of 1996), medium (by 2000) and long term (by 2005). It defined the main goal of reform as rendering the MVD 'capable of guaranteeing the unfailing protection of individuals, society and the state from criminal encroachments':

> Owing to changes in Russia's economic, political, and social life, as well as the deteriorating criminal situation and growing public demands on the MVD during the development of a democratic and legal state, the MVD must be reformed. (Concept of Development for the Internal Affairs Agencies and Internal Troops of Russia, 1996)

According to the Concept, reform was to be achieved through the introduction of positive changes to the MVD's main areas of operational activity and improvements to the results of its activities to socially acceptable levels, with the aim of restoring and maintaining public respect. In order to reach these goals, various key outcomes were developed, including improvements to: management efficiency; the legal framework; work with personnel; levels of professionalism; cooperation with other law-enforcement agencies and NGOs; international relations; the financial and material base; legal and social protection for employees; and internal discipline. The main tasks placed before the militia were to:

(1) Achieve a turning point in the fight against crime;
(2) Ensure the visibility of positive changes in terms of priority objectives;
(3) Adopt a maximum public-oriented approach;
(4) Mobilise all social resources to counteract criminal expansion.

It was anticipated that by 2005 the major part of the reform process would have been implemented, including the creation of new legal, organisational, financial and material/technical conditions for the optimal functioning of the reformed MVD system; the transfer to a new system of selection, training and appointment of militia personnel; the technical re-equipping of the militia and internal troops; and the provision of legal and social guarantees and conditions for MVD staff. For these tasks to be completed successfully, priority had to be given to policing functions, and it was therefore envisaged that other functions would be transferred to relevant bodies. Accordingly, in 2000 the penitentiary system was transferred to the Ministry of Justice, and in 2001 the fire department was transferred to the Ministry of Civil Defense, Emergencies and Disaster Relief,

---

3. Order no. 145.

relieving the MVD of a significant logistical burden and allowing it to focus on its core law-enforcement tasks.[4]

In order to facilitate the achievement of these tasks, various changes were envisaged and made to the legal status, organisational structure and operational policies and work patterns of the militia, as outlined and reviewed below.

Changes in the legal status of the militia

The legislative framework that existed at the end of the 1980s for the organisation and work of the militia bore the stamp of a totalitarian regime and did not meet the requirements of a legal and democratic state. Russia inherited a plethora of legal acts pertaining to the militia, including more than 4000 acts from the Soviet MVD, some of which directly infringed civil rights, and many of which were not available in the public domain.[5] The adoption of the Law on the Militia in 1991 was therefore heralded by some as a watershed for setting out the role and duties of the militia for public view for the first time, although critics argue it only served to publicly endorse the powers that the militia had been awarded secretly under Soviet rule (Handelman, 1995).

The law defined the legal status and organisational structure of the Russian militia, and thus its place and role in society and as part of executive power. With its adoption, its provisions, including legal safeguards for the life, health, human rights and freedoms, property, and the interests of society and the state from criminal and other unlawful acts, were given the maximum force of law – at least on paper. The law established international humanitarian values as the militia's guiding principles: legitimacy, humanism, social justice, political neutrality, impartiality and respect for, and observance of, human rights. In accordance with international guidelines, the militia must protect any person irrespective of their citizenship, nationality, political convictions and other circumstances. Officers are obliged to defer only to the law, and the creation and activity of political parties or other organisations pursuing political aims are proscribed. In practical terms, this law was a significant step towards narrowing the functions of the militia. It was intended to free individuals and society from the comprehensive police supervision and intrusion that had characterised previous decades.

The law thus provides for many of the principles required for the development of democratic policing in Russia, which is to be applauded, but in practice very few of the law's provisions appear to be adhered to, which is a problem of Russian society as a whole. As succinctly noted by Gilinskiy (2000: 176), 'In Russia, officially proclaimed and legally fixed principles and norms have

---

4. These measures were also required as a result of Russia's obligations to the Council of Europe.
5. For example the Regulation 'On the Soviet Militia' was authorised in 1973, but only published in 1985 some 12 years after its adoption.

always been at variance with reality, including the practice of administering justice, law enforcement and the work of the executive power.' In terms of the Law on the Militia, this means that its provisions are routinely ignored in different ways. For example:

(1)   Human rights abuses by the militia are well documented, especially against ethnic minorities, who tend to be stereotyped as 'terrorists' and 'drug dealers' (Shelley, 1999; Amnesty International, 2002; Human Rights' Watch, 2003). It is clear therefore that militia actions are often arbitrary and not everyone can expect to be treated the same by them.

(2)   Many militia officers are ambivalent to the law in general (Gustafson, 1998).

(3)   Militia activity is far from politically neutral (Timoshenko, 1997).

In terms of assessing the success of militia reform, this last point is particularly interesting. Although the police are 'inherently and inescapably political' (Reiner, 1985: 2) police legitimacy demands impartiality. However, just as political affiliation was the norm under Soviet rule, there has been little real change in the relationship between the militia and political structures in Russia since the collapse of the Soviet Union. At the national level, the Minister of Interior is a government minister appointed by the President. The incumbent Minister, Boris Gryzlov, is one of the leaders of the United Russia ('*Yedinaya Rossiya*') political party, which supports the President. Questions have been raised about his dual role of Minister and party leader, as well as de facto head of the militia, given that the latter are supposed to be politically neutral. At the regional level, police chiefs remain directly subordinated to the President, and even at the local level, the municipal militia (where they exist) are likely to be beholden to the local authorities, on whom they are dependent for office premises, housing and other resources. Officers at grass roots level may in turn be influenced by their superiors, even though the militia are prohibited from engaging in political activity within their jobs.

In this respect, it is difficult to blame the militia for the situation they find themselves in, since they are to a great extent pawns or 'objects of political manipulation' (Gilinskiy, 1999: 177): for example, whereas the heads of the local branches of the Interior Ministry (as well as the FSB, Prosecutors' Office and Tax Police) used to be under the *de facto* control of the regional governors, that control is now exercised by the presidential envoys appointed to each of the seven federal regions. The creation of security councils in each region, comprising the regional heads of law enforcement, military and intelligence agencies has further deprived regional elites of a 'serious support base' (Kryshtanovskaya, 2003).

The Law on the Militia therefore appears less a significant step towards the creation of democratic policing than simply more window dressing. This is also true of its provisions for legal and social guarantees for militia employees. For example, among other benefits, the law provides for a maximum forty-hour week, compensation for overtime (including work on days off, holidays and night shifts) and the right to join trade/professional unions. However, interviews with militia officers suggest that employees' rights are also routinely infringed for various reasons such as a lack of resources and extenuating circumstances. For example, the appearance of terrorist activity during recent years has led to lengthy states of alert, resulting in 12-hour shifts without additional pay becoming the norm for many police personnel, including police cadets. Similarly, although some trade unions were created to represent members of the militia, their organisers and members have been subject to harassment (Shelley, 1999), invalidating the law's provisions.

Changes in organisational structure and policies

As already established, the militia form part of the MVD, which is responsible for regular policing functions such as maintaining public order, investigating and preventing crime, and traffic control, but also for vehicle registration, transportation security, and issuing visas, passports and residence permits.[6] Organisational change within the militia has been the norm since the collapse of the Soviet Union, but it has tended to be superficial, rather than substantive (Gilinksiy, 2000), and there has in fact been a great deal of underlying continuity in structure and policies. For example, the militia remains an essentially militaristic force: employees wear uniforms and have ranks very similar to the armed forces, including officer classes from private up to general of the militia.[7] The ranking system has many inherent problems, including being far removed from routine policing or investigation, ignoring officers' day-to-day achievements and personal abilities, and largely discouraging initiative by new recruits as well as any interest they may have in acquiring special skills (Timoshenko, 1997).

While uniforms and ranks are a superficial indicator of militarisation (Wright, 2002), more significant is the fact that the militia is one of Russia's three armed power structures alongside the military and federal security services. Members of the militia are routinely armed and entitled to use guns to defend themselves and members of the public: 759 cases of deaths and injuries were caused by militia use of firearms in 2001, and during 2002 more than 250 regular militia officers were killed while on duty (*Moscow Times*, 2003).[8] This last figure does not

---

6. The '*propiska*' system of residence permits was introduced in the 1930s to control the number of people moving from the countryside to the cities. In order to secure work in the cities, it was a requirement to have a valid residence permit provided by the police. Although the system is acknowledged as being anti-constitutional (Shelley, 1999), it is still widely used in Russia's larger cities.
7. Stalin was responsible for militarising public services during the 1930s, including introducing quasi-military ranks and promotions systems, as well as departmental uniforms to many public agencies (Timoshenko, 1997).
8. According to an interview with Boris Gryzlov, this high number of fatalities showed that a sense of responsibility prevailed within the militia.

include fatalities in Chechnya, which provides a further example of militarisation: the militia are routinely deployed to trouble spots, such as Chechnya, even though they do not possess the heavy artillery and other special equipment of some of the MVD's more specialised units (e.g. the OMON riot police and Internal Troops). Nevertheless militia units are a permanent feature in conflict areas within the country.

The last major restructuring within the MVD occurred in 2001 and resulted in the creation of the Criminal Militia, the Public Security Militia and the Logistics Service, which are headed by the Minister of Internal Affairs' deputies.[9] These services include most of the main directorates (police command units) and independent directorates within the Ministry's Headquarters. Main directorates were also created in each of Russia's seven federal regions, which are overseen by presidential envoys.

A draft law currently before parliament (the *Duma*) provides for major structural change with the creation of municipal forces (to be responsible for local issues such as patrolling the streets and ensuring security at stadiums and other crowded venues); a federal police force (to combat nationwide problems such as economic and general crime, migration issues, policing the roads and public safety at national events); and a federal investigations service and national guard, which will largely retain the functions of the Ministry's existing investigative committee and interior troops respectively.[10] The bill, which is expected to come into force on 1 January 2005, appears to be a major step towards decentralising at least part of the MVD. Its main aim, however, is to redistribute power among federal, regional and local government. According to the Russian Constitution, local authorities are responsible for ensuring public order: the bill will ensure they have guaranteed budgets to do so by rerouting funding through the federal budget, which will also prevent regional leaders from exerting undue influence on the local police, thus providing some degree of local autonomy (*Moscow Times*, 2002).

In 2002 Boris Gryzlov spoke of the need for further changes to the structure and management of the MVD as a result of continued 'negative trends' in the country's social and crime situation. According to Gryzlov, the MVD had failed to achieve any qualitative successes in the fight against serious organised crime, drugs' trafficking and economic crimes: similarly, the level of street crime remained high, while controlling migration continued to present serious problems.[11] Moreover, militia employees were still guilty of contravening rules and regulations by committing crimes and showing insensitivity and disrespect to members of the

---

9. President Putin signed the Decree 'On the Essential Reform of the Ministry of Internal Affairs System' in June 2001.
10. Federalniy Zakon 'Ob Organakh okhrany obshestvennogo poryadka v Rossiiskoi Federatsii' (The Federal Law 'On Bodies for the Protection of Public Safety in the Russian Federation').
11. From a speech given by Boris Gryzlov on 19 October 2002 at a conference in St Petersburg to mark the 200th anniversary of the MVD.

public. Many militia officers appeared still to consider it their main job to supervise, rather than protect citizens and maintain their own legitimacy, suggesting that little has changed in militia behaviour since reforms began.

In this respect, militia culture may be partly to blame: it is firmly entrenched in the day-to-day practices of its employees and recruitment and training procedures have failed to promote or produce change in either attitudes to work or police practice For example, in terms of selection procedures potential recruits are supposed to undergo psychological, fitness and suitability tests, but interviews with militia officers suggest that such vetting is far from stringent, partly as a result of personnel shortages.[12] Similarly, although by law recruits are not accepted if they have a criminal record, media reports suggest that this stipulation is routinely ignored, and that officers charged with breaking the law may be allowed to return to work (Feifer, 2003).

In terms of training, efforts have been made in recent years to try to counteract the force of existing informal cultures within the police, including the development of new training programmes for recruits to introduce ideas and concepts more suited to democratic policing, such as human rights' training. However, it appears that old habits die hard and interviews with teaching staff highlight the problems encountered by graduates once they leave education to begin work in the militia: 'It doesn't matter how keen they start off: after a few years in the militia they are as degraded as the rest of them.'[13] This infers that, while the ideas and concepts more suited to a democratic society and police force may have been introduced to police training, they are not yet having the anticipated impact on police culture and behaviour, perhaps because expectations of what can be achieved are too high (Buerger, 1998). Teaching staff also argue that the system of centralised control ('Moscow's domination') of the training and education agenda is also problematic, insofar as it rules out local or regional initiatives. Much more fundamental a problem, however, is the law-based education offered to cadets, which produces lawyers rather than the public servants required to change the nature of the service offered by the Russian militia to the public. A public-service orientation would require much greater emphasis to be placed on skills' training rather than the formal system of legal education currently in use.

Although no disqualification process was applied to the militia post 1989, it has experienced a significant degree of organisational instability (Gilinskiy, 2000). In particular, large-scale turnover has had an impact on all levels and services within the militia.[14] Turnover has been affected by many factors, including ministerial

---

12. From interviews conducted with militia officers in Russia, June 2003.
13. From an interview with a senior MVD academic, June 2003.
14. Data from the MVD show that length of service figures vary for different units within the militia: for example, in the criminal militia around 60% of staff average 3–10 years of service, while 15% have less than three years' experience and 20% have 10–20 years. In the public security militia around half of all staff have 3–10 years' experience, compared with 27% with less than three years and 17% with 10–20 years (MVD, 2001).

changes, which routinely result in the reshuffling of posts in the upper echelons of the militia (Gilinskiy, 2000), thus giving the impression of progress being made, but without any substantive change (Bayley, 2001). Other reasons for high turnover include a perceived lack of career prospects, and poor working conditions, including low pay. More recently, the fight against corrupt officers has resulted in tens of thousands of officers being sacked from their jobs (Kosals, 2002), indicating an intensified campaign against the so-called 'bandits' or 'werewolves' in uniforms (Abdullaev, 2003).

Changes in operational policies and work patterns

A major policy initiative developed by the Minister of Interior is a reorientation of militia activity towards the public: 'Turning the militia to face the public in order to restore [public] trust and confidence in them' (*Komsomolskaya Pravda*, 2003). The development of a responsive public service orientation is a key element of democratic policing identified by Bayley (2001) and in Russia will involve closer work with the public and a role for them in the evaluation of militia performance.

Working with the public
The Soviet public were heavily involved in crime prevention and control, which was organised on a supposedly 'voluntary' basis and focused on various community groups, including street or block committees, youth groups, and street patrols – the *druzhiny* (Mawby, 1990). These groups were distinct from the regular state militia, but worked closely with them. Their main loyalties, however, were to the Communist Party rather than to the police (ibid.). Community involvement in law and order peaked in the 1960s under Khrushchev, but in recent years plans have been mooted to revive it. The spontaneous appearance of neighbourhood watch activities following terrorist attacks in Moscow in 1999, which left 300 people dead, perhaps served as a catalyst for the revival of community participation in crime control. A new law has recently been drafted by the Moscow city administration on citizens' involvement in crime prevention. Media coverage, however, has not been favourable, with critics hailing a return to the 'supervision' and 'snooping' of the past and even the covert creation of an additional security force to serve the purpose of the city authorities (Paton Walsh, 2003).

Measuring police performance
Two significant changes introduced to the militia in recent years are the requirement to record every incident reported by the public and a new appraisal system. These changes are closely interrelated: it has long been the case that the appraisal system for law-enforcement activity, which relied almost exclusively on detection and clear-up rates, encouraged the manipulation and outright falsification of crime statistics (Faverel-Garrigues, 2000). This was practised at various levels, from rank and file militia officers, who would fail to register crimes they believed they had

little chance of solving, to more senior officers seeking to paint an optimistic picture of their forces' success in terms of crime prevention and detection. Such behaviour was further encouraged by the existence of performance targets, which put additional pressure on the militia to 'cook the books' by, for example, fabricating evidence, framing suspects and getting convicted offenders to take the blame for previously unsolved crimes. Such practices led to the concealment of a sizeable proportion of crimes (Goryainov *et al.*, 2001), which served to undermine public confidence in the militia even further.

In an attempt to remedy this situation, two initiatives were developed: first, the militia were ordered to register all incidents reported to them by the public, and secondly, to compensate for the anticipated increase in recorded crimes, a new set of criteria was developed to measure performance. Instead of relying exclusively on detection and clear-up rates, the new system will consider national and departmental statistical reporting, local conditions (geographical, demographic and socio-economic factors), and perhaps most importantly – public opinion of militia activity.

The new appraisal system was piloted in nine administrative jurisdictions during 2001–02, after which it was declared a success by the Ministry and plans were made to roll it out across the whole of Russia. Compulsory registration of all crimes reported was introduced in 2001, along with warnings that cases of concealment would be taken very seriously and lead to disciplinary sanctions being taken against officers found guilty of not registering crimes. The public were also forewarned by the deputy Minister of Internal Affairs to expect a significant increase in recorded crime figures, as had occurred when a similar initiative was introduced during the mid 1990s (Saradzhyan, 2001).[15] However, the expected increase did not happen: in fact officially recorded crime fell by 17% from around 3 million in 2001 to 2.5 million in 2002 (MVD, 2003). The fall was largely attributed to changes in legislation, which saw a reclassification of some minor crimes as administrative offences, while the head of the MVD insisted that the militia were following the new regulations, 'even with a strict requirement to register all citizens' complaints, fewer than 3 million crimes were registered in 2002' (*Komsomolskaya Pravda*, 2003). We are therefore left to ponder sceptically the relationship between the official account of crime and the vastly different accounts offered by other sources, including victim surveys (Zvekic, 1996; MVD Research Institute, 2001; Beck and Robertson, 2002). It would appear that the self-deception of Russian police statistics has developed into a vicious and durable circle, the paradox being that the MVD, and the militia in particular, would probably gain in terms of funding and resources if they presented a more accurate picture of crime.

---

15. In 1998 the then Interior Minister, Sergei Stepashin, tried to encourage the registration of all crimes, but his campaign floundered when some regional police chiefs failed to act as instructed and he was subsequently reprimanded by President Boris Yeltsin for allowing crime to increase by 20% (Saradzhyan, 2001).

Changes in supervision and control

Supervision and control of the police are crucial components of a democratic system. In Russia the militia are supposed to be accountable to the law. Official supervision and control of militia activity is exercised internally by the MVD's Internal Security Service *(Sluzhba sobstvennoi bezopastnosti)* and by the Minister. External supervision is exercised by the Prosecutors' Office and ultimately the President. Informal supervision is provided by the media and human rights groups. As yet there is no provision for civilian supervision.

To all intents and purposes, the militia therefore primarily police themselves. The remit of the Internal Security Service, which was upgraded in 2001 to a full main directorate, is to detect and prevent 'illegal' behaviour within the militia. In 2001 around 10,000 officers were called to account and more than 1000 faced criminal proceedings for abusing their power.[16] In 2002, more than 21,000 police officers were censured for criminal and other offences, 17,000 of whom were sacked (Kosals, 2003), suggesting that efforts are being made to curb police deviance, including corruption.

Corruption is one of the most serious problems within the militia, and for many taking bribes is considered normal practice. However, corruption takes different forms, from the small-scale petty bribe taking that is widespread throughout Russian, as well as other former Eastern European societies (Lovell, Ledeneva and Ragachevskii, 2000; Miller, Grodeland and Koshechkina, 2001) to more serious large-scale corruption, which sees law-enforcement colluding with organised crime and other criminal groups and individuals (Handelman, 1995). Many factors play a role in militia corruption, including low wages, poor legal consciousness, and lack of respect for the law (Shelley, 1999). Although recent events suggest that the fight against corruption within the militia has been stepped up[17] – indeed it has been made a priority by Boris Gryzlov (Abdullaev, 2003), the culture of corruption remains a significant obstacle to democratic reform. What is required is not only the continued rooting out of corrupt officers, but also the establishment of transparency and accountability. In this respect, the introduction of external supervision, including some form of civilian supervision, could serve to discipline the militia, although it may be late in the day to prevent small-scale abuses and corruption from becoming entrenched in the thinking and habits of the militia (Bayley, 2001). Without some form of independent external supervision, it is difficult to see how the Russian militia can break out of the cycle of corruption in which they appear to be caught.

---

16. From a report by the Deputy Minister of Interior given to the international conference, 'Preventing Police (Militia) Corruption', Moscow, 11–12 February 2002.
17. Although a clampdown appears to have begun in Moscow of senior officers suspected of corruption, critics have argued that this amounts to little more than propaganda linked to the forthcoming elections (Latynina, 2003).

Discussion: the extent of democratic police reform in Russia

As stated in the introduction to this volume, there is a general consensus that democratic policing rests on three main principles: legitimacy, professionalism and accountability. The goals of democratic police reform should therefore be sustained legitimacy, skilled professionalism, and effective accountability, but very little genuine progress appears to have been made in these three areas in Russia. For example:

Legitimacy infers that the police have gained the trust of the communities they serve, but opinion polls suggest that this is not the case in Russia: in fact the militia continue to be the public agency least likely to enjoy the trust of the public (MVD, 2003), although some surveys show that public attitudes towards the militia improved slightly during 2002 (*Komsomolskaya Pravda*, 2003). Moreover, as discussed above, the militia still show signs of partisanship, although the way in which the militia are funded and controlled forces local police chiefs into a position of dependency on local, regional and national political structures and other groups.

A *professional* force has the skills to balance effectiveness and justice, which remains far from the case in Russia. Professionalism encompasses principles of fairness, integrity and sensitivity, concern for human rights, impartiality, commitment to law and use of minimum force. Various human rights' groups produce annual reports suggesting that the Russian militia have a long way to go before they meet these criteria (Amnesty International, 2002; Human Rights Watch, 2003).

Accountability to outsiders is crucial, but centralised and militaristic systems provide minimal local or civilian accountability (Mawby, 1999). Little has changed in Russia in this respect; in particular, there has been no institutional change that would promote a more accountable police force.

The overall assessment of police reform in Russia is therefore largely negative. It is clear from this chapter that policy makers in Russia have a clear understanding of the types of policies required for the introduction of more democratic policing practices, and that attempts have been made to introduce the necessary legal, organisational and operational reforms. The problem with such reforms, however, is that they do not automatically translate into changes in militia behaviour. As Bayley (2001: 21) states, police behaviour cannot be changed by formal reorganisation or restructuring on a national basis, 'because it does not touch the "culture" of an organisation'. The fact that organisational and professional culture is firmly entrenched within the militia presents a major obstacle to the successful implementation of reform, but not one that is necessarily insurmountable (Bowling and Foster, 2002).

Given the way in which militia reform has been conceptualised and implemented, it is perhaps not surprising that real change has been slow to occur. For example, the militia have been expected to reform from within, but this is unlikely if they perceive no benefit from reform. This applies to employees throughout the militia hierarchy (Bayley, 2001): they all have vested interests in maintaining the status quo, either through legal or illegal means (Gilinskiy, 2000). Moreover, although the militia are one of the main stakeholders in the reform process, there is little evidence of any consultation with them or attempts to involve them: the introduction of new rules and regulations has only served to increase the burden placed upon them without any compensatory incentives in the form of increased resources and improved working conditions. In fact working conditions have deteriorated in recent years: shortages of equipment including guns, ammunition, patrol vehicles and petrol are now worse than during the Soviet era (Shelley, 1999), and although militia wages were doubled in July 2002, according to Kosals (2002) many employees have to rely on second jobs, both legal (e.g. providing security services, retail trade or taxi services) and illegal (taking bribes, registering stolen cars, dealing in drugs and arms, selling fake passports). Given these circumstances, it is perhaps not surprising that the culture of reform has not been embraced by the MVD.

Finally, it is important to recognise that one of the main obstacles to reform applies not only to the militia, but more broadly to Russian society as a whole: the legal framework may have improved, but until the rule of law is genuinely established in Russia the problem of enforceability will remain. If laws continue to be broken or circumvented with impunity by the militia themselves, there is little, if any, hope of sustained reform.

In terms of the lessons that might be learned or taken from Russia's experience, perhaps the most important, therefore, is that to compromise on transparency and accountability undermines democratic development. The aim must be to promote democracy through increased transparency and accountability, both internal and external. This will not be easy: policing in Russia has a long history of being authoritarian and the concept of democratic governance remains relatively alien. There is also the constant danger that emerging problems, such as the growing threat of terrorism, will stop reform in its tracks and push policing backwards rather than forwards. On the other hand, reform of the Russian militia can only be a long-term process (Shelley, 1999), given that the task of transforming it into a relatively clean and accountable force is monumental and will take decades, rather than years. This appears to be the opinion of Boris Gryzlov, who remains optimistic that militia reform will happen: 'It has to be understood that the MVD is a large, complicated and, as in any other country, very conservative body. But this does not mean that it will not change' (*Komsomolskaya Pravda*, 2003).

References

Abdullaev, N. 2003. 'Gryzlov promises to fight dirty cops'. *Moscow Times*, 25 June 2003.

Amnesty International. 2002. Report on Russia.

http://www.amnesty.org/russia/briefing.html

Bayley, D. 2001. *Democratizing the Police Abroad: What to Do and How to Do It*. Washington.

Beck, A. and Robertson, A. 2003 'Crime in Russia: exploring the link between victimisation and concern about crime'. *International Journal of Crime Prevention and Community Safety*. vol. 5, no. 1

Bowling, B. and Foster, J. 2002 'Policing and the police', in Maguire, M., Morgan, R. and Reiner, R., eds. *The Oxford Handbook of Criminology, 3rd Edition*. Oxford.

Buerger, M. 1998. 'Police training as a pentecost: using tools singularly ill-suited to the purpose of reform'. *Police Quarterly*, vol. 1, no.1.

Dashkov, G.V. 1992. 'Quantitative and qualitative changes in crime in the USSR'. *British Journal of Criminology*. vol. 32, no.2.

Faverel-Garrigues, G. 2000. 'Implementing struggle against economic crime in Russia: bureaucratic constraints and police practices', in Pagon, M., ed. *Policing in Central and Eastern Europe: Ethics, Integrity, and Human Right*. Ljubljana.

Feifer, G. 2003. 'Police corruption chokes progress', in *Johnson's Russia List*, 20 Mar. 2003. http://www.cdi.org/russai/johnson/7070-12.cfm

Gilinskiy, Y. 2000. 'Challenges of policing democracies: the Russian experience', in Das, D. and Marenin, O., eds. *Challenges of Policing Democracies: A World Perspective*. Amsterdam.

Goryainov, K.K., Ovchinskiy, V.S. and Kondratyuk, L.V. 2001 *Ulusheniye vzaimootnosheniya grazhdan i militsia: dostup k pravosudniyu i sistema viyavleniya, registratsiya i ucheta prestuplenii* (Improving the relationship between the public and the police: access to justice and the system of detecting, registering and recording crimes.) Moscow.

Gustafson, T. 1999. *Capitalism Russian-Style*. Cambridge.

Handelman, S. 1995. *Comrade Criminal*. London.

Human Rights Watch. 2003. Briefing Paper on the situation of Ethnic Chechens in Moscow. http://www.hrw.org/backgrounder/eca/russia032003.htm

Kazakov, V.G. 2001. *Istoriya organov vnutrennykh del*. Moscow.

Komsomolskaya Pravda. 2003. 'Inter'vyu Ministra vnutrennykh del Rossii, Borisa Grylova'(Interview with the Minister of Internal Affairs, Boris Gryzlov.), *Komsomolskaya pravda newspaper*, Moscow, 08/05/03.

Kosals, L. 2002. *Informal Economic Activities of the Police in Russia: Sociological Analysis*. Unpublished report of Institute of Population Studies. Moscow.

Kryshtanovskaya, O. 2003. 'Putin's dangerous personnel preferences'. *Moscow Times*, 2 July 2003.

Kudriavtsev, V.N. 1999. '*Sovremenniye problemy borb'y c prestupnost'iu v Rossii*'. *Vestnik Rossiiskoj Akadamii Nauk* (The contemporary problems of fighting crime in Russia.), vol. 69, no. 9, pp. 790–7.

Latynina, Y 2003. 'Arresting PR and electoral intrigue'. *Moscow Times*, 2 July 2003.

Lotspeich, R. 1995. 'Crime in the transition countries'. *Europe-Asia Studies*, vol. 47, no.4.

Lovell, S., Ledeneva, A. and Rogachevskii, A. 2000. *Bribery and Blat in Russia: Negotiating Reciprocity from the Middle Ages to the 1990s*. London.

Mawby, R.I. 1990. *Comparative Policing Issues: The British and American Experience in International Perspective*. London.

Mawby, R.I. 1999. 'The changing face of policing in Central and Eastern Europe'. *International Journal of Police Science and Management*, vol. 2, no. 3.

Militsiya 1993 'Interview with General A. Aslakhanov, former deputy of the Supreme Council of the Russian Federation'. *Militsiya*, 1993 # 3, p. 3.

Miller, W.L., Grodeland, A.B. and Koshechkina, T.Y. 2001. *A Culture of Corruption: Coping with Government in Post-communist Europe*. Budapest.

Morozov, V.M. and Sergevnin, V.A. 1996. 'Utilisation of the international experience of the police recruiting, selection and training in the Russian Federation', in Pagon, M., ed. *Policing in Central and Eastern Europe: Comparing Firsthand Knowledge with Experience from the West*. Ljubljana.

Moscow Times. 2002. 'Kozak outlines plans for police overhaul', *Moscow Times*, 21 Nov. 2002.

Moscow Times. 2003. '250 policemen killed', *Moscow Times*, 14 Jan. 2003.

MVD. 1996. *Kontseptsiya razvitiya organov vnutrennykh del i vnutrennykh voisk MVD Rossii* (The Concept of Development for the Internal Affairs Agencies and Internal Troops of Russia). Moscow.

MVD. 2001. *Spravka po rabote c lichnyn sostavom* (Personnel Information Booklet). Moscow.

MVD. 2003. *Izucheniye obshchestvennogo mneniya o sostyanii kriminogennoi obstanovki i otsenki deyatel'nosti organov vnutrennikh del* (A study of public opinion on the crime situation and evaluation of the activity by law-enforcement bodies). Moscow.

PatonWalsh, N. 2003.'Moscow seeks spies in suburbs'. *Guardian*, 16 July 2003. http://www.guardian.co.uk/russia/article/0,2763,998986,00.html

Prenzler, T. and Ransley, J., eds. 2002. *Police Reform: Building Integrity*. Bayswater.

Reiner, R. 1985. *The Politics of the Police*. London.

Saradzhyan, S. 2001. 'Gryzlov to overhaul lagging police force'. *Moscow Times*, 3 July 2001.

Shelley, L. 1996. *Policing Soviet Society: The Evolution of State Control*. London.

Shelley. L. 1999. 'Post-socialist policing: limitations on institutional change', in Mawby, R.I., ed. *Policing Across the World: Issues for the Twenty-first Century*. London.

Timoshenko, S. 1993. 'Moscow (Russia)', in Alvazzi del Frate, A., Zvekic, U. and van Dijk, J., eds. *Understanding Crime: Experiences of Crime and Crime Control*. Rome.

Timoshenko, S. 1997. 'Prospects for Reform of the Russian Militia'. *Policing and Society*, vol. 8.

Timoshenko, S. 1998. 'The International Crime Victim Survey in Moscow (Russia) 1996', in Hatalak, N., Alvazzi del Frate, A. and Zvekic, U., eds. *The International Crime Victim Survey in Countries in Transition: National Reports*. Rome.

Wright, A. 2002 *Policing*. Cullompton.

Zakon RSFSR. 1991. '*O militsii*' (*Law on the Militia*). http://zakon.kuban.ru/sayt/milo1.shtml

Zvekic, U. 1996. 'Policing and attitudes towards police in countries in transition: preliminary results of the International Crime (Victim) Survey', in Pagon, M., ed. *Policing in Central and Eastern Europe: Comparing Firsthand Knowledge with Experience from the West*. Ljubljana.

Zvekic, U. 1998. *Criminal Victimisation in Countries in Transition*. Rome.

Chapter 15

Reform of the Militia in Ukraine

Adrian Beck, Alexei Povolotskiy and Alexander Yarmysh

Introduction

Ukraine is situated in the south-eastern part of Central Europe, sharing land borders with Russia, Belarus, Moldova, Slovakia, Romania, Hungary and Poland, and sea borders with Russia, Georgia, Bulgaria, Romania and Turkey. It regained independence in 1991 after the collapse of the Soviet Union, inheriting many of the structures and problems associated with the previous authoritarian regime, some of which continue to hamper its development (Jasinski, 1999; Koszeg, 2001; Shelley, 1999). Since 1991 Ukraine has seen considerable change in its economic, political and social landscape and many government agencies have introduced a wide range of reforms to bring them more into line with demands for greater democracy, transparency and accountability. The Ukrainian militia (police)[1] have not been immune from this process, although some argue that it has been one of the agencies slowest to introduce change, partly caused by self interest and an understandable desire by some senior ranking officials to retain positions of power and influence enjoyed under the previous regime (Polokhalo, 1994; Smith, 1996). Growing levels of crime, increased public dissatisfaction with the service they receive and recognition by the militia that public support is essential if they are to meet the challenges of the future has seen the issue of reform rarely far from the top of the political agenda (Beck and Chistyakova, 2002; Jasinski, 1999).

Unlike many of the states emerging from the Soviet Union, independence for Ukraine did not bring sweeping political change and many of the 'new' ruling elite were previously senior members of the communist party who were not in a hurry to bring about significant political and structural change (Bandurka and Dreval, 1999; Smith, 1996). This lack of a 'revolutionary' transformation from the previous regime partly explains why the Ministry of Interior (MIA) has retained a strong centralised structure and lacks clarity about its future role in Ukrainian society (Kravchenko, 1998). Political and ideological ambiguity has led to uncertainty about how the militia should be reformed from one previously focused on serving the state and 'collective' interests to one meeting the needs of the individual and local

---

1. The term 'militia' is used throughout rather than 'police'. Although the Ukrainian word *militsia* may eventually be replaced by *politsia*, the former continues to be the name by which the police in Ukraine are popularly known.

communities. This chapter begins by highlighting some of the key reforms undertaken by the Ukrainian Militia in the years since independence, and then goes on to detail the significant factors that have impeded this process. It concludes by reflecting upon future priorities and the prospects for developing a more democratic policing model in Ukraine.

Militia reform

Prior to formal independence, a new law governing the work of the militia was passed by the Parliament of the Ukrainian Soviet Socialist Republic in December 1990. Article 1 of this law outlined the main role of the militia as being 'the state armed body of executive authority that protects the life, health, rights and liberties of citizens, the property, environment and interests of society and the state from illegal encroachments upon them'. The Act publicly stated the key activities and responsibilities of the militia, which included: the maintenance of public order; carrying out preliminary investigations and holding inquests on cases within its jurisdiction; crime prevention; the protection of individual, collective and state property; administration of gun permits; the managing of special facilities for homeless people and isolation wards for infected offenders; the administration of immigration control (passport control and registration of foreigners); managing traffic safety; and supervising recently released prisoners. It also put the rights of the citizen before those of the state, a significant change in emphasis from the previously accepted doctrine that the militia were the 'punishing sword of the Communist Party of the Soviet Union'.

For many commentators, however, a more symbolic step in the reform process was the adoption of the Ukrainian Constitution, although the considerable lapse in time between December 1991 when participation in the Soviet Union was terminated and the eventual adoption of the Constitution in 1996, speaks volumes of the lack of political commitment to change and the dominance of the nomenklatura in creating reforms designed to preserve the previous political and economic system (Smith, 1996). The Constitution set the overall parameters within which the militia were to operate:

> The human being, his or her life, health, honour and dignity, inviolability and security are recognised in Ukraine as the highest social value. Human rights and freedoms and their guarantees determine the essence and orientation of the State. The State is answerable to the individual for its activity. To affirm and ensure human rights and freedoms is the main duty of the State (Article 3, Constitution of Ukraine, 1996).

The new Constitution was accompanied by the Conception of the Development of the Ministry of Internal Affairs (MIA) System of Ukraine (Ministry of Interior, 1996), which outlined the need for change, and despite little political consensus within Parliament on how the militia should be reformed (a recurring theme throughout post-Soviet Ukrainian history), several key components were agreed. These were:

1. The militia should focus on protecting the life, health, rights and freedoms of the individual and the interests of society and the state.
2. The structure of the MIA should be simple, flexible and cost-effective.
3. The work of the MIA should be focused at the local level.
4. The public should have free access to information about the work of the MIA.
5. Consideration should be given to the way in which support services are organised and the pay and rank structure should be reviewed.
6. There should be close co-operation between the militia and local authority bodies in order to maintain public order.

The key notions of democratic policing (legitimacy, accountability and professionalism) can be seen within these statements. Legitimacy in terms of meeting the needs of the individual first, and being focused at the local level; accountability in terms of access to information and to a certain extent in co-operation with local authority bodies; and professionalism in the recognition of the need to review structure and pay, and become more flexible. How these sentiments were to be transformed into policy and practice was less clear, however, although Ukrainian academics and police practitioners at the time felt that there should be a general move away from the previous Soviet model towards the development of a system based upon accepted best practice from the rest of the world.

Since 1990 there have also been a number of other notable laws, presidential edicts and government decrees passed covering the work of the militia. These include laws on Operational and Investigational Activity (1992); the Organisational and Legal Basis of Tackling Organised Crime (1993); Tackling Corruption (1995); Public Participation in Maintaining Public Order and State Borders (2000); the General Structure and Strength of the Ministry of Internal Affairs (2002);[2] and Presidential Edicts on Complex Targeted Programme of Tackling Crime (1996–2000); Concepts of Tackling Corruption (1998–2005); Complex Programme of Crime Prevention (2001–05); Establishment of Local Militia (2001); and Further Measures for Strengthening Law and Order, Securing the Rights and Freedoms of Citizens (2002). In addition, in 1998 the responsibility for prisons was moved from the MIA to the State Department of Ukraine for Matters of Implementing Punishments, although the MIA continues to carry out a wide range of functions beyond those normally associated with the police (see below). This plethora of legislative activity, however, has seen relatively little change in the day-to-day working practices of the militia and the way in which they are perceived by the public. In some respects it can be portrayed as rearranging the deckchairs on the

---

2. The various laws passed by the Verkhovna Rada of Ukraine can be viewed at: http://www.rada.kiev.ua

Titanic – a programme of root and branch reform is still required rather than mere alterations to the existing structure.

Obstacles to reform

For many commentators, the reform of the police in Ukraine has been piecemeal and partial, lacking a systematic and systemic approach (Fogelsong and Solomon, 2001; Shelley, 1999). It is a country almost always on the verge of reform, but has become bogged down by a whole host of interrelated factors that have combined to reduce not only the impact of reforms introduced to date, but also conspire to inhibit the entire reform process. It is instructive, therefore, to consider the current obstacles to police reform in Ukraine.

The sovietised reform process

The unique political milieu within Ukraine at the time of independence had a powerful influence upon the nature and pace of proposed militia reform. The compromise negotiated between the former Ukrainian communist leadership and the nationalists, which essentially left the previous ruling oligarchy in power, meant that opposition to change was built into Ukrainian political transition (Fogelson and Solomon, 2001). Whereas some other states emerging from the Soviet Union sought to remove much of the previous *nomenklatura*, including many of the senior ranks within the militia (such as the Baltic countries, which declared the previous law-enforcement agencies as institutes of a foreign state), Ukraine was characterised by the continuing dominance of the previous ruling elite. This in turn has seen much of the former Soviet style of political control and decision-making, based upon centralisation, obfuscation, secrecy and diktat, remaining the overriding approach adopted. The influence of this can be seen in the numerous laws, presidential edicts and governmental decrees relating to militia reform passed since 1991, which are strong on rhetoric but extremely weak on detail and often lack the necessary enabling legislation or financial support. The Soviet culture of plans and reports without any interposing action seems evident in much of the reform process in Ukraine. This is particularly characterised by the official crime statistics, which seem to have more to do with sustaining an illusion of efficiency and control than reflecting the current state of crime and the militia's response to it (see below).

Organisation and management

Much of the previous Soviet structure and organisation, which is based upon a highly militarised authoritarian model of control and decision-making, remains within the Ukrainian militia (Bandurka, Bezsmertniy and Zuy, 2000). Indeed, the years since independence have seen an increase in the overall number of those holding senior ranks within the organisation (Bandourka, 1996). This is partly explained by the ongoing link between rates of pay and rank – militia personnel can only improve their level of recompense by achieving a higher position. Indeed, duties that were previously fulfilled by those in a civilian position now proffer a rank upon those holding the post. This 'rankification' process has reinforced the militarised nature of the police in Ukraine, which in turn further acts to stultify the reform of the organisational structure.

In addition, recent research has shown that the militia remains a highly bureaucratic organisation, with perhaps as few as one-quarter being employed directly to protect public order or tackle crime (Bandurka, 1996; Frolov, 2001). There has also been a continuation of a sovietised model of control, reducing officer discretion to a minimum through close supervision, and a stringent hierarchy of decision-making from above. The flow of information is strictly controlled and is primarily from the bottom up, and the extensive use of record-keeping maintains an occupational culture of conservatism (Jefferson, 1990). Moreover, concerns persist about the ongoing influence of nepotism and personal relations in the promotion process, 'it is dangerous when promotion is dependent not on the basis of special knowledge and personal characteristics, but on informal relations' (Lyashenko, 2002: 449).

Militia managers also maintain a monocratic system of routinised superior–subordinate relationships (Angell, 1971; Kelling and Moore, 1988). Recent research conducted in Kyiv highlighted the continuing reliance upon an authoritarian and disciplinarian model of management with militia managers being perceived by junior ranks as lacking leadership and 'people management' skills (Beck, Barko and Tatarenko, 2003). These views were particularly strong among female officers and younger male officers. Work is now underway to develop new management courses to address these issues, although at the moment they are only being provided for the most senior ranks within the militia (Beck, Barko and Tatarenko, 2002).

While a number of political moves have been attempted to develop a more decentralised militia structure (see, for instance, the Presidential Edict on the Establishment of Local Militia, 2001), the overarching Soviet model of central control and command remains firmly entrenched. Where a more decentralised model has been piloted (for instance in the cities of Berdiansk, Kyiv and Kharkiv) local Ukrainian researchers have described the results as impressive: 'it helped to establish militia/public partnerships, to bring the militia under efficient democratic control, and compelled the local authorities to improve the financial and technical upkeep of the militia and social welfare of its employees' (Bandurka, 1996: 97). As yet, however, the necessary enabling legislation to facilitate the rest of Ukraine to adopt this approach has not been passed by the Ukrainian Parliament and as such the militia remain a highly centralised organisation, with little local input into the setting of, or control over, their plans, priorities and indeed practices.

Performance indicators: the Soviet mythology of success
A key stumbling block in the reform process has been the continuation of Soviet practices of measuring crime and the performance of the militia. Like police agencies throughout the world there is a strong reliance upon official statistics to

assess levels of crime, which take little account of unrecorded and unreported crime and act more as a measure of the administrative (in)efficiency of the police than a true indicator of the level of criminality in society (Maguire 1994). Estimates suggest that towards the end of the Soviet period the militia in Ukraine failed to register roughly one-third of the crimes reported to them, although this is now thought to be an underestimation (Fogelson and Solomon, 2001). More critically, however, the key performance indicator for the militia remains the crime clear up rate, which compared with other non-Eastern European countries, continues to be staggeringly high. It generally hovers around the 90% rate and for certain offences (such as murder) it is often 100% (compared with for instance the UK where it is about 25%). This seemingly impressive rate of success, however, has more to do with dubious militia accounting practices than the way in which the militia are organised or perform their duties.

Centrally agreed targets for clear-up rates and associated sanctions for non-compliance act as a powerful incentive for the militia not to record crimes that will prove difficult to solve such as car crime and burglary. Most Western commentators tend to agree that as a measure of police performance, the clear up rate and levels of crime are poor indicators, offering only a partial reflection of the way in which the police perform (Crawford, 1998; Griffiths, 1999). Scepticism and cynicism about the veracity of police crime statistics is now so common in Ukraine that many procurators advocate the transfer of control over data registry to civilian authorities (Zelenetskiy, cited in Foglesong and Solomon, 2001: 73).

This mythology of success causes three key problems in the reform process. First, it acts to perpetuate existing practices (if it works don't fix it). Secondly, it undermines societal confidence in the extent to which the militia have become more accountable and transparent (a service-oriented approach is seen to be subservient to organisational priorities). Thirdly, it can undermine attempts to persuade Ukrainian politicians and indeed oversees agencies that additional funding is required to reform the militia (existing levels of funding are already producing outstanding results).

Militia – public relations
Another key obstacle to reform is the public's apathy and general hostility towards the militia. Recent research shows that the majority of respondents considered the militia to be inefficient and not ready to help ordinary citizens (Beck and Chistyakova, 2002). One recent commentator painted a gloomy picture where most Ukrainians fear the police and agents of law enforcement organs more than they do criminals (Byrne, 2000). Surveys of the public regularly highlight concerns about corruption, rudeness and low professionalism within the militia (Beck and Chistyakova, 2002; Zvekic, 1998). More positively, research has shown that both the militia and the public recognise the importance of improving the relationship between them and two-thirds of the public surveyed were willing to establish closer links, providing it was well organised and perceived to be the right thing to do (Beck and Chistyakova, 2002). A recent pilot study in the city of Kharkiv, funded by the

UK government, had some notable success in beginning to bridge this gap, and developing alternative ways of organising the militia at the local level (see Beck and Chistyakova, 2001, 2002, 2003). How the results from this experiment will be incorporated into the ongoing reform process and disseminated more broadly throughout Ukraine, however, is still not clear.

Training and selection

When independence was declared in 1991, Ukraine did not have a recognised structure of law enforcement training and research. Most of the high-level research and training centres were located in Russian cities such as Moscow, Leningrad and Omsk, leaving a vacuum that needed to be filled. There was only one militia higher school in Kyiv, and militia schools in some regions, which carried out basic training of rank and file militia, and provided some special courses for militia officers responsible for fighting economic crimes (for example in Kharkiv).

This situation has since been improved and there is now a network of training and research institutions, with the two most significant being the National Academy of Internal Affairs based in Kyiv and the National University of Internal Affairs in Kharkiv. These two centres annually train more officers than all the other institutions in Ukraine put together, and now employ a wide range of specialists carrying out a wide range of research and training programmes.

Nevertheless, the system for training police officers faces a number of problems that need to be resolved. There are few links between theoretical courses and practice; a weak system of professional training; and insufficient training in communication skills and methods of working with the public. According to one Ukrainian academic,

> the main focus of improving the education system today is a reorientation from an informative type of education to one that allows cadets to prove and develop cognitive and creative leanings and to develop their professional qualities to ensure their effectiveness ... these need to become core components of the education of future militiamen. (Venedictov, 2002: 245)

There is also a continuing strong emphasis (particularly for those attending higher education establishments) on teaching the law rather than providing training relevant to the requirements of being a police officer. Graduates of these programmes are awarded a Diploma in Law and many decide to take these skills into the private sector where pay and conditions are far superior to those offered by a career in the militia.

The relatively poor level of pay and the significant reduction in social status associated with the militia has also had a negative impact upon the number and quality of candidates applying to join the militia. The Ukrainian militia is currently 12% under strength and there is widespread concern that the current selection process is admitting candidates who are unsuitable for work in the police, often lacking basic levels of education.

Problem of corruption

The problem of corruption is a major obstacle not only to the reform of the militia, but more broadly, the economic and political well being of the country (UFE Foundation, 1997; Ledeneva, 1998; Rose-Ackerman, 1999). For some it has become endemic, leeching into every facet of Ukrainian society, severely undermining the prospects for developing a democratic society (Miller *et al.*, 2001). Western businesses cite corruption as one of the main reasons why they are unwilling to invest in Ukraine, and the Corruption Perception Index ranks it as one of the countries with the highest rate of corruption in the world, rated 85th out of 102 countries surveyed (Internet Center for Corruption Research, 2003). While the debate about the causes of corruption in post-Soviet societies continues (some argue that Ukraine was never governed by the legal rationality associated with Weberian bureaucracy, and much of what outsiders call corruption reflects traditional exchange relationships; see Foglesong and Solomon, 2001), what is clear is that the militia are regularly highlighted as one of the state groups most involved in corrupt practices.

Very little data is available on the scale and extent of the problem; it has been estimated that only between 2% and 5% of bribery cases ever reach the criminal justice system (Shalgunova, 2001), and in the year 2000 some 15,000 civil servants were convicted (5% of the total) (Foglesong and Solomon, 2001). Various surveys suggest that as much as 60% of government officials' income comes from bribes (Shelley, quoted in Foglesong and Solomon, 2001). The militia account for 26% of those called to account for corruption (Vysotski, 2001), and bribery makes up for 13.6% of all crimes committed by members of the militia (Shalgunova, 2001). While much of the corruption can be regarded as relatively insignificant, often committed by employees of the State Automobile Inspectorate (GAI), other more serious incidents committed by the militia are evident, such as performing 'services' for wealthy individuals, criminal group and businesses. This can take the form of selling information, providing protection services, or negotiating with fire, health and tax inspectors (Kravchenko, cited Foglesong and Solomon, 2001).

The gravity of the problem of corruption cannot be underestimated and will play a major role in undermining efforts to develop a more democratic policing system in Ukraine. The impact on the public perception of police integrity and efficacy is considerable and no doubt helps contribute to the scale of unreported crime and the public's ongoing scepticism about the militia's raison d'être.

Supervision and control

For the most part, the pre-independence structure of supervision and control has remained largely unchanged, although there have been some notable changes. Reports of instances of abuse of power, corruption and torture persist (see European Roma Rights Center, 1997; Liga Online, 2001a, 2001b; Ukrainian Truth, 2001; US State Department, 2001) and calls for greater accountability continue. When the 1996 Constitution of Ukraine's 'Transitional Statutes' expired, only the courts were left with the right to issue arrest warrants, although how strictly this is adhered to by militia officers is open to debate. The creation of the Ombudsman's Office, supervision of the Minister of Interior by the Verkhovna Rada of Ukraine (the Parliament), the creation of special committees set up by local authorities to monitor the work of the militia and, perhaps more significantly, the revised role of the Procurator's Office, which became the highest supervisory body charged with controlling observance of the law by all Ukrainian subjects (Law on the Procurator's Office, 1991, which included Article 5 'ensuring that bodies which fight crime and misdemeanors observe the law'), have all brought some modicum of greater supervision and control over the militia. Indeed the Procurators office annually uncovers about 15,000 crimes 'concealed' by the militia and opens criminal investigations into another 15,000 cases that the militia unjustifiably decided not to investigate (Fogelsong and Solomon, 2001). There is ongoing concern, however, about the lack of independence of the Procuracy and uncertainty about its future role and function (Fogelsong and Solomon, 2001).

In June 2003, a new law was adopted entitled On Democratic Civilian Control over Military and Law Enforcement Bodies of the State. According to Article 7 of the law, the system will consist of control by: parliament, the President, executive authorities and local authorities, judicial bodies and the prosecutor's office and the public. This new act continues to give primary responsibility for overseeing observance of the law to the Prosecutor's Office, although Articles 19 and 20 give the public and the media (in theory) greater access to information about the militia: 'the mass media can, as laid down, ask for and receive (free of charge) from ... law enforcement bodies open information, documents, and materials within their competence...' (Article 20). In addition, the MIA have begun to make more information available to the public through the annual publication of regular reports on its activities and a new ethical code has been introduced for MIA employees. It is too soon to say how these new initiatives will work in practice, although it is hoped that it will bring about greater levels of accountability and control over the militia.

Future priorities

A recent Ukrainian document, perhaps inadvertently, neatly summarises the current situation. It states that the MIA has recently started to draft a new reform programme, with the help of the National University of Internal Affairs. Those working on the project state that 'the *reformed* militia will comply not only with Ukrainian legislation but also with the norms of international humanitarian law, the standards of democratic police activity and the interests of Ukrainian citizens, society and the state as a whole' (emphasis added; National University of Internal Affairs, 2003). Simple deduction would suggest that the current Ukrainian militia are not meeting these norms, standards and requirements.

The legacy of the Soviet Union continues to pervade all aspects of the militia in Ukraine and the attempts to reform it since independence in 1991. It is a country that recognises the necessity for change but lacks the political will to design and deliver a programme that necessities a radicalised approach to the creation of a new structure and ethos. The notion of democratic policing as defined by many western scholars is for the most part singularly absent in Ukraine (for definitions see Brodeur, 1998; Das, 2000; Kratcoski and Cebulak, 2000; Marenin, 2000). Undoubtedly democratic ideals can be seen in much of the law making over the past ten years, but there has been little evidence of this being translated into operational policies and rules for working. As Marenin states (2000: 313), 'the challenge for democratic policing ... is to translate principles into rules of work which can be taught, enforced, rewarded if properly done and sanctioned if abused.' To date the policing culture in Ukraine is such that implementing the existing legal rhetoric, observing the rule of law and delivering many of the other practices of democratic policing (such as accountability, transparency and so on) seem emasculated by a Sovietised tradition still focused on protecting the elite and maintaining the status quo.

More specifically, emphasis needs to be given to developing the service function of the militia, which is not only concerned with partnerships between the militia and the public, and the development of a respectful and attentive attitude to all citizens, but is also focused on putting individuals' rights and interests at the centre of all militia activity. This in turn will help to overcome some of the hostility ordinary citizens have for the militia and improve levels of accountability.

There needs to be a rationalisation of the functions of the MIA. This has already begun (with the removal of responsibilities for prisons) but other tasks could be reallocated such as: registration of motor vehicles and driving tests; prevention of air and reservoir pollution by motor transport and farming machinery; passport and immigration control; providing quarantine measures during epidemics; and responsibility for bringing infected and ill people to hospital and reporting them to the medical services for obligatory examination and treatment (Kravchenko, 1998). This would enable the militia to focus more on their core functions of public order, crime control and crime prevention.

The MIA has been plagued by a lack of financing. Observers suggest that the Ministry receives only around one-third of the funding it requires (Ministry of Interior, 2003). Between 1997 and 2000 wage delays were a regular occurrence for militia officers, whose average salary is now around $100 per month. In addition, militia officers have lost a number of social guarantees, such as free public transport and housing benefits, which has put further pressure upon their incomes. Severe financial constraints also make it difficult to retain staff (in the last three months of 2002, 5537 MIA employees resigned); attract high quality trainees; purchase much needed equipment, renovate buildings; and even provide petrol for police cars (the MIA state that they will only receive 9% of the necessary funding for non-salary costs in 2003).

Undoubtedly, considerable challenges face the reformers in Ukraine and it could take a generation before any significant change takes place (Roberg, 1994; Shelley, 1999). There are many able and committed people working within the MIA who seek to create a Ukrainian militia that is committed to the notions of democratic policing. Whether they will be successful is highly dependent upon a sea change in thinking among the ruling elite, something which to date has been largely absent.

References

Angell, E. 1971. 'Alternatives to police organisation'. *Criminology*, vol. 9.

Bandurka, O. 1996. *The Basics of Management in the Bodies of Internal Affairs*. Kharkiv.

Bandurka, O., Bezsmertniy, O. and Zuy, V. 2000. *Administrative Activity*. Kharkiv.

Bandurka, O. and Dreval, Y. 1999. *Parliamentarianism in Ukraine*, Kharkiv.

Beck, A., Barko, V. and Tatarenko, A. 2002. 'Developing police management training in post-Soviet societies: understanding the context and setting the agenda'. *Policing Quarterly Journal*, vol. 5, no. 4.

Beck, A., Barko, V. and Tatarenko, A. 2003. 'Women militia officers in Ukraine: exploring their experiences in a post-Soviet policing organisation'. *Policing: An International Journal of Police Strategies and Management*. Forthcoming.

Beck A. and Chistyakova, Y. 2002. 'Crime and Policing in Post-Soviet Societies: Bridging the Police/Public Divide'. *Policing and Society*, vol. 12, no. 2.

Beck, A. and Chistyakova, Y. 2001. Crime and policing in Ukraine: The Kharkiv Crime Survey 2000. Leicester.

Beck A. and Chistyakova, Y. 2003 'Closing the gap between the militia and the public in post Soviet Ukraine: a bridge too far?'. *Police Practice and Research: An International Journal*. Forthcoming.

Beck, A. and Tatarenko, A. 2001. *Developing Police Management Training in Post-Soviet Societies*. Leicester.

Brodeur, J. 1998. *How to Recognize Good Policing. Problems and Issues*. Washington.

Byrne, P. 2000. 'Many fear the police more than they do criminals'. *Kyiv Post*, 23 Mar. 2000.

Crawford, A. 1998. *Crime Prevention and Community Safety: Politics, Policies and Practices*. London.

Dantzker, M. 1999. *Police Organisation and Management*. Boston.

Das, D. 2000. 'Challenges of policing democracies: a world perspective', in Das, D. and Marenin, O., eds. *Challenges of Policing Democracies: A World Perspective*. The Netherlands.

European Roma Rights Centre. 1997. *The Misery of Law: The Rights of Roma in the Transcarpathian Region of Ukraine*.
http://www.arts.uwaterloo.ca/minerals/archive/05081997-07:47:10-4795.html

Foglesong, S. and Solomon, P. 2001. *Crime, Criminal Justice and Criminology in Post-Soviet Ukraine*. Washington.

Frolov, M. 2000. *Departments of the Bodies of Internal Affairs in the Conditions of Law Reform*. Kharkiv.

Griffiths, C. 1999. *Canadian Police Work*. Toronto.

Internet Centre for Corruption Research. 2003. http://wwwuser.gwdg.de/~uwvw/corruption.cpi_2002_data.html

Jasinski, J. 1999. 'Crime: manifestations, patterns and trends of crime 'traditional' versus 'new' crime; juvenile crime; fear of crime'. *European Journal of Crime, Criminal Law and Criminal Justice*, vol. 7/4.

Jefferson, T. 1990. *The Case Against Paramilitary Policing*. Philadelphia.

Kőszeg, F. 2001. 'Introduction', in Kádár, A., ed. *Police in Transition*. Budapest.

Kratcoski, P. and Cebulak, W. 2000. 'Policing in democratic societies: a historical overview', in Das, D. and Marenin, O., eds. *Challenges of Policing Democracies: A World Perspective*. The Netherlands.

Kravchenko, Y. 1998. *Problems of Reforming the Bodies of Internal Affairs (Organizational and Legal Questions)*. Candidate's Thesis, University of Internal Affairs. Kharkiv.

Ledeneva, A. 1998. *Russia's Economy of Favours*, Cambridge: Cambridge University Press.

Liga Online. 2001a. http://www.liga.kiev.ua/lenta/get.html?id=13765

Liga Online. 2001b. http://www/liga.kiev.ua/lenta/get.html?id=14152

Lyashenko, N. 2002. 'Career growth in the bodies of internal affairs'. *Vistnyk of the National University of Internal Affairs*.

Maguire, M. 1994 'Crime statistics, patterns, and trends: changing perceptions and their implications', in Maguire, M., Morgan, R. and Reiner, R., eds. *The Oxford Handbook of Criminology*. Oxford.

Marenin, O. 2000 'Democracy, democratization, democratic policing', in Das, D. and Marenin, O., eds. *Challenges of Policing Democracies: A World Perspective*. The Netherlands.

Miller, W., Grodeland, A. and Koshechkina, T. 2001. *A Culture of Corruption?* Budapest.

Ministry of Interior. 1996. *Conception of the Development of the MIA System of Ukraine*. Kyiv.

Ministry of Interior .2003. Retrieved 14 Aug. 2003, from http://mvsinfo.gov.ua.

National University of Internal Affairs. 2002. *Propositions of the NUIA on the Reform of the System of the Ministry of Interior of Ukraine, up until 2006*. Kharkiv.

Polokhalo, V. 1994. 'The neo-totalitarian transformation of post-communist power in Ukraine'. *Politychna Dumka*, no. 3.

Roberg, R. 1994. 'Can today's police organisations effectively implement community policing?', in Rosenbaum, D., ed. *The Challenge of Community Policing. Testing the Promises*. London.

Rose-Ackerman, S. 1999. *Corruption and Government*. New York.

Rushenko, I. and Sobolev, V. 2000. *Results of Sociological Research Conducted Within the British-Ukrainian Project.* Kharkiv.

Shalgunova, S. 2001. 'Ways of improvement of activity of territorial bodies of internal affairs'. *Protection of rights, freedoms and legal interests of citizens of Ukraine in the process of enforcing the law.* Donetsk.

Shelley, L. 1999. 'Post-Socialist Policing: Limitations on Institutional Change', in R. Mawby, R., ed. *Policing Across the World: Issues for the Twenty-First Century.* London.

Smith, G. 1996. *Reforming the Russian Legal System.* New York.

UFE Foundation. 1997. *Lviv Integrity System.* Report Presented to USAID, Kyiv. Lviv.

Ukrainian Truth. 2001. *Likvidovano nametove mistetchko.* http://www.brama.com/survey/messages/7509.html

US State Department. 2001. *Ukraine, Country Reports on Human Rights Practices, 2000. Released by the Bureau of Democracy, Human Rights, and Labor.* http://www.state.gov/g/drl/rls/hrrpt/2000/eur/index.cfm?docid=854

Venedictov, V. 2002. 'The problem of higher education of personnel of the bodies of internal affairs of Ukraine'. *Vistnyk of the National University of Internal Affairs.*

Verkhovna Rada of Ukraine. 1996. *Constitution of Ukraine.* Kyiv.

Vysotski, D. (2001) 'Liquidation of corruption as a condition of providing for human rights and freedoms'. *Protection of rights, freedoms and legal interests of citizens of Ukraine in the process of enforcing the law-enforcement.* Donetsk.

Zvekic, U. 1998. *Criminal Victimisation in Countries in Transition.* United Nations Interregional Crime and Justice Research Institute (UNICRI), Publication No. 61. Rome.

PART VI

CONCLUSION

Chapter 16

Process and Progress in the Reform of Policing Systems

Marina Caparini and Otwin Marenin

Fundamental and sustained reform of the regular policing system has proven to be one of the most difficult tasks faced by the new democratic regimes in Central and Eastern Europe.[1] The descriptions and analyses of police reforms in the countries included in this volume raise the question whether the reforms achieved so far – the changes in rhetorical aspirations, organisational arrangements, legal bases and functional assignments of the police – amount to progress towards democratic forms of policing. The general answers given in the various chapters seem to suggest that is not yet the case. On the whole, many institutional reforms have been implemented but success in implementing democratic control and accountability of the police has been relatively modest. Much remains to be done and what remains are probably the more difficult aspects of reform. The easier changes have been done and now the hard work of changing the working values, habits and practices of the police, at all ranks in the hierarchy, is at hand.

Generally, reforms to police systems in Central and Eastern Europe have been slow in taking form, have sometimes lacked coherence, and have usually not been guided in practice by a systematic plan or strategy to address related components that feed back into the effectiveness of police reforms, such as the judiciary and the criminal justice system. Although the idea of democratic policing has begun to make inroads on certain formal structures and in declaratory statements of various political and policing figures, it does not yet appear to have effected fundamental change towards a service mentality among police officers, acceptance of the notions of policing by consent, public accountability and external supervision. Many police organisations throughout the region are still strongly influenced by the model of Soviet policing, and remain more centralised and militarised than is the case in Western societies. These policing structures still tend to display certain authoritarian tendencies and to lack public trust and confidence, factors exacerbated by chronic underfunding and lack of effectiveness in combating crime. There also

---

1. For earlier examination of the challenges of police reform in Central and Eastern Europe, see the collection of articles in Andras Kadar, ed., *Police in Transition* (Budapest: Central European University Press, 2001) and the chapters on Central European countries in Dilip Das and otwin Marenin, eds., *Challenges of Policing Democracies. A World Perspective* (Reading, UK: Gordon and Breach Publishers, 2000).

continue to be deficiencies in police accountability and ineffective or non-existent external civilian supervision mechanisms.

One of the participants at the Prague Workshop, Milan Pagon, suggested a heuristic analogy. Watching the reforms of policing in Central and Eastern European states, he said, is like observing a fashion show. The models come out, walk down the runway, return to the changing rooms, and glide down the runway again, but in different outfits. Police reforms, he thought, had similar qualities. The models wear different outfits (the police pronounce a different rhetoric and their appearance has changed), but the structural conditions, often the models themselves, and the practices and habits of the show are largely and still the same. Reforms at the surface matter (rhetoric and declared aspirations are not irrelevant) but they are only the beginnings of progress. Only changes in the structural conditions which surround and determine the nature and work of the police, and changes in the habits of the police during their interactions with the public, will constitute progress towards democratic forms.

The analogy is more accurate for some countries than for others. In some countries, not just the clothes but the models have changed, and the runway is not what it used to be, nor is the audience the same. The question is what has led to such differences in the reform experience among countries? What conditions have been supportive of reforms which also are progress? As the chapters make clear, much depends on contexts and unique events.

The chapters in this volume have provided a snapshot of the status of police reform throughout Central and Eastern Europe. The countries under consideration vary greatly in terms of the sizes of their territories and populations, the nature of the regime change to democratic systems, as well as the rates at which they have subsequently transformed their political and economic systems. Yet all must deal with the decades-long legacy of state socialist regimes which used the police first to support the ruling party elite and suppress opposition, and only to a lesser extent to provide public safety. All of the countries under consideration began the transformation with police agencies (often called militias) that were often highly centralised and militaristic in approach and organisation, with close links to state security and used to employing authoritarian practices. All of the post-communist states also encountered a marked increase in crime, both regular and organised, as well as corruption following the change in regime and the liberalisation of various aspects of their governments and societies.

A certain number of the case study countries, mainly the independent successor states of former Yugoslavia, have the added burden of delayed transition due to recent involvement in inter-ethnic violence and armed conflict. Police were often directly involved in the conflict, and sometimes, especially special units, were implicated in wartime abuses. The task of transition for such states, then, is even more difficult, as police must shift back to an essentially civilian and law enforcement function after having been subject to military command, discipline and use in combat roles.

Below, we briefly compare approaches among the four sub-regional groups of states in terms of various key issues. We then describe some of the lessons which come from these analyses and how such lessons are different from the advice, standards and lessons which have been pronounced – West to East – so far. We then place police reform within the broader context of security sector reform (SSR) and examine what this comparative analysis has told us about SSR; and finally, we suggest what remains to be done and future directions for research.

Sub-regional trends

The countries in the Central Europe grouping include Hungary, the former GDR, Poland, the Czech Republic and Slovenia. This group of countries is generally acknowledged in the literature on democratisation to be the most advanced in terms of democratic consolidation and the creation of market economies. In the field of police reform, too, they tend to stand out as among the most advanced in moving towards efficient and democratic policing, yet there is variation across certain categories. The former GDR stands as the most advanced of the grouping, benefiting from the significant manpower and material resources invested from Western Germany in the reform process. In all of these countries legislative reform is at an advanced stage, and progress towards both depoliticisation and demilitarisation has been realised. Decentralisation of policing has been slower to take root, however, particularly in Hungary and Poland. And the record on protection of human rights by police is mixed, with problems notable especially in the Czech Republic and Hungary vis-à-vis the Roma and other visible minority groups. While the publics in these countries tend to accord a moderate level of legitimacy to policing, there is much yet to be achieved in the dealing with citizen complaints about police misconduct. There is a strong likelihood that police reforms will continue in view of the stringent conditions of the ongoing EU accession process and international (Western) pressures to deal more effectively with transborder crime.

Romania and Bulgaria, through their accelerating integration into Euro-Atlantic structures, while still lagging behind the Central European group generally, appear to be moving closer to the experience of these neighbours. The chapter on Romania describes the insularity of the Ceausescu-era police from the rest of society, which in combination with the regime's deliberate policy of secrecy about criminality and the close ties of police to the Romanian Communist Party, resulted in the evolution of mythology surrounding the police and the propagation of widespread societal fear of the police. After 50 years of totalitarian repression this ultimately backfired on the regime in December 1989, when the police became the lightning rod for pent-up societal fear and anger. Police reform was delayed for several years after the overthrow of the Ceausescu regime and resisted by police in Romania, however. It was not until 1996, then, that there was political will for police reform, peaking with significant legislative changes in 2002. With EU accession now definitely on the horizon, Romania has moved quickly since to formally demilitarise its police force, one of the first to do so in the region.

Bulgaria similarly experienced delay in fundamental reforms to the police until about 1997, when a national consensus emerged on the need for Bulgaria to integrate with Euro-Atlantic structures, namely the European Union and NATO. As in Romania, these objectives have in Bulgaria functioned as major drivers for institutional reform. Nevertheless, the author of the Bulgarian chapter warns that a sustained failure of the state to address public fears of crime, corruption and personal insecurity may undermine the legitimacy of the new democracy.

Police reform in the Western Balkan group of states must overcome not only the legacy of decades of state socialism, but more recent authoritarian rule and involvement in armed conflict with the disintegration of former Yugoslavia. The legacy of the Titoist state was broadly similar to other state socialist regimes in Central and Eastern Europe in the sense that police functioned as a key instrument of state security and state control of the population, resulting in a centralised and militarised force that, through its close links with state security police, directly served the interests and protected the ruling regime. With the outbreak of the Yugoslav wars in the early to mid-1990s, police across the region became directly involved in violent conflict. In certain countries (Serbia) they also became highly politicised. Inter-ethnic conflict had directly influenced the composition of the police throughout the region, which typically went from being fairly ethnically diverse to homogenous in each of the republics and enclaves. Police were drawn into conflict through efforts to massively increase police strength, equip them with heavy arms and equipment, and deploy them in military security-type roles. Efforts to rapidly expand the police resulted in the decline of professionalism, as normal education and training requirements were shortened and standards lowered.

In Croatia, the involvement of police in the war for independence had the effect of creating high public esteem and a legitimate indigenous police force divorced from the repressive Yugoslav militia. Involvement of police in the conflict, however, also served to reinforce and strengthen the traditional code of silence and bonds of professional loyalty among police officers. The consequence is that rooting out police corruption or creating internal controls over police misconduct has been made more difficult.

As a result of their recent involvement in conflict, most of the states in the Western Balkans are subject to the assistance and pressures of international and regional organisations such as the United Nations, NATO, EU, OSCE and Stability Pact. The Western Balkan states have been the focus of sustained efforts at the multilateral and bilateral levels to shape the transformation of the police towards more decentralised, professional and democratic patterns. This has been pursued through the monitoring performed by UN peacekeeping forces (UN Mission for Bosnia and Herzegovina, followed by the EU Police Mission in January 2003), international efforts to train police, the legitimising of distinct, ethnically-based police and state structures at the entity and even cantonal level through the Dayton Peace Agreement in Bosnia-Herzegovina, and the efforts of the OSCE to promote and coordinate root and branch police reform in Serbia and Montenegro. The results of international assistance have been mixed, however. In BiH, the Dayton Agreement is believed to have frozen the ethnically partitioned state, whose divisions are reflected in ethnically homogenous police forces in the entities. Pressure to reform the police in BiH arises only from external actors. In view of the declining commitment of international donors to the region, the question arises of the sustainability of the reforms already undertaken. In other states, there is also pressure from within to professionalise and modernise the police. The presence and attention of international actors means that police reform tends to reflect current thinking in major donor states about what is democratic policing. Ironically, the states throughout the region are also now subject to donor fatigue, raising the question of whether the pace of reforms can be sustained by states experiencing the gradual withdrawal of foreign actors and assistance.

The Western Balkan group of states moreover share a problem in the form of criminal networks which have emerged from the wars and which now use the states as transit corridors for the trafficking of humans, and smuggling of drugs, arms and other contraband. Frequent scandals suggest close links between state and political authorities and organised crime groups.

Both of the case studies drawn from the former Soviet Union are 'hard' cases. They demonstrate the lingering effects and attitudes of the centralised, militarised and authoritarian policing characteristic of the Soviet period, the persistence of former ruling elites in positions of power and systemic resistance to root and branch reform in the militia (police). Both Russia and Ukraine are experiencing serious problems due to corruption and rule of law cannot yet be said to exist throughout these societies.

Positive developments include the onset of a gradual rationalisation of policing functions to remove from the police responsibility for functions that are not related to combating crime and ensuring law and order. In Ukraine, this has notably included removing responsibility from the militia for administering prisons. However, the Ukrainian militia retain responsibility for many other administrative duties, such as registering motor vehicles, monitoring vehicles for pollution emissions, and passport and immigration control. The Russian Federal MVD (Ministry of the Interior) similarly is no longer responsible for fire-fighting or for the penal system, but its militia retains many of the same administrative functions as listed for Ukraine.

Russia also experiences security threats that arguably differ in degree and nature from those facing most of the other countries under consideration in this volume. The threat of terrorism or insurgency in Chechnya, for example, has resulted in the deployment of militia to such areas. This is one factor that helps to sustains the militaristic character of the Russian militia.

The Russian case study highlighted the fact that there are some practices from the Soviet era which may at first glance bear a resemblance to the principles of democratic policing that are being promoted today. These practices included extensive community involvement in local crime prevention and control through the formation of street committees, youth groups and street patrols. However, the politicised nature of these 'community policing' initiatives stands in contrast to the community-level initiatives, such as neighbourhood watch programmes, that are viewed as markers of civil society and social capital in Western democracies. In contrast, the suspicion lingers today in Russian neighbourhoods that the renewal of voluntary citizen participation in law enforcement marks a return to state surveillance and informants.

The Russian case also underscores that implementing reforms to the legal framework of policing is necessary but not sufficient in itself to ensure transformation towards a more democratically accountable and efficient police organisation. Restructuring the organisation without addressing professional and organisational culture will not result in fundamental transformation. The police exist as a part of a system, and in order to effect fundamental change all major components of the system must be attended to. Inculcating a culture of reform necessitates addressing all major aspects of policing as a profession and as an essential service. Further, establishing a sound legal framework for policing in the absence of rule of law and reliable mechanisms for disciplining those police and citizens who flout the law cannot be seen as an indicator of reform.

In a similar way, concentrating the education of police officers on legal issues and omitting much of the essential practical knowledge and skills of police work will not result in effective or democratic policing. Moreover, as is noted in the Ukrainian case, such legally trained members of the militia are more likely to seek better-paid employment as civilian lawyers in the private sector.

Policing efficiency is a major component of police legitimacy. A police organisation that is widely perceived as ineffective, passive or corrupt, such as the Russian or Ukrainian militias, will lack public trust. Further, the development of a service ethic is essential to fostering the confidence of citizens that the militia are concerned first with the safety of ordinary individuals.

The Russian and Ukrainian case studies also highlighted the need for external civilian supervision mechanisms and the contribution they could make to stemming corruption in the militia and increasing public trust in the institution and its members. The Ukrainian militia reflects the state of public institutions generally since independence in terms of the carryover in positions of power of many members of the ruling elite from the Soviet period, and hence structural opposition to reform. The militia remains highly militarised, hierarchical and centralised, and continues to exhibit Soviet-era practices through authoritarian management, minimal local input and excessive secrecy.

In both Russia and Ukraine, authorities use detection or clearance rates to measure crime and as indicators of militia performance in solving and preventing crime. Militia performance is measured according to detection rates (percentage of cases cleared). In reality, the detection rate does not accurately reflect either the efficiency of the police or the actual level of criminality. As the primary indicator to measure performance, the detection rate became subject to manipulation and these figures are often exaggerated to the extreme. In the Soviet period, detection rates were extremely high, often exceeding 90%. The unrealistic clearance rates tend to result in the militia under-registering many crimes reported to it in both countries, especially those crimes that are harder to solve. As a result, those crimes that tend to affect the greatest number of people, such as burglaries and car thefts, often go unregistered and are not reflected in official statistics. The emphasis on detection rates also means that police have an incentive in not registering those crimes that are unlikely to be solved. Reforms implemented by the Russian authorities to require the registering of every crime reported by the public and to base appraisals on many more factors than clear-up rates has been one effort to reduce systemic incentives to under-register crimes and falsify detection and clear-up rates.

General lessons learned

Rhetoric and action
There is a general sense among the authors that police reformers in Central and Eastern European countries have learned to talk the right democratic language but that they have not yet been able to translate knowledge of goals, values, good practices and appropriate models into sustainable police progress. Clearly, police leaders and reformers have an intimate knowledge of international standards and human rights concerns, the basic notion that democratic policing is a service, the ideologies and practices loosely grouped under the rubric of 'community policing', and the importance of civic society involvement in accountability practices. No one, even when security conditions have deteriorated, as they have in all states, uses the discredited policing rhetoric of the former socialist policing systems. The impression exists, as well, that police leaders are serious when they use the new language and are committed to seeing it transformed into practice.

There are instrumental and philosophical reasons why the new language is used. Instrumentally, the facility in language points to one important conditions for reform, which can be observed in all Central and Eastern European states (with the possible exception of Slovenia),[2] and that is the pressure exerted by the regional and international community on the political and police leadership of these states. All chapters note the importance of membership in the larger regional European community, desired mainly for economic reasons, but also for the psychological

---

2. The argument that Slovenia's reforms were the result of internal actions rather than international pressures is correct as far as the process of reform itself is concerned. But the content of reforms – from basic notions of democratic policing to specific ideologies such as community policing – reflected a profound familiarity by internal reform agents with the practices and policies of the police in Western societies and the efforts to promote reforms in other Central and Eastern European states. The mechanisms and pressures for reforms may have been different, but the goals and substance of reforms, and the problems encountered, are quite similar to the experiences of other states throughout the region.

benefits. But in order to gain accession (to the EU or NATO), countries have to meet threshold conditions for a democratic society, including the security system. Pre-accession demands, guidelines, assessments and assistance have mandated changes in Central and Eastern European systems, and only if such demands are met will accession proceed. In some cases, such as Serbia (and in Kosovo)and Bosnia-Herzegovina, international advisors effectively control the process of reforming the policing system of the past. In short, international demands and supervision and the desire for accession have placed Central and Eastern European states into a regional classroom in which their performance is graded by existing members of the European community by standards which reflect Western democratic concepts and values.

Philosophically, reformers know that the old systems need to be replaced and reformed. There really is no choice, given the movement towards democratic governance and market reforms in the region. The goals of professionalism, the notion of service, the norms embedded in codes of conduct, and the need to legitimise new security systems are accepted by reformers, even when there may be some reservations about specific aspects of democratic reforms, such as external supervision and accountability.[3] In the long run, reformers expect that reforms will make the police more effective, will lead to greater acceptance of the police by the public, and make the job of policing easier – and that is all to the good.

International pressure, itself, reflects in its substantive provisions changing conceptions of policing which have crystallised in Western democracies in the last quarter century. Community policing, for example, is an innovation everywhere. That its ideology has found its way into international models and assistance programmes, and pressures for reform, is not surprising. Nor is it surprising that police reformers in Central and Eastern European states want to be associated with the latest, 'cutting-edge' developments in policing. International models and examples may be imposed or demanded but they are also objects of imitation and accepted standards against which to judge the modernity and professionalism of police forces.

International demands have been both an offence to sentiments of national sovereignty and distinctiveness but, and more importantly, have provided internal reformers with a powerful argument and tool for reform. It has become impossible to speak of policing in any other terms than those characteristic of Western democracies. Even a re-emerging nostalgia for the old times – when there was repression, to be sure, but also greater sense of personal protection from ordinary crime – which arises routinely as crime explodes and organised crime takes over

---

3. Resistance by the police to external supervision is not unusual among police forces, even those considered to be quite responsive to public demands and committed to democratic norms. External supervision clashes with professional values – the values of expertise, knowledge of the practicalities of street work, demands for autonomy, and the right for self-discipline – and will be resisted in practice, even when accepted in rhetoric, as it will be by other professional groupings, such as lawyers or doctors.

much of economic life, cannot hide the fact that the discourse of policing has changed. People want more security but not a return of the repressive state apparatuses which used to be the police.

The pragmatic question is how long the new rhetoric can be sustained, if no effective reforms are accomplished, before new conceptions of policing lose their lustre, and before civic society and the state delegitimise the goals and policies of reform. At some point, reforms must become visible in the lives of ordinary people (especially marginal groups) and in the way they are treated by the police in encounters. If the police have not changed, or are not seen to have changed, in how they behave in the routines of their work then all other legal, organisational and rhetorical reforms will mean little. The payoff for police reforms is on the street. And that will require, most fundamentally, a specific police culture.

Determining whether the proper police culture is being brought into existence is not an easy research project, nor is it well understood which personnel practices (recruitment, education, training, discipline and rewards), managerial strategies, organisational arrangements, and relational tactics (with civic society and other state agencies) will produce the needed cultural norms and attitudes. One of the real gaps in these chapters (with minor exceptions) is the absence of the voice of street level police officers. What do they think about reforms matters, for they will have to implement the reforms, convert the rhetoric into practice.

More research is needed, not just for curiosity's sake or to employ researchers but for effective policies. If the pay-off for democratic policing is on the street (as a shorthand term for all the encounters and interactions of the police with civic society) then understanding how to create a police culture (rather than let it develop haphazardly and by the interests of the police) which will guide discretion into appropriate behaviour is essential.

The politics of reform

A second impression gained from these analyses is the complete enmeshing of police reform efforts in the larger political dynamics of the country. Policing is power. Controlling the police makes one powerful. Losing control makes one weaker. Proposed reforms of policing systems will always be assessed, by all internal actors (civic groups, political leaders, police managers, domestic and international reformers) by how much reforms will redistribute control and power as well as by criteria of justice and effectiveness. There is no neutral, apolitical way to talk about the police, to assess their roles and performance. Of course, the language of justice and effectiveness will clothe support for and opposition to reforms.

The chapters are replete with examples of the politics of the police. The police are part of politics everywhere. Yet in Central and Eastern European states, which are in transition towards new forms of politics, economic organisation and state–society relations, the political roles of the police and the impacts of police reforms on the likely outcomes of transition are more visibly apparent and understood by all. Each chapter details the dynamics of advocacy and opposition, of seeking control of reforms.

The politics of policing can be seen in diverse examples. Efforts to directly manipulate the police and the creation of specific police forces for political and personal gain can be found in all these states. Changes in political fortunes and governments will be connected to changing the personnel and priorities of the police. Another example is 'ceaseless innovation' in policing law. New political leaders will try to 'fix' what they see as inappropriate, biased towards the wrong values, and ineffective in past police reforms. The result is organisational instability and ineffective policing as the police attempt to determine what are their jobs and priorities and how to adapt and adjust to new external demands. Competition for resources, which, almost by definition, are scarce in transitional societies will limit the capacity of the police to recruit new members and equip the police with needed tools. A common occurrence, in all Central and Eastern European states, is the drain of police officers to private, and sometimes criminal, employment which pays better. The police become the training and proving ground, at the taxpayers' expense, for private security agencies. The ethnic, class and gender composition of police forces are political issues, whether reformers seek to hire the best candidates irrespective of their background, or whether political figures and civic groups try to stack the police with their 'own' people. Merit will conflict with perceived political allegiance and group loyalties.

The crucial role of politics is understood by international reformers but, one has a sense, in an abstract and largely negative way. And there is a sense that international reformers downplay the role of politics in their own reform advocacy and efforts. Donor competition and lack of cooperation are well known facts;[4] as is the advocacy of national styles or 'models' of policing.

Reformers know that policing is subject to politics but think that political influence should be minimised in the practices of the police. But politics is essential for the legitimisation of new policing systems. In short, police reform is a political process, not just the transfer or creation of technical, managerial or evaluation skills.

Constitutional and legislative reforms are necessary but not sufficient for transforming police

The enshrining of basic human rights and the creation of supervision mechanisms and requirements in laws governing the police are essential to their democratic control and accountability. Further, there are important legal provisions which the societies in transition have needed to implement in order to deal with increasing criminality, especially serious and organised crime. One example is the provision for providing immunity to witnesses who were part of a criminal group and who testify against it (see the Polish case). Yet while legal reform is necessary, it is not sufficient to ensure democratic and effective policing. Organisational culture must also undergo a transformation, and individual police officers must be made to feel, and must be held, responsible for misconduct and abuse of human rights. As Pagon

---

4. Renata Dwan, ed., *Executive Policing: Enforcing the Law in Peace Operations*, SIPRI Research Report No. 16 (Oxford: Oxford University Press for SIPRI, 2002).

notes in his contribution, persistent problems such as a traditional police subculture, an us-versus-them mentality and police brutality

> cannot be solved by passing new laws and regulations. They have to be solved by working with people on a daily basis, changing their attitudes and perceptions, managing their experiences and the consequences of their behaviour, setting an example, establishing an appropriate moral climate, managing social relationships, etc.

Moreover, legal reform may serve as 'window dressing' for a lack of fundamental reform, as was seen in Russia with the continued politicisation of the militia.

The contents of reforms: three little d's and one big D

One conceptual scheme for capturing the goals of reforms is common to many of the chapters, namely that the three small d's of decentralisation, demilitarisation, depoliticisation will lead to the larger D of Democratisation. The three small d's are largely a reaction to the policing systems typical of socialist, state and party-controlled, repressive and politicised systems of the Soviet period. The three d's seek to rid the policing systems of traits which made them instruments of state and elite power and non-responsive to civic society demands. Democratic policing is frequently defined as policing in the service of civic society, or people, and not the party or the state. Accomplishing the three d's will go a long way towards preparing the ground for meaningful democratic practices. Conversely, if not accomplished, reforms of the police cannot achieve democratic standards.

The three d's are advocated mostly in reaction to the past but also because they are perceived as inherently or necessarily connected to democratic forms of policing. The danger is that in reacting to the past, often without knowing exactly why abuses happened, democratic values and practices may be short-changed.

Decentralisation

Centralisation/decentralisation can refer to the organisational structure of the police. All authority for decisions rests in the apex of the command hierarchy, which itself was controlled in state socialist systems by parallel party command bodies. In centralised systems every police force (regular or militia, state security, border forces) is controlled at the highest political level. Centralisation/decentralisation can also refer, as it does in notions of community policing, to the dispersion or shift of authority and discretion to lower levels of the organisation. In a decentralised system, even though the structure may be formally centralised, officers have the devolved capacity to make and implement policies and decisions (within broad legal and organisational limits) which reflect local conditions and their professional judgement.

In state socialist systems policing was highly centralised in terms of control and hierarchy, even though organisational arrangements had the look of dispersion and local control. Control was always centralised and nothing was done in disregard of central, party-issued and party-approved directives and priorities. Largely, this was a matter of internal culture and managerial practices. Police officers were socialised into doing only what they were told, not to take initiatives, and certainly not to do anything which might go against central or organisational priorities without checking first with superiors. One of the most widely described aspects of policing in Western democracies – the ability of the individual police officer to use personal discretion in his or her work – was rarely observed to be found in socialist policing systems.

A common problem in most of the states surveyed is the continued *de facto* centralisation of policing organisations, although community policing is slowly spreading and gaining popularity, at least on a declaratory level. In certain states, initial efforts were made to decentralise but were not followed through or were reversed (Hungary, Macedonia). In other states, decentralisation has been very slow to take root. Jobard maintains that, based on the experience of the former GDR, decentralisation of the police was a *sine qua non* of its democratisation. However decentralisation of decision-making, which is a core prescription for community policing, will not be achieved by reconfiguring organisational charts but requires a concomitant change in the way the police see their capacity for discretion. But more starkly, without discretion there is little hope that community policing will be implemented. Yet most of the decentralisations which have occurred in Central and Eastern European states have been at the organisational chart levels. Reforms have reacted to the centralised nature of socialist systems rather than to the need for new capacities for discretion. There has been, not unexpectedly, a sense that discretion is not a goal of reforms. Discretion sounds too daring, implies arbitrariness and lack of consistency, invites corruption and abuses of power, and complicates external supervision and accountability. Plus it is difficult to conceptualise as a policy or practice, hence hard to plan for, difficult to teach, and almost impossible to evaluate. The last thing you want to convey in reform advocacy is that the police should have the right to make some of their own decisions.

At the micro level, several authors noted that individual citizens should be encouraged to take part in local law enforcement activities and cooperate with police. However, in most of these countries there was a communist-era involvement of citizens in policing activities that were driven by ideological and material interests and incentives. Moreover, the communist-era police forces often engaged in an intense form of 'community policing', whereby certain officers walked the beat of streets or offices in the areas where they themselves lived. The proximity of these police officers and the active interest they took in the personal lives of citizens, facilitated, however, their surveillance activities, and the information they gathered could be passed on to the political police. Indeed, the model of 'community policing' practised in communist states such as the GDR could be said to exceed that practised in any other Western system. There is also the perception that while the necessary legal protections were introduced for prisoners and those accused of crimes with the onset of transition, the rights of victims were not equally advanced, contributing to a sense of resentment, helplessness and unwillingness to assist police by stepping forward as witnesses to crimes. The failure to address citizen dissatisfaction with law enforcement and the criminal justice system may result in vigilante initiatives whereby individuals take the law into their own hands.

Demilitarisation

As with decentralisation, demilitarisation can refer to different aspects of policing. It is generally accepted that the police, being a service that has civic society (especially victims) as clients and stakeholders, should be organisationally distinct from the military. The danger of militarising policing is largely a question of ethos and culture in the organisation, rather than one of institutional affiliation. Of course, being part of the military will infect the police with military values, attitudes and behaviours which are inappropriate for a service. The military fights and aims to kill an enemy by whatever means it takes; the police protect society, victims and offenders in a legally circumscribed manner and turn their work over to other agencies. The danger is that a militarised police will begin to treat its service clients as enemies who must be destroyed, eliminated or immobilised by any means.

Demilitarisation of the ethos and culture is essential and that can be done more easily if institutional affiliations with the military are removed. The militarisation of many of the police organisations throughout the region provides one explanation for why police leadership continues to be authoritarian in nature, and policing often repressive in character. Police organisations structured with a highly centralised military-type hierarchy and command system do not tend to foster a sense of individual responsibility for upholding the human rights of citizens on the part of police officers, nor support the honing of professional discretion advocated by Western police organisations.

Depoliticisation

The police in socialist systems were a tool of state and party power. They did what the political leadership ordered irrespective of constitutional rights, legal prohibitions, or local demands (unless approved by higher authority). Taking the police out of the political process has been a major goal of reforms. Depoliticisation entails changing the function of the police from protecting the political regime or government to ensuring public safety, with police powers and responsibilities defined by law. A democratic police force is subject to the rule of law and not political demands.

Depoliticisation and political neutrality of the police are a common challenge confronting all of the police organisations throughout the region. Given the recent history of communist party control of the police and the use of the police to protect the former political regime, depoliticisation was not surprisingly one of the first reforms undertaken by many of the young democracies. Continuing politicisation of the higher levels of the civil service, however, is a trend that commonly characterises the transition states, and this is also reflected in the domain of policing.

Nevertheless, the danger of over-reacting to the past is the almost wholesale deprivation of political rights for police officers. The police in most states have been denied even some of the most basic political rights any citizen is entitled to. It is likely, as has been argued in Western democracies, that if the police themselves are not treated with respect for their democratic rights, they in turn will not treat citizens with such respect. Democracy implies a distinct level of trust and risk-taking in what people will do. And that includes, or should include, police officers.

Gains and losses

The gains from reforms which have been implemented are pretty clear. In the short run, there will be a greater likelihood that the police will gain acceptance from the public and, in the long run, greater legitimacy.

Less clear is what will be lost. One common phenomenon in the countries reviewed in this study is the explosion of crime. Reforms mean some degree of organisational turmoil, loss of personnel for various reasons (vetting, private employment, age and educational disqualifications), and increasing demands by civic society for harsher, more repressive policing and less justice or due process-oriented policing. In the short run, such demands will be hard to resist by the police or political leaders, and supporters of due process (mostly international and local NGOs) will be ostracised and condemned (e.g. ICHRP, 2003).

Another consequence of reforms which is noted in some of the chapters is the discrepancy in state socialist-era policing systems between informal and formal arrangements. In some systems, such as in Slovenia and the former GDR, socialist police were knowledgeable about and responsive to local communities (or local leaders). The new systems, in their efforts to control political influence, have removed the police further from their communities, even when community policing has been the advocated ideology. In short, not all socialist policing was alike, nor was it centralised and removed from local conditions.

Accountability and legitimisation

While improvements can be noted in the development of structures for police accountability, these are often mostly internal to the police or ministry of interior. Internal investigation of complaints against police predominate, typically with a very low incidence of disciplinary action and sanctions. One exception is Bosnia-Herzegovina, where policing was administered by the UN authorities, and is now being monitored by the EU police mission. Some countries have devised external civilian supervision bodies which may include the police in their remit. Hungary's parliamentary ombudsmen for human rights, minority rights and data protection are a notable example. Parliamentary supervision is notable for being largely absent apart from a brief mention in most of the chapters, leading to the tentative conclusion that it remains relatively weak as a supervision mechanism over the domain of policing. The office of the procuracy usually plays a prominent role in these states in launching investigations into allegations of wrongdoing by police. The role of the courts as a mechanism of supervision, however, generally appears to be inadequate, and seeking remedy before the courts is not as common a phenomenon as in Western countries.

Public trust in the police still appears, on the whole, to be low. Central and Eastern European publics continue to be reluctant to report all crimes to the police, often in the belief that they will not register the crime, or will not pursue it actively. The Russian and Ukrainian case studies in particular explore this reluctance to call on the police and lack of confidence in the police.

In the case of some of the Yugoslav successor states, the active role played by the regular police in the wars for independence (Slovenia, Croatia) tended greatly to increase public trust, and therefore legitimacy, of the police. However accountability appeared to be undermined because of the effect of shared combat experience on strengthening the sense of mutual loyalty among police colleagues and reinforcing the code of silence, as described in the chapter in Croatia.

One of the correlates of the low public trust in police is the moderate to high level of corruption involving police and other state authorities. All of the states under consideration experienced increases in crime rates, including organised crime. The growth in crime rates across the region highlighted the need to increase the efficiency of the police in crime prevention and detection. The emergence of organised crime and high-level corruption further underscored the inadequacies of the existing policing organisations. It is recognised throughout the region that greater transnational police cooperation is needed to combat cross-border crime such as trafficking, and developments are visible both on the bilateral and multilateral dimensions, in particular with the European Union. Whether the push for greater transnational police cooperation is accompanied by an emphasis on democratic accountability is open to question.

One explanation for the slow and sometimes superficial reforms to policing systems in the region is that governments may have been reluctant to bring in radical change when social, economic and cultural changes have put additional pressure on criminal justice systems, that is, when crime is increasing. Post-communist countries have all witnessed a significant increase in crime, many almost to levels found in Western states. Fear of crime is prevalent in these societies, and growing crime rates often lead to public demands for a return to repressive approaches to crime and social control. The socio-political context in many post-communist societies is such that increasing crime rates and fear of crime have tended to result in the prioritising of maintaining order and cracking down on crime, with less concern for maintaining respect for human rights and civil liberties and little sympathy for accused criminals and prisoners.

The growth in crimes rates also served to reduce incentives for implementing more muscular supervision and control mechanisms. Instead, efforts to make the police more effective and efficient took precedence in a number of case study countries. In some countries, such as Hungary, the police are viewed by some as having successfully used the wave of public concern about increasing criminality to try to take control of the reform process. In other words, the primary concern of the public in environments characterised by high crime and public insecurity appears to be community safety rather than democratic policing. Political instability or rising crime can be, and has been, used to justify maintaining a strong police. Yet police in these countries have also been accused of using the growth in crime rates and heightened public fears of crime to consolidate their institutional interests and resist calls for greater transparency and accountability.

The role of the police in security sector reform

Police reforms are part of a larger, more comprehensive process of change in transitional societies, both in the societal conditions of these countries, and more particularly in the 'security sector'. The notion of security sector reform (SSR) has recently emerged as a framework for understanding and guiding changes which would lead to a more effective, legitimate, accountable, and sustainable security system and sense of safety among individuals and groups in society.

This volume has contributed to the emerging literature on security sector reform by setting out the challenges in reforming policing systems facing a region of states that for the past 15 years has been actively seeking to transform the entire security architecture and the underlying rationale of security institutions. While the focus on police reform is but one part of the security sector, it is a vital part, and one that is not always well understood by those who look at other sectors, such as the armed forces and intelligence agencies. The lessons learned on public security and reforming policing system outlined above may be instructive for specialists in the other spheres of security. The volume also suggests some new lines of enquiry for security sector reform research.

A security sector reform perspective sensitises us to the inter-relationships and inter-dependencies of different security agencies and their respective reform programmes. One such issue that this project briefly touched upon was the requirement for police reform to be accompanied by reform of the judiciary and broader criminal justice system in transitional societies. As with police reform, judicial and criminal justice reform require more than merely organisational changes; they are also political undertakings that require changing mind-sets, attitudes and expectations within the judiciary and criminal justice system, and externally among politicians, policy-makers and the general public.

Another relationship – that between police reforms that improve public security on the one hand, and on the other hand sustainable economic development, is one that cuts to the core objective of security sector reform. The linkage has been mentioned in passing but has not yet been studied in depth. It may even be premature to attempt to do so before we understand the parameters of each component sector of security. More work is needed, for example, to draw out the conceptual linkages between sectors and to assess them in empirical terms, in order to arrive at more effective policy formulation and assistance programmes. Nevertheless, there are interesting avenues for research already apparent, such as the relationship between the public security climate and level of trust in law enforcement systems on the one hand and direct investment on the other. Countries with high levels of corruption and organised crime generally appear to be avoided by foreign investors, and even by diaspora groups who may send money back to their country of origin in the form of remittances and spend money when they come back to visit, but who decline to invest capital locally. Establishing a secure environment, including the rule of law, helps build business confidence and ultimately promotes economic development.

The transitional societies under examination also witnessed rapid development of private policing and security firms, often a response to inadequate public security amid spiralling rates of criminality and the emergence of organised crime and high-level corruption. A security sector reform perspective would explore the ramifications of the growing private security sector on public conceptions of their security and on the legitimacy of the state's security institutions. Also of interest would be the movement of personnel from police to private security firms and the impact this drain has on the attitudes and practices in policing and the overall impact on public security. Similarly, there has been insufficient attention to the impact of having demobilised soldiers, especially in post-conflict contexts, and former state security or intelligence agents join policing structures. While there has been discussion of vetting practices, there is little consideration of the implications of the horizontal movement of personnel between security sectors for professionalism and operational practice.

The contributions to this publication also clearly suggest that the international community can play an important role in initiating reforms in the police and broader security sector. International attention and assistance have proven helpful in transferring knowledge and expertise to reforming police organisations, when that assistance has been sustained and focused. It is proving particularly useful in building up the capacities of policing bodies throughout the region to counter organised crime. The countries of Central and Eastern Europe are the focus of much attention by Western governments and their police agencies in the effort to build local capacities to deal more effectively with organised crime and other transborder threats. Nevertheless, there also exists the possibility that Western agendas for assistance, which are currently focused on combating organised crime and illegal immigration, are skewing policing priorities in recipient states and are creating privileged sectors within the policing community, such as border policing, which benefit more from international assistance, resources and attention than the lower-profile areas of regular policing. A security sector reform perspective reminds us that police reform, like any other area of public policy, is not a mere technical exercise but a profoundly political one, both in its domestic and international dimensions. Assistance, leverage, sanctions and conditionality are all means by which actors seek to protect and advance their interests.

At the same time, one should not necessarily over-state the influence of international actors on police reform processes. International assistance and pressures are to a considerable degree responsible for the police reforms initiated and implemented to date in the international protectorate of Bosnia and

Herzegovina, yet the sustainability of those reforms is not certain in the context of gradual withdrawal of international community. In other contexts such as Slovenia, international influences on police reform have been described as being limited to the strictly operational-technical level, as police remain distrustful of foreign ideas and approaches. Thus while international assistance can influence the shape and pace of security sector reform, it cannot substitute for domestic consensus or political will to sustain and implement the spirit of the reforms.

Lessons, policies, futures

Perhaps the most important lesson that one can derive from this study is this: Meaningful reforms of the police cannot be achieved without a deep and accurate understanding of the totality of conditions and contexts which influence the ideologies and work of the police. Piecemeal reforms – whether organisational innovations, new forms of interactions with the community, structures and processes of accountability, or specific crime control techniques – will fall by the wayside if they are not connected systemically and systematically to other factors which shape police performance.

For example, accountability mechanisms, which are essential, are just structures and words if not connected to general policing ideologies, managerial practices, and civic involvement. It is a safe generalisation that no internal or external accountability mechanisms works well in any society simply by the activities of people involved in those mechanisms. They may work hard and conscientiously but that is all. There will be no accountability consequences to their work.

Future research could focus more precisely on how these states are trying to build police cultures where respect for fairness, human rights and the dignity of the individual is a facet of all policing activities. What are the mechanics of shifting the perceptions of the police from the governing regime's instrument of force to a public service that upholds and protects human rights? What is the role of police leadership in transitional states in effecting changes in attitudes and behaviour? Is there a debate or even discussion about ethics in policing in these societies? A related topic might be the impact of transnational policing and increasing contacts with police colleagues from other states on the domestic police culture.

While national boundaries are of decreasing relevance both in terms of the occurrence of criminality and its prevention and detection, police agencies, criminal justice systems, and accountability and control systems are still based on the national context. A final useful direction for further research would be to examine the disparity between growing international cooperation among policing and state security authorities and the largely static accountability mechanisms and procedures in place at the national level. Having particular influence on on the evolution of policing legislation and practices throughout the Central and Eastern European region are multinational legal arrangement such as the European Convention on

Human Rights, the EU Schengen agreement, and the extremely rigorous EU accession process. The area of Justice and Home Affairs has become the European Union's most dynamic policy area in recent years, and although developments in this field fundamentally affect the relationship between the state and its citizens through such areas as policing, there has been very little advancement in democratic oversight of the decisions and procedures of this policy area. The articles in this collection have underscored the continuing deficiency of national-level civilian controls and accountability mechanisms for police throughout the post-socialist region. As these countries move closer towards European integration and develop more effective means of combating cross-border crime, care must be taken to ensure that these deficiencies do not deepen.

The transformation of policing will never be accomplished, in any society, to the satisfaction of all groups who have a stake in the process, be these other government agencies, international sponsors, representatives of civic society, political leaders or the police themselves. Transformation is, as well, a continually ongoing and open-ended process which will be debated in terms of ultimate goals, policy objectives and implementation mechanisms. In a democracy, and in countries seeking to democratise, this fluidity of institutions, laws and policies may be a drawback (for crime control and the maintenance of order) but it is also a crucial strength for it indicates the capacity and willingness of stakeholders to engage in debate about one of the fundamental elements of a democratic society – a system of policing that is both effective and just. By this consideration, the fact that the countries discussed in this book are only part way along the road to that goal is not reason for dismay. What matters more is that the process of transformation is being pursued and that this process is guided by and seeks to adhere, ias it is in these countries, to standards which can lead to democratic policing systems.

References

Das, Dilip and Marenin, Otwin, eds. 2000. *Challenges of Policing Democracies. A World Perspective.* Reading, UK: Gordon and Breach Publishers.

Dwan, Renata, ed. 2002. *Executive Policing: Enforcing the Law in Peace Operations*, SIPRI Research Report No. 16. Oxford: Oxford University Press for SIPRI.

ICHRP (International Council on Human Rights Policy) 2003. *Crime, Public Order and Human Rights. Draft Report for Consultation Mar. 2003)*, Geneva: ICHRP.

Kadar, Andras, ed. 2001. *Police in Transition*. Budapest: Central European University Press.

Statewatch, 16 June 2003, http://www.statewatch.org/news/2003/jun/16safe.htm

Appendix

Tables compiled by Michael Jaxa-Chamiec

Table A.1   Summary Table: Western Balkans

	Bosnia & Herzegovina	Croatia	Macedonia	Montenegro	Slovenia	Serbia
Personnel strength (2003)	20,000	20,000	Approx. 5000	Numbers secret: estimated 4750 uniformed policemen and further 10,000 special police	6882 policemen, 716 detectives	Total of 26,000 (including detectives and scientific support personnel)
Ratio: policemen/ 100,000 inhabitants	Roughly 500/100,000	428/100,000	250/100,000	Difficult to establish	274 (+ 36 detectives)/100,000 (official figures: 241)	280/100,000
Reform of legislative framework of police	Many introduced, but mainly forced by UN and rushed	Highly advanced and specific; vast enforcement problems	Adequate	Inadequate; drafts now in circulation	Adequate	Inadequate; drafts circulating for some time, held back by pervasive weakness of the overall state legal framework; no Constitution yet
Depoliticisation	Partial; increasing	Partial	Partial; high on the agenda, but problematic	Low; highly politicised	Adequate in legal terms; varied in practice	Poor

	Bosnia & Herzegovina	Croatia	Macedonia	Montenegro	Slovenia	Serbia
Demilitarisation	Partial; increasing	*	Partial; increasing, albeit vested with problems	Partial; low	Partial; some relics in mentality and organisational structure	Partial; low
Decentralisation	High; though not necessarily a virtue: reflects and fuels regionalisms	Partial; high in operational terms; central command	Increasing; very high on the agenda since 2001	Low	Partial; conflicting tendencies prevail	Limited
Human rights/policing ombudsman	Schemes/institutions exist (incl. ombudsman); varies in practice	Adequate both legislatively and in practice	Institutionally and legislatively installed, but often problematic in practice	Poor; no ombudsman	Ostensibly adequate mechanisms but documented cases of violence and abuse	Poor; currently no ombudsman
Civilian review/ supervision board	Poor; mainly UN-inspired, irregular, of limited capabilities and sustainability	Yes; annual reports to parliamentary committees; important role of the independent media	Elaborated, multi-layered, both within the state and non-state structures; in practice, however, significant part of activity and reporting remains classified	Annual reports to Parliament; no legal role for general public, but some consultation mechanisms in place; internal control much stronger	Limited in actual competences	Indirect, 'one-way' and limited; bi-annual reports, press conferences, website; many new solutions pending
Internal control of police (by police hierarchy/MOI)	Limited; international agencies file and consider problems	Always the first step; in practice, often the last	Always the first step; rarely proceeds further	MOI particularly strong: both in promotions (keep secret) and reprimands	Yes; members of the public appointed as observers	Relevant mechanisms established very recently: difficult to assess, but surely vested with problems

	Bosnia & Herzegovina	Croatia	Macedonia	Montenegro	Slovenia	Serbia
Judicial supervision	Inadequate	Adequate	Inadequate	Inadequate	Inadequate	Poor
Representation of women	[Generally inconclusive data]	High (20% of the force)	Currently inadequate; increasing	Negligible	Inadequate	Although significantly improved in recent years, still inadequate (a total of 750)
Representation of minorities	Poor; increase attempted; mixed results; especially poor at high ranks	Adequate: reflecting the ethnic composition of the country	Currently inadequate; but high on the PR agenda and increasing	No good data, but clearly inadequate	Inadequate	Generally inadequate; good locally (south Serbia)
Legitimacy	Locally/ethnically varied; trusting 'their' local police, not 'other'	Medium levels; decreasing	Medium levels; increasing with the emphasis on community policing and public relations	Low; because of the level of politicisation, police remains an isolated service	Varies*	Low
Rates of effectiveness of complaints (complaints found justified, sanctions applied)	Fairly effective, though done by the highly-empowered UN authorities (UNMBIH)*	Good mechanisms in place; however, usually poorly implemented	Poor in practice; very limited number of applied sanctions	Poor; police servicemen enjoy particular state protection	High percentage of processed complaints, but too low/infrequent sanctions	Official data diverge from NGOs reports, but certainly inadequate

	Bosnia & Herzegovina	Croatia	Macedonia	Montenegro	Slovenia	Serbia
Complaint procedures	Exclusively UN-nts made to relevant UN uthority	Personal accountability of officers for misconducts	Many options and institutions to resort to, both state and non-state	Internal complaints system; both police and MOI	Submissions in writing,	Inspector General office - began functioning, this year
Code of ethics?	Yes	Yes	Yes	Yes, recently adopted	Yes.	No; courses on ethics delivered by OSCE
Rates of Personnel Turnover	Medium	High. Recently began to decrease.	Inconclusive	Inconclusive	Inconclusive	Not totally clear; seems high, especially at medium-higher ranks
Level of professionalism	Increasingly higher; better at upper ranks	Increasing; emphasis on specialised training, instead of 'general practice'	Increasing: good in comparison with other states of the region	Low	High	Low
What priority is fighting organised crime?	Important problem, difficult to tackle due to decentralisation and corruption	At present inadequately tackled, due to corruption in the ranks and govt	High, despite lack of experience	Low	Too low	Top priority *
Corruption	High	High	High	High	Medium	Very high

	Bosnia & Herzegovina	Croatia	Macedonia	Montenegro	Slovenia	Serbia
International assistance	Vital (UN introduces, conducts most of the reforms)	Fairly low; only limited EU incentives, selectively applied	High and intensive; advanced participation of EU, USA and OSCE on many levels	Limited, but important in gearing for the reform (EU, OSCE)	Limited	High; OSCE; Council of Europe, Danish Centre for Human Rights
International influence on reforms	High	Limited; mainly EU	Medium	Essential, given politicisation of the internal sector	Limited	Medium; limited

BiH:
* At the beginning of the year, EU police mission began taking over UNMBIH tasks.
** Note the dual-ethnicity of Ministers across Cantons problem (page 000). Efforts now being made to converge into a single, ethnicity-independent, chain of command.
***Less in RS canton.
Croatia:
* Problematic: organisationally secured, but given the recent war past, where the police were performing defence functions, and defence was an absolute budgetary priority, well entrenched in the personnel mentality.
Slovenia:
* In general, the police isolate themselves as a part of much criticised 'culture' or 'mentality', though the public are expressing willingness to cooperate, especially in the preferred community policing projects.
Serbia:
* This year saw the assassination of the Serbian Prime Minister Djindjić, attributed to his efforts at fighting far-reaching organised crime.

Table A.2 Summary Table: Central and South-Eastern Europe

	Bulgaria	Czech Rep.	Former GDR	Hungary	Poland	Romania
Personnel strength (2003)	No data	41,000 (additional 10,000 civilians)	No data	Approx. 38,500	103,000	Approx. 52,000. Plus 18,000 Gendarmerie and 20,000 Public Guards
Ratio: number of policemen/ 100,000 inhabitants	No data	410/ 100,000	No data	380/100,000	Approx. 375/100,000	Approx. 400/100,000 (including Gendarms and Public Guards)
Reform of legislative framework of police	Major reforms pending	Fairly advanced; more pending	Good; adopted overall German legislation	Adequate	Adequate	Adequate, following major reform of 2002
Depoliticisation	Partial/ fairly high, especially in recruitment and training	Fair	High	Fair	Fairly high	Partial
Demilitarisation	Partial [inconclusive]	Partial	High	Fair; low in some organisational respects	Fair	Fairly high, increasing
Decentralisation	Partial	Partial	Very high (Länders)	Low; some tendencies recently re-appeared	Low, increasing	Partial; high in some respects

	Bulgaria	Czech Rep.	Former GDR	Hungary	Poland	Romania
Human rights/policing ombudsman	Mixed evidence; Ombudsman law pending	Poor: pervasive outstanding problem of racial prejudice; no track of wrongful acts kept; no external controls	Good	Fairly poor; evidenced cases of abuse, especially against minorities; Ombudsmen with limited power	Ombudsman yes; many mechanisms in place	Fair; Ombudsman instituted; human rights high on the agenda
Civilian review/supervision board	Adequate mechanisms on central decisions; poor on operational	Inadequate; primarily indirect/ through media	Varies by Länder	Parliamentary committees, ombudsmen; low level of empowerment though	Adequate; both parliamentary and local supervision mechanisms	Adequate; Parliament, media, civil associations, 'open-door' schemes
Internal control of police (by police hierarchy/ MOI)	Yes; two internal inspectorates	Solely; no external control	Varies by Länder	Yes; internal inspectorates; controls by police superior	Yes; Internal Affairs Bureau	Yes- General inspectorates in cooperation with other specialised bodies and civilian supervision

	Bulgaria	Czech Rep.	Former GDR	Hungary	Poland	Romania
Judicial supervision	Some, though questionable in practice	Inadequate	Adequate	Currently inadequate	In principle adequate; note the pervasive general problems of the judiciary in Poland though	In principle adequate
Representation of women	Improved, still inadequate	Inadequate	Varies by Länder	15.1%	Inadequate (10 percent)	Currently inadequate, improving
Representation of minorities	Inadequate; some better local initiatives	Inadequate; but in some cases reflecting societal prejudice against, in particular, the Romany group	Varies by Länder	Inadequate; although official data cannot be obtained under current law	Not really an issue	Currently inadequate, improving
Legitimacy	Varied; high support for particular high-level police/MOI officials; otherwise fairly low	Medium; increasing	Medium; lower than the Western German Police	Varied; fairly low	Medium; increasing	Medium; fairly high in relative terms (5th most trusted institution)

	Bulgaria	Czech Rep.	Former GDR	Hungary	Poland	Romania
Rates of effectiveness of complaints (complaints found justified, sanctions applied)	Despite both politicians' and the public apparent satisfaction with the system, the effectiveness remains elusive	Few filed; half dismissed readily; 10% result in charges	No aggregated figures	Very low; 80% of investigations ineffective	No data	No data
Complaint procedures	The complaints are filed and considered by the internal inspectorates; external controls also in place	Only internal dealing with complaints	Vary by Länder	Complaints filed by relevant head of (local) police, but the investigation exclusively internal; military court may follow; some civilian measures exist, but are rarely resorted to	Filed locally; can also be addressed to central command and civil courts	No specific discussion
Code of ethics?	Yes	Outlined in Police Acts	Yes	No specific reference	Yes	Yes
Rates of Personnel Turnover	Fairly high *	Failry high, but not necessarily seen as a drawback	Varies by Länders	High	No data	No data

	Bulgaria	Czech Rep.	Former GDR	Hungary	Poland	Romania
Level of professionalism	Medium/ increasing	Medium/ increasing	Medium/ increasing; intensive training schemes in place	Low/medium; increasing, especially with foreign assistance	Medium/ increasing	Medium/ increasing
What priority is fighting organised crime?	Medium/high	Not top of the list	Not top of the list	Medium/high	High	High
Corruption	Medium	Medium	Fairly low	High	High	Fairly high
International assistance	Fairly high	Limited	Low	Fairly high	Medium; more bi/multilateral cooperation	Fairly high
International pressure for reform	High; especially pre-accession EU	Limited	Low (already EU member)	Considerable pre-accession pressures by the EU	Medium; EU pre-accession requirements	High

Bulgaria:
* There's an observable trend for leaving the service in favour of private security establishments.

Table A.3   Summary Table: Eastern Europe

	Russia	Ukraine
Personnel strength (2003)	Approx 1.1 million (total of the MVD system employees)	Approx 350,000 (total of MIA employees) *
Ratio: number of policemen/100,000	Approx 750 MVD personnel/ 100,000. No better breakdown available.	Approx 700 MIA personnel/ 100,000. No better breakdown available.
Reform of legislative framework of police	Wide divergence between theory and practice	Strong on rhetoric, but weak in practice
Depoliticisation	Low	Low
Demilitarisation	Low	Low
Decentralisation	Low; reform pending (2005)	Low; some attempted, but limited success
Human rights/policing ombudsman	Very poor	Ombudsman instituted; records still very poor
Civilian review/supervision board	None instituted; external controls by President	Parliamentary supervision, also local committees, Procurator; also (in theory) the media; questionable effectiveness in practice
Internal control of police (by police hierarchy/ MOI)	Internal Security Service, Minister of Interior	Strict control by hierarchy, often exercised on informal basis
Judicial Supervision	Poor	Poor
Representation of women	Poor	Poor
Representation of minorities	Poor	Poor
Legitimacy	Very low	Extremely low

	Russia	Ukraine
Rates of effectiveness of complaints (complaints found justified, sanctions applied)	Many sackings, though following internal proceedings, on all sorts of misdemeanours: around 10% of officers called into account are charged; note this may include cases brought forward by citizens or else	Unclear, given poor recording and widespread procedures of concealment
Complaint procedures	Unclear; inadequate	Unclear; inadequate
Code of ethics?	No	Recently introduced
Turnover rates of personnel? (high?)	High	High
Level of professionalism	Low	Low
What priority is fighting organised crime?	High, but limited effects	Not entirely clear
Corruption	Very high	Very high
International assistance	Low	Limited
International pressure for reform	Low	Limited

Ukraine: Currently understaffed by 12%.

Index

accountability (general) 5-9, 14-16, 70, 80, 100, 123, 321, 322, 327-8, 330, 332, 334-6, 338-9

adaptation 10-11, 60-1

Amnesty International 39, 41, 58, 83, 122, 293, 300

Bayley, David 4, 12, 16, 34-5, 38, 56, 59, 297, 299, 301

Bonn-Pertersberg Agreement 172, 176

Bosnia and Herzegovina 169-93, 324, 328
>   accountability 172, 181
>   corruption 177, 186, 190
>   crime 171,173-5, 181-2, 189
>   decentralisation 171
>   demilitarisation 177-181
>   human rights 183-7
>   legal framework 174
>   supervision and control 183
>   training 179, 182, 186, 188-9

Brčko (arbitration) 168-171

Bulgaria 131-145, 323, 324
>   accountability 133, 138-40
>   corruption 138, 140
>   crime 135, 137-8, 140-2, 144
>   human rights 140
>   legitimacy 141
>   supervision and control 138-40
>   training 133, 136-8, 140-1

Bundesgrenzschutz polizei (BGS) 45-7

Bundeskriminalamt (BKA) 46, 56

Chechnya 294

civilian supervision, control 7-8, 82, 299, 322, 326, 334, 339

code(s) of conduct 6-7, 70, 80, 169, 173, 328

communism 10, 70, 111, 289

community policing 10, 14, 47, 56, 59, 61, 75, 122, 124, 326-8, 327 (ft. 2), 331-2, 334

Continuous Professional Development (Montenegro) 259, 261

Crime (general) 7, 11, 14, 18, 321-4, 327-9, 335-6

Criminal Procedure Code (Croatia) 209, 212

Croatia 195-219, 324, 335
>   accountability 197-8, 200, 203, 207, 210
>   corruption 213-17
>   crime 197, 201-02, 205, 208-09, 212-13, 215
>   demilitarisation 200, 204
>   demystification 200

About the contributors

Pavel Abraham is the President of Romania's Anti-Drugs Agency and is a Secretary of State in the Romanian Ministry of Interior. He holds degrees in Law and Criminology from the University of Bucharest. His professional activities have included a wide spectrum of official posts in policing and anti-corruption. He is also a Professor of Law at the University of Bucharest, and Assistant Professor of Penal Law At European University I.C. Dragan, Lugoj. He is a member of the International Political Science Association and the International Society for Criminology. He served as an independent expert tackling the reform of law and justice system for the Soros Foundation, and as a NATO scholar addressing relations between police and community in the period of transition to the rule of law. Dr Abraham has authored and co-authored 42 academic publications.

Dusko Bakrac, LLB (University of Montenegro), is a 'special ministerial adviser' to the Minister of Internal Affairs of the Republic of Montenegro. He has spent his career in the police service, serving in both State Security and Public Security Departments, a fairly unusual career path. He occupied a number of senior posts in recent years, such as the Chief of City of Budva Police Service and Head of Herzeg Novi Public Security Centre, comprising all the Border Guard and Coast Guard Units at the Montenegrin-Croatian and Montenegrin-Bosnia and Herzegovina Borders. He has extensive experience in fighting organised crime. Mr Bakrac is also a postgraduate student at the International Graduate Management School in the European Centre for Peace and Development at the University for Peace, established by the United Nations.

Adrian Beck is a Senior Lecturer in Crime and Policing at Scarman Centre, University of Leicester, UK. Mr Beck has worked at the Scarman Centre since its inception in 1989. His research interests include crime and policing in Eastern Europe and crime against organisations. He has recently received a number of research grants from the UK's Department for International Development and Foreign and Commonwealth Office, to look at a wide range of issues in Russia and Ukraine. These include police corruption, context-driven community policing schemes, police management training and burglary reduction initiatives in transitional societies.

Marina Caparini is Senior Fellow at the Geneva Centre for the Democratic Control of Armed Forces, responsible for research and coordination of the working groups on internal security and civil society, and PhD candidate at the Department of War Studies, King's College, London. She has published articles on civil-military relations and security sector reform, including most recently the article 'Security Sector Reform and NATO and EU Enlargement' in the *SIPRI Yearbook 2003* (Oxford University Press for SIPRI), and co-editor of the book *Security Sector*

Reform and Democracy in Transitional Societies (2002), published by NOMOS Verlagsgesellschaft.

Michael Jaxa-Chamiec holds a BA degree is Social and Political Sciences from Downing College, University of Cambridge, specialising in Social Psychology, Sociology of Crime and Deviance and Sociology of Media and Culture. He is currently in the process of obtaining a Diplôme des Etudes Approfondis in International Relations in the Graduate Institute of International Studies in Geneva. His current research interests focus on the alternative politics of urban youth cultures in world cities of late modernity.

David A. Jenks, PhD, is an Assistant Professor at the School of Health and Human Services in the California State University in Los Angeles. He coordinates and advises on a number of programmes on law enforcement, youth and gang violence, dispute resolution and many others. He holds degrees from University of Akron, University of North Carolina and Florida State University. His current research interests include international and comparative criminal justice systems, policing and violence against police, social learning theory and criminal justice education.

Fabien Jobard is a full-time researcher at the Centre de recherches sociologiques sur le droit et les institutions pénales (CNRS/French Ministry of Justice). He was also post-doctoral research fellow for one year at the Max Planck Institute for Human Development in Berlin. His research areas presently include police and human rights, police and regime changes, and police violence in France. He recently published his PhD thesis, *Bavures policières. La force publique et ses usages* (Paris : La Découverte 2002), and 'Usages et ruses des temps. La réunification de la police berlinoise (1989-90)', *Revue française de science politique*, June 2003.

Éva Keresztes Dimovné is currently a SJD (Doctor of Juridical Science) candidate at Central European University, Budapest. In 2001 she received her LLM in Comparative Constitutional Law, with a specialisation in human rights, also at Central European University, Budapest. She received her first law degree from Eötvös Loránd University (ELTE), Faculty of Law, Budapest in 2000.

Sanja Kutnjak Ivkovich received her LLB degree from the University of Zagreb, Croatia, a doctoral degree in Criminology (PhD) from the University of Delaware, and a doctoral degree in law (SJD) from Harvard Law School. She is a member of the Croatian bar. Dr Ivkovich has been pursuing a variety of topics in criminology, criminal justice, and sociology of law. A particular area of her interest and expertise is policing, but her interests also include the court system and legal decision-making. She has studied participation of lay persons (jurors, lay judges) as decision-makers in criminal and civil cases, both in the United States and abroad. In the arena of international jurisprudence, she undertook a project focusing on the delivery of justice by the International Criminal Tribunal for the Former Yugoslavia to the victims of war crimes. Dr Ivkovich has published a book and numerous journal articles and book chapters in the areas of policing, comparative criminology/criminal justice, and sociology of law. Her work has appeared in journals such as *Journal of Criminal Law and Criminology, Law and Social Inquiry, Stanford Journal of International Law, Law & Policy, International Journal of Comparative and Applied Criminal Justice, International Criminal Justice Review, Journal of Crime & Justice*, among others. She is currently writing the book *The Fallen Blue Knights: Controlling Police Corruption* (Oxford University Press, forthcoming).

Otwin Marenin is Professor of Political Science and Criminal Justice at Washington State University. He has written extensively on comparative policing, police reform and democratisation processes. Recent publications in this area include the edited book with Dilip Das, *Challenges of Policing Democracies. A World Perspective*, and numerous journal articles and seminar papers.

Milan Pagon is Dean and Professor of Police Administration and Management at the Faculty of Criminal Justice, University of Maribor, and Professor of Organisational Behaviour at the Faculty of Organisational Sciences, University of Maribor, Slovenia. He received his ScD from the University of Maribor, and his PhD from the University of Arkansas, Fayetteville, USA. His current research interests include police stress, corruption and deviance, and comparative aspects of policing.

Ken Palmer is completing his PhD in sociology at the University of North Carolina at Chapel Hill. His dissertation, entitled *Power-Sharing Extended: Policing and Education Reforms in Bosnia-Herzegovina and Northern Ireland*, examines how the interaction between external agents (other states and international organisations) and local power structures impacts on institutional outcomes in two post-peace agreement societies.

Emil W. Plywaczewski, PhD, is the Director of Department of Criminology and Organised Crime Issues in the Bialystok School of Law. He is also Professor of Law in University of Bialystok.

Alexey Povolotskiy works at the National University of Internal Affairs, Kharkiv, Ukraine. He is currently working as a coordinator of the British-Ukrainian project entitled 'Introducing Community Policing in Ukraine'.

Annette Robertson is a Researcher at the Scarman Centre, University of Leicester. She is currently co-ordinating a three-year project funded by the British Government's Department for International Development (DfID) on 'The Development of Crime Reduction Schemes for At-Risk Groups: Context Specific Approaches for Transitional Societies'. Her main research interests are policing, crime prevention, crime and victimisation in Russia and the former Soviet states.

Dr Zeljko Sevic (LLB[Hons], LLM, MSc, PGDipl., SJD, PhD [FinEcon], PGCE, PGDipl., ILTM) is Principal Lecturer in Accounting and Finance and Head of the

Accounting and Finance Subject Group in the University of Greenwich Business School, where he teaches a wide range of courses in finance, specialising in area of Banking and Financial Management, Management Accounting and Treasury Management. He has published over 50 different papers including two books in Serbo-Croatian (*Undisclosed Agency Operations (Commission Transactions) in Banking Law* and *Central Bank: Position – Organisation – Functions*) which are standard postgraduate textbooks. He also co-edited, with Prof. G. Wright, *Transition in Central and Eastern Europe*, in two volumes. He has taught in Belgrade and Dundee and was a visiting professor in Japan, Germany, Ukraine and Russia. He has been a consultant to a number of firms in Central and Eastern European countries, assisting with their restructuring and privatisation programmes. Dr Sevic is a member of the Editorial Board of *Economist*, an academic journal or transitional studies, and also serves as the First Vice-President and CEO of the Balkan Center for Public Policy and Related Studies, and the convenor of the Public Sector Finance and Accounting Group under the auspices of the NISPAcee.

Vladislav Shopov served as an EU integration advisor to the Minister of Home Affairs of Bulgaria during the period between October 1997 and February 1999 and subsequently as a Counsellor at the Bulgarian Mission to the EC in Brussels dealing with justice and home affairs, human rights and minorities (February 1999 until July 2001). He is currently completing his doctorate on contemporary ideologies at Sofia University. He holds degrees from the University of Sofia and the London School of Economics and Political Science.

Marijana Trivunovic is an independent consultant at the Constitutional & Legal Policy Institute (COLPI)/Open Society Institute (OSI), Budapest, Hungary, where she previously worked as a designer and manager of anti-corruption initiatives in Central and Eastern Europe, Central Asia and Mongolia. She has previously acted as an advisor/resource person for anti-corruption activities for OSI network, particularly Soros national foundations as well as supervised the joint COLPI–OSCE/ODIHR Fund for an Open Society Macedonia police education reform project initiated in 1999. She holds degrees from University of Virginia and Central European University, Budapest.

Alexander Yarmysh is Rector of the National University of Internal Affairs, Ministry of Interior of Ukraine. He is a Doctor of Juridical Sciences, Professor, Corresponding Member of the Academy of Law Sciences of Ukraine, Adviser to the Committee on Law Enforcement of the Verkhovna Rada of Ukraine (the Parliament), and an Honored Jurist of Ukraine. His research interests include state and legal history, history of policing in Ukraine and post-Soviet countries and police reform in Ukraine.

Islam Yusufi is International Policy Fellow at the Centre for Policy Studies, Budapest, Hungary, and Assistant to National Security Adviser of the President of the Republic of Macedonia. Previously he held a fellowship at the Woodrow Wilson International Center for Scholars in Washington DC and Research Fellowship at

NATO. He holds an MA in International Relations from the Bilkent University and post-masters degree in international affairs from the University of Amsterdam.

Geneva Centre for the Democratic Control of Armed Forces (DCAF)

Established in October 2000 on the initiative of the Swiss government, the Geneva Centre for the Democratic Control of Armed Forces (DCAF) encourages and supports States and non-State governed institutions in their efforts to strengthen democratic and civilian control of armed and security forces, and promotes security sector reform conforming to democratic standards.

The Centre collects information and undertakes research in order to identify problems, to gather experience from lessons learned, and to propose best practices in the field of democratic governance of the security sector. The Centre provides its expertise and support, through practical work programmes on the ground, to all interested parties, in particular governments, parliaments, military authorities, international organisations, non-governmental organisations, and academic circles.

Detailed information on DCAF can be found at www.dcaf.ch

Geneva Centre for the Democratic Control of Armed Forces (DCAF):
rue de Chantepoulet 11, PO Box 1360, CH-1211 Geneva 1, Switzerland
Tel: ++41 22 741 77 00; fax: ++41 22 741 77 05; e-mail: info@dcaf.ch;
website: www.dcaf.ch

Wissenschaftliche Paperbacks
Politikwissenschaft

Hartmut Elsenhans
Das Internationale System zwischen Zivilgesellschaft und Rente
Gegen derzeitige Theorieangebote für die Er-
klärung der Ursachen und die Auswirkungen
wachsender transnationaler und internationaler
Verflechtung setzt das hier vorliegende Konzept
eine stark durch politökonomische Überlegungen
integrierte Perspektive, die auf politologischen,
soziologischen, ökonomischen und philoso-
phischen Ansatzpunkten aufbaut. Mit diesem
Konzept soll gezeigt werden, daß der durch Pro-
duktionsauslagerungen/Direktinvestitionen/neue
Muster der internationalen Arbeitsteilung gekenn-
zeichnete (im weiteren als Transnationalisierung
von Wirtschaftsbeziehungen bezeichnete) ka-
pitalistische Impuls zur Integration der bisher
nicht in die Weltwirtschaft voll integrierten Pe-
ripherie weiterhin zu schwach ist, als daß dort
nichtmarktwirtschaftliche Formen der Aneignung
von Überschuß entscheidend zurückgedrängt
werden können. Das sich herausbildende internationale System ist deshalb durch miteinander
verschränkte Strukturen von Markt- und Nichtmarktökonomie gekennzeichnet, die nur unter
bestimmten Voraussetzungen synergetische Effekte
in Richtung einer autonomen und zivilisierten
Weltzivilgesellschaft entfalten werden. Dabei
treten neue Strukturen von Nichtmarktökonomie
auf transnationaler Ebene auf, während der Wie-
deraufstieg von Renten die zivilgesellschaftlichen
Grundlagen funktionierender oder potentiell zu
Funktionsfähigkeit zu bringender, dann kapitali-
stischer Systeme auf internationaler und lokaler
Ebene eher behindert.
Bd. 6, 2001, 140 S., 12,90 €, br., ISBN 3-8258-4837-x

Klaus Schubert
Innovation und Ordnung
In einer evolutionär voranschreitenden Welt sind
statische Politikmodelle und -theorien proble-
matisch. Deshalb lohnt es sich, die wichtigste
Quelle für die Entstehung der policy-analysis,
den Pragmatismus, als dynamische, demokratie-
endogene politisch-philosophische Strömung zu
rekonstruieren. Dies geschieht im ersten Teil der
Studie. Der zweite Teil trägt zum Verständnis
des daraus folgenden politikwissenschaftlichen
Ansatzes bei. Darüber hinaus wird durch eine

konstruktiv-spekulative Argumentation versucht,
die z. Z. wenig innovative Theorie- und Me-
thodendiskussion in der Politikwissenschaft
anzuregen.
Bd. 7, 2003, 224 S., 25,90 €, br., ISBN 3-8258-6091-4

Politik: Forschung und Wissenschaft

Klaus Segbers; Kerstin Imbusch (eds.)
The Globalization of Eastern Europe
Teaching International Relations Without
Borders
Globalization and fragmentation, weakly
controlled flows of information and knowledge,
increasing cleavages in societies undergoing rapid
change, flows of migrants, services and capital,
bypassing the control of national governments,
life styles and consumption patterns produced
by electronic media and advertising – all
these developments already have a significant
impact on post-Soviet regions. And all kind of
actors – decision makers, journalists, experts,
students – perceive the environment beyond their
respective national borders increasingly as the
"playground" they have to take into account, and
as a framework for action.
The chapters in this volume are produced by
experts in the so called transformation countries
in Eastern Europe. They address various
questions on inter- and transnational relations,
thereby offering a framework for reflection
and for analysis of macro-trends around policy
fields relevant for the countries in Central and
Eastern Europe. The product certainly mirrows
the specific environment of researchers, teachers
and students in these countries. At the same time,
it reflects a process of intensive discussion on the
state of IR literature worldwide. Furthermore, this
book demonstrates how useful teaching tools for
universities and institutes not only in Eastern and
Central Europe can be produced.
Bd. 1, 2000, 600 S., 35,90 €, br., ISBN 3-8258-4729-2

Hartwig Hummel; Ulrich Menzel (Hg.)
**Die Ethnisierung internationaler Wirt-
schaftsbeziehungen und daraus resultierende Konflikte**
Mit Beiträgen von Annabelle Gambe,
Hartwig Hummel, Ulrich Menzel
und Birgit Wehrhöfer

LIT Verlag Münster – Hamburg – Berlin – Wien – London
Grevener Str./Fresnostr. 2 48159 Münster
Tel.: 0251 – 23 50 91 – Fax: 0251 – 23 19 72
e-Mail: vertrieb@lit-verlag.de – http://www.lit-verlag.de

"Die Ethnisierung der internationalen Wirtschaftsbeziehungen und daraus resultierende Konflikte"
lautete der Titel eines Forschungsprojekts, das
diesem Band zugrunde liegt. Es geht um die
Themen Handel, Migration und Investitionen. In
drei Fallstudien werden die Handelsbeziehungen
zwischen den USA und Japan, die Einwande-
rung nach Deutschland bzw. Frankreich und das
auslandschinesische Unternehmertum untersucht.
Die Ergebnisse des Projekts sehen Hummel und
Menzel in den späteren Ereignissen bestätigt:
Ethnisierende Tendenzen können sich in der
Handelspolitik und der Investitionstätigkeit von
Unternehmen nicht durchsetzen, während die
Ethnisierung im Bereich der Migration andauert.
Bd. 2, 2001, 272 S., 30,90 €, br., ISBN 3-8258-4836-1

Theodor Ebert
**Opponieren und Regieren mit gewaltfreien
Mitteln**
Pazifismus – Grundsätze und Erfahrungen für
das 21. Jahrhundert. Band 1
Das grundlegende und aktuelle Werk eines
Konfliktforschers, der über Jahrzehnte in pazi-
fistischen Organisationen, in sozialen Bewegun-
gen und in Gremien der Evangelischen Kirche
gearbeitet hat. Ebert breitet in anschaulichen
Berichten und doch in systematischer Ordnung
die Summe seiner Erfahrungen aus und entwickelt
Perspektiven für eine Welt, die mit der Gewalt
leben muss, doch Gefahr läuft, an ihr zugrunde
zu gehen, wenn sie auf die Bedrohungen keine
neuen, gewaltfreien Antworten findet.
Aus dem Vorwort: "Es gibt eine pragmatische
Befürwortung des gewaltfreien Handelns in in-
nenpolitischen Auseinandersetzungen durch eine
Mehrheit der Deutschen, und dies sollten wir
als tragenden Bestandteil der Zivilkultur nicht
gering schätzen. Doch die Frage, wie man mit
gewaltfreien Mitteln regieren und sich gegenüber
gewalttätigen Extremisten durchsetzen kann und
wie man sich international behaupten und Be-
drohten helfen kann, ist bislang kaum erörtert
worden ... Dieses Buch soll klären, was unter
politisch verantwortlichem und doch radikal ge-
waltfreiem Pazifismus zu verstehen ist, und wie
mit gewaltfreien Mitteln nicht nur opponiert,
sondern auch regiert werden kann."
Bd. 3, 2001, 328 S., 20,90 €, br., ISBN 3-8258-5706-9

Theodor Ebert
Der Kosovo-Krieg aus pazifistischer Sicht
Pazifismus – Grundsätze und Erfahrungen für
das 21. Jahrhundert. Band 2
Mit dem Luftkrieg der NATO gegen Jugoslawien
begann für den deutschen Nachkriegspazifismus
ein neues Zeitalter. Ebert hat sich über Jahr-
zehnte als Konfliktforscher und Schriftleiter der
Zeitschrift "Gewaltfreie Aktion" mit den Möglichkeiten gewaltfreier Konfliktbearbeitung befasst.
Von ihm stammt der erste Entwurf für einen
Zivilen Friedensdienst als Alternative zum Militär.
Aus dem Vorwort: "Wer sich einbildet, auch in
Zukunft ließe sich aus großer Höhe mit Bomben
politischer Gehorsam erzwingen, unterschätzt die
Möglichkeiten, die fanatische Terroristen haben,
in fahrlässiger Weise. Jedes Atomkraftwerk ist eine stationäre Atombombe, die von Terroristen mit
geringem Aufwand in ein Tschernobyl verwandelt
werden kann. Wir haben allen Grund, schleunigst
über zivile Alternativen zu militärischen Einsätzen
nachzudenken und die vorhandene Ansätze solch
ziviler Alternativen zu entwickeln."
Bd. 4, 2001, 176 S., 12,90 €, br., ISBN 3-8258-5707-7

Wolfgang Gieler
**Handbuch der Ausländer- und
Zuwanderungspolitik**
Von Afghanistan bis Zypern
In der Literatur zur Ausländer- und Zuwanderungspolitik fehlt ein Handbuch, dass einen
schnellen und kompakten Überblick dieses Poli-
tikbereichs ermöglicht. Das vorliegende Handbuch
bemüht sich diese wissenschaftliche Lücke zu
schließen. Thematisiert werden die Ausländer-
und Zuwanderungspolitik weltweiter Staaten
von Afghanistan bis Zypern. Zentrale Fragestel-
lung ist dabei der Umgang mit Fremden, das
heißt mit Nicht-Inländern im jeweiligen Staat.
Hierbei werden insbesondere politische, soziale,
rechtliche, wirtschaftliche und kulturelle Aspek-
te mitberücksichtigt. Um eine Kompatibilität
der Beiträge herzustellen beinhaltet jeder Bei-
trag darüber hinaus eine Zusammenstellung der
historischen Grunddaten und eine Tabelle zur
jeweiligen Anzahl der im Staat lebenden Auslän-
der. Die vorgelegte Publikation versteht sich als
ein grundlegendes Nachschlagewerk. Neben dem
universitären Bereich richtet es sich besonders
an die gesellschaftspolitisch interessierte Öffent-
lichkeit und den auf sozialwissenschaftlichen

LIT Verlag Münster – Hamburg – Berlin – Wien – London
Grevener Str./Fresnostr. 2 48159 Münster
Tel.: 0251 – 23 50 91 – Fax: 0251 – 23 19 72
e-Mail: vertrieb@lit-verlag.de – http://www.lit-verlag.de

Kenntnissen angewiesenen Personen in Politik, Verwaltung, Medien, Bildungseinrichtungen und Migranten-Organisationen.
Bd. 6, 2003, 768 S., 98,90 €, gb., ISBN 3-8258-6444-8

Harald Barrios; Martin Beck;
Andreas Boeckh; Klaus Segbers (Eds)
Resistance to Globalization
Political Struggle and Cultural Resilience in the Middle East, Russia, and Latin America
This volume is an important contribution to the empirical research on what globalization means in different world regions. "Resistance" here has a double meaning: It can signify active, intentional resistance to tendencies which are rejected on political or moral grounds by presenting alternative discourses and concepts founded in specific cultural and national traditions. It can also mean resilience with regard to globalization pressures in the sense that traditional patterns of development and politics are resistant to change. The book shows the that the local, sub-national, national, and regional patterns of politics and development coexist with globalized structures without yielding very much ground and in ways which may turn out to be a serious barrier to further globalization. Case studies presented focus on Venezuela, Brazil, the Middle East, Iran, and Russia.
Bd. 7, 2003, 184 S., 20,90 €, br., ISBN 3-8258-6749-8

Ellen Bos; Antje Helmerich
Neue Bedrohung Terrorismus
Der 11. September 2001 und die Folgen.
Unter Mitarbeit von Barry Adams und Harald Wilkoszweski
Die terroristischen Anschläge des -11. September 2001 haben die Weltöffentlichkeit erschüttert. Ihre weitreichenden Auswirkungen auf die Lebenswirklichkeit des Einzelnen, den Handlungsspielraum der Nationalstaaten und das internationale System stehen im Mittelpunkt des Sammelbandes. Er basiert auf einer Ringvorlesung, in der sich Wissenschaftler der Ludwig-Maximilians-Universität München aus den Fächern Amerikanistik, Jura, Geschichte, Politik-, Religions-, Kommunikations- und Wirtschaftswissenschaft mit den geistigen Hintergründen und den Konsequenzen des Terrorismus auseinandersetzten.
Bd. 9, 2003, 232 S., 19,90 €, br., ISBN 3-8258-7099-5

Heinz-Gerhard Justenhoven; James Turner (Eds.)
Rethinking the State in the Age of Globalisation
Catholic Thought and Contemporary Political Theory
Since Jean Bodin and Thomas Hobbes, political theorists have depicted the state as „sovereign" because it holds preeminent authority over all the denizens belonging to its geographically defined territory. From the Peace of Westphalia in 1648 until the beginning of World War I in 1914, the essential responsiblities ascribcd to the sovereign state were maintaining internal and external security and promoting domestic prosperity. This idea of „the state" in political theory is clearly inadequate to the realities of national governments and international relations at the beginning of the twenty-first century. During the twentieth century, the sovereign state, as a reality and an idea, has been variously challenged from without and within its borders. Where will the state head in the age of globalisation? Can Catholic political thinking contribute to an adequate concept of statehood and government? A group of German and American scholars were asked to explore specific ways in which the intellectual traditions of Catholicism might help our effort lo rethink the state. The debate is guided by the conviction that these intellectual resources will prove valuable to political theorists as they work to revise our understanding of the state.
Bd. 10, 2003, 240 S., 19,90 €, br., ISBN 3-8258-7249-1

Geneva Centre for the Democratic Control of Armed Forces

Heiner Hänggi; Theodor H. Winkler (Eds.)
Challenges of Security Sector Governance
The war in Iraq in spring 2003 was a further indication of the 'resecuritisation' of international relations triggered by the terrorist attacks of September 11, 2001. However, the new (or renewed) primacy of security will be of a rather different nature as compared to the Cold War period. The underlying assumption of the essays in this volume is that security issues will increasingly be approached from a governance perspective and that, in this context, the internal dimension of security governance – security sector governance – is an issue whose rapidly growing importance has not yet been duly recognised.
Bd. 1, 2003, 312 S., 23,90 €, br., ISBN 3-8258-7158-4

LIT Verlag Münster – Hamburg – Berlin – Wien – London
Grevener Str./Fresnostr. 2 48159 Münster
Tel.: 0251 – 23 50 91 – Fax: 0251 – 23 19 72
e-Mail: vertrieb@lit-verlag.de – http://www.lit-verlag.de